Product Release Planning

Methods, Tools and Applications

BOOKS ON SOFTWARE AND SYSTEMS DEVELOPMENT AND ENGINEERING FROM AUERBACH PUBLICATIONS AND CRC PRESS

CAD and GIS Integration
Hassan A. Karimi and Burcu Akinci
ISBN: 978-1-4200-6805-4

Applied Software Product-Line Engineering
Kyo C. Kang, Vijayan Sugumaran, and Sooyong Park, eds.
ISBN: 978-1-4200-6841-2

Enterprise-Scale Agile Software Development
James Schiel
ISBN: 978-1-4398-0321-9

Handbook of Enterprise Integration
Mostafa Hashem Sherif, ed.
ISBN: 978-1-4200-7821-3

Architecture and Principles of Systems Engineering
Charles Dickerson, Dimitri N. Mavris, Paul R. Garvey, and Brian E. White
ISBN: 978-1-4200-7253-2

Theory of Science and Technology Transfer and Applications
Sifeng Liu, Zhigeng Fang, Hongxing Shi, and Benhai Guo
ISBN: 978-1-4200-8741-3

The SIM Guide to Enterprise Architecture
Leon Kappelman, ed.
ISBN: 978-1-4398-1113-9

Getting Design Right: A Systems Approach
Peter L. Jackson
ISBN: 978-1-4398-1115-3

Software Testing as a Service
Ashfaque Ahmed
ISBN: 978-1-4200-9956-0

Grey Game Theory and Its Applications in Economic Decision-Making
Zhigeng Fang, Sifeng Liu, Hongxing Shi, and Yi LinYi Lin
ISBN: 978-1-4200-8739-0

Quality Assurance of Agent-Based and Self-Managed Systems
Reiner Dumke, Steffen Mencke, and Cornelius Wille
ISBN: 978-1-4398-1266-2

Modeling Software Behavior: A Craftsman's Approach
Paul C. Jorgensen
ISBN: 978-1-4200-8075-9

Design and Implementation of Data Mining Tools
Bhavani Thuraisingham, Latifur Khan, Mamoun Awad, and Lei Wang
ISBN: 978-1-4200-4590-1

Model-Oriented Systems Engineering Science: A Unifying Framework for Traditional and Complex Systems
Duane W. Hybertson
ISBN: 978-1-4200-7251-8

Requirements Engineering for Software and Systems
Phillip A. Laplante
ISBN: 978-1-4200-6467-4

Software Testing and Continuous Quality Improvement, Third Edition
William E. Lewis
ISBN: 978-1-4200-8073-5

Systemic Yoyos: Some Impacts of the Second Dimension
Yi Lin
ISBN: 978-1-4200-8820-5

Architecting Secure Software Systems
Asoke K. Talukder and Manish Chaitanya
ISBN: 978-1-4200-8784-0

Delivering Successful Projects with TSPSM and Six Sigma: A Practical Guide to Implementing Team Software Process^{SM}
Mukesh Jain
ISBN: 978-1-4200-6143-7

Product Release Planning

Methods, Tools and Applications

Günther Ruhe

CRC Press
Taylor & Francis Group
Boca Raton London New York

CRC Press is an imprint of the
Taylor & Francis Group, an **informa** business
AN AUERBACH BOOK

Auerbach Publications
Taylor & Francis Group
6000 Broken Sound Parkway NW, Suite 300
Boca Raton, FL 33487-2742

Printed in the United States of America on acid-free paper
10 9 8 7 6 5 4 3 2 1

International Standard Book Number: 978-0-8493-2620-2 (Hardback)

Library of Congress Cataloging-in-Publication Data

Ruhe, Günther.
Product release planning : methods, tools, and applications / author, Günther Ruhe.
p. cm.
Includes bibliographical references and index.
ISBN 978-0-8493-2620-2 (hardcover : alk. paper)
1. New products--Planning. 2. Product management. I. Title.

HF5415.153.R86 2010
658.8'02--dc22 2010017615

Visit the Taylor & Francis Web site at
http://www.taylorandfrancis.com

and the Auerbach Web site at
http://www.auerbach-publications.com

Contents

PART D: APPLICATIONS

Foreword

"Plans are nothing. Planning is everything." This is how former US president Dwight D. Eisenhower emphasized the importance of good planning processes already during his active duty in World War II. The real purpose of effective planning is not only to make plans but to change the thinking of impacted stakeholders and decisions makers. Planning facilitates learning. It is not the exact plan, generated with some form of computer support, which counts most. Instead, it is the understanding of the direction to go and what risks, obstacles and dependencies exist that is most important.

Planning is a means for achieving stated goals, not the end. It is intended to provide directions, not final solutions. Planning is a continuous effort because we are living in a world of fast change. An initial plan provides guidance in which direction to go. No one would expect this to remain valid without adjustment for a longer period of time. Planning implies re-planning.

Over time I have created a simple checklist with ten elements which I walk through with my clients in product and portfolio management. It applies to this book and to guide you as a reader. Just have a brief look at the following list and decide for yourself and your company, how many of the following topics you would mark as *yes* or *true* for your organization:

1. Business goals not aligned with product and technology decisions
2. Lack of alignment with many different voices in the company
3. Unclear ownership of business decisions
4. Focus on the "paper" and "plan" instead of on people and commitments
5. Unknown value and impacts of features and releases
6. Surprises and ad-hoc decisions
7. More re-active than pro-active planning mode
8. Lack of transparency of product decisions
9. Insufficient stakeholder commitment
10. Inadequate resource consideration

If you had more than three topics marked, I strongly recommend this book in order to learn best product planning and management practices. You might want to select an appropriate chapter and just start reading or first focus on methodology and then look to concrete case studies.

This book presents methods and tools to apply sound planning to product development and product management. This is called product release planning.

Product release planning is a management instrument for forecasting and planning evolution paths for a product and its versions and variants to best meet market and customer needs both operationally and strategically. It highly interacts with road mapping and strategic planning to align different stakeholders in the company around research, engineering, technology evolution, product management and marketing, sales, competence management and of course projects. As such, product road mapping is part of strategic management as illustrated in the Figure 1.

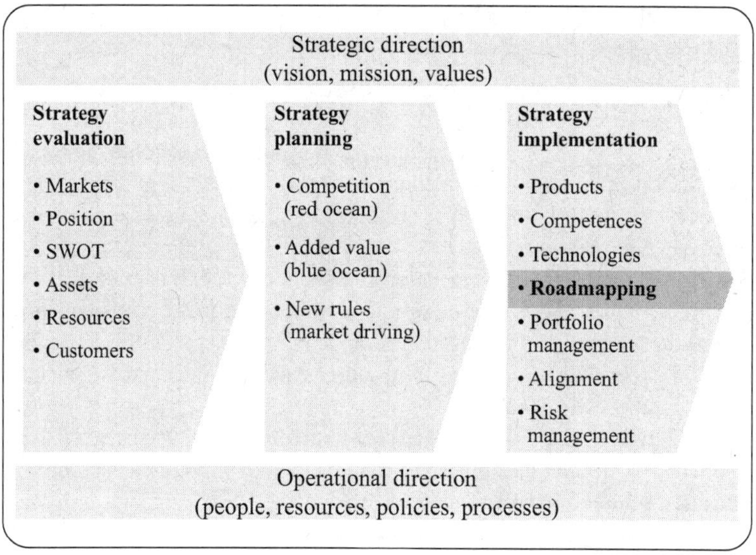

Figure 1 Positioning of roadmapping

Release planning is a challenging problem because of its complexity and dependencies, the number of stakeholders involved in it, the variety of variables that need to be looked at, and the uncertainty of the information it is relying upon. The overall goal is to determine a "most promising" release plan such that the total degree of satisfaction of all the different stakeholders is maximized. The capability to react quickly to changed demands and to exploit efficiently the opportunities of new technologies is a driving factor of a company's success.

The ambition and objective of release planning is to efficiently and effectively translate strategy to concrete milestones and concrete deliverables that make an impact on the market. Product release planning therefore is the process of creating, maintaining and aligning product-related roadmaps. While strategic planning provides the long-term outlook and aligns vision, mission and overall evolution of the organization, and portfolio management translates strategy into plans for action and planned outcomes, product release planning is the process for translating these plans into concrete steps for action and for highlighting the interdependencies between customer and market needs on one side, and availability of competencies and technologies, product development milestones, readiness of production technology and facilities, market demand, sales, etc. on the other side.

Release decisions address the early stage of a product's life-cycle. They are part of product management, an emerging discipline that aims at improving the whole process of development ranging from product requirements to design, implementation, product launch and service. In its essence, release planning is the process of defining the functionality of a sequence of product releases as part of incremental development. Customers and stakeholders are continuously asking for more features or revision of existing ones. But, which ones should finally be selected for the next release and why? Which features are not attractive enough and are better left out or postponed?

Release planning delivers a mapping of technologies, components and features to future products. Although different types of products must all be synchronized in their individual releases, there is a clear distinction regarding the individual ownership and focus. Release planning applies top-down in translating strategies to products and bottom-up in coining products that best address a multitude of needs, features, variabilities and contents. Release plans are evidently never frozen. Concrete timelines must be maintained but periodic updates are required in line with updating of assumptions and outcomes of regular risk assessments. Once a plan is established, this plan needs adjustment to accommodate all the changes occurring down the road.

Release planning is useful for various reasons. Better product roadmaps will help product managers to deliver according to commitments and thus to improve business performance. Wrong decisions are hard to reverse afterward, especially in the early stages of the process when fundamental design decisions are made. Planning is part of the pro-active effort to avoid pitfalls in the later stages. Good release planning saves 5-30% of product development budget by different levers:

- Visible, committed and achieved milestones and results.
- Trust and alignment across R&D, marketing, finance and sales.
- Harmonizing product and technology decisions with business needs.
- Baselined assumptions.
- Early removal of inconsistencies.
- Simplified monitoring of performance and results.
- Increasing accountability for results across the corporation.
- More effective resource utilization.
- Competitive and more realistic product, technology and competence evolution.
- Variant management. Planned reuse. Less resources wasted.
- Transparent and clear rules for termination or not proceeding.

This book for the first time gives a comprehensive introduction into the field of product release planning. Authored by renowned expert Günther Ruhe, it provides a guided tour through the methodology and usage of release planning starting with technology and market needs and proceeding to product planning and finally to development projects. The dependencies of stakeholders and between related fields of business strategy, technology strategy, and project and product portfolio management are nicely illustrated. Often overlooked by overly technical research, the necessity of vertical and horizontal cross-functional communication is highlighted.

Case studies and exercises partially based on Günther's ReleasePlanner™ tool offer opportunities to underpin methodologies with practical examples. The book thus complements participants' knowledge and problem-solving competences in release planning and enables them to implement more effective release management processes in their companies.

The techniques presented in this book are not supposed to be the ultimate truth, but a direction to go to support the human decision-making, to better understand the rational of the decisions made, and to grow in the capability of mastering the whole planning process. Thus, it is important to enter the continuous planning and learning process. It will help you as well as your organization to grow your maturity. For this matter I wish you all the best and good success. With all planning do not forget the wisdom of another great leader, Winston Churchill, who once said: *However beautiful the strategy, you should occasionally look at the results.*

Christof Ebert

Stuttgart

Acknowledgments

Writing this book has been part of my life for about five years. It would have been impossible to ever get it finished without the collaboration, friendship, love and support of so many people. I would like to explicitly mention them here and acknowledge their importance for finally reaching the finish line. Collaboration with other researchers and students has always been a fascinating part of my life. It is stimulating to share ideas, to get comments and suggestions, and to jointly create solutions. During the five-year period, and in the context of this book, I was fortunate to work with many people across the world.

Research is the result of discussion and interactions. Des Greer (Queens University of Belfast) was the one with whom I started to look at the whole area of product release planning in 2002, when we developed the first ideas and a systematic solution method called EVOLVE. This collaboration is still ongoing, and has substantially contributed to this book. Both Dietmar Pfahl (University of Oslo) and Armin Eberlein (American University of Sharjah) have provided constructive comments and suggestions on earlier versions of the book. Their support was tremendously helpful to make the text more readable and easier to understand.

An Ngo-The (Pelsea, Calgary) has been a close collaborator of mine since 2003. His background and expertise were very valuable for developing some of the methods and techniques presented in this book. Among the many others, I want to explicitly mention Joerg Denzinger, Michael M. Richter, Jonathan Silito from University of Calgary and Luigi Troiano (University of Sannio) and Tom Zimmerman (Microsoft Research). The ATMAN collaboration project with the Helsinki University of Technology gave me the opportunity to collaborate with a number of colleagues, especially with Ville Heikkilae, Kristian Rautiainen and Jarno Vahaniitty.

Research is the result of discussion and interactions. Working with students is one of the most fascinating things in my professional career. My former and existing students Jingzhou Li, Gengshen Du, Omolade Saliu and Ahmed Al-Emran deserve special acknowledgement for their contribution to Sections 9.2, 9.3, 9.4 respectively 9.5 of the book. The work of Anas Jadallah and Emad Livani has been of great help to perform the case studies of Chapters 7, 12, and 13. Comments and feedback to earlier versions of chapters of the book were provided by Sebastian Maurice, Jim McElroy, Elham Paikari, Mainur M. Rahman, Christoph Streb and Irfan Ullah.

The decision support tools presented in this book have been implemented over a period of six years. A number of students and professionals have contributed to that. Special thanks for their work are due to Amandeep Azad, Eric Bauld, Pankaj Bhawnani, Stephen Bosch, Brad Cossette, Devlin Dunsmore, Martin Echtner, Johannes Fischer, David Goodladd, Julian Gamble, Mark Przepiora, Greg Spiers and Kenny Tsang. The tools have matured over time as a result of a large number of trial users and a substantial number of graduate and undergraduate student projects conducted at the University of Calgary's departments of Computer Science as well as Electrical and Computer Engineering.

I cannot stress enough the importance of the interaction with industry from the very beginning. Their immediate response and ongoing request to address new questions have been a stimulating factor: Ville Hamalainen (Stonesoft), Janne Jarvinen, (F-Secure), Eduard Kaiser and Andreas Reh (Siemens Audiology), Puneet Kapur (Chartwell Technology), Franz Kudorfer (Siemens Corporate Technology), Mike McAllister (SAP Canada), Peter McCurdy (Nortel Networks), Ludger Meyer (Siemens Corporate Technology), Joseph Momoh (Trema Laboratories), the late Andrew Smith (Chartwell Technology), Hamid Sarreshtehdari (National Research Council) and Mark Stanford (iGrafx).

Parts of the research have been supported by various funding agencies. The financial support of the Alberta Informatics Circle of Research Excellence (iCORE), the Natural Sciences and Engineering Research Council of Canada NSERC, the National Research Council of Canada NRC, and the Alberta Ingenuity Fund AIF is highly appreciated.

Many thanks are also due to the publishers from CRC Press. Special thanks to John Wyzalek for his never-ending patience and support.

Friends and family always provided the essential emotional support to keep the fire burning. In particular, it was and is Kornelia Streb who has done even more than that. Her technical excellence has helped to visualize things I could not express myself. She has devoted endless patience and energy to design figures, prepare tables, screen-shots and finally putting the whole text together.

Part A: Foundations

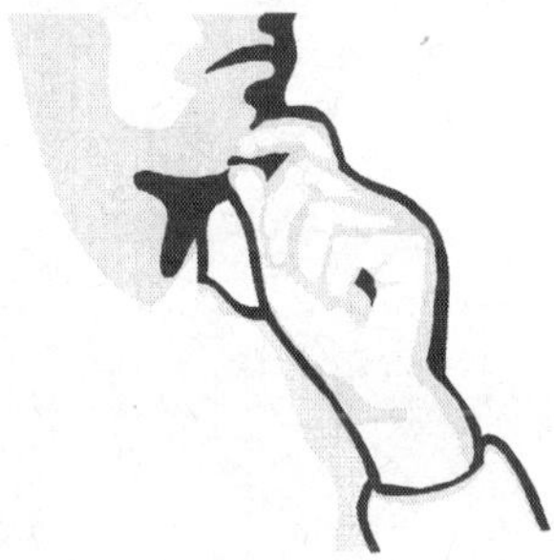

CHAPTER 1

OVERVIEW AND INTRODUCTION

1.1 WHAT IS RELEASE PLANNING AND WHY DO WE CARE?

Writing a book is not an easy task, nor is its reading. There should be a number of questions clarified to the reader up-front before entering the endeavor of studying a book like this. This overview and introduction chapter is devoted to giving an answer to a number of questions:

- What is product release planning?
- Why writing a book about this topic?
- What is the current status of release planning?
- What is the book's structure?
- What are the underlying assumptions behind writing this book?
- Who are the different types of reader supposed to read the book?
- What is the expected benefit from reading the book?

Size and complexity of today's product is continuously growing. This is true not only for software products, but is valid for many other products in information and communications technology, electronics and manufacturing. As a response to that, products are often developed more evolutionary than monolithic. This allows accommodation of early user feedback and facilitates better project planning and control. As a consequence, the likelihood of a product becoming successful is expected to increase. This is directly linked to the intended overall business success.

Product release planning is the process of planning for the next release of an evolving product. Customers and stakeholders are continuously asking for more or better features. But which ones to finally select for the next release and why? And which features are not attractive enough and are better left out (or postponed)? To give proper answers, many aspects need to be taken into account. These aspects range from (changing) customer needs over resources and time periods available, to the consideration of the technical feasibility of the proposed implementation plans.

Product release planning relates to other well-established disciplines of (incremental) development:

i. Requirements management, especially requirements prioritization,
ii. Project planning and management and
iii. Change and configuration management.

A major part of the responsibility of a product manager is to balance a variety of needs from markets, customers and stakeholders, and align them into an optimized allocation of sparse resources [Ebert '07]. Release planning is a challenging problem because of its size, the number of stakeholders involved in it, the variety of variables that need to be looked at and the uncertainty of the information it is relying upon. The overall goal is to determine a "most promising" release plan such that the total degree of satisfaction of all the different stakeholders is maximized.

The capability to react quickly to changed demands and to exploit efficiently the opportunities of new technologies is a driving factor of a company's success. Proposals for shortening the design and implementation time of a product have been made elsewhere [Blackburn et al. '96], [Smith and Reinertsen '98]. The emphasis of this book is on the preceding phase of planning what should be designed and implemented. The reason for this emphasis is that failures made in this early stage of the product life-cycle are hard to compensate afterward.

In this chapter of the book, an overview and introduction is given. There are a number of misconceptions about release planning. Their rebuttal is the content of Section 1.2. The logical dependency of the different chapters is outlined in Section 1.3. For the whole book, there are a number of underlying assumptions, which are presented in Section 1.4. The explicit description of these assumptions is intended to facilitate the understanding of the contributions of the book.

A variety of use case scenarios for the book are specified. In Section 1.5, some guidance is provided on which chapters of the book might be most relevant for different groups of readers. The expected benefits of these scenarios are categorized in Section 1.6.

1.2 MISCONCEPTIONS ABOUT RELEASE PLANNING

Product and service organizations are aiming at maximum business performance. They are trying to provide products and services that are attracted by customers and delivered in time and within budget. The role of planning in this process is an ongoing debate. Steve McConnell has formulated the *Nine Deadly Sins of Project Planning* [McConnell '01] and emphasized the importance of (proper) planning. At the other end of the spectrum, [Mankins and Steele '06] surveyed 156 senior executives and found that only 11% of them were highly satisfied with the cost-effectiveness of strategic planning. Where does product release planning fit into this spectrum, and how product decisions are made? And how should they be made? To better position the book, some of the existing misconceptions about release planning are analyzed.

1.2.1 Misconception #1: Release planning is useless

Why perform (release) planning at all? Isn't reality changing so quickly that any plan once established is deemed to be no longer valid after a short time? And does not the product manager know anyway what the customer wants?

Mike Cohn has written a book about agile estimation and planning [Cohn '06]. Emphasizing the effectiveness of the processes and focusing on their flexibility, he has provided five functions supported by planning in general: Reducing risk, reducing uncertainty, supporting better decision-making, establishing trust and conveying information. What does all this mean for planning of product releases? There are, in general, very good reasons why release planning is *useful*, not useless:

i. *Reducing risk:* Continuous planning and re-planning of releases will highlight some possible roadblocks. These roadblocks can be related to lack of resources needed or lack of time available. From performing continuous planning and re-planning, an update is obtained all the time about the likelihood of achieving the stated goals, either the original ones or the ones refined accordingly.

ii. *Reducing uncertainty:* Release planning involves a number of uncertainties, which are caused by the business conditions, the development processes and the people involved. Release planning allows easily varying or adjusting the underlying assumptions and analyzing their consequences. That way, the impact of uncertainty can be systematically elaborated and finally reduced.

iii. *Supporting better decision-making:* Good decisions are based on proper understanding of the problem and well-defined responsibilities for how to approach it. Planning supports both parts. Good decisions also rely on the best information available. Planning is not just generating the plan, but also the process to qualify all pre-requisites for it. This automatically qualifies decision-making as well.

iv. *Establishing trust:* A release plan gives the customer an outlook of which features can be expected in which release and which release can be expected when. If this plan is then also implemented that way, this likely creates trust on the customer side. This is even more so if the features planned are the ones the customer is expecting. This adds to the trust in the sense that customers feel well understood.

v. *Conveying information:* A release plan communicates the next stages of the product life-cycle to all involved stakeholders. With all the release plan information, stakeholders have a chance to compare with other products (when the stakeholders are the customers) or to organize the work to achieve stated milestones (when they are the development team).

1.2.2 Misconception #2: Release planning takes too much effort

Once some usefulness is confirmed, the next question is: *How much planning is enough?* This question is hard to answer in general because the impact (and thus the return of investment) of release planning depends on the product, the organizations, and the business domain. Under the pressure of time and project complexity, release decisions are often made "on-the-fly". This approach, however, often results in one or more of the following pain scenarios:

Pain in quality and in customer satisfaction: Often, the product delivered is not what the customers expected, leading to customer dissatisfaction. According to [Standish '09], *only about 20% of the features and functions specified get used.* This tendency of overwhelming the user with features relates to the belief that *the more features a product has, the better the product.* Too many (unused) features are not only a waste of effort, but they can also confuse the user. Besides, the complexity of the product is growing, which eventually has an impact on its performance.

A second deviation from customer expectation refers to the lack of offering expected features. Even if only 20% of the features offered are really used, are these the ones expected by the users and customers? Consciously or unconsciously ignoring customer expectations increases the risk of losing these customers. A careful analysis of customer needs is mandatory for business success.

Pain in business: The products offered by the company do not really penetrate the market. Competitors are more successful in bringing the right features at the right time to the right customers. A recent survey with response from 675 organizations revealed that only 6% of them classified their market evidence as *excellent* [Paquet '09]. The average revenue of these organizations is 114 million dollar, where 45% of the companies reported less than $50 million in revenue.

In daily life, pain often causes people and organizations to make changes. The question becomes: How much pain is an organization willing to accept as a result of immature product management? Proper release planning is considered one (but essential) part of this change. Problems prevented are problems solved. Optimization of complex processes and performing proactive what-if analysis with possible scenarios of the future will help find possible problems early. The earlier possible shortages or even conflicts are found, the earlier they can be mitigated. This can be a huge cost savings factor.

1.2.3 Misconception #3: Release planning is only possible with complete information

Meaningful data for release planning is hard to gather and uncertain in its nature. Features and requirements constantly change as the project progresses. Other parameters such as the number of stakeholders, business priorities or resources available also change with time. Estimates of the available effort, dependencies of features and definition of preferences from the perspective of involved stakeholders are difficult to gauge. In consideration of that: Why still planning?

The real purpose of effective planning is not to make plans but to change the microcosm, the mental models that ...decisions makers carry in their heads [De Geus '97]. Planning facilitates learning. It is not the exact plan, generated with some form of computer support, which counts most. Instead, it is the understanding of the direction to go for which is most important. The offerings by the methods and tools presented in this book are not supposed to be the ultimate truth, but a direction to go to support the human decision-making, to better understand the rationale of the decisions made, and to grow in the capability of mastering the whole process.

Thus, it is important to enter the continuous planning (and learning) process. It will help the individual product manager as well as the organization to move up to the next level of maturity.

1.2.4 Misconception #4: Planning is only useful if there are no changes once planning has been completed

Planning is a means for achieving stated goals, not the end. It is intended to provide directions, not final solutions. Planning is a continuous effort, as things are continuously changing. As in daily life, an initial plan gives you guidance in which direction to go. No one would expect this to remain valid without adjustment for a longer period of time. Planning implies re-planning. The same applies for product release planning. Once a plan is established, this plan needs adjustment to accommodate all the changes occurring down the road.

1.2.5 Misconception #5: Release planning is too complex

"Good" release plans are indeed hard to generate. Size and complexity of the planning endeavor are major problems for product managers when choosing release plans — some projects may have hundreds or even thousands of features. There are competing objectives such as cost and benefit, time-to-market and quality, and it is unclear which objectives should be emphasized and by how much. Some of the criteria are hard to formulate explicitly, such as the functional cohesiveness of the set of additional features or the smoothness of integration into existing product.

Release planning methods and tools need customization toward the organizational and project context. The level of granularity, its focus and scope, and the level of detail in the computation are decided by the user in response to the purpose of planning. At the beginning, a more coarse-grained and simple approach might be sufficient. At a later stage, further aspects and a higher level of detail can be taken into account. All this is not a *yes* or *no* decision about (release) planning, but a decision to find the right scope and level of detail.

1.2.6 Misconception #6: Intuition and experience is sufficient to create plans

Intuition and experience are necessary and important for making good release decisions. However, they are not sufficient. The size and complexity of the problem, and the possibility of forgetting to consider the most relevant factors in the planning process, make it risky to decide just based on individual judgment or methods of trial and error. There is substantial risk that such decisions are misdirecting. This is because they ignore important aspects of the whole process.

Intuition alone is not enough to solve complex problems. In the same way, formality, for example, as offered by mathematics, alone is insufficient as well. Optimization of complex processes and proactive analysis of possible future scenarios requires a method for systematic support of human decision-making that involves intuition whenever needed.

1.3 HOW THE BOOK IS STRUCTURED

Different groups of readers will have different backgrounds, interests and expectations of the content of a book on product release planning. This book is organized in four main parts including 15 chapters. The structure reflects the main components considered important for maturing the process of making product release decisions. The four main parts are:

Part A: Foundations	Chapter 1 to 3
Part B: Methods	Chapter 4 to 9
Part C: Tools	Chapter 10
Part D: Applications	Chapter 11 to 15

A graph of logical dependencies between the chapters is drawn in Figure 1.1. An arrow between two nodes (representing chapters) indicates that the origin node (chapter) is a preparation for the destination chapter.

Besides this overview and introduction, the *Foundations* part describes the background of decision-making (Chapter 2) and features prioritization (Chapter 3). Some of the decision-making concepts are illustrated by concrete problems from the area of release decisions. These problems will be used later on in the book to illustrate the proposed solution methods. Prioritization of features is positioned as a first step toward making release decisions. In general, all methods and techniques studied in this book are considered from a process perspective. That means it is specified which steps need to be done, who should conduct these steps, and what the results are. This process perspective is chosen to facilitate application and customization of the methods.

The *Methods* part is devoted to product release planning. In Chapters 4 to 6, a more strategic and also is taken at release planning. This is often called *roadmapping*. An overview of existing methods for release planning is given in Chapter 4. More in-depth modeling options related to business, resource, risk, and technological constraints are presented in Chapter 5. A customizable method for conducting systematic release planning called *EVOLVE II* is the subject of Chapter 6. EVOLVE II is highly flexible and emphasizes the involvement of relevant stakeholders at the different stages of the process.

Once a roadmap is established, guidance is needed to accommodate change. All underlying planning assumptions are candidates for change. It begins with the arrival of new features and the need to change existing ones. It continues with modifications of the business priorities, which have an impact on the content and priority of the planning objectives. Also budgets are often changed, and so is the availability of human resources. Chapter 7 provides a method for re-planning the ongoing release, trying to accommodate changes in the best possible way.

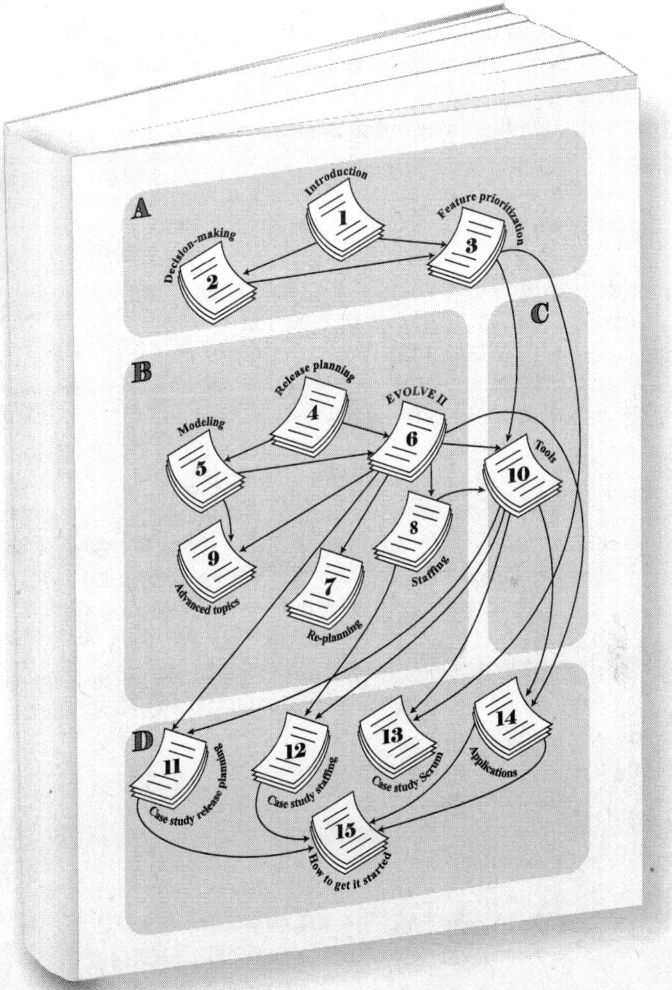

Figure 1.1 Graph of logical dependencies between the 15 chapters of the book

Another implication of an existing roadmap is the need to plan for its operational implementation. This is called *operational planning* and includes the scheduling and staffing of the tasks providing the features. Different formulations of this problem are given in Chapter 8. All of them take into account that developers have different productivity profiles. The challenge is to find the operational plan where the best available developers are assigned to the right tasks.

As the final chapter of Part B, Chapter 9 presents four advanced topics of research. They are related to effort and resource estimation with emphasis on release planning, the explanation of decision support generated from machine learning techniques, the consideration of design constraints in the course of making release decisions, and the prediction of the impact of uncertainty in operational planning.

Part C is denoted to tool support. Three release planning tools are presented in Chapter 10. The three tools have different focuses and different levels of detail. *VeryBestChoice*^{Light} aims at the prioritization of features and subsequent analysis of prioritization results obtained from different stakeholders and with respect to different criteria. The *ReleasePlanner*™ decision support system is used for generating optimized product release planning alternatives. Finally, *RASORP* optimizes staffing and scheduling of the implementation of features defined for the next release. Trial user accounts are provided for the first two tools to allow the reader to become more familiar with the tools. For both of them, the login information for the (read only) user account is *user name* = *book* and *password* = *trial.*

Another important part of the book is devoted to *Applications*. Three case studies are presented to give further insight into the practical realization of the proposed methods. They are devoted to product release planning (Chapter 11), staffing for product releases (Chapter 12) and decision support for adoptable project management following Scrum (Chapter 13). In addition to these case studies, five application scenarios are outlined in Chapter 14. In all of the five scenarios, it is shown how the problems behind the scenarios can be reformulated to allow the application of the EVOLVE II planning method and its related tools. The five applications are:

- Roadmapping for multiple products
- Release planning with consideration of quality demands
- Agile project management following Scrum
- Planning for competitiveness of products
- Project portfolio planning

The final Chapter 15 gives operational instructions how to get it started with the process of product release planning.

1.4 SOME ASSUMPTIONS TO SHARE

1.4.1 About assumptions

This book is not written in a vacuum. As most of the things studied in science and engineering, the methods, tools and techniques proposed and discussed are based on some key assumptions and beliefs. Describing these key assumptions early on will help the reader to better understand the book. The assumptions formulated later in this section are fundamental and address the role of models, planning, and decision-making. There are other assumptions formulated later in this book which are more specific and related to a single method or technique.

Assumptions express certain beliefs at the start of an investigation. The reader does not necessarily need to share all assumptions in order to benefit from reading the book. Different assumptions might be true in different contexts and environments.

1.4.2 The need for balancing art and science

This is the common theme of the whole book: Balancing art and science, intuition and discipline. *Art* stands for all the unique skills, feeling and competencies associated with the human experts. *Science* stands for the design and analysis of rigorous methods and techniques, their controlled application for the purpose of solving a tacit problem. Art is as important as science. One cannot successfully apply one without the other. Release decisions exclusively based on intuition will likely miss business opportunities and waste resources. On the other hand, just following formal models, method and techniques is insufficient to accommodate implicit concerns of human decision-making. What is needed is the synergy between the two worlds. While this is easy to admit, the hard part is: How do we actually achieve this synergy? As its main goal, the book tries to provide a constructive answer for creating synergy between art and science for the sake of making better release decisions.

1.4.3 To prevent problems is to solve problems

Planning is useful for various reasons. Wrong decisions are hard to reverse afterward, especially in the early stages of the process when fundamental design decisions are made. Planning is part of the proactive effort to avoid pitfalls in the later stages.

While this seems to be generally accepted, there is always the debate: How do we measure the "goodness" of a plan? One possible answer to this question is to measure the impact of problems that have been prevented from early planning activities. What-if analysis often helps detect the lack of resources and the lack of time to achieve the originally stated goal. Understanding these and possible other problems in advance reduces the risk that the (product development) project fails or does not achieve its stated goal.

1.4.4 The only stable thing is change

Planning is important, but it needs to be understood as a continuing activity. Roadmaps are blueprints for future product development. They give a direction, but cannot be expected to be the ultimate pathway and being valid and stable for a longer period of time. Instead, plans need to be adjusted. What counts is a good plan, but even more the understanding that this (good) plan is just the beginning of getting the plan implemented. That means that one permanently has to react to change.

1.4.5 Good products require good up-front planning and design

To say it by a quote again: *A man who does not think and plan long ahead will find trouble right at his door* (Confucius BC 551–BC 479). This is assumed to be true in general and for product development in particular. Decisions resulting in the selection of the wrong features cannot be compensated by highly efficient implementation. Up-front planning cannot provide guarantees, but will reduce the risk of making the wrong things and of making things wrong.

1.4.6 The role of modeling: Approximation of the truth and its implications

This book emphasizes modeling as a means to formulate, understand, communicate and discuss the (different) views about the reality of making release decisions. These decisions are tremendously complex with all the possible factors impacting them. It is simply impossible to accommodate all of them. Instead, the most important ones need to be selected. As already stated by Aristotle (384 BC–322 BC): *It is the mark of an instructed mind to rest satisfied with the degree of precision to which the nature of the subject admits and not to seek exactness when only an approximation of the truth is possible.*

Being aware of the model limitation is as important as being satisfied with an approximation of the truth. Models are a means, not the end. Models are as good as they are helpful for the purpose for which they are designed. Understanding the limitations of the model increases the chances to make meaningful conclusions out of them.

1.4.7 What counts is insight, not numbers

In this book, there is some emphasis on models and their use for systematic analysis. Often, this analysis is quantitative. As extensively argued by [Sassenburg '05], numbers matter, but are not enough. There is too much uncertainty in making release decisions. Uncertainty is related to people, processes, technologies, markets and primarily to the goals of the actual (product) development. It would be too simple to assume all these things could be mapped into something as precise as numbers. Numbers serve as indicators, not as truth evaluators. But numbers, although quantitative, help us to understand reality from a qualitative perspective. They help to better understand things; that is, they help to *gain insight*.

1.4.8 The importance of proper processes and process integrated tools

Edwards Deming (1900–1993) formulated the importance of (explicit) process as follows: *If you can't describe what you are doing as a process, you don't know what you're doing*. Release planning is a process, and needs to be understood as such. For its performance, there are a number of steps to be looked at in the proper order of sequence. The right people need to be involved in the process to ensure its best results. Organizing all this in a proper way and deciding who is responsible for what is what is called *the process*.

Processes need to be conducted efficiently. Tools have the potential to help on that, if the tools are the right ones for their requested purpose. Tools and processes need to be harmonized. Their combined effect has the potential to make the difference. If not integrated, things might become worse than without tool support.

1.4.9 Investments into better product planning and decision processes pay off

A study including one-to-one interviews with 14 senior marketers from brand-name companies and a quantitative survey of product marketing professionals from a wide range of industries [BPMForum] revealed significant pain points in the product decision-making process:

- 70 percent of respondents classify their opinion of the quality of data being conveyed between product marketing and other internal constituencies as being from *average* to *very low.*
- Despite the implementation of big-ticket technology infrastructures, up to 80 percent of respondents rely on internal data generated and communicated through outdated spreadsheets.
- Almost 70 percent express displeasure with the technologies they use for product forecasting, pricing, product portfolio planning and competitor analysis.

1.4.10 Decisions need to be managed holistically at corporate level

Release planning decisions are one part of the whole chain of company decisions to be made. Just improving on one of them will have low impact if the others remain unchanged. Qualifying the roadmapping process needs to go hand-in-hand with qualifying other organizational processes. The key need is to establish a holistic enterprise strategic decision management infrastructure with the goal to align roadmapping with systems engineering, business strategy and (human) capability management [IEEE '08].

1.5 WHO SHOULD READ THIS BOOK?

The development and selling of products is the key scope of doing business. Products are ultimately everywhere. There is the whole spectrum of software products (with all the different categories such as business administration, enterprise resource planning systems, databases, e-commerce, business intelligence, security and e-learning). But the methods, tools and applications presented in this book are not at all limited to software products. Examples of other products are:

- Telecommunication products (mobile phones, faxes, modems, routers, voice over IP products, communication devices, GPS devices)
- Medical devices (hearing aid, diagnostic devices, monitoring devices)
- Electronic devices (computers, home theaters, monitors, printers)
- Transportation products (cars, trains, buses, airplanes)
- Governments and municipalities (services, business practices)

The above list is not intended to be complete, but illustrative. The commonality in all these product planning applications is the search for the best orchestration of features in consideration of budget and resource capacities.

A situation similar to planning for product roadmaps can be found in the area of composition of services. While services can differ in their content and nature, the same question arises: Which blend of services is most attractive to be offered at which point in time? As all the services consume some effort, the same prioritization and selection challenge applies as for selection of the most attractive product features.

All product release, project portfolio and service managers are facing the same challenge: To plan and organize for a process enabling the best business based upon a sequence of product, project or service releases. In project management, the term *releases* is often replaced by quarterly or annual *milestones*.

The book is intended to attract readers from both academia and practice. This may sound attractive, but it also incorporates a substantial risk. The risk is that none of the two camps feels sufficiently satisfied in their needs and their way of thinking. Both camps speak different languages, and there is sufficient evidence that they don't always understand each other [Kaindl el al '02]. Patience from the researcher's side is requested because (intentionally) not all the technical details are provided. However, there are always scientific journal or conference publications to find further technical details. Patience from the practitioner's side is requested, as some formalized descriptions, including formula's, have been unavoidable.

One way to mitigate the risk of a diverse readership is to provide different pathways for reading the book. The assumption is that all groups of readers start with Chapter 1 to receive an overview. Without being prescriptive, Table 1.1 offers some suggestions for *who (classified according to roles and abbreviated by R1 to R9) should read what?*

Table 1.1 Suggestions for *who* should read *what*

Role	#	Recommended chapters
Executives	R1	If there is time for reading two chapters, then read Chapters 10 and 15.
Product managers	R2	If there is time for reading five chapters, then read Chapters 3, 4, 10, at least one of {11,12,13, 14} and 15.
Practitioner	R3	All chapters should provide some practical value. The highest level of formality is in Chapters 5, 7 and 8.
Researchers	R4	Chapters 2 to 9.
Undergraduate students	R5	Chapters 2, 3 and 4.

Table 1.1 (continued)

Role	#	Recommended chapters
Main interest in applications	R6	Chapters 11 to 15.
Main interest in tools	R7	Chapter 10.
Project managers	R8	Chapters 7, 8, 10, 12, 14 and 15.
Marketing and sales representatives	R9	Chapters 3 and 10.

1.6 EXPECTED BENEFITS

In general, the expected benefits will depend on the background of the reader and on how much time is spent with the book. The main benefits include the following:

- Getting an overview of existing methods in product release planning.
- Gaining detailed knowledge about the release planning method EVOLVE II.
- Understanding the foundations of making product release decisions.
- Understanding the application of the different methods from going through different case studies.
- Becoming skilled in the application of prioritization and planning tools.
- Becoming skilled in adjusting to change.
- Becoming skilled in performing voice-of-the-stakeholder analyses.

The expected benefits for the different readers are summarized in Table 1.2. It is up to the reader to either confirm the projected outcome or report other experiences. The reader is encouraged to take this journey and to communicate their learning experience to the author. Have things be properly described? In an understandable way? And which ones? Answering these and other questions from the perspective of the different types of readers helps to incorporate in later editions of the book for the benefit of future learners. For any type of comments or suggestions, the author can be reached at ruhe@ucalgary.ca.

Table 1.2 Potential benefits for the different groups of readers R1 to R9

	R1	R2	R3	R4	R5	R6	R7	R8	R9
Getting an overview of existing methods in product release planning	X	X	X						
Gaining detailed knowledge about the release planning method EVOLVE II			X	X					
Understanding the foundations of making product release decisions		X	X	X	X				
Understanding the application of the different methods	X	X	X			X			
Becoming skilled in adjusting to change			X					X	
Becoming skilled in performing voice-of-the-stakeholder analyses			X						X

CHAPTER 2

DECISIONS AND HOW TO MAKE THEM

2.1 INTRODUCTION

Decision-making is a complex process with different stages and players involved. Decisions have to be made all the time in product development. The focus of this chapter is on the process of making product decisions. Special emphasis is on prioritization and planning of features and the decisions about staffing for their implementation. All these decisions have tremendous impact on the success of the company. The information available is typically uncertain and incomplete. Often, information is changing. Decisions are further complicated by a range of criteria and constraints that need to be taken into account. In some cases, the formulation of these criteria and constraints is a problem itself. Despite all this, decisions need to be made as qualified and fact-based as possible. The scope and level of detail of this process is determined by the context.

The discipline of *Decision Science* is encompassing all of these and even more aspects. Decision Science (or *Decision Analysis*) is a well-established and truly interdisciplinary discipline [Keeney '82], [Clemen '96]. It has strong links and interactions to many other disciplines such as Economics, Operations Research, Logic, Organization Theory and Sociology. At its very core, decision-making is the process of creating and defining alternatives, evaluating them and determining the one that is most appropriate to the original problem context. Decision-making is happening at very different levels ranging from strategic to tactical to operational. Decisions depend on each other, and decision-making happens everywhere and anytime.

Depending on the nature of the decisions to be made, intuition can play an important role. However, solely relying on intuition reduces the transparency and trustworthiness of decisions. Simultaneously, it increases the risk of ignoring important factors resulting in decisions of lower quality. But how does combining human intuition with the rationality and exactness of the computer produce better decisions? The advantage of the computer-based decision-making approach is exactly where the human-based approach fails: The capability to effectively manage and analyze large amounts of information. The advantage of the human intelligence-based approach often is that it is able to handle soft and implicit objectives and constraints.

Decisions are the focal points for business success in general, and for any product development in particular. It is difficult to compensate for wrong or weak decisions at later stages of the process. The emphasis of this section is not to give an overview of all the different types of decision problems but to provide the necessary background for the subsequent chapters.

Three sample product release decision scenarios are introduced in Section 2.2. They will be studied later in the book after methods for their solution have been described. A pragmatic classification of (tamed) decision problems is the content of Section 2.3. The difference between decision-making and decisions support is highlighted in Section 2.4. The process of decision-making is studied in Section 2.5. It is defined as part of evolutionary problem solving in Section 2.6. Finally, the role of decisions is put into a more comprehensive context in Section 2.7 when looking at the *Enterprise Strategic Decision Management* initiative [IEEE '08].

2.2 THREE PRODUCT RELEASE DECISION SCENARIOS

During the process of planning and implementing product releases, various decisions have to be made at different process stages. Three typical decision scenarios have been selected. They are related to *feature prioritization, re-planning of product releases*, and *staffing for implementation of features*.

2.2.1 Feature prioritization for product release planning

John is the product manager for a mid-size telecommunications software-intensive product company called *SIP Inc*. For their flagship product, on average, new releases are offered every six months. The number of new features being added per release depends on their size. The number typically varies in the range between 20 and 30. The commitment to these features is the result of a prioritization process that typically includes about 60 candidate features. But how does one select the "right" ones?

The company's products are distributed worldwide to more than 100 customers. One of John's tasks is the ongoing prioritization of existing and new arriving features. Features are constantly changing, often as a result of feedback from customers having used early prototypes as well as alpha or beta product versions. In addition to that, some of the already existing features do not meet customer expectations and need to be revised.

John needs to classify features into (i) those that are so important that they are practically mandatory, those (ii) that are not considered right now, and (iii) the remaining set of features where closer consideration is required. For example, in the case where the top three customers of SIP Inc. have requested the same feature on their wish list for the next product release, John will emphasize that this feature indeed will be implemented in the next release. On the other side, if the market is not yet ready for the feature or the feature is extremely risky in its implementation, then it will be put aside, at least for now. All together, John will focus on selections that avoid losing customers or violate laws and contracts.

Overall, this sounds like a simple and straightforward process. However, John knows that it is not as simple or straightforward as it sounds. Different stakeholders have different opinions about which features are more important than others. And what actually is the meaning of *importance?* Does it refer to customer satisfaction, to business value or to urgency? Very likely, what needs to be done is to look at a combination of all of these and maybe even other criteria.

Thus far, effort to implement these features has not been taken into account. This, however, is the biggest concern John has all the time: The capacity is by far not sufficient to allow implementation of all the features of interest. Overall, John has to make a number of difficult decisions such as:

- Which people (or stakeholders) should I listen to for their opinion?
- Which questions (prioritization criteria) should I ask the stakeholders to look at?
- How much effort is (likely to be) consumed by the candidate features?
- How can the projected value of features and their combination be estimated?
- Which features should make it into the next release, which ones to the following release, and which ones come later?

On top of that, the criteria and opinions for making these decisions are often multiple and contradicting. The best compromises are needed in these cases.

2.2.2 Re-planning for product releases

Once the next product release features are announced, the process of their implementation gets started. However, the arrival of new feature ideas and the modification of already existing features do not stop because of this. On the contrary, John, our product manager for SIP Inc., is under an ongoing demand to ensure the implementation of the already agreed upon features, but also to accommodate very important and very recent requests for changes. To make his life even more challenging, the company has recently changed its business strategy, and John is expected to align with these new directions as well.

The inclusion of a new feature has at least two implications:

i. As the available development capacity has not changed, inclusion of a new feature typically means removing one or more others.
ii. The originally announced feature plan of the release needs to be revised. With more than 100 customers, John needs good arguments to explain the necessary changes to them and to demonstrate that the revised release is of more value than the original one.

The re-planning situation becomes even more complex as ideas and suggestions for new features can occur continuously. In an extreme case, should a large portion of the already agreed upon features be replaced by more attractive ones? In this context, John has to decide a number of things:

- When is a good point in time for re-planning?
- How often can one re-plan during a release?
- Who should be asked for their opinion on the importance of features?
- What is important for company SIP Inc. at this point in time?
- How many features should be replaced?
- How can the balance be kept between the attractiveness of new features and the degree of change to an already announced product release?

Overall, John not only needs to make the best possible (compromise) decisions, he also needs to make his decisions transparent to all the shareholders of the company to get their buy-in.

2.2.3 Staffing for product releases

John, the product manager at SIP Inc., is working closely with Jane, one of the project managers at the company. Jane's responsibility is to ensure that the plans and re-plans created by John are properly scheduled on a task level, and that the assignment of developers to perform the individual tasks is feasible and efficient.

What Jane is looking at is a list of features already committed for the next release. Each feature unit represents a kind of mini-project with effort devoted to its design, implementation, testing and documentation. Different tools and skills are needed to perform these tasks. From having worked in the company, Jane has a good overview of the specific skills and competencies of all their developers. The challenge is to assign them in a best possible way utilizing their strengths and avoiding their weaknesses.

In the case of re-planning, already existing assignments have to be changed. Ideally, the degree of changes should be kept as low as possible for stability reasons. Stability of announced plans represents a value of its own because it helps developers focus on the once assigned tasks and avoids unnecessary communication overhead. For performing staffing, effort estimation per feature-specific task is mandatory. Jane is also maintaining an effort database with records of features developed in past releases including their estimated versus their actual efforts. This information is useful to perform estimation based on analogy, where actual efforts from former features being similar to the new one are taken to predict the effort for the new one.

The staffing becomes even more complex because the availability of personnel is uncertain. Key developers might become unavailable at very short notice, and re-allocation needs to be performed to fill the gap. The overall goal of this re-planning is to provide the new release within the announced release date. In addition, the quality of the release needs to be ensured by all means, as this is the key success factor of SIP Inc.

Jane has to make weekly staffing decisions related to the following questions:

- Which features will be implemented next?
- Who is working on what?
- How do we react to changed and new features?
- How do we incorporate necessary bug fixes?
- How do we react to changes on the availability of personnel?

2.3 CLASSIFICATION OF DECISIONS

In the case of all three scenarios just described, decisions need to be taken even though information is incomplete and uncertain. The priorities assigned by stakeholders might vary over time, and the understanding of the feature might be incomplete. The effort estimates made are to the best of the expert's knowledge, but they need adjustment typically over time. This is even more true for the projection of the feature's market value. All these difficulties are consciously ignored for now, and the formulation of decision problems in its simplest forms is started. Following [Bouyssou et al. '06], a decision problem can be described by a

(2.1) Set A = {a(1), a(2), …} of alternatives (these alternatives are not necessarily described explicitly), and a

(2.2) Set G = {g(1), g(2), …,g(n)} of criteria to evaluate each alternative of A from different perspectives.

Often, the formulation of both the criteria and the (feasible) alternatives is the harder problem than the algorithmic solution itself. Three main categories of decision problems can be defined.

(2.3) *Selection*: Select one alternative a* from A or a subset of alternatives $A^* \subset A$.

(2.4) *Triage*: Assign each alternative a* from A to one of the given set of classes.

(2.5) *Ranking*: Arrange all alternatives in A according to an order $a(1) \geq a(2) \geq \ldots$ (where $a \geq b$ means *alternative a is at least as good as b*).

Three examples are given. As an example for the *selection* category, Scenario 2 is considered with its request to select features of the upcoming release for being replaced by new, more attractive arrivals.

As an example for the *triage* category, Scenario 1 is considered. When planning two releases ahead of time, each feature is assigned either to the next release, or to the next plus one release, or it is postponed.

As an example for the *ranking* category, Scenario 3 is considered with its request to rank features according to their perceived risk.

In most of the practical cases, decision-making is a complex process. There are different kinds of complexity to think of:

- **Computational complexity**

In its easiest form, computational complexity [Garey and Johnson '79] classifies (decision) problems into those for which a (deterministically) polynomial solution algorithm is known and those for which it is not (assuming both classes in fact are different, which is still an open research problem). *Polynomial solution algorithm* refers to an algorithm whose time and space requirements represent a polynomial function of the size of a problem. These problems are considered *easy* in the sense that they are solvable even for large scale problems in a reasonable amount of space and time.

- **Cognitive complexity**

Cognitive complexity refers to the difficulty to explicitly formulate the decision problem. The above descriptions of selection, triage and ranking belong to the category of well defined and formulated problems. They are also called *tamed* decision problems. At the other side of the spectrum, there are *wicked problems* as introduced by [Rittel and Webber '84]. Planning and design problems are typical representatives of this class of problems. Several characteristics have been defined. One of them says that there is no definite formulation of the problem. Another one states that wicked problems have no stopping rule applied to terminate the solution process. While tamed and wicked problems are the two extremes, it can be expected that most decision problems are some form of combination of the two extremes.

- **Decision-making complexity**

The actual decision is typically made by humans. Looking at decision-making complexity refers to whether there is either a single person or a group decision situation. The single person case is easier, as no conflicts between the involved humans can occur. In the case of group-decision making, synchronization, balancing and negotiation between different opinions is necessary. Different types of agents are used to assist human decision-making within this process. For release planning, this idea is studied and implemented in [Denzinger and Ruhe '04].

- **Information complexity**

The nature of information used for decision-making can be deterministic or stochastic. In case of deterministic information, the measurement of attributes is expressed by a single value. For example, the feature implementation effort can be considered a point estimate of 12 person days. For the same example, the effort could be considered stochastic as well. In this case, a probability distribution is defined describing the probability that certain effort values will occur. This distribution can have different forms such as those described by normal, triangular or constant functions.

Independent of complexity considerations, but looking at the scope and time horizon, [Turban et al. '05] identify three levels of decisions: strategic, tactical and operational. *Strategic decisions* concern the goals of an organization with its products and services. They have a large scope of impact (all the activities in an organization or a project) and a long-term time horizon (life-cycle of a product, duration of a project). A typical example is defining the product strategy for the next five years.

Tactical decisions address the planning of resources, time or tasks to achieve the goals (decided at the strategic level). They are usually made at the middle level of management with a smaller scope of impact and shorter time horizon. A typical example is *project planning* and related decisions such as *How much resources should be allocated to different tasks?* or *How do we schedule the tasks?*

Operational decisions are made at the operative level by requirement engineers, developers or testers while performing specific tasks to realize the project according to the plan. Decisions such as *When to stop testing?*, *Which portion(s) of the code should be re-factored?* or *Which bug should be fixed by whom?* all belong to this category.

2.4 DECISION-MAKING VERSUS DECISION SUPPORT

2.4.1 Decision support — why?

Decision support has been successfully designed, developed and applied in many areas such as logistics, manufacturing, health care, energy and agriculture. The idea of offering decision support always arises when decisions have to be made in complex, uncertain or dynamic environments. In the context of product development, what type of support can be expected in which situation?

Many decisions have to be made as part of product development. They relate to processes, products, resources, tools, methods and techniques. From a decision-making perspective, all these questions are facing different objectives and constraints, a huge number of variables under dynamically changing requirements, processes, actors, stakeholders, tools and techniques.

How are these decisions currently made? Some observations from current decision-making in real-world situations are summarized below [Ruhe '03]:

- Decision problems are often poorly understood and described.
- Decisions are done at the last moment and under time pressure.
- Decisions are not relying on empirically evaluated models, best knowledge and experience and a sound methodology.
- Decisions are made without considering the perspectives of all the involved stakeholders.
- Decision-making takes too much effort or too much time (meetings).
- Decisions are not explained or made transparent to those involved.

Providing support in complex and uncertain situations of decision-making is a comprehensive endeavor. Decision support systems typically are specific to the context of the decisions to be made. They couple the intellectual resources of individuals and organizations with the capabilities of the computer to

- Generate and evaluate (new) solution alternatives,
- Allow more transparent decisions (to be better understood by involved people),
- Analyze decisions proactively,

- Better react to changes in the problem parameters (re-planning),
- Make more effective (trade-off) decisions (improved quality), and
- Allow more efficient decisions (improved cost-benefit).

While this sounds like the ultimate achievement, it is a substantial effort and challenge to provide meaningful support. Despite a number of successful systems (for example [Capilla et al. '08], [Collofello et al. '98], [Neubauer and Stummer '07], [Shaw et al. '07]), there is still a substantial gap between the reality of applying decision support and what seems possible. On the other hand, once decision support systems have been established, there is an acceptance problem as well. The main obstacle here is human-related. This topic is discussed further in Section 9.3 of the book.

Methodologically, decision support can be the result of a variety of different analytical contributions. The architecture of a decision support system for product development is shown in Figure 2.1. There is a bi-directional relationship between all the supporting methods and techniques and the different activities in a product life-cycle. The product life-cycle is represented in a simplified manner by the three main stages of planning, development and evolution. The intermediate layer provides the communication platform for and between the involved decision-makers and stakeholders.

2.5 THE DECISION-MAKING PROCESS

Similar to product development, there exist a number of variants for the process of decision-making. Any concrete decision process needs to be adjusted to each specific situation in terms of its scope, level of detail and overall effort. Six stages of the decision-making process are considered:

- **Define problem:** The art of understanding and formulating the problem with the degree of detail possible and necessary. The problem definition typically includes definition of criteria and constraints.
- **Define alternatives:** Alternatives can be defined either explicitly (e.g., architectural alternatives) or implicitly. The implicit definition is done by giving a number of constraints that need to be satisfied to become a (feasible) alternative. A large part of Chapter 5 is devoted to this effort.
- **Evaluate alternatives:** Evaluation of alternatives is done based upon the stated objective(s). The evaluation method can be the formal computation of the objective function value(s). In case this is not possible, it can be done more subjectively, for example, by expert judgment. Besides the impact toward the stated objectives, evaluation of alternatives might also include the prediction of other possible impacts of the decision.
- **Decide:** The actual decision can be the selection of the most preferred alternative. Following the former classification, it could also be triaging alternatives or providing their ranking.

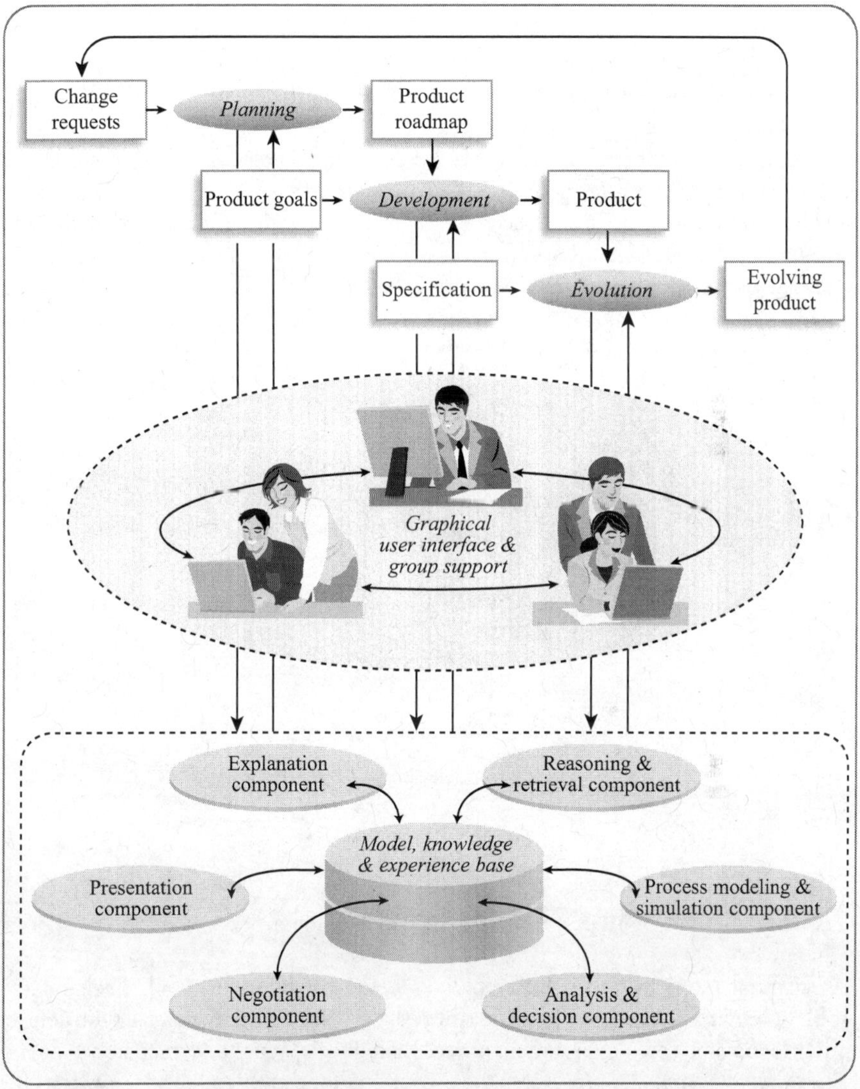

Figure 2.1 Architecture of a decision support system for product development

- **Implement decision:** Implementation of a decision really means to make it happen. This often requires the buy-in from all the stakeholders. If the decision is related to a new technology, customizing and learning processes need to be initiated. In general, the implementation of decisions looks into all these details and often creates follow-up questions and decisions.

- **Evaluate decision:** Once decisions are made and implemented, it is important to follow their life-cycle even further. Did the decision provide the expected outcomes? If not, what might have caused the deviations from them? Retrospective evaluation is an important means to improve the quality of decision-making.

The execution of the process steps can be done in different ways, quite similar to the key product development phases. The (strict) waterfall type of decision process is illustrated in Figure 2.2. Each process step is followed without feedback by the next one. Similar to the waterfall software development life-cycle process, the strictly sequential process only occurs when the problem is well understood with all its alternatives, objectives and constraints. In addition, the structure of the problem does not change over time.

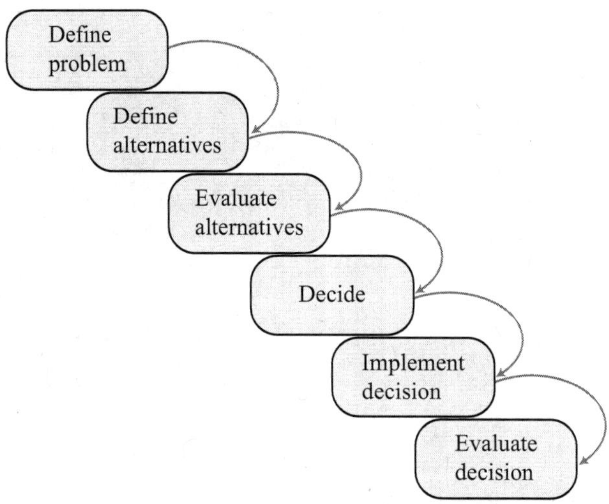

Figure 2.2 Waterfall type of decision process

As demonstrated by an experiment conducted by [Conklin '01], decision (or "problem-solving") processes do not necessarily follow the waterfall structure. Similar to the software development process, feedback loops to former stages occur.

The curve in Figure 2.3 represents the evolution of the problem-solving process for the experiment [Conklin '01]. The content of the experiment refers to the design of an elevator control system. The waterfall model curve is going through six main stages (in correspondence to the description of the decision-making process introduced above). The other curve describes the varying stages of the problem-solving process. The higher the level on the y-axis, the closer is the state of the human problem solver in the level of understanding and formulating the problem (problem space). From proactive analysis of prototype solutions (low level on the y-axis), a more complete problem understanding can be expected.

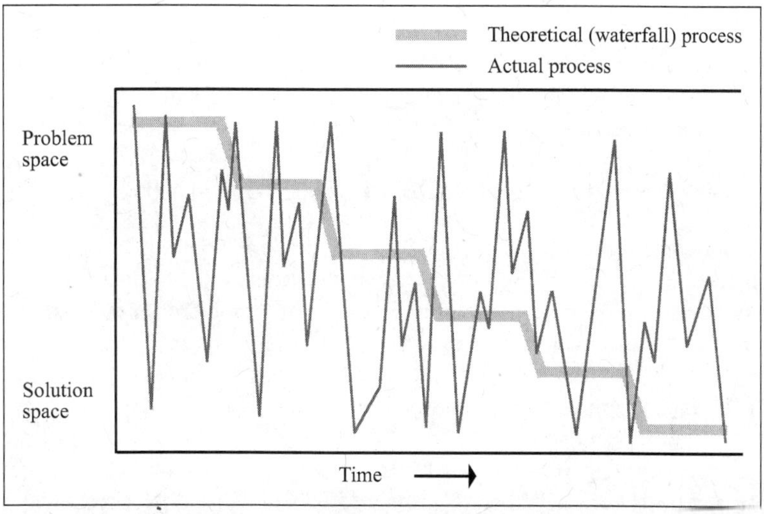

Figure 2.3 Pattern of cognitive activity of one designer (adapted from [Conklin '01])

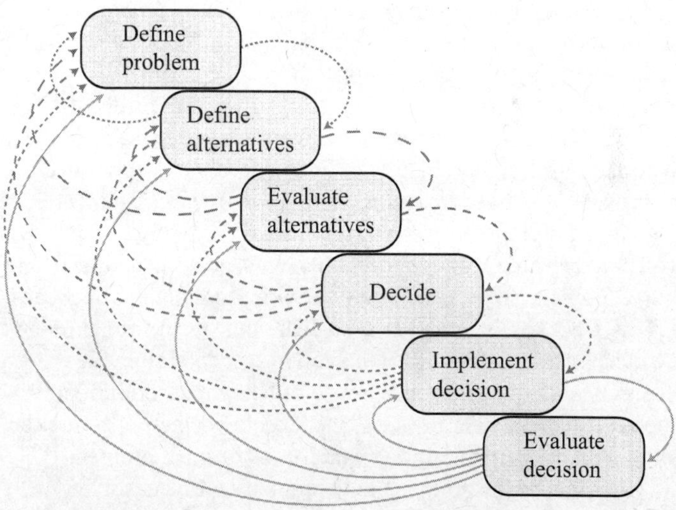

Figure 2.4 Decision-making process with feedback loops

It was pointed out by [Conklin '01] that the actual process curve looks different for different subjects. The above experiment tells us that the decision-making process might be more complex than performing a strict sequence of steps. In dependency of the problem understanding, feedback loops are important in the process. As a result, the process described in Figure 2.4 is considered more realistic.

From each stage of the process, there is the possibility to return to one of the former steps. The key rationale for that is the evolutionary nature of the process of understanding the problem For the problem of product release planning, the risks of problem (mis-) understanding are mitigated by involving significant stakeholders and allowing them to participate at the different stages of the process.

2.6 EVOLUTIONARY PROBLEM SOLVING

The theories of *natural selection* and the *survival of the fittest* have been based on principles extracted from observations and analyses of changes in living organisms over a long period of time. Evolutionary problem solving is partially inspired by those ideas and involves the evolution of problem comprehension and the corresponding solution alternatives. It starts with the premises that (i) problem formulation is as important as its solution and (ii) problem formulation, in a strict sense, is an evolutionary process.

The problem-solving process described in Section 2.4 is further studied, now from the perspective of whether to provide feedback. The difference of problem solving with and without feedback is illustrated in Figure 2.5. In both cases, the real-world situation is considered as a starting point. Modeling is performed to create a formalized description of the original problem. Based on that, formal methods can be applied to generate solution(s) in an analytical way. *Formal methods* here subsumes all methods and techniques applicable in the context of the stated problem such as reasoning, analysis, simulation or optimization.

In the upper part of the figure (problem solving without feedback), the solutions gained from the application of the formal methods are projected back and interpreted in the context of the original problem. No further feedback is provided on how well the solution provided really addresses the original problem. The inherent risk is that whenever the modeling fails, the resulting solutions are likely to fail as well.

The lower part of Figure 2.5 follows the same process with the one essential difference that problem solving includes early and continuous feedback from the real-world. This feedback is intended to validate the stated formal model. Problem solving here means a continuous effort in evolving models, allowing them to become more and more meaningful for their purpose of being a description of reality. Now, from having validated models in place, the likelihood increases that the solutions gained from this process are highly relevant for the original problem.

A further refinement of the process of evolutionary problem solving with feedback is illustrated in Figure 2.6. On the left side, the evolution of models is illustrated. At each of its steps, the inner white shape represents the reality which is evolving as well. Comparing these shapes top-down, changes in reality are visualized by changes in the inner white shape.

The outer shape represents the description of the reality by a formalized model. In the course of evolution, a better and better approximation of the inner shape by the outer one is assumed. In fact, the inner shape (reality) is never exactly known. The outer one is an explicit description of the perception of the real-world, having the additional value of being amenable to the application of formal algorithms.

At each step of the evolution it is assumed that feedback is obtained from evaluating the proposed planning alternatives. This is a necessary condition for success of this process, but not a sufficient one. In general, evolution and evolutionary processes do not necessarily lead to progress. This is due to lack of knowledge and the presence of all the uncertainty as well as the inherent risk of incorrect modeling.

In EVOLVE II, the planning method described in Chapter 6, feedback is provided at the different stages of the process by human experts. This assumes a human capability to judge the quality of the solutions obtained from the current model.

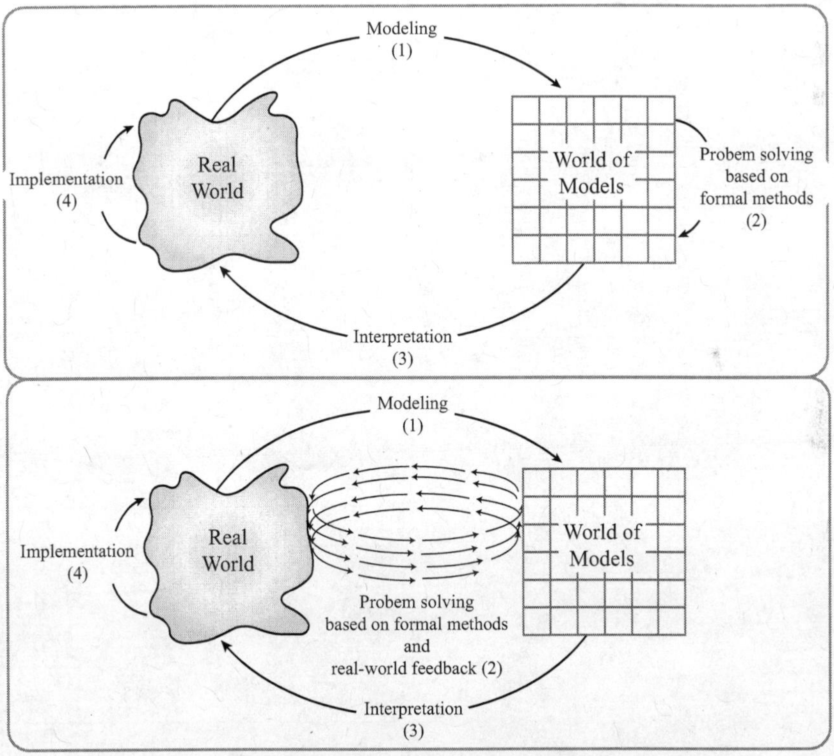

Figure 2.5 The principal approach of problem solving without (top) and with feedback (bottom)

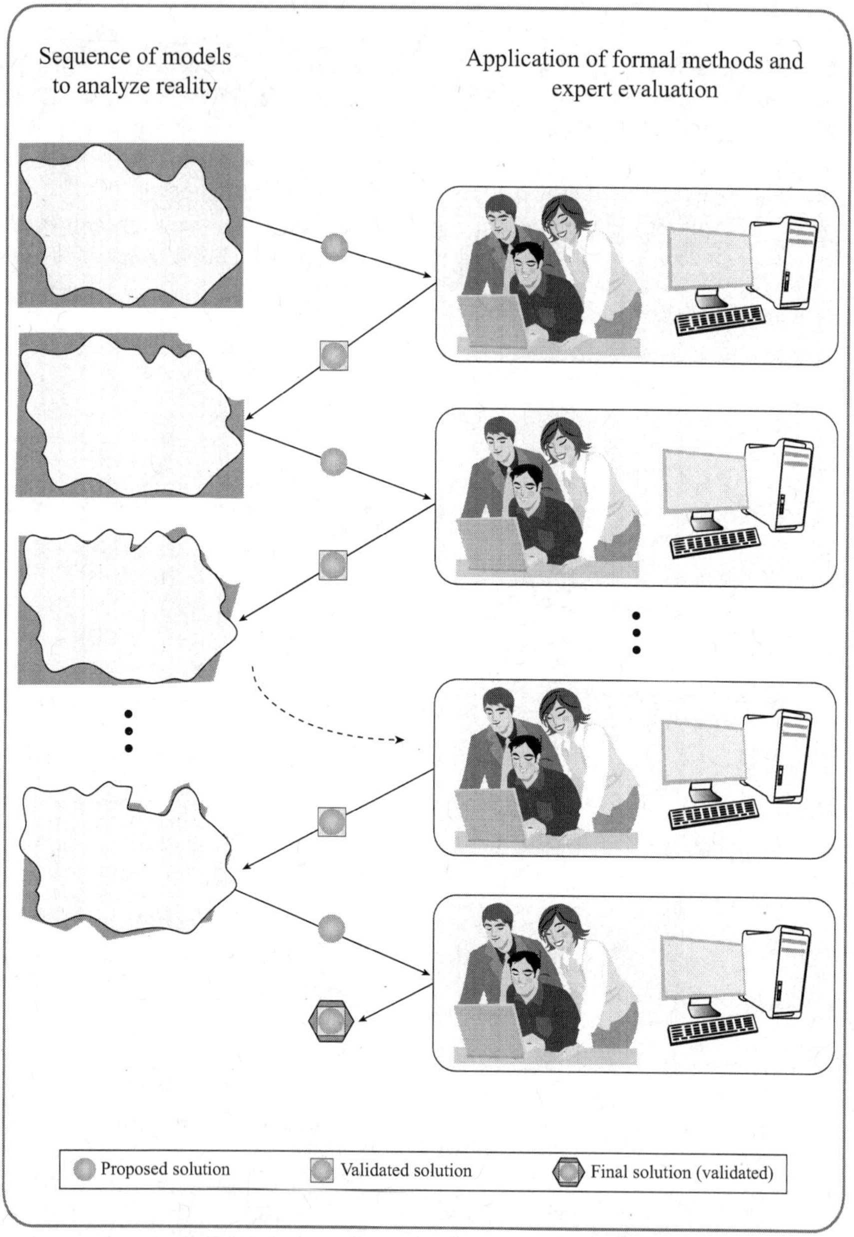

Figure 2.6 Evolutionary problem-solving process

2.7 AN INTEGRATED APPROACH TO DECISION-MAKING

In this chapter, the nature of decisions and their underlying processes has been studied. The process of decision-making has been emphasized as a key driver for achieving good decisions. In the forthcoming chapters of this book, product release planning decisions are analyzed more thoroughly.

[Van De Weerd et al. '06] developed a reference framework for software product management, in which key process areas such as portfolio management, product roadmapping, release planning and requirements management are identified.

Decisions have to be made across all parts of an organization. All these decisions often depend on each other. From an organizational perspective, qualified decision-making needs to be made a joint, corporate-wide initiative. [DeGregorio '00] described the pioneering work at Motorola in providing an integrated, strategic decision-making, requirements management and roadmapping process. The main purpose of their *Enterprise Strategic Decision Management* initiative, which is in the process to become an IEEE Standard, is to enable common decision management methods to be used across all parts of an enterprise. It defines *common methods and work products for (i) decision planning, analysis, traceability and execution, (ii) collaboration within and among enterprises and (iii) linkages with other business processes* [IEEE '08].

The premise of the working group is that there is a lack of a framework for the management of all the decisions across the organization. The cost to business and government of making decisions in an incomplete or incorrect context is in the hundreds of billions of dollars per year, based on the improvements achieved in pilot implementations at a number of Fortune 500 companies [IEEE '08].

CHAPTER 3

FEATURES AND THEIR PRIORITIZATION

3.1 INTRODUCTION

The input for the release planning process is a set of features that are evolving over time due to changing user requirements and better problem understanding. Intuitively, features are key distinctive characteristics of a product. Features are an abstraction from requirements that both customers and developers understand. They are seen as the "selling units" of a product.

Prioritization of features is the process of assigning a priority to them. This is typically done by multiple stakeholders and related to multiple criteria. Prioritization sounds simple but it is not. Already on a conceptual level, you need to specify who is doing the prioritization, what is being prioritized, according to which criteria, and based upon which scale. And how should the different stakeholder opinions related to the different criteria be combined?

Features are the key objects of study of this whole book. There is no universally applied definition of what constitutes a feature. Intuitively, a set of logically related requirements will be called a feature in this book. Features, their definition and their classification are the subject of Section 3.2. Product release planning assumes that the candidate features are well defined as a result of a feature elicitation process. This elicitation is discussed in Section 3.3. Feature elicitation is an ongoing process. Once a set of features is defined for planning purposes, then feature prioritization can be done. Feature prioritization is in the category of a triage decision problem (using the terminology introduced in Chapter 2). Criteria for feature prioritization are the content of Section 3.4. A process and criteria for the selection of stakeholders participating in the prioritization of product features are studied in Section 3.5.

Prioritization precedes assignment of features to releases. The prioritization process can be performed in a variety of ways. [Firesmith '04] gives an overview of requirements prioritization criteria and techniques. An evaluation of requirements prioritization techniques has been done by [Karlsson et al. '98]. Different prioritization methods were compared in [Berander and Andrews '05] in terms of their scale, granularity and sophistication. For our purposes, one prominent technique (the *Analytic Hierarchy Process [AHP]*) is described in Section 3.6. AHP will be used later in other parts of the book. In Section 3.7, a multi-criteria and multi-stakeholder scoring technique called *Multi-score* is proposed. This technique is one of the key process phases in the systematic product planning method EVOLVE II as described in Chapter 6. Among others, it offers a variety of options for analyzing the different types of results obtained form the multi-dimensional prioritization process presented in Section 3.8. The different options are the content of Section 3.9.

3.2 FEATURES

Features represent the value-unit to the customer. Definitions of features are abundant in the literature. The notion is perceived differently according to the context of the problem in consideration or the characteristic of the approach. FODA (Feature Oriented Domain Analysis) [Kang et al. '90] defines a feature as *a prominent and distinctive user visible characteristic of a system*. In [Reid Turner et al. '99], three informal definitions are proposed: *subset of system requirements*, *subset of system implementation*, and *aggregate view across life-cycle artifacts*. Wiegers has defined a product feature as *a set of logically related requirements that provide a capability to the user and enable the satisfaction of business objectives* [Wiegers '03]. In this book, Wiegers' definition is followed.

The concept of a feature is applicable and important for any product development paradigm. However, it is especially important for incremental development. As an abstraction of requirements, the identification of features is mainly based on the exploration of requirements. The task is not trivial and needs a systematic approach. This motivates many researchers who deal with feature modeling. The end result of a feature model is a classification scheme. According to their usage, [Griss et al. '98] distinguishes three categories of features:

i. *Mandatory features*: These are the features used to identify the product. For example, for a mailing system, the mail client must have the ability to type messages.
ii. *Optional features*: These features, when enabled, add some value to the core functionality. For the example of the mailing system, a dictionary might be an optional feature.
iii. *Variant features*: These are alternative ways to describe optional or mandatory features. For example, some e-mail clients may offer text editors with varying functionality in terms of importing and exporting files.

Another classification scheme uses the external visibility of features (how a feature is visible to the end user) as the distinguishing attribute [Lee et al. '02]. This scheme assigns features into four layers in which the first one is the closest, that is, most visible, to the user.

i. Capabilities (distinct services, operations or non-functional characteristics, which can be identified by the user),
ii. Domain technology (the way the operations or services are implemented),
iii. Implementation technique (generic techniques used to implement operations or services), and
iv. Operating environments (where the application operates).

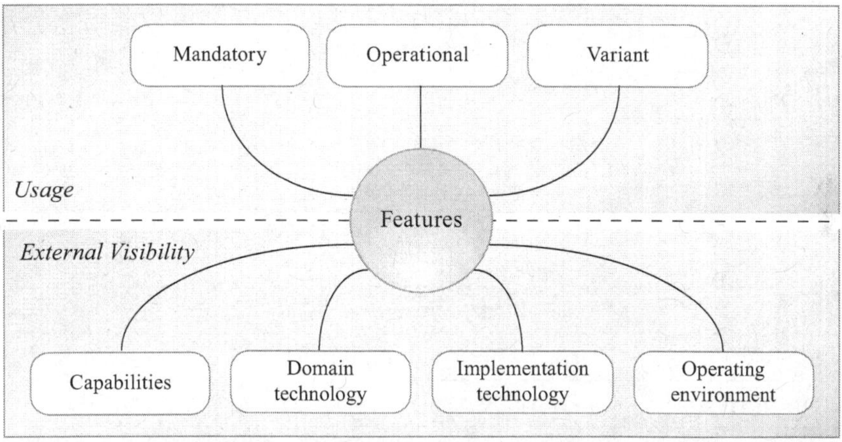

Figure 3.1 Classification of features according to usage and external visibility

In Figure 3.1, the two schemes are put together into a joint one. For the actual description of features, different types of information need to be collected in a feature repository. This information typically relates to the name, ID, description, origin, dependencies and status for each of the features. As an example for a description scheme, in Table 3.1, a structure is given which largely follows the scheme suggested by [Regnell and Brinkkemper '05]. An example attribute from this scheme is the *state* of a feature. It refers to the features life-cycle status ranging from *candidate* to *released*. To keep the feature repository up-to-date, it needs to be changed whenever some feature-related information (such as its state) changes. While all of these attributes are somehow relevant, it is not expected that all this information is available all the time.

Maintenance of the feature repository is one of the responsibilities of the product manager. Even if not all information is available for all features, it should be as complete as possible. For prioritization and product release planning, a pre-selection of features is typically done to keep the process more time-efficient. At this point it becomes clear how important it is to synchronize the release planning process with other accompanying processes such as effort estimation, needs elicitation, customer relationship management, as well as project tracking and control.

Table 3.1 Feature characterization scheme (based on [Regnell and Brinkkemper '05])

Attribute	Value
State	Candidate / approved / specified / discarded / planned / developed / verified / released
ID	Unique identity
Submitter	Who issued it?
Company	Submitter's company
Domain	Functional domain
Description	Short textual description
Contract	Link to sales contract enforcing requirement
Priorities	Prioritization for different criteria by different stakeholders on a nine-point scale
Motivation	Rational: Why is it important?
Line of business	Market segment for which feature is important
Specification	Link to use cases, textual specification
Dependencies	Precedence, coupling or other dependencies between features
Resource estimation	Estimated effort per defined resource type
Risk	Projected risks of implementation and market penetration
Design	Link to design documents
Test	Link to test documents
Novelty	Novelty of the features when compared to competitors
Release version	Official release name for which the feature is planned

3.3 FEATURE ELICITATION

Understanding stakeholders, especially understanding customer needs, is still one of the key success factors for product development. Without the early effort to elicit customer needs, there is a substantial risk that the product delivered is not what the customer needs or what the customer is expecting. This is exactly the motivation for the early effort on feature needs elicitation and prioritization of a set of candidate features.

The process of feature elicitation is *the art of determining the needs of the stakeholder* [Davis '05]. Dieste et al. have conducted a comprehensive analysis of existing elicitation techniques and their performance [Dieste et al. '08]. From looking at 30 studies (since 1987), the authors found 43 different techniques. It is widely acknowledged that the term *stakeholder needs* is a somewhat fuzzy concept. It varies between stakeholders and also varies over time. The difficulty of the elicitation process not only results from the variety of possible techniques, and the question of deciding on which ones to use, but also from the fact that elicitation is so time and context specific.

In the feature elicitation process, a number of inherent difficulties exist:

i. The stakeholder does not yet know precisely what he or she wants.
ii. The stakeholder changes his or her opinion on what is wanted.
iii. The stakeholder does not properly express what is wanted.
iv. The requirements engineer does not properly understand what the stakeholder wants.
v. The description and specification given by the requirements engineer are ambiguous and misleading.

Existing elicitation techniques have different capabilities to address some of these difficulties. The portfolio of techniques ranges from the different styles of interviewing (with or without prepared structure), protocol analysis, scenario playing, brainstorming and group meetings to the different types of prototypes offered to the stakeholder in order to better allow him or her to understand and judge features. For further discussion of the strengths and weaknesses of individual techniques, take a look at [Davis '05] and [Zowghi and Coulin '05].

The actual choice of the technique depends on, and is impacted by the content and the domain of the feature, the depth of knowledge available and requested, the time available for running the process, the number and the size of the features, and the commitment of the involved people. In general, it might be worthwhile to look at a combination of techniques having complementary strengths.

3.4 CRITERIA FOR FEATURE PRIORITIZATION

Once a set of candidate features is agreed upon, the question of what constitutes *the right features* needs to be answered in the specific context of the project. In fact, the question of what is *right* is harder to answer than actually selecting the features. In what follows, a list of prioritization criteria is provided. Without trying to be complete, the criteria give different interpretations of what might be considered to be *attractive*.

- Customer satisfaction

The needs of the customers are of key importance, and the degree of match between their needs and the proposed features is called *customer satisfaction (with a specific feature)*. An attractive feature will largely match the expectations of the key stakeholders, especially customers and users.

- Customer dissatisfaction

If we look at a specific feature ABC, then there is a slight difference between being *very satisfied if ABC is delivered in the next release* versus *being very dissatisfied if ABC is not delivered in the next release*. The first statement does not automatically imply the second. In other words, the planning can be directed toward high customer satisfaction or toward low customer dissatisfaction.

- Risk of implementation

How risky is the implementation of the feature? How novel is the feature? How well is the process of implementation already known and understood? At which part of the overall project will the feature be implemented? Is its implementation targeted at a stable or more unstable component? How many components are impacted by this implementation? All of these questions are related to the risk of implementation. The lower the risk, the more attractive the feature becomes.

- Risk of acceptance

How risky is the acceptance of a feature by customers? Is the feature the result of a careful voice-of-the-customer analysis? Or is it more speculative? Having a lower risk of acceptance will contribute to the attractiveness of a feature.

- Financial value

High customer satisfaction typically implies good business value. However, it is not exactly the same. Products can have features that impact the price of the product, but not primarily the customer satisfaction. A feature can eventually be so dominant that its presence strongly supports the acceptance and thus the financial value of the whole release, more or less independent of the remaining features.

- Cost

The different features have different (estimated) costs for their implementation. This primarily relates to the total amount of resources requested for a feature's implementation. Even though the cost is hard to estimate in detail, a sufficiently detailed classification would be useful early-on.

- Urgency

To provide the right feature at the right time is another challenge of planning. Certain features are more urgent than others. Urgency can be caused by the needs of the customers or the need to stay competitive in the marketplace.

- Readiness

Is the feature ready for implementation? Besides a clear understanding of its functionality, readiness also refers to the status of implementation (e.g., the availability of resources or the healthiness of the target component).

- Frequency of use

Is it true that *the more features are offered the better the product is*? The downside of this premise is that the user has more and more difficulty handling a myriad of features. Looking at the frequency of use would help us to concentrate on the ones most likely to be expected and used by customers [Wiegers '00].

- Ease of use

Similar to frequency of use, features could be also judged by their *ease of use*.

Sophisticated but difficult to use features can create disappointment on the customer side, and the potential value needs to be balanced against the risk that this value is not materialized.

Ideally, features fulfilling all of the above-mentioned aspects simultaneously with a *good* or *very good* rating would be the ones the product manager is looking for. However, such features seldom exist. So, the final decision depends on how important the different attributes are in the context of the project. Furthermore, the cost of implementation of the features will play an important role for making the final release decisions.

Prioritization of features depends on the criterion chosen, but also on the stakeholders selected. Similar to the variation between criteria when looking at just one stakeholder, there is the possibility that for one fixed criterion there are completely different opinions between stakeholders. What we can learn from this is that "the battle for the right features" (as another term for release planning) starts with the proper definition of the features, with a careful selection of stakeholders, and with a company and project-specific commitment on what goals are most important to be achieved.

3.5 SELECTION OF STAKEHOLDERS

Once the candidate features are defined and the prioritization criteria are agreed upon, the nomination of stakeholders needs to be undertaken. What is a stakeholder in the process of product release planning? [Sharp et al. '99] collected a number of possible definitions of what constitutes a stakeholder. Without going into the details here, the *stakeholder* term is used for anyone influenced by or influencing the release planning process and its resulting product.

Stakeholders can play very different roles for the definition of the product planned for. They can be related to the design or development of the product, they can have a financial interest by the sale or purchase of the product, they can be responsible for the introduction and maintenance of the product, or they can have an interest in the use of the product. All of these roles and perspectives are relevant, and their opinions often are contradictory. One of the challenges of product release planning is to determine a well-balanced product plan that addresses the most relevant concerns. In Figure 3.2, a number of these roles are arranged in what is called a *stakeholder network*.

Despite the obvious importance of stakeholders, there is a lack of constructive guidance on how to find "the right set" of stakeholders. [Sharp et al. '99] presented an approach addressing this gap. The starting point of their method is to define what they called *baseline stakeholders*. Under this category, four groups of stakeholders are summarized:

i. Users and customers,
ii. Legislators (such as professional bodies, trade unions, legal representatives, safety executives or quality assurance auditors),

iii. Developers, and
iv. Decision-makers of a company (such as the CEO or shareholders).

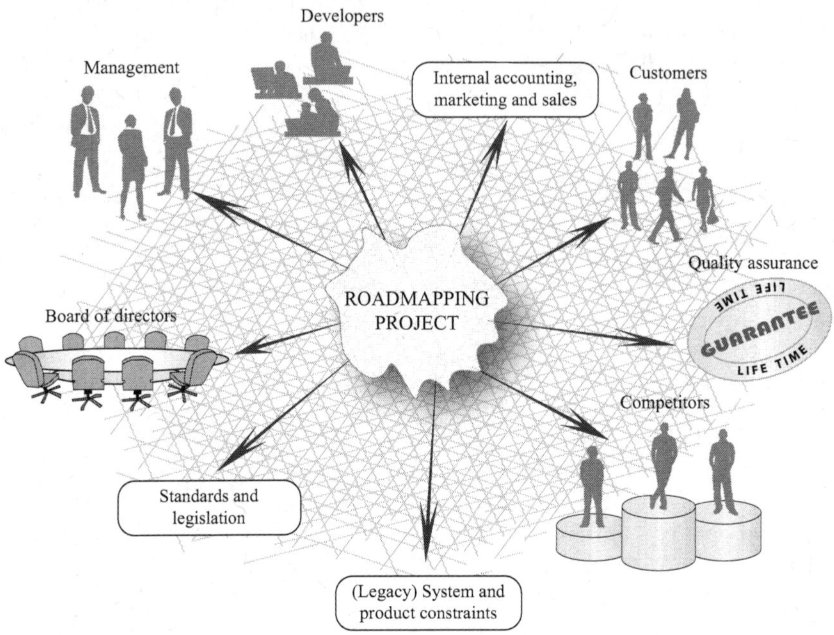

Figure 3.2 The stakeholder network

Once the baseline stakeholders are established, the authors suggest a five-step procedure to add further stakeholders to one of the four established groups. With the stakeholders defined and the criteria set-up, the process gives stakeholders access to a prioritization scheme. This access defines who is prioritizing what and how prioritization is done. A process needs to be prepared where stakeholders can articulate their preferences in a time-efficient manner. Meetings to bring all the relevant parties together are very costly and hard to realize in practice. In Chapter 10, Web-based tool solutions are described allowing stakeholders to provide their priorities and feedback at any time and anywhere. On top of that, if needed, meetings can be held to focus on specific conflicts, narrowing the scope of discussion and thus reducing the total effort needed.

3.6 PRIORITIZATION BY COMPARISON: THE ANALYTIC HIERARCHY PROCESS AHP

3.6.1 Overview

Preferences or relative importance of competing alternatives are often not explicitly known. AHP is a quantification technique of subjective judgments and allows decision-makers to model a complex problem in a hierarchical structure. This structure relates the goal, objectives (criteria) with the possibility to include sub-objectives, and alternatives of the problem.

AHP has been developed at the Warton School of Business by Thomas Saaty [Saaty '80]. AHP is based on three basic principles: decomposition, comparative judgment and hierarchic decomposition or synthesis of priorities [Saaty '94]. The decomposition principle is used for stepwise refinement of a stated goal against sub-goals (or criteria). The principle of pair-wise judgment is applied to evaluate pairs of alternatives from the perspective of a stated criterion or to judge the importance of sub-goals in the light of the stated goal. Finally, the principle of synthesis of priorities provides an aggregation of the local priorities determined from pair-wise comparison into global priorities for the stated alternatives.

AHP allows decision-makers to assign ratio scale priorities to alternatives applying a sequence of pair-wise comparisons. The comparison itself is based on a nine-point scale expressing the degree of preference between the two alternatives under consideration. Assuming two options (which can be alternatives or criteria) called A and B, a nine-point scale is used based on the following transformation from verbal into numerical judgment: If A is *verbal judgment* to B, then *numerical value*. The different combinations between verbal and numerical judgement are summarized in Table 3.2.

A pair-wise comparison matrix is used to determine relative weights of criteria and sub-criteria as well as the evaluations of alternatives. The decision-maker is looking at all pairs from the perspective of just one criterion. At this point, all the other criteria are ignored.

Table 3.2 Nine-point scale for pair-wise comparisons in AHP

Verbal judgment	Numerical value
Equally preferred	1
Equally to moderately preferred	2
Moderately preferred	3
Moderately to strongly preferred	4
Strongly preferred	5

Table 3.2 (continued)

Verbal judgment	Numerical value
Strongly to very strongly preferred	6
Very strongly preferred	7
Very strongly to extremely preferred	8
Extremely preferred	9

At the end of the process, AHP will provide a complete ranking between candidate alternatives. The generation of alternatives is crucial for any decision-making activity. For making good decisions, it should be ensured that all possible candidate solutions are considered. If essential alternatives are missed then the suggested solution will not be the best possible, but just the best among the ones considered. That is why this step is of crucial importance. At the end of this process, a set of (ranked) alternatives is established.

3.6.2 Illustrative example

For illustrative purposes, the question to define some priority level for three groups of features to be developed for the next generation of a product is studied. For finding the right mix between these feature groups, three groups of users are taken into consideration. They represent the layer of objectives:

- Novice users (C1)
- Advanced users (C2)
- Expert users (C3)

The feature group alternatives are:

- Group of analysis features (A1)
- Group of reporting features (A2)
- Group of data exchange features (A3)

The hierarchical structure, representing the three layers and their dependencies, is shown in Figure 3.3. Ignoring the details of all the pair-wise comparisons for the three criteria (user groups) from the perspective of the overall business attractiveness, a vector of normalized degrees of relative importance called Weight(0) is obtained in (3.1).

(3.1) $\text{Weight}(0) = (0.644, 0.271, 0.085)$

The first component of the vector corresponds to the first group of users. It can be concluded that the novice users are considered by far the most attractive group, while expert users are the least attractive among the three. For each of the three criteria, another cycle of comparisons is done for comparison between the groups of features from the perspective of a specific user group. When looking at novice users, the comparison produces in the following results:

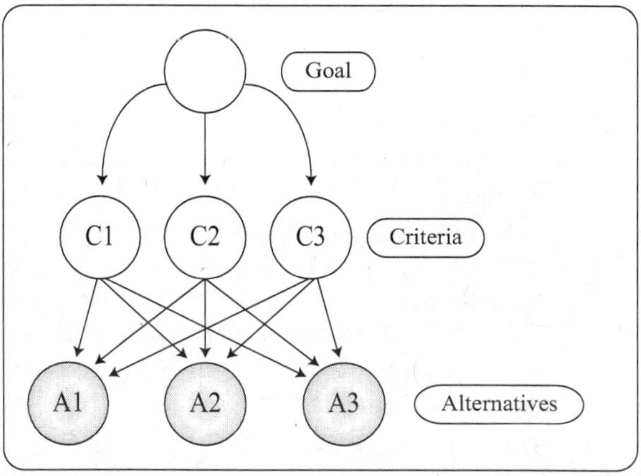

Figure 3.3 Hierarchical graph structure

- The group of analysis features is equally to moderately preferred to the group of reporting features (value = 2)
- The group of analysis features is strongly preferred to the group of data exchange features (value = 5)
- The group of reporting features is moderately strongly preferred to the group of data exchange features (value = 4)

These pair-wise comparisons result in degrees of relative importance for the alternatives (groups of features) summarized in a vector Weight(1) given in (3.2).

(3.2) Weight(1) = (0.570, 0.333, 0.097)

In the same way, it is assumed the comparisons were done from the perspective of the other two user groups resulting in weighting vectors Weight(2) and Weight(3) given in (3.3) and (3.4).

(3.3) Weight(2) = (0.100, 0.300, 0.600)

(3.4) Weight(3) = (0.117, 0.683, 0.200)

All these results are combined by multiplication of the vector of weights of the criteria with the matrix composed by the weights of the alternatives as determined from the perspective of the individual criteria. In our example, this results in the global weight vector (0.404, 0.354, 0.242) suggesting the first feature group being overall of highest attractiveness, followed by the second one, and the third one being the least attractive. In our case, this result was obtained from doing $4 \cdot 3 = 12$ pair-wise comparisons and some eigenvalue computations supported by tools such as Expert Choice [www.expertchoice.com '08].

3.6.3 Applicability

AHP has been successfully applied in different decision scenarios. For an overview of the great variety of applications, the reader is referred to [Vaidya and Kumar '06]. The definite strength of AHP is its conceptual clarity and ease of application. The AHP method is compensatory in the sense that is allows one to consider alternatives from the perspective of different objectives and to bring them together.

There is a well-known scalability problem with the AHP method. The method is comprehensively based on conducting a series of pair-wise comparisons. But already for a relatively small problem with $n = 10$ alternatives and just $K = 5$ criteria, a number of $K \cdot n \cdot (n-1)/2 = 5 \cdot 10 \cdot 9/2 = 225$ comparisons needs to be conducted. This is substantial, and it gets easily prohibitive for larger problems. Efforts have been made (such as [Harker '87]) to decrease the number of comparisons. On the downside, this reduces the ability to identify inconsistent judgments [Karlsson et al. '98].

3.7 PRIORITIZATION BY SCORING

3.7.1 Scoring with one criterion

Scoring will become an essential element of the prioritization process being part of the EVOLVE II method presented in Chapter 6. Scoring is the (often applied) process of classifying alternatives. This is expressed by assigning a score to them. Scoring can be done in different ways depending on the number of criteria used, the number and role of participants, the process of scoring, the total number of scores available per participant, and the number of scores that can be assigned per individual alternative. In our context, the scorer is a stakeholder in the process of prioritization of features.

For the scoring itself, a scale as defined in Table 3.3 is introduced. With the same arguments as for the AHP process, a nine-point scale is considered sufficiently detailed to differentiate between features. In principle, any other ordinal scale could be used instead. For simplicity reasons, it is also assumed that each stakeholder is scoring each feature. Both the scoring and the subsequent analysis remain applicable for the case that a stakeholder has "no opinion" related to a feature, eventually, because the feature is not understandable to the stakeholder.

Table 3.3 Correspondence between priority level and numerical score

Priority	Score value
Extremely low	1
Between low and extremely low	2
Low	3
Between low and average	4

Table 3.3 (continued)

Priority	Score value
Average	5
Between high and average	6
High	7
Between high and extremely high	8
Extremely high	9

3.7.2 Illustrative example

The feature prioritization case study introduced in Section 2.2.1, Chapter 2, is reconsidered. Eight stakeholders are invited to provide their input into the prioritization process. The stakeholders are selected to represent the most important internal roles in the SIP organization (Product Manager, Chief Executive Officer, Chief Technology Officer, Chief Financial Officer) as well as the four key customers representing different regions called *East, West, North* and *South*:

Architect	(Stakeholder 1)
Customer East	(Stakeholder 2)
Customer West	(Stakeholder 3)
Customer North	(Stakeholder 4)
Customer South	(Stakeholder 5)
Product Manager	(Stakeholder 6)
CEO	(Stakeholder 7)
CTO	(Stakeholder 8)

In order to allow differentiation in the importance of stakeholders, a nine-point scoring classification is applied in the same way as defined in Table 3.3. The weights of the eight stakeholders selected for the case study example are given in Table 3.4.

Table 3.4 Degree of importance (weights) for the eight stakeholders

Stakeholder	1	2	3	4	5	6	7	8
Weight	5	6	6	6	6	7	9	8

In Table 3.5, the result of the scoring process for 20 candidate features with eight stakeholders is shown. To make the prioritization results more meaningful, an explicit prioritization perspective *Frequency of use* is given. This will later be combined with a perspective on the features' *value*. Typically, different perspectives are relevant, and the results will differ among the different perspectives taken. From the scores given by the stakeholders, it is observed that the feature *Cost Reduction of Transceiver* received the highest priority from Stakeholder 2. Just looking at the same stakeholder, it can be seen that all features of Group E are considered to be of between *low* and *extremely low* importance.

In Table 3.5, the column *Weighted average score* provides the information about the average score from all eight stakeholders where stakeholder scoring is multiplied by their degree of importance. The feature with ID = 1 has the highest weighted average score.

There are a number of limitations when using this approach. The first limitation relates to the usage of just one criterion. The importance of feature can hardly be judged by just looking at their *frequency of use*. The second limitation comes from the observation that the number of scores allocated by the different stakeholders varies substantially. Stakeholders 5 and 8 have allocated 65 scores in total. On the other side, stakeholder 7 has spent 114 scores. This means, the scores assigned by that stakeholder will have a higher impact on average. Both of these limitations are overcome by the prioritization method presented in Section 3.8.

Table 3.5 Prioritization of 20 features by 8 stakeholders for *frequency of use*

Feature			Stakeholders								
ID	Group	Name	1	2	3	4	5	6	7	8	Weighted average score
1	A	Cost Reduction of Transceiver	6	9	7	6	5	6	6	7	6.49
2		16 sector, 12 carrier BTS	4	7	7	5	5	4	1	4	4.40
3		Expand Memory on BTS Controller	1	3	3	3	2	2	5	2	2.75
4		Next Generation BTS "In a Shoebox"	3	4	4	3	3	4	4	4	3.68
5	B	Pole Mount Packaging	4	5	5	5	4	5	6	4	4.81
6		FCC Out-of-Band Emissions Regulatory Change	4	2	2	2	2	3	5	3	2.98
7		Patching Improvements/Upgrade Enhancements	3	7	7	7	5	5	1	3	4.51
8		CIU and SRM Management Enhancements	2	3	2	2	2	3	8	2	3.26

Table 3.5 (continued)

Feature			Stakeholders								
ID	Group	Name	1	2	3	4	5	6	7	8	Weighted average score
9	C	SMS Cell Broadcast	4	3	3	3	3	3	8	4	4.09
10	C	Traffic Allocations Enhancements	2	3	2	3	3	3	7	3	3.47
11	C	eBSC CR: CCMC Removal	3	4	4	4	4	4	9	3	4.60
12	C	3 of N Band Class Support	4	2	2	2	2	3	9	3	3.66
13	C	EVRC-B Capacity Enhancements	6	4	4	4	4	4	8	4	4.87
14	D	Mobile Recovery Algorithm	4	4	4	3	4	3	7	3	4.11
15	D	Quick Paging Channel Power Offset	3	2	3	2	3	3	6	2	3.13
16	D	Access Optimized IMSI Paging	5	5	5	5	6	6	6	5	5.42
17	E	EBSC REX Testing	3	2	2	3	2	2	3	3	2.53
18	E	CSVS Robustness Enhancements	2	2	2	3	2	3	5	3	2.91
19	E	EBSC Outage Footprint (Flight Recorder)	2	2	2	2	2	2	7	1	2.70
20	E	MFRM Flight Recorder Enhancements	3	2	2	2	2	3	3	2	2.40

3.8 PRIORITIZATION METHOD MULTI-SCORE

Multi-score is an advanced scoring method where scoring is done for each of a set of criteria. Typically, the different criteria will generate different ranking of features. Scoring itself is based on a nine-point scale as specified in Table 3.3.

Cumulative scoring (called 100-Dollar-test in [Berander and Andrews '05]) allows only the allocation of a limited amount of scores among the alternatives (features). As an implication, if the total available amount of scores is small enough, cumulative scoring implies that not all alternatives can be ranked as having high importance. Typically, each stakeholder has some high priority alternatives. Then, cumulative scoring enforces the process of thinking about which of the alternatives might be less important (in order to stay within the scoring budget).

Cumulative scoring can become complex if the number of alternatives becomes large. At this point, grouping features might be a useful technique to reduce complexity. With a partition of the set of all features into subsets of smaller size, the idea of cumulative scoring can be applied in hierarchical manner [Berander and Joensson '06]: First allocating scores between all the groups, and second allocating scores within each group.

Formulated for the case of prioritization of features, *Multi-score* contains the following main steps:

1. Definition of features (prioritization objects) and their groupings (if any)
2. Nomination of stakeholders (prioritization subjects) and their groupings (if any)
3. Definition of prioritization criteria and their weights
4. Definition of prioritization mode with the two dimensions
5. Decision about cumulative versus non-cumulative scoring and
6. Definition of scoring assignments: which stakeholder is assigned to which group of features and to which criteria?
7. Scoring by stakeholders according to the defined mode
8. Analysis of scores

The scoring is intended to provide the decision-maker (in our case, the product manager) further insight into the preference structure of features, thus facilitating decision-making. For that purpose, a collection of possible analysis options is explained in the next section.

3.9 VOICE-OF-THE-STAKEHOLDER ANALYSIS

3.9.1 Overview

In order to provide a more rigorous description of a variety of analysis options, some key notation is introduced. It is assumed that scoring is performed for all combinations of

- Features f(n) (n = 1…N),
- Prioritization criteria denoted by crit(k) (k = 1…K), and
- Stakeholders denoted by stake(p) (p = 1…P).

Definition (score): A *score* is a value denoted by score(n,k,p) expressing the judgment of stakeholder stake(p) toward feature f(n) from the perspective of criterion crit(k). □

Once stakeholders have given their scores, data analysis tries to provide insight into the overall preference structure between features. This is also called *voice-of-the-stakeholder analysis*. Differences and commonalities in the scoring between (groups of) stakeholders, (groups of) features, and between the different criteria are detected and different forms of ranking and comparisons are done.

In what follows, a variety of 10 analysis options will be described. It is the product manager who finally decides which one is chosen in the context of a concrete feature prioritization project.

Analysis Option 1:	Ranking of features based upon a single criterion
Analysis Option 2:	Ranking of features based upon multiple criteria
Analysis Option 3:	Ranking of features based upon the level of disagreement between stakeholders (single criterion)
Analysis Option 4:	Ranking of stakeholder scores for a fixed feature based upon single criterion (Pareto analysis)
Analysis Option 5:	Comparison of stakeholder scores for a fixed feature based upon multiple criteria
Analysis Option 6:	Trade-off analysis for stakeholder scoring
Analysis Option 7:	Comparison of weighted averages of stakeholder scores for feature groups based upon multiple criteria
Analysis Option 8:	Comparison of frequency distributions of stakeholder scores on features based upon single criterion
Analysis Option 9:	Per feature scoring comparison between groups of stakeholders
Analysis Option 10:	Comparison of frequency of scoring between groups of features and between groups of stakeholders

For each option, its main content is briefly explained in the following subsections. In addition, it is illustrated by an example how the analysis chart created from the stakeholder scores helps us to understand and address the original question. The example is the same features prioritization scenario introduced in Section 2.1, with some detailed data already provided in Table 3.5. Besides the criterion *frequency of use*, the features were also evaluated from the perspective of their anticipated business value. *Business value* relates to the expected impact of the feature on revenue of the product.

All the screen-shots shown were generated from the Web-based decision support system called VeryBestChoice^{Light} [VBC^{Light}], which is described in further detail in Section 10.2.

3.9.2 Ranking of features based upon a single criterion

Analysis Option 1: For a given prioritization criterion and the whole set or a group of features, the features need to be ranked according to their weighted average priorities.

The definition of a weighted average follows the standard formulas given in descriptive statistics [Black '06]. The (complete) ranking of features gives the order of their anticipated frequency of use. In Figure 3.4, the ranking results for the criterion *frequency of use* are presented. According to that, the feature *Cost Reduction of Transceiver* (ID = 1) is most preferred. The weighted average score of the feature is 6.49. The least attractive feature is *MFRM Flight Recorder Enhancements* (ID = 20) with a weighted average score of 2.40.

In addition to the ranking of features based on the weighted average score, the disagreement value between stakeholder scores per feature is given. It can be seen that there is substantial agreement between stakeholders that feature f(20) is the least important. The disagreement measure is explained in more detail in Section 3.9.4.

3.9.3 Ranking of features based upon multiple criteria

Analysis Option 2: Instead of looking at just one criterion for ranking the features, it can be important to consider several criteria in conjunction. To keep the method sufficiently simple, the issue becomes ranking the features for the (weighted) sum of all the weighted average priorities.

For the case study example, Figure 3.5 shows that feature f(1) is ranked highest in total, although feature f(9) would be most important when just looking at *urgency* in isolation. For what is called *indirect* criteria such as risk or volatility, it is true that *the lower the score, the higher the priority of the feature* (which is opposite from direct criteria). To combine different criteria, the weighted average value z of an indirect criterion needs to be transformed into another value z' = 10 – z. This needs to be done in order to keep the semantics between the criteria consistent.

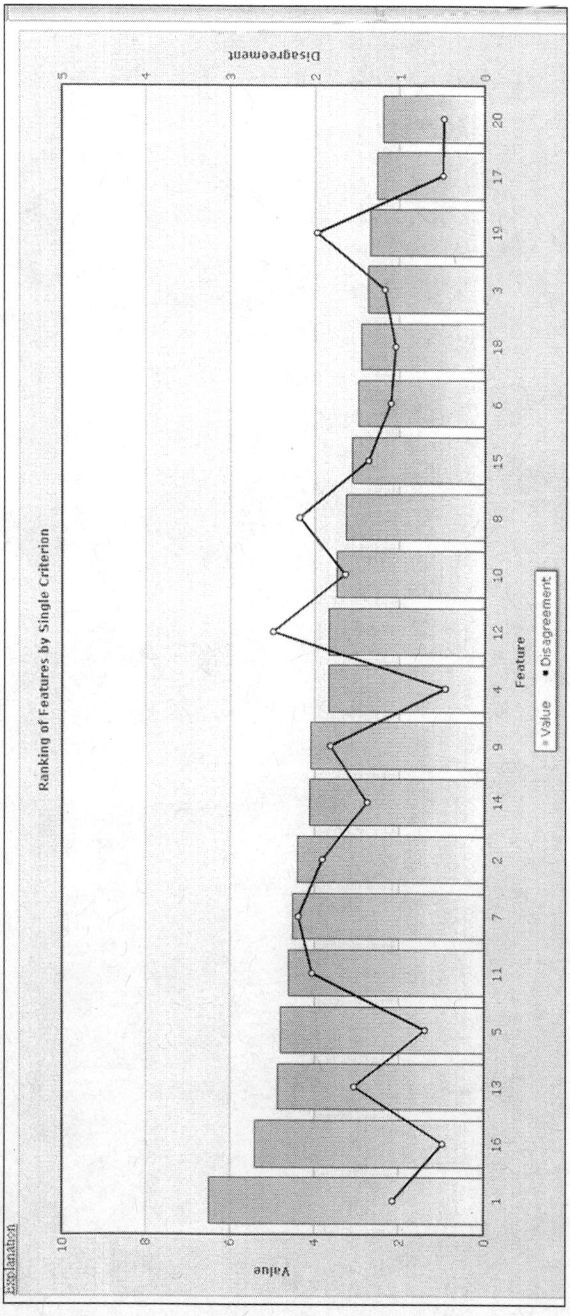

Figure 3.4 Ranking of features based upon their *frequency of use*

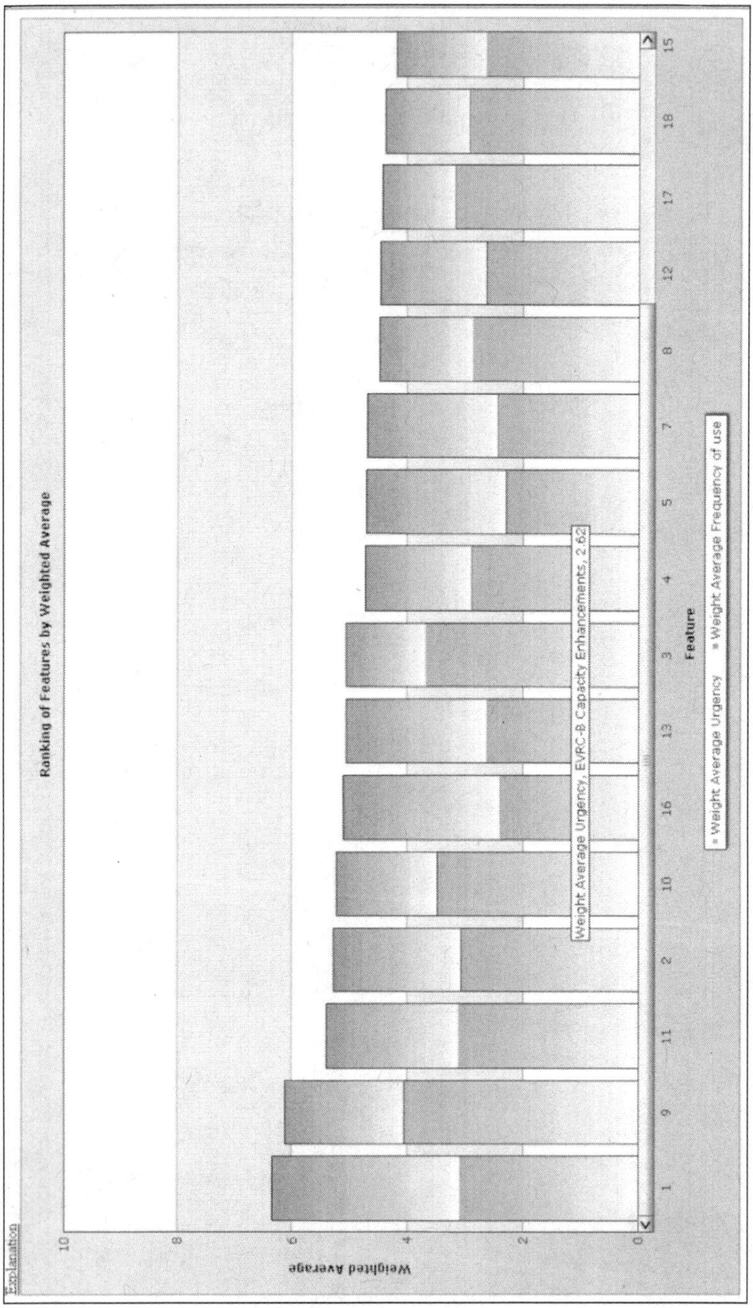

Figure 3.5 Ranking of features based on the sum of weighted averages of stakeholder scores for two criteria

3.9.4 Ranking of features based upon the level of disagreement between stakeholders for single criterion

Analysis Option 3: For deciding about features, besides their weighted average stakeholder scoring, it is also important to know about the level of disagreement between stakeholders related to the feature. If there is a stronger level of disagreement, this should initiate some further analysis into its root-cause.

The level of disagreement is measured by the statistical standard deviation [Black '06]. For our example, Figure 3.6 offers a ranking of the features in decreasing order for the scores on *frequency of use* given in Table 3.5. It becomes clear that the feature *3 of N Band Class Support* (ID = 12) overall creates the highest controversy among stakeholders. This might be used by the product manager as an indication to further look into the definition of this feature (if it unambiguously defined) or to discuss the controversial opinions directly with the stakeholders. On the other hand, a low level of disagreement (as for features f(4), f(16), f(17) and f(20)) is an indicator of reliability in the consideration of the features' priority.

3.9.5 Ranking of stakeholder scores for a fixed feature based upon single criterion (Pareto analysis)

Analysis Option 4: For a given feature f(n) and a given prioritization criterion crit(k), all the priorities score(n,k,1) … score(n,k,P) provided by the P stakeholders are considered. The question is how the stakeholders are ranked based on their score given to this feature.

Figure 3.7 illustrates the analysis. Based on the priorities described in Table 3.5, stakeholder priorities assigned to feature f(7) are ranked. All the stakeholders who have provided their priority are ranked in decreasing order. Besides the ranking, the Pareto chart also shows the range of scores assigned to this feature (in this case, from 7 to 1).

The graph is accompanied by a line graph, which shows the cumulative totals of scores, taken from left to right. For example, the cumulative percentage of the total number of scores gives the information that 51.28% of the total amount of scores is provided by the top three stakeholders, and that 76.92% of the total amount of scores being given to this feature are provided by the top five stakeholders. In case of a larger number of stakeholders, and especially in the case of stronger variation between stakeholder scores, the results of the Pareto analysis are considered a valuable piece of information in the context of stakeholder prioritization analysis.

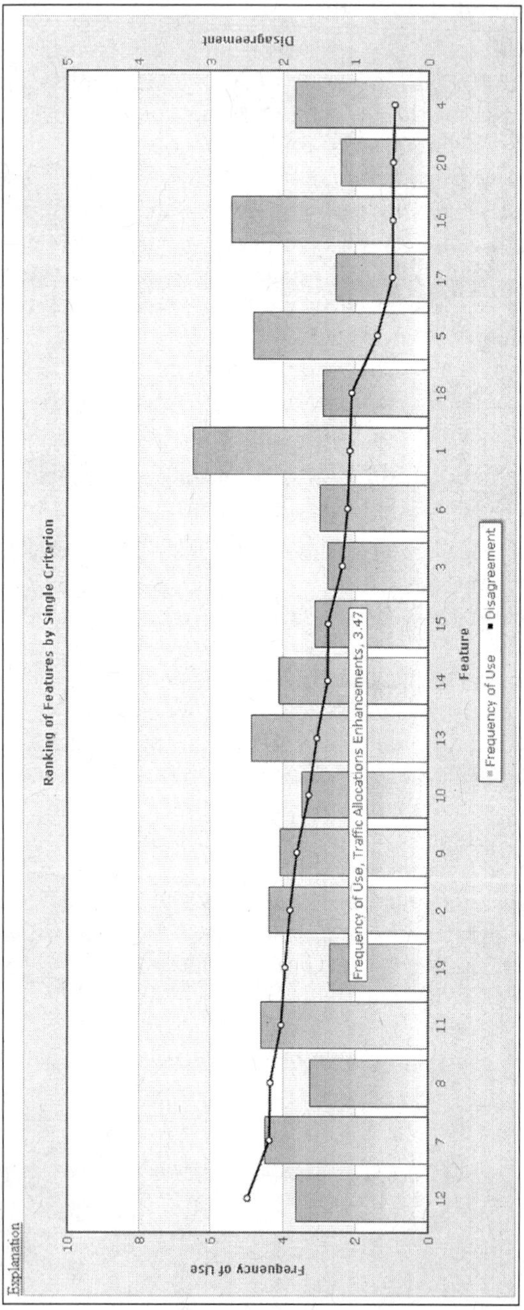

Figure 3.6 Ranking of features based on the level of disagreement between stakeholders for single criterion

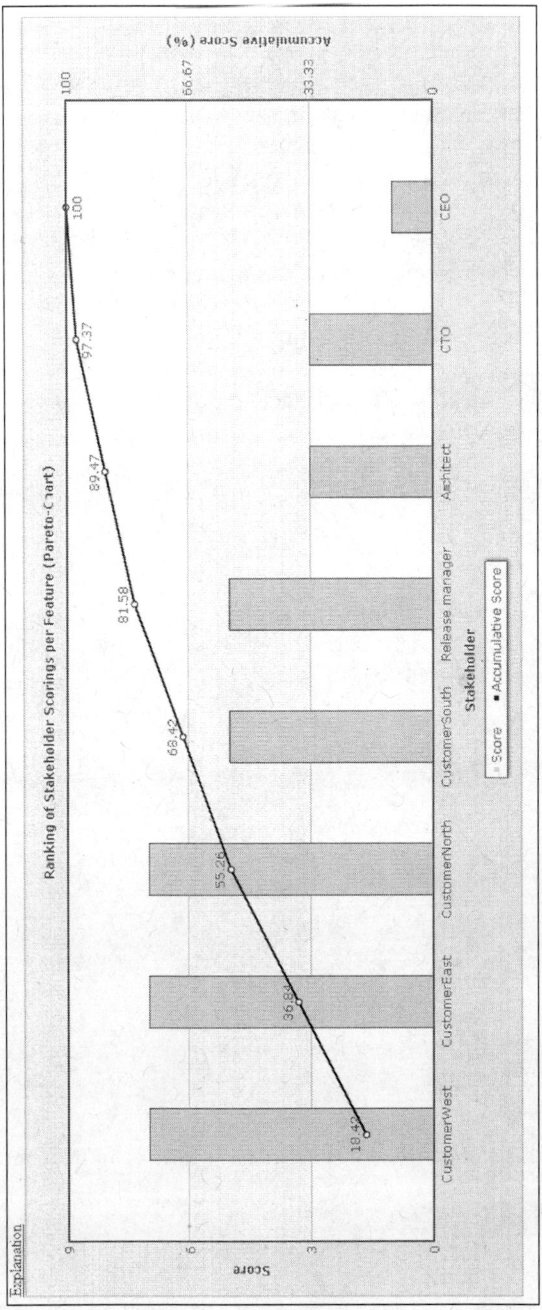

Figure 3.7 Ranking of stakeholder priorities for feature f(7)

3.9.6 Comparison of stakeholder scores for a fixed feature based upon multiple criteria

Analysis Option 5: For one specific feature under consideration, the question under consideration is to compare the scores given to this feature between the different stakeholders and between the different criteria.

This analysis allows both the comparison of the scores between both the stakeholders and between criteria. For a fixed feature and a fixed criterion, the user can compare the scores of the different stakeholders. On the other hand, for a fixed feature and a fixed stakeholder, one can see how the different criteria were ranked.

Looking at the Telco example project data again, feature f(8) is considered as an example. In addition to the evaluation of the feature in terms of *frequency of use*, Figure 3.8 also shows the stakeholder scores for *urgency*. It can be seen that there is a discrepancy between the scoring for the two criteria as most of the stakeholders have considered *urgency* more critical than the actual expected *frequency of use*. The only exception to that is the CEO stakeholder who has the opposite opinion in that matter.

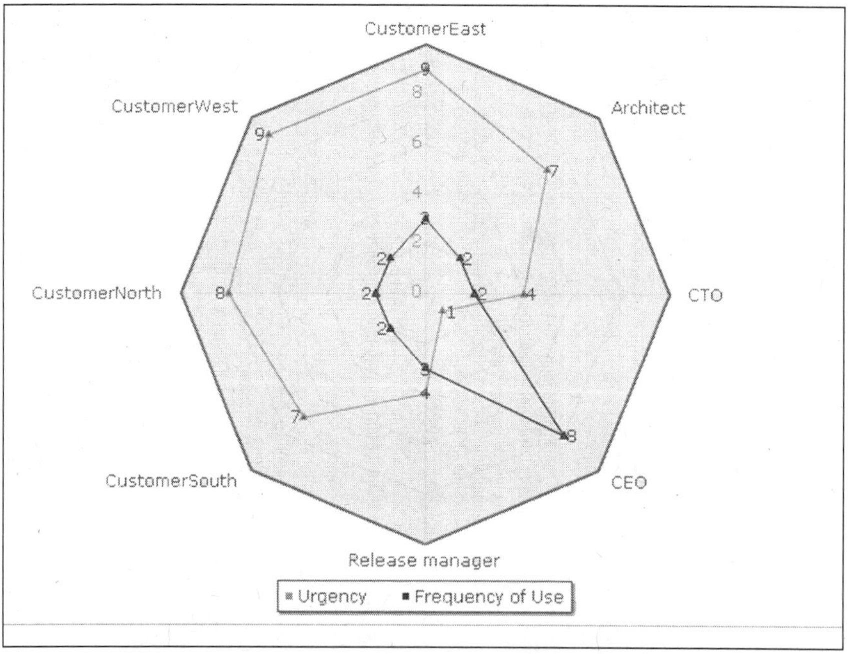

Figure 3.8 Comparison of stakeholder priorities for feature f(8)

3.9.7 Trade-off analysis for stakeholder scoring

Analysis Option 6: For a given set of features, the question here is to compare the features in terms of their weighted scoring averages gained for two selected criteria.

Comparison of all objects in terms of two criteria is called *trade-off analysis.* It allows us to look at the weighted average scores of all (or a selected group of) features. The trade-off analysis shows which features perform favorably for both criteria, which ones perform below average for one of the two criteria, and which ones are below average for both criteria.

Figure 3.9 illustrates this analysis for our example by showing the trade-off analysis when looking at both *urgency* and *frequency of use*. Consequently, the feature *Cost reduction of transceiver* in the upper left quadrant looks most promising, while features positioned in the lower left quadrant look to be the least promising ones when taking both criteria into account.

3.9.8 Comparison of weighted averages of stakeholder scores for feature groups based upon multiple criteria

Analysis Option 7: For this analysis option, feature groups are considered. The question is to compare the weighted average scores defined for the groups of features. The comparison is between groups for different criteria.

For each group, the weighted average score for both criteria of our illustrative example is shown in Figure 3.10. It is observed that the *urgency* score is consistently higher for all five groups compared to the *frequency of use* score. The features of Group A have received the highest average priority rating in both criteria. The difference between the two criteria is biggest for Group E (Robustness features).

3.9.9 Per feature scoring comparison between groups of stakeholders

Analysis Option 8: The question is to compare between the features in terms of the frequency of scores assigned to this feature. This information gives an aggregated view of all the frequency distribution of individual stakeholder scores.

To make this comparison easier, the original nine-point scale is transformed into a more coarse-grained three-point scale. The three classes are defined in (3.5) to (3.7):

(3.5) Class A *(Low)*: Priorities 1, 2 and 3 of the nine-point scale

(3.6) Class B *(Average)*: Priorities 4, 5 and 6 of the nine-point scale

(3.7) Class C *(High)*: Priorities 7, 8 and 9 of the nine-point scale

To facilitate the comparison, features are arranged in decreasing order in terms of their weighted average stakeholder priority. The results of our illustrative example are provided in Figure 3.11. The criterion used is *frequency of use*. For example, the first feature (ID = 1) has been prioritized by 37.5% (i.e., 3 out of 8 stakeholders) of the stakeholders as of being in category *high*. The rest of the stakeholders have classified the feature as having *average* priority, with no one scoring it as *low*. These portions of the three categories change when you compare to lower ranked features.

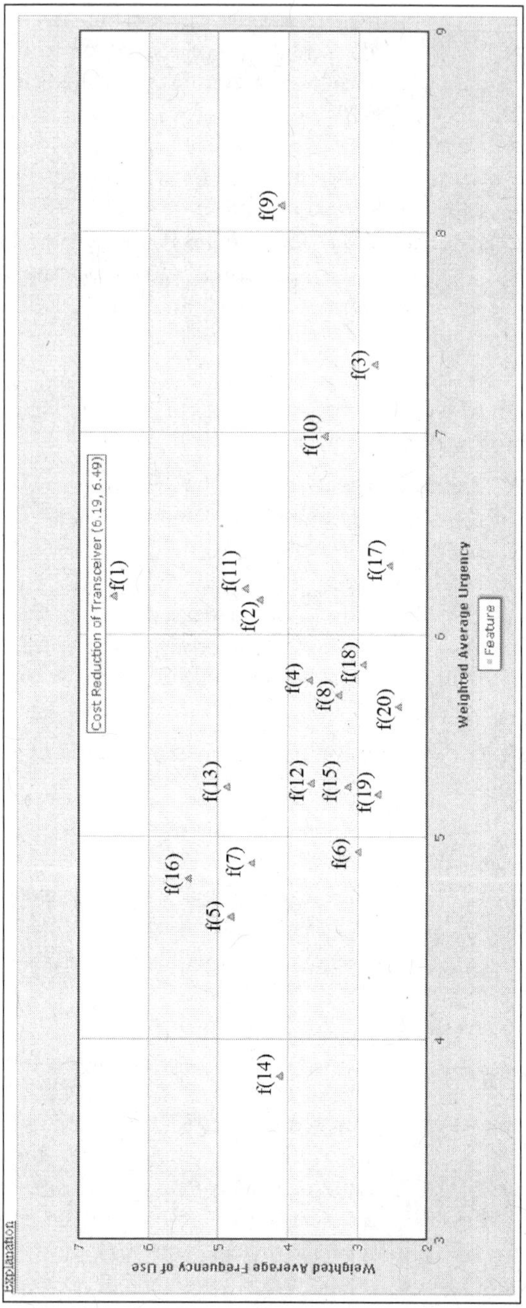

Figure 3.9 Trade-off analysis for *frequency of use* versus *urgency* criteria

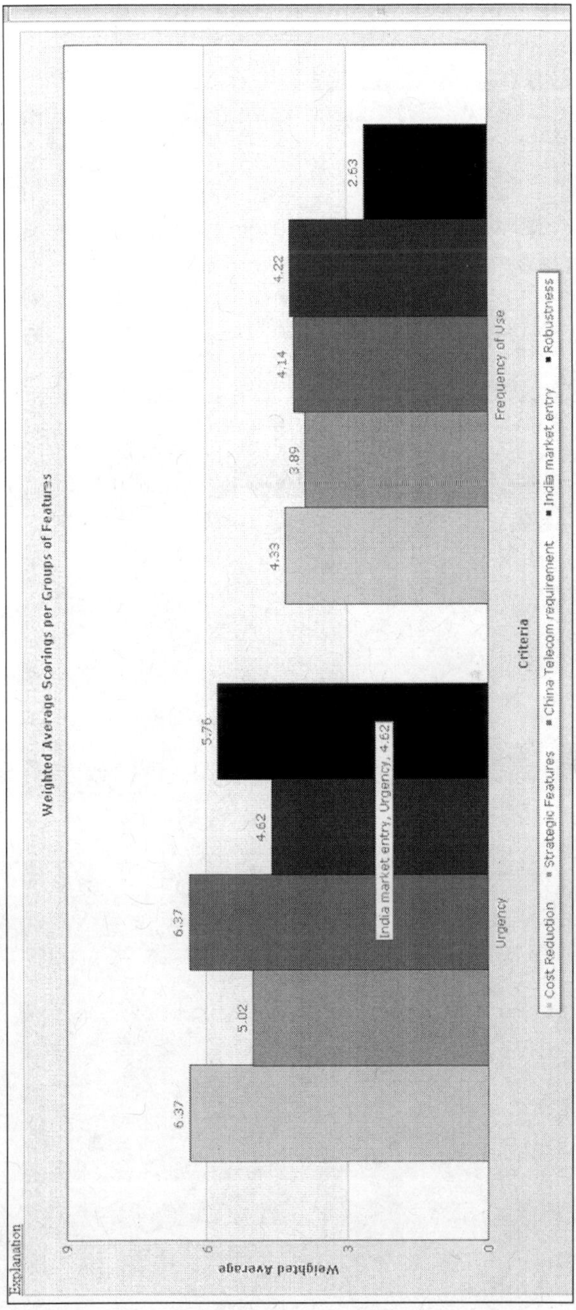

Figure 3.10 Comparison of weighted averages of stakeholder scores for five feature groups and two criteria

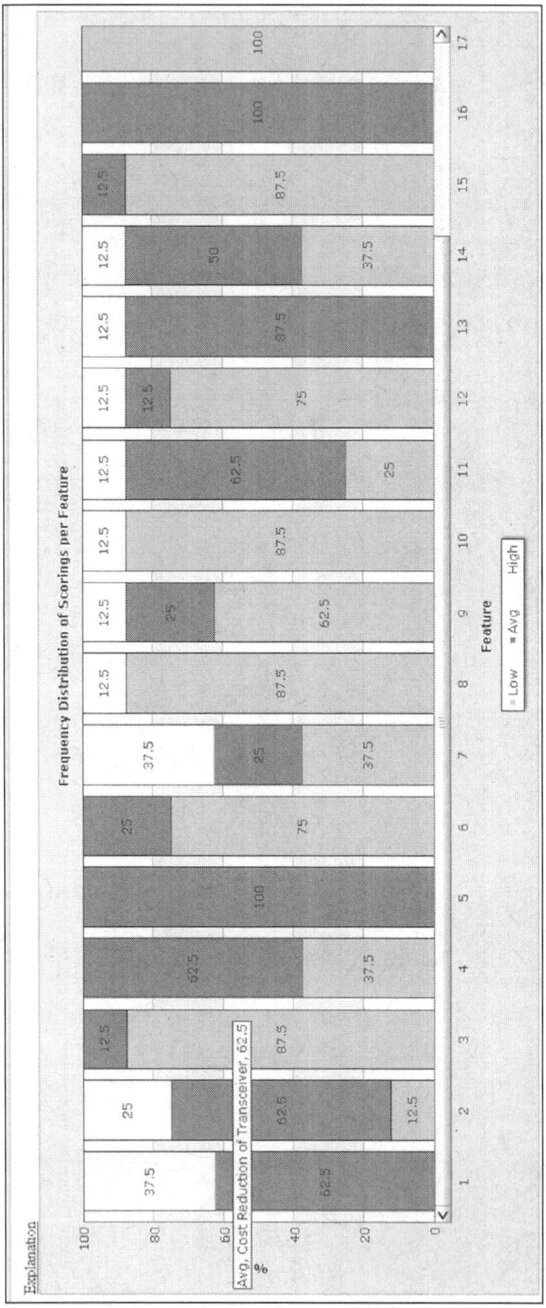

Figure 3.11 Frequency distributions of scoring categories *low*, *average* and *high* for the data from Table 3.5

3.9.10 Comparison of frequency of scoring between groups of stakeholders

Analysis Option 9: For a given criterion, the question is to perform a per feature comparison of the frequencies in scoring categories as defined in (3.5) to (3.7) between two given groups of stakeholders.

The motivation for this question might be that the product manager wants to find out commonalities and differences in the priority profiles between groups of stakeholders. The profiles might vary for different groups of clients. Similarly, a comparison between internal and external stakeholders might be of substantial interest.

In Figure 3.12, the comparison is made between internal stakeholders (CEO, CTO, release manager, chief architect) and external stakeholders (four sales representatives). For all 20 features, the difference between the absolute number of occurrences is studied for all three defined categories. Only bubbles of those features are shown where any deviation occurred. The bigger the bubble in a category, the more significant is the difference between the two stakeholder groups in their scoring related to this category. For example, if feature f(7) *Patching Improvements/Upgrade Enhancements* is considered, differences in all three categories can be observed. The largest differences for this feature are in the *high* and *low* categories. This is a clear indication that there are good reasons to perform a root-cause analysis to better understand the reasons for the deviations. On the other hand, only minor differences (in the *low* and *average* category) were observed for features f(5) and f(19).

If the perception of importance of features considered between internal and external stakeholders is significantly different, then it cannot be automatically assumed that the internal stakeholder represents all stakeholders (as it is sometimes the case in reality).

3.9.11 Comparison of frequency of scoring between groups of features and between groups of stakeholders

Analysis Option 10: A given set of (groups of) features is considered. The question of investigation is to compare the frequency of scoring between different groups of stakeholders for the different groups of features under the premise that the prioritization criterion is fixed.

This question is motivated by the study of scoring patterns between groups of features and groups of stakeholders. If a group of features is selected, then it would be interesting to see if there is a pattern between the frequencies of scoring when comparing the scores of different groups of stakeholders.

The question is illustrated in Figure 3.13. It is observed that the distribution for the fourth group of features looks quite different between internal and external stakeholders. Of the internal stakeholders, 25% have assigned high scores to features from this group, while there is no *high* score from the external stakeholders for this feature group. On the other side, the scores for the third group of features look quite similar between the two groups of stakeholders.

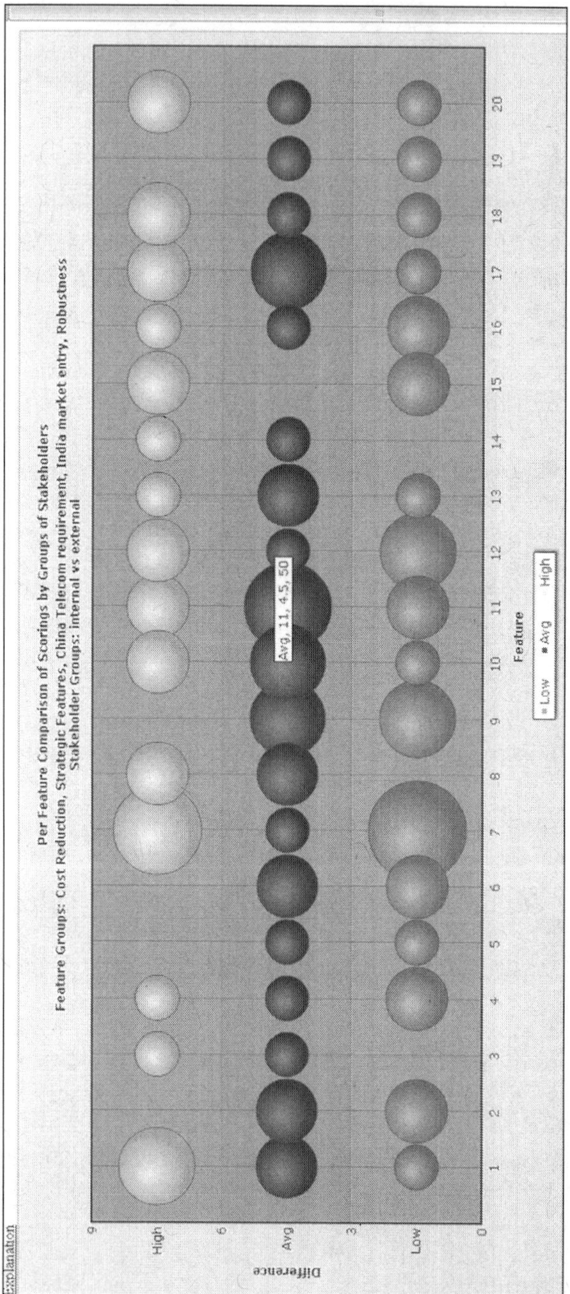

Figure 3.12 Per feature comparison of scoring categories between internal and external stakeholders

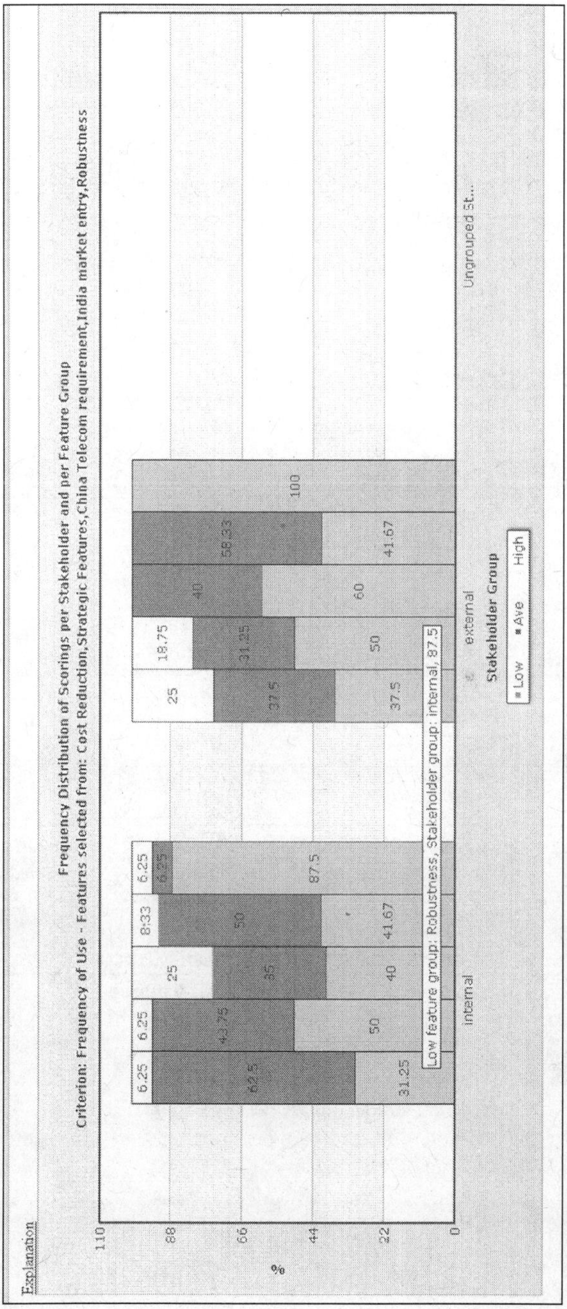

Figure 3.13 Comparison of frequency distribution of *urgency* scores for two groups of stakeholders and five groups of features

3.9.12 Summary

In total, 10 different analysis options for stakeholder scoring have been presented. In Table 3.6, a classification of all the different options has been made. While the list is not intended to be complete, it offers a variety of alternatives the decision-maker can chose from to make final priority and release decisions.

Table 3.6 Classification of options for analyzing stakeholder scores

Analysis option	Type of analysis	Object of analysis	# of features	# of criteria	# of stake-holders
1	Ranking	Weighted average scores per feature	All features or group(s) of features	1	All
2	Ranking	Weighted average scores per feature combined for all criteria	All features or group(s) of features	More than 1	All
3	Ranking	Level of disagreement between stakeholder scores	All features or group(s) of features	1	All
4	Ranking (Pareto analysis)	Stakeholder scores per feature	One selected feature	1	All
5	Comparison	Stakeholder scores per feature	One selected feature	More than 1	All
6	Comparison (trade-off analysis)	Weighted average scores per feature	All features or group(s) of features	2	All
7	Comparison	Weighted average scor-ing per group of features	Groups of features	More than 1	All
8	Comparison	Frequency distribution of stakeholder scores per features	All features or groups of features	1	All
9	Comparison	Frequency distribution of stakeholder scores per group of stakeholders	All features or groups of features	1	Groups of stake-holders
10	Comparison	Frequency distribution of stakeholder scores per group of features and per group of stakeholders	Groups of features	1	Groups of stake-holders

Part B: Methods

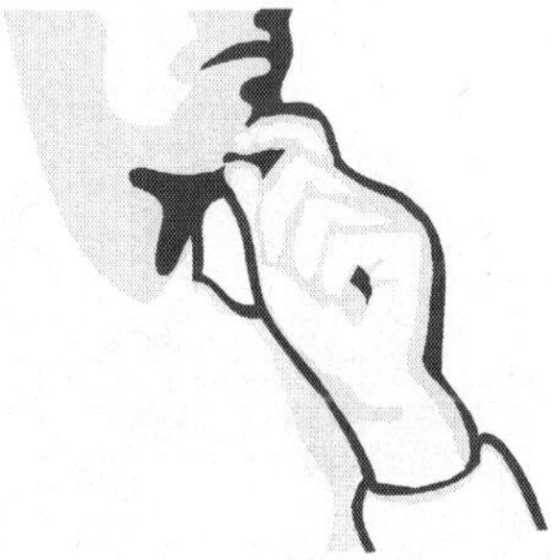

CHAPTER 4

PLANNING FOR PRODUCT RELEASES: AN OVERVIEW

4.1 INTRODUCTION

Already being late in the process of creating the next release of an evolving product, your customers and stakeholders are continuously changing their opinion, are asking for new or revised features and services. Their actual expectations are different from what the product manager thought they were. In total, their wish list far exceeds the capacity of the development resources available. Some of the resources originally planned for are at risk of not being available. Looking at the individual customer's wish lists in more detail, their preferences differ quite substantially between each other. But how can you satisfy the needs of one stakeholder without ignoring the needs of the others?

Most critical product decisions are made in the early phases of the product life-cycle. Any failures or omissions done at this stage usually have a larger impact compared to later stages. Consequently, qualifying the early stage process may affect directly the product success [Smith and Reinertsen '98]. Planning the right sequence of product releases is an essential part of this effort. The challenge of the product managers is to make release decisions in consideration of multiple criteria such as time-to-market, customer satisfaction, business value, competitiveness, and risk. Under the pressure of time and project complexity, the release decisions are often done ad hoc, mainly relying on intuition and experience. The result of this might be one or more of the following deficits:

Deficit in quality: Because of having committed to the "wrong" set of features and the lack of resources available to realize them, trade-offs need to be made in the quality of the delivered product releases in order to maintain the agreed upon release dates.

Deficit in business: Your products do not really penetrate the market as your competitors are more successful in bringing the right features at the right time to the right customers. Key business opportunities have been missed, resulting in a lack of profit.

Deficit in process: In the course of implementing the committed next release, it becomes clear that there is a lack of resources to provide all the announced features at the announced release date. Re-planning and process changes have to be implemented, creating additional risks for timely shipping of the product.

Deficit in customer satisfaction: The product delivered is not what the customers expected, leading to customer dissatisfaction. Satisfied customers are critical for the business and the image of the company.

In this chapter, an overview about product release planning is given. In Section 4.2, release planning is positioned as part of a hierarchy of planning activities. An overview of the process and content of release planning is the content of Section 4.3. Some rigorous release planning methods are explained and compared to each other in Section 4.4. As a result of performing a series of semi-formal interviews and doing a questionnaire, a reflection of the current state-of-the-practice is given in Section 4.5.

4.2 THE PLANNING ONION

Planning of product releases is part of a hierarchy of planning activities. Their principal relationship is described by the planning onion introduced by [Cohn '06] and is illustrated in Figure 4.1.

The planning onion describes the hierarchical relationship between the different objects of planning. This relationship is valid independent of the actual product development paradigm. Daily operational planning is the refinement of planning for iterations. Different iterations constitute a release, and releases describe the evolution of a product. This evolution is often also called a *product roadmap*. A combination of different products constitutes a product portfolio. At the highest level, planning is done based on portfolios constituting the company's strategy.

The planning onion has an operational perspective at the core and gradually moves to a strategic perspective. Daily planning assigns human resources to specific tasks and sub-tasks. Strategic planning looks into the future, for example, three years from now. The overall business success of a company depends on a synchronized process between all these layers. Daily and operational planning becomes difficult if the proper release plan is missing. In the same way, release plans need to be well-aligned with the product and portfolio strategy of a company.

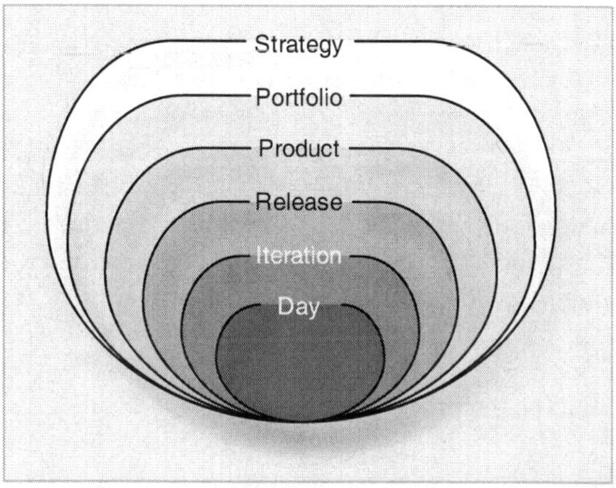

Figure 4.1 The planning onion ([Cohn'06] Agile Estimating and Planning, 1st, ©2006. Electronically reproduced by permission of Pearson Education, Inc., Upper Saddle River, New Jersey)

Release planning differs from iteration planning in the scope and the level of detail. Roughly speaking, release plans are major milestones in the evolution of a product. The time periods for a release depend on the type of the product, the underlying business model, and the type of development processes applied. Iteration plans (again, independent of the development paradigm) are refinements of a release plan. For the next release period, iterations are defined in which the sequence of the release functionality will be developed. This includes assignment of resources to individual tasks, as studied in Chapter 8 of this book. Iteration planning and release planning are going hand-in-hand. One without the other will result in weaker results.

4.3 RELEASE PLANNING IN A NUTSHELL

As software and other products are getting more and more complex and larger in size, incremental and iterative development is rapidly replacing monolithic product creation approaches [Larman and Basili '03]. The key difference between phased (subsuming iterative and incremental) development and the monolithic approach is the concept of creating the overall product in different stages. The key idea of incremental development is the delivery of a sequence of increments. Developing systems through incremental releases first requires providing essential operating functions, then providing system users with improved and more and more capable versions of a system at regular intervals [Basili and Turner '75]. One of the most prominent issues involved in incremental and iterative software development is to plan for its releases.

Release planning is the critical process of deciding which features are implemented in which releases. In reality, the set of features is permanently updated because new features continually arrive and become integrated into the product. Other (existing) features need to be revised. In most cases, both the resources and the timing are not sufficient to implement everything in one release. Consequently, features need to be postponed or sometimes even completely rejected.

Release planning needs to be continued as long as the product evolves. In Figure 4.2, release planning is illustrated as part of an ongoing product evolution process. In this example, planning is done for the next three release periods. These periods are generally called k, k+1 and k+2. Let's assume that 13 versions of an evolving product have already been released. The feature repository maintains all features proposed, all the ones existing, and all the ones requested for an update. The product planning is then done for releases k = 14, k+1 = 15 and k+2 = 16. At the end of each period, the resulting release is called product release 14, 15 and 16, respectively.

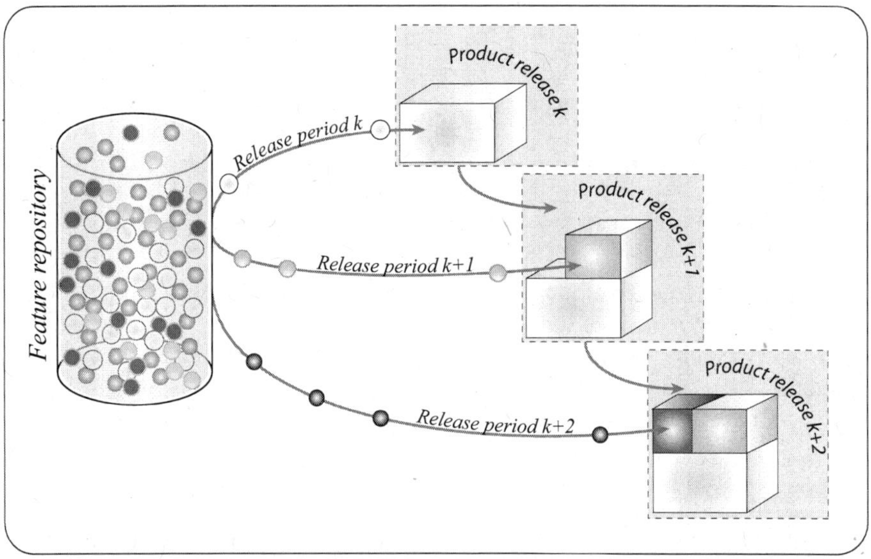

Figure 4.2 Release planning as the selection and assignment of features to releases

4.4 RIGOROUS RELEASE PLANNING METHODS

4.4.1 Overview

Different models and related release planning methods have been proposed over the last decade. In this chapter, six methods are briefly explained. All these methods use some formalized problem description. As such, they are different from *informal* planning, also called *planning on-the-fly*. More specifically, the following methods are studied:

- Greedy release planning
- Optimizing value and cost in requirements analysis [Jung '98]
- The next release problem [Bagnall et al. '01]
- The incremental funding method [Denne and Cleland-Huang '04]
- Software release planning: An evolutionary and iterative approach [Greer and Ruhe '04]
- Software product release planning through optimization and what-if analysis [van den Akker et al. '08]

4.4.2 Greedy release planning

Creating a release plan based on the information of both the feature priority and the resource consumption is often done in reality using some form of a greedy approach. Greedy algorithms are a widely applied iterative solution technique aimed at finding a good global solution by determining the local optimum choice at each stage [Cormen et al. '06].

What is provided here is an easy variant of the general greedy algorithm which does not consider any type of dependencies between features. If there are dependencies, the procedure needs to be adjusted correspondingly. The key principle of greedy release planning is to elaborate the features top down according to their overall value. The process starts with the feature of highest overall value. It is continued with the next best feature. The process is continued as long as the available resource capacities are not exceeded. If the addition of any of the new features violates any of the cost or resource constraints, the feature is dismissed and the next best feature is considered for inclusion. If no further feature can be added that way, the composition of the next release is started with the best of all the leftover features.

The subsequent *greedy release planning* procedure is based on the following assumptions:

(4.1) A set of features F = {f(1) … f(N)}

(4.2) Features consume resources called cost (1) … cost(N), respectively

(4.3) Features have estimated values called value(1) … value(N), respectively

(4.4) Planning is performed for the next K releases

(4.5) Each release k has total cost capacity called TotalCost(k) (k = 1 .. K)

(4.6) The results of planning are sets of features Release(1) … Release (K)

A pseudo-code description of the process is given in Table 4.1. Its application is acceptable if optimality is not important or is difficult to obtain. The small example presented next, although simplified, is intended to illustrate the risk you take when following the greedy technique and when primarily looking at value.

Table 4.1 Greedy release planning

```
Begin
// Assume value(1) ≥ value(2) ≥ .. ≥ value(N)
For k = 1...K Do
// k denotes the release index//
        Begin
        ActualCost(k) = 0, ActualValue(k) = 0, Release(k) = Ø
        For n = 1...N Do
        // n denotes the index of the feature under consideration //
                Begin
                If f(n) in F and ActualCost(k) + cost(n) ≤ TotalCost(k)
                Then
                        Begin
                        Release(k) := Release(k) + {f(n)}, F = F - {f(n)},
                        ActualCost(k) := ActualCost(k) + cost(n)
                        ActualValue(k) := ActualValue(k) + value(n)
                        End
                End
        End
End
```

Example

As an example, a problem with N = 10 features and planning for K = 2 releases is considered. Features are assumed being arranged in decreasing order of value. The sample data is summarized in Table 4.2.

Table 4.2 Data for sample example for application of greedy release planning

Feature	f(1)	f(2)	f(3)	f(4)	f(5)	f(6)	f(7)	f(8)	f(9)	f(10)
Value	9	8.5	8	7.5	7	6.5	6	5.5	5	4.5
Cost	100	90	25	23	22	20	10	30	30	30

With capacities TotalCost(1) = 100 and TotalCost(2) = 90, the procedure would initially consider f(1) and assign this feature to the first release. As the whole capacity of the first release is already consumed, the procedure subsequently looks at the second release (k = 2). The remaining set F now consists of {f(2) … f(10)}. Feature f(2) is considered first, as it has the highest value. Again, one feature consumes the whole cost capacity of that release. Consequently, there is no other feature that could be assigned to one of the two releases.

The process terminates with the two sets Release(1) = {f(1)}, Release(2) = {f(2)} and related cost ActualCost(1) = 100 and ActualCost(2) = 90. This would result in a total value of 9 and 8.5 in releases 1 and 2, respectively. However, the result obtained from the application of this procedure is far from optimal. What is (based on the given numbers) a better plan is to assign features to releases as shown in (4.7) and (4.8).

(4.7) Release(1) = {f(3), f(4), f(5), f(6), f(7)}, ActualValue(1) = 35

(4.8) Release(2) = {f(8), f(9), f(10)}, ActualValue(2) = 15

Features assigned to later releases are typically assumed to create reduced value compared to offering them in the first release. If you weight the value of the second release just half the benefit of the first one, the greedy solution achieves a total value of 9 + 0.5·8.5 = 13.25. This is a portion (9 + 0.5·8.5)/(35 + 0.5·15) = 13.25/42.5 of what is totally possible. In other words, in this case, the greedy assignment of features results in a plan having about 31.2% of the value of the best possible solution.

Even though the numbers were created synthetically, the example shows how badly the greedy approach might perform. While generating relatively good solutions on average, the solution quality is unknown for any specific case in consideration.

4.4.3 Optimizing value and cost in requirements analysis

Jung first proposed a cost-value requirements analysis using mathematical programming [Jung '98]. This was an improvement of the manual inspection method proposed by [Karlsson and Ryan '97] who proposed to use the Analytical Hierarchy Process [Saaty '80] and subsequent application of intuitive inspection to determine the most valuable requirements. Instead of relying on intuition alone, Jung applied a rigorous algorithm to decide which requirements should be assigned to the next release.

Jung's approach is to formulate the optimal feature selection as a knapsack problem (see [Kellerer et al. '04] for knapsack problems). The approach is applicable whenever the problem is not too large and if the only interest is on cost-benefit ratio optimization. Each feature f(n) of set F has an associated cost and an associated benefit. For a given capacity, a two-stage method was proposed. At the first stage, the maximum benefit Value* was determined as the solution of the knapsack problem having variables x(n) in correspondence to features f(n) for all n = 1...N. The knapsack problem is known to be NP-complete [Garey and Johnson '79]. The maximum value Value* can eventually be achieved by different compositions of feature sets. In a second phase, the set causing the least cost among the ones having maximum benefit is determined.

4.4.4 The next release problem

The next release problem as approached by [Bagnall et al. '01] looks exclusively at the cost per feature. There is no involvement of stakeholders in the prioritization of features because a customer gets either all or nothing. The scope of planning is just the next release. Compared to [Jung '98], this approach allows modeling of some feature dependencies. The specific model the authors considered assumes a list of features and a weight for each customer. Feature dependencies are expressed by an acyclic graph. Each feature has an associated cost which is the total cost created from all types of resources involved in its implementation.

Each customer has a wish list of features. Some of them are requested exclusively, others are requested jointly by a number of customers. In general, a feature can only be offered when all the enabling features are provided. These enabling features do not directly contribute to the satisfaction of a customer, but they are needed as enablers for the features being on the wish list.

The objective of planning is to achieve the highest value subset of customers under the condition that the total cost consumed for achieving this does not exceed total capacity. In general, it will not be possible to fulfill the expectations of all customers. The reason for this is that all the features consume some cost, and the total amount of cost is limited. Some of the customers are more important than others, and some of them have higher expectations than others.

The authors have mapped this problem formulation to a knapsack problem with some additional constraints. They have applied three solution methods to solve the resulting problem. On the smallest problem with 100 customers and 140 features, the integer programming algorithm was successful in providing the optimal solution. For larger problems with up to 500 customers and 3250 features, the exact algorithms were unable to find a solution, and the simulated annealing technique [Van Laarhoven and Aarts '87] proved more applicable.

4.4.5 The incremental funding method

The incremental funding method aims at *delivering functionality in chunks of customer-valued features, carefully sequenced to optimize the project's net present value* [Denne and Cleland-Huang '04]. The method plans for what is called *minimum marketable features* (MMF). These MMFs are small, self-contained features that can be delivered quickly and that provide market value to the customer. The model assumes business dependencies between the MMFs. The method relies on estimates for the projected net present value of each MMF for each feasible period. It performs a greedy-type of heuristic to decide in which sequence the MMFs should be offered.

The method does not make any consideration of resources. It is very focused on the maximization of the overall financial value. The method was proven to generate good (in terms of the stated financial objective) solutions for randomly generated examples with 10 to 12 MMFs. The scalability of the method, however, was not investigated.

4.4.6 Software release planning: An evolutionary and iterative approach

An iterative approach for solving release planning called EVOLVE has been offered and is described in more detail in [Greer and Ruhe '04]. EVOLVE conceptually differs from the former methods in the following aspects:

- It is the first method to look ahead for more than one release.

- It is based on the opinions and input of the stakeholders. It assumes prioritization of features by all selected stakeholders in terms of urgency and value of the features. The method tries to balance the conflicting stakeholder opinions to achieve the highest degree of satisfaction with the resources available.
- It considers technological constraints for coupling and precedence relationship between features.
- It assumes an evolutionary process of planning with features added and removed between all planning iterations (releases).
- As a solution method, it generates more than one alternative. Each alternative represents a trade-off between fulfillment of stakeholder expectations and the total benefit of the proposed plans.

The goal of the optimization procedure is to maximize a function G(x) defined for each plan x. G(x) is composed as a linear combination of a penalty function G1(x) and a benefit function G2(x) by a factor α as

(4.9) $G(x) = (\alpha - 1)\, G1(x) + \alpha\, G2(x)$ (with $0 \leq \alpha \leq 1$)

The penalty function G1(x) defined for plan x is describing the degree of violation of the *consistency* property between all pairs of features for all stakeholders having expressed their priorities. Consistency is looking at the partial order between features defined by the scoring of one stakeholder in comparison to the releases the features are assigned to.

The benefit function G2(x) is based on feature scores of the stakeholders and the actual assignment of features to releases according to the plan x under consideration. The function (4.9) is supposed to become of maximum value. For the different values of α, more emphasis is lead to minimize the penalty (low value of α) or to maximize the value (high α).

4.4.7 Software product release planning through optimization and what-if analysis

van den Akker et al. applied mathematical programming to provide a solution for the next release problem [van den Akker et al. '08]. Their main planning criterion is based on projected revenue of the features. Different types of feature dependencies are taken into account:

- Implication (one feature can only be implemented if another feature is implemented)
- Combination (one feature only makes sense in combination with another one)
- Exclusion (either the one feature or the other, but not both of them)
- Revenue-based (revenue of groups of features is no longer just additive)
- Cost-based (cost of groups of features is no longer just additive)

The emphasis of their next release planning approach is on different scenarios related to teams needed to implement the feature. In the easiest case, there is only one team, and this team is assumed to execute all parts of the features. This option is a simplification of reality as mostly there are teams having specialized skills and expertise for doing the individual types of jobs. This situation is considered in a second scenario to have different teams with specialized expertise, but to not allow any type of exchange between teams. Finally, different teams and exchange between teams is considered as well as hiring external personnel or extending the release date.

Managerial steering mechanisms are used to run what-if analysis for changed project parameters. The individual models and their possible integration ended up in an integer linear programming problem. The authors developed a prototype tool based on the ILOG CPLEX software library [ILOG]. The largest problem studied included 99 requirements and 17 teams. Near optimal solution of proven degree of optimality could be generated for that problem.

4.4.8 Comparative analysis

For two of the methods described in this chapter, a comparative analysis is done in this section with what is called *on-the-fly planning*, which performs release planning exclusively based on intuition and some form of communication. On-the-fly planning assumes an experienced product manager and is often used in practice. The results of this approach are considered to become more risky, the more complex the planning situation becomes (size, number of resources, dependencies, number and involvement of stakeholders, planning criteria). In Chapter 6, another comparison is done with a new method called EVOLVE II.

In Table 4.3, the comparison between methods is related to some of the key aspects of release planning:

- *Time horizon* considers the number of releases looked ahead when planning for the releases.
- *Objectives* looks at the number and the definition of the objectives considered for planning.
- *Stakeholder involvement* asks for the degree of involvement and the number of stakeholders involved. This aspect of the comparison also includes the type of involvement.
- *Solution method* considers the way actual release plans are generated.
- *Quality of solutions* is judged against the stated objectives.
- *Feature dependencies* looks at the dependencies between features, which are considered by the respective methods.
- *Human resource constraints* ask if there is the possibility to handle constraints related to human resources.
- *What-if analysis* asks for the explicit support of running different scenarios with varying problem parameters.
- *Integrated tool support* looks at the possibility for the user to enter and maintain online all the relevant release planning information.

Table 4.3 Comparison between two release planning methods and on-the-fly planing

	Method		
Characteristics	Greedy	On-the-fly planning	[van den Akker et al. '08]
Time horizon	Next release, but applicable more general	Next release	Next release
Objectives	Flexible, but typically value-based	Vague and not explicitly described	Maximize financial value function
Stakeholder involvement	Not directly supported	Opportunistic and by communication	Not directly supported
Solution method	Greedy heuristic	Intuition and experience-based	Integer linear programming (ILP)
Quality of solutions	Good on average, but unknown for specific cases	Difficult to judge. The more risky, the more complex the problem	Near-optimal solutions based on ILOG
Feature dependencies	Typically not considered	Implicitly, hard to consider for more complex problems	Precedence, coupling, *either or* dependencies
Human resource constraints	If at all, then just cumulative effort	Implicitly, hard to consider for more complex problems	Yes, including staffing of teams
What-if analysis (explicit support)	No	No	Yes
Integrated tool support	No	No	Prototype based on usage of ILOG

Over the last decade, there has been progress in the capability to solve product release planning problems more systematically. However, there is still lack of methods with associated tools maintaining a feature repository, thus allowing ongoing updates of features and their data. This, on the other hand, is in general the strength of existing general-purpose commercial tools. These tools, however, mostly do not aim at quality of release decisions. Another current deficit is the lack of industrial evaluation of the proposed methods. Most methods have just been initially evaluated by small or randomly generated test examples.

4.5 RELEASE PLANNING IN PRACTICE: THE STATUS QUO

4.5.1 Overview

To evaluate the current state-of-the-practice of product release planning, a survey and 25 semi-structured interviews with product and project managers were performed. All these subjects were involved in product release planning in their organization. The companies were from different domains with different types of offerings (software products, services, embedded products). In addition to these interviews, practical experience as reported in [El Emam and Madhavji '95], [Carlshamre et al. '01], [Carlshamre '02], [Amandeep et al. '04], [Ruhe and Saliu '05], [Lehtola '06], [Momoh and Ruhe '06], [Ebert '07], [Cao and Ramesh '08], and [Lindgren et al. '08a] was included. Most recently, a comprehensive product management survey was conducted by [Paquet '09]. Some of these results are included in this analysis, too.

The results reported from all these efforts are providing some significant findings, but do not claim to be general practices or statistically significant. In what follows, the most significant observations are summarized.

4.5.2 Status and impact of product management

The role of the product manager and its impact for the success of a product was studied by [Ebert '07]. The product manager is often titled the *mini CEO* because of the broad range of responsibilities and the need to link marketing, sales, engineering, finance, quality and operations. Following [Paquet '09], 90% of the 789 responding companies have a dedicated product manager. More than two thirds of the companies report having even more than one.

The results of an empirical field study at Alcatel covering 178 projects of one business unit revealed that duration (time to market), schedule adherence and product quality improve with strengthening of a coherent product management role [Ebert '07]. It was demonstrated that with a focus on systematic and rigorous product management techniques, cycle time in the business unit was reduced by 36% compared to the stated initial baseline.

Project delays are defined as *the relative delay of the actually achieved milestone compared to the milestone committed at project start* [Ebert '07]. It was shown that project delays were reduced by 80% as the result of the application of systematic and rigorous product management techniques. The same level of improvement was achieved for quality, defined here as the percentage of total defects found after hand-over of the product to the customer compared to the totality of reported defects found during the product life-cycle.

4.5.3 Impact of rigorous planning

Performing an electronic survey, 12 product and project managers answered detailed questions about the expected impact of performing a more rigorous release planning process. Their answers were given on a five-point scale ranging from *very strong* to *no impact*. The results of the survey are shown as Figure 4.3. More than 70% of the respondents expected from more rigorous release planning processes a strong or even very strong impact on a better match of customer expectations. Similarly, about 25% expected very strong impact on a reduced rate of failed projects and products.

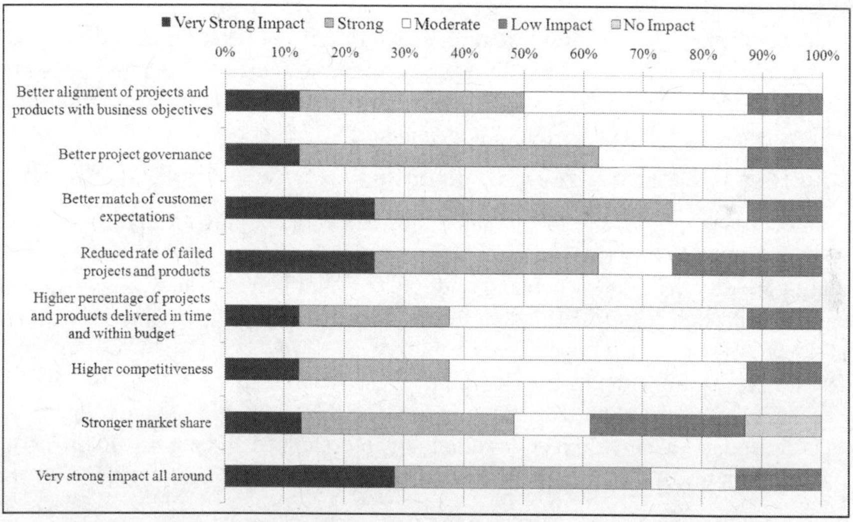

Figure 4.3 Survey results for evaluation of the impact of a rigorous release planning process

4.5.4 Existence of a planning process and potential for its improvement

Typically, companies have a process in place, and the process is also largely followed. There was no evaluation possible at this point about the quality of this process. When asked for potential improvements of the existing processes, a number of directions have been mentioned. Only those are given, which were mentioned by at least 50% of the participants:

- Stronger emphasis on strategic objectives
- More objectivity of the planning process
- Broader involvement of stakeholders, especially of customers
- Stronger consideration of resources and budgets required
- Consideration of risk factors
- Ability to run proactive what-if analysis
- Documentation of the process for better transparency

4.5.5 Quality of feature decisions

It is difficult to find the "right" set of features. Almost all respondents agree that this is typically not achieved. Cases have been reported in which features have been offered which were never used. In parallel, attractive features requested by customers have been missed (for example, the copy & paste feature in the first versions of the iPhone). Lack and quality of stakeholder involvement was considered one of the key reasons for both of these weaknesses by the participants.

The decision about inclusion of features is partially based on the anticipated value of the feature. However, the value of a feature is mostly hard to predict and often time-dependent. A given feature might create value if delivered in the next release but might be of much less value afterward. Another difficulty comes into play when looking at features in conjunction. Certain combinations of features create additional value, which is considered hard to model and hard to predict.

4.5.6 Reactive versus proactive planning

In most cases, offering of features in a new release is largely a response to (key) customer demands or fixing existing deficiencies of features. This type of reactive planning mode only acts on demand and makes it unlikely that new, innovative or even breakthrough features are taken into account. However, these are the features that potentially create a competitive advantage.

Proactive planning mode tries to look ahead with features not yet known or expected. It is less applied than reactive planning. And in case proactive planning was performed, it was seldom done following an organized and controlled process.

4.5.7 Prioritization practices

Prioritization of features is considered key input for release planning. The current practice is to look into the next release. [Lehtola '06] interviewed 25 practitioners from seven software companies in order to understand the existing practices. It was found that *prioritization practices are informal and prioritization methods are not widely used in the industry. However, they appear to be similar mental models that practitioners use as a basis for their prioritization decisions. The most common hidden idea in the practices is to evaluate implementation costs versus the business value gained by implementing the feature. In addition, the companies aim to utilize their product development resources evenly as a function of time used for the implementation* [Lehtola '06].

4.5.8 Number of releases and release dates

The survey [Paquet '09] analyzed 715 responses on the number of product releases per year. Including major and minor releases as well as patches, the average number found was 4.4 releases, with a distribution shown in Figure 4.4.

In terms of release times, there are two fundamental types of release planning problems: (i) release planning with fixed and pre-determined time intervals for implementation, and (ii) planning with flexible intervals. In the second problem type, the decision about the length of the interval to implement the assigned features is not pre-determined. Release dates are often driven by business logistics. External events such as peak sales periods or the capability of the user to upgrade the running system are considered for deciding the release date. The same is true for features and releases offered by main competitors

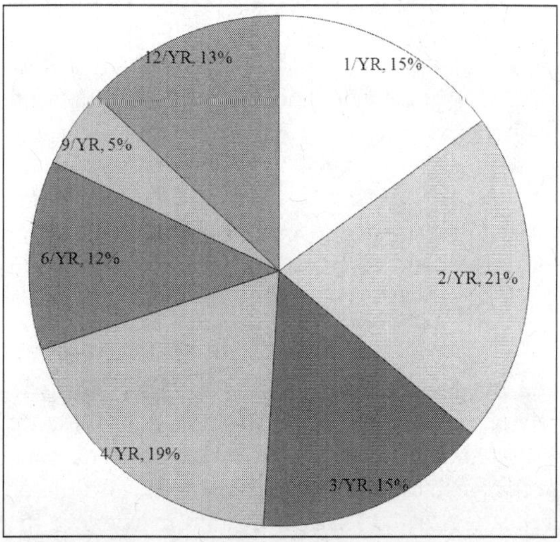

Figure 4.4 Distribution of the number of releases per year [Paquet '09]

4.5.9 Consideration of resources as part of the planning

There is a general lack in consideration of more specific resources other than just effort. One reason for that is the lack of a qualified estimation procedure. This is partially due to the strong variation between software features, where it is more difficult to find similar cases from the past as, for example, in the case of hardware features. The existence of an effort database with effort, and feature-related attributes is more the exception than the rule. The same is true for post-mortem analysis of project performance where former estimates are compared with actual efforts and reasons for deviations are analyzed.

4.5.10 Consideration of feature interdependencies

A study of requirements repositories in telecommunications domain by [Carlshamre et al. '01] analyzed that only about 20% of the features were singular or independent of each other. The authors discussed six different types of possible requirements interdependencies (all of them are studied in more detail in Chapter 5). Ideally, the user would receive support in the elicitation, formulation and verification of feature dependencies. Among the companies interviewed, dependencies have been largely ignored. This causes later changes in the implementation process (when detected later) or makes certain features impossible to use for some time (when detected after delivery).

4.5.11 Frequency and scope of re-planning

There is a continuous need for re-planning due to changed or new requirements, modified constraints, or priorities [Stark et al. '99]. Once the model and the initial project data are made available to apply a computer-supported solution procedure, the actual re-planning becomes easier to perform as well. Even after implementation commences, requirements could change or projects may be heading toward crisis because of unrealistic release plans.

The frequency of re-planning strongly varies between organizations. This has a lot in common with the volatility of features (less volatile features imply less need for re-planning) and the stability and maturity of the overall development process (stable and more mature processes tend to require less re-planning).

4.5.12 Re-planning process

Re-planning in general is considered important. The actual re-planning process is often coordinated by the change control board. This process and the resulting decisions are largely based on intuition. In some cases, acceptance of new features also implies hiring more people to get it done by the pre-determined release date.

For the degree of change, there are limits to how much can be modified of an already announced product feature. An at least 90% conformance level to features already committed to customers was reported. This is equivalent with the limitation of the degree of change by 10% of an announced product release after its implementation has started.

4.5.13 Planning for one versus multiple products

Most companies maintain a variety of products. The survey [Paquet '09] revealed that *the average product manager is responsible for 3.3 products*. Resources for implementation of product features are largely allocated on a per-product base. Usage of resources across products is more the exception than the rule. In most cases, each product is largely planned independent from the other. If synchronization is needed between the products, then this is often tried to be achieved *on-the-fly*, which makes it hard to achieve the goal without additional delays.

In case of embedded product where software is an (essential) part of what is creating the overall value of the product, release planning for software features was reported determined by the cycles of the hardware features.

4.5.14 Tool support

Different types of tool support are used to facilitate the planning and to implement its results. The support ranges from spreadsheets, requirements management tools (such as DOORS®, Requisite Pro®) to the different forms of project management tools (such as Microsoft Project®, Primavera®). The survey conducted by [Paquet '09] asked for the disposition in terms of importance and usefulness for a variety of tool functionality. The results of the 686 responses are shown in Figure 4.5.

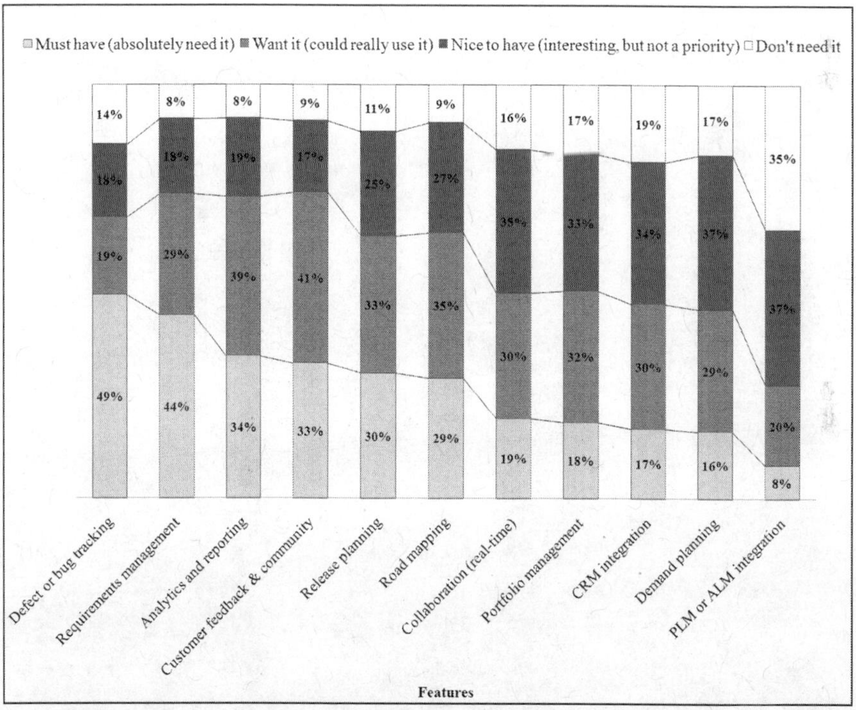

Figure 4.5 Percent distribution by value for different support tool functionalities [Paquet '09]

According to [Paquet '09], Microsoft technologies (specifically the Office suite) are the most commonly used tools to document requirements. From the 25 conducted semi-formal interviews, tools are seen to be limited in two directions: (i) they do constitute the status quo and do not offer any new ideas or strategies, and (ii) tool support is more happening on a micro level than on the strategic or macro level.

CHAPTER 5

MODELING FOR PRODUCT RELEASE PLANNING

5.1 INTRODUCTION

Modeling is an art. It is the art of describing essential parts of reality for the purpose of its further analysis. Depending on what we hope to achieve and also depending on the data and information available, the models will be more or less detailed.

> *The mere formulation of a problem is far more essential than its solution, which may be merely a matter of mathematical or experimental skills. To raise new questions (and), new possibilities, to regard old problems from a new angle, requires creative imagination and marks real advances in science.*
>
> ***(Albert Einstein, 1879-1955)***

Models in general are abstract and simplified descriptions of reality. According to the objectives and the specific topic under investigation, models are always focusing on specific aspects of reality. Many concerns have to be left out to keep the model tractable. In the cases where reality is dynamically changing, models have to be adapted correspondingly.

This chapter is devoted to modeling for the purpose of product release planning. The decision about the level of detail of the model is important. Its answer depends on the scope of the planning and the level of detail expected from the planning results. As expectations from planning are varying, there is no *one size fits all* type of model. Instead, the content, size and granularity of the model are context specific.

In this chapter, different components of release planning models are studied. A variety of modeling options is presented. As a result, the readers will have different possibilities to find the most appropriate model components, applicable for their specific purposes. This model is then used as an input for Chapter 6 when utilized for planning.

5.2 DECISION VARIABLES AND HORIZON OF PLANNING

Decisions in product release planning are primarily related to features and their assignment to releases. Consequently, decision variables are related to a set of features under consideration. Let F = {f(1),…,f(N)} be a set of candidate features. At this point, the assumption is that the features are known and are well described. Their (given) description is used to prioritize them.

It needs to be specified how far in advance planning should be done. This is the number of product releases to consider for planning purposes. Our model allows us to go beyond just looking at the next release. In general, K releases of the product are considered. In case of K equal to one, planning is just for the next release.

Even though the degree of uncertainty grows for each later release, it is often useful to have a more long-term perspective. Customers want an answer regarding when a specific feature is planned to be provided. This information is closely related to the competitiveness of the product. If a company is able to provide key features ahead of their competitors, then this is attractive from a sales and marketing point of view. In addition, the release plan of a product also provides guidance for the development team on the sequence of features to be implemented.

The decision variables x(n) (n = 1…N) describing the proposed strategy for handling features f(n) provide answers to two questions:

i. Is feature f(n) part of any of the next K product releases?
ii. If *yes*, at which release is the feature f(n) offered?

Each individual release plan x describes the assignment to releases for all candidate features. It is characterized by a vector x = (x(1),…,x(N)) defined by (5.1) and (5.2).

(5.1) x(n) = k if feature f(n) is offered at release k (n = 1…N)

(5.2) x(n) = K+1 if feature f(n) is postponed, i.e., it is not offered in one of the next K product releases (n = 1…N)

5.3 DEPENDENCIES BETWEEN FEATURES

A number of additional constraints need to be considered for the decision about features and their assignment to releases. From analyzing industrial software product release planning projects in the domain of telecommunications, [Carlshamre et al. '01] observed that features are often dependent on each other. For the projects and the domain analyzed, the percentage of features being dependent in one way or the other was as high as 80%.

There is a variety of types of dependencies. In [Carlshamre et al. '01], six different types were analyzed. In what follows, a list of eight types of dependencies is presented in more detail. The term *dependency* here can mean different things. It can be related to dependencies in the

- Implementation space (two features are "close" in their implementation and should be treated together), or
- Feature effort space (two features are impacting each other in their implementation effort if provided in the same release), or
- Feature value space (two features are impacting each other in their value if provided in the same release), and
- Feature usage space (two features are only useful for the user if provided in the same release).

Feature dependencies can be visualized by a feature dependency graph. The vertices of the graph correspond to the features, and the arcs (directed connection between vertices) and edges (undirected connections between vertices) correspond to one of the different types of dependencies illustrated in Figure 5.1.

5.3.1 Type 1: Coupling

Feature A *is coupled* to feature B means that both features should be offered in the same release. The reason for this is that both features depend on each other. For a text processing system, the user would expect the feature *Copy* and the feature *Paste* to be in the same release. Alternatively, the coupling relationship can also be based on another form of dependency such as the closeness in the implementation of the features, that is, whenever one of the features is implemented, the other one should be implemented as well.

5.3.2 Type 2: Either or

Features A and B are in an *either or* dependency relationship if exactly one of them needs to be taken. That means, if A is selected then B cannot be selected and vice versa. *Selection* here means that the feature is offered in one of the product releases under consideration.

5.3.3 Type 3: At least one

For a set of features A, B, C ... the *at least one* dependency means that among the features, at least one should be selected for one of the releases in consideration. Consequently, choosing none of the features would violate this dependency condition, while choosing more than one would not.

5.3.4 Type 4: At most one

For a set of features A, B, C ... the *at most one* dependency means that among the features, at most one should be selected for one of the releases in consideration. Consequently, choosing more than one of the features would violate this dependency condition, while choosing none of them would not.

5.3.5 Type 5: Weak precedence

Features A and B are in a *weak precedence* dependency (A weakly precedes B) if feature A cannot be offered in release later than feature B. However, feature A can be offered in the same release as feature B.

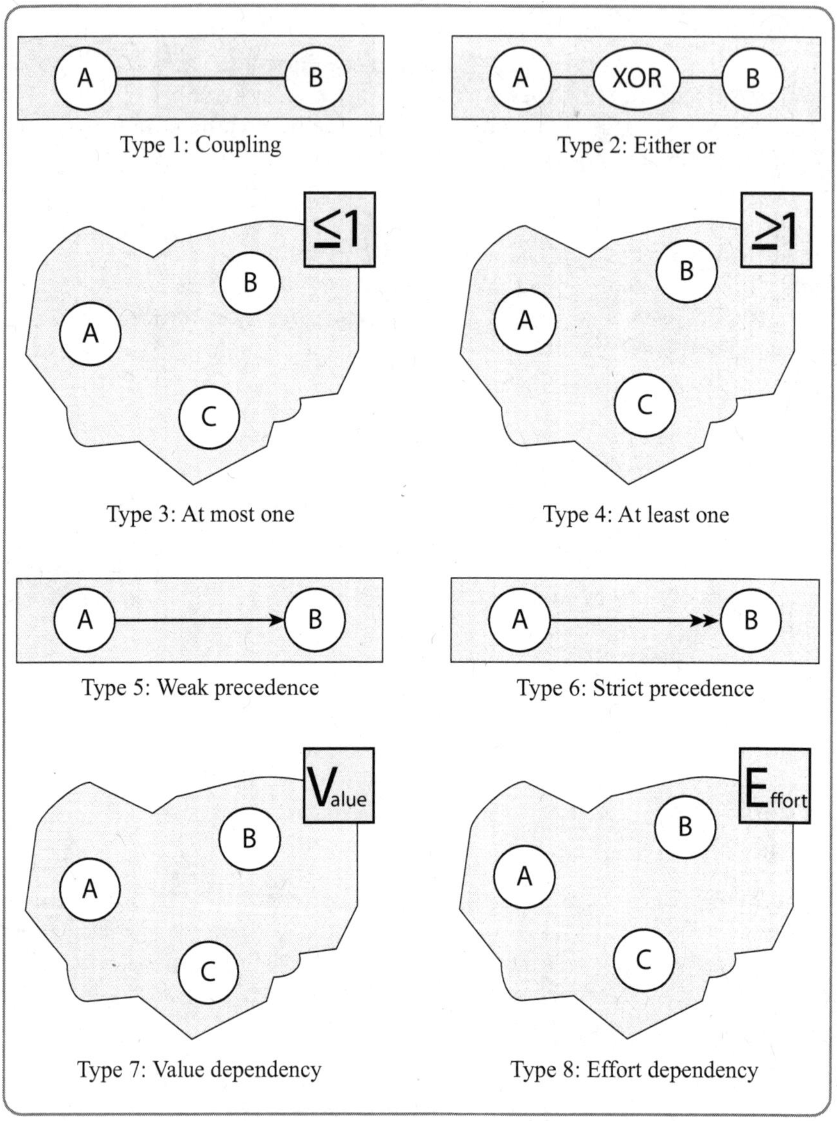

Figure 5.1 Types of features dependencies and their visualization

5.3.6 Type 6: Strict precedence

Feature A and B are in a *strict precedence* dependency (A strictly precedes B) if feature A has to be offered at an earlier release than feature B. In the strict precedence relationship, both features cannot be offered in the same release.

5.3.7 Type 7: Value dependency

A set of features A, B, C ... are in a value dependency if the features are offered together in the same release, and the value of the features in conjunction exceeds the value from taking the sum of all the single values. Value dependency offers a bonus in the case that a certain number of features are offered in conjunction.

5.3.8 Type 8: Effort dependency

A set of features A, B, C ... is in an effort dependency if the features are offered together in the same release, and the total effort of the features is less than the effort from taking the sum of all the single values. Effort dependency is motivated by possible synergies between features when they are implemented in the same release.

5.4 PRE-ASSIGNMENTS

5.4.1 Overview

Pre-assignment of a feature to specific release is one possibility of enlarging the modeling options for the human user. The general purpose of release planning is to assign features to releases. For making this decision, the (subjective) priorities assigned to features by the different stakeholders and the (estimated) amount of resources consumed by the features are taken into account. Both types of information are geared toward making a largely objective decision.

Independent of the method selected for fact-based planning, there might be situations and scenarios where the assignment of features to releases is prescribed. These situations can be related to important legal constraints, aspects of competitiveness (a feature should not be released later than a given release), or (non-) availability of resources. In other words, pre-assignment makes the human decision (assigning a feature to a release) more important than what any computer-supported planning method is proposing.

Pre-assignment can be done in two principal ways. First, a feature can be prescribed to be assigned in exactly one specific release. Second, a feature can be prescribed to be assigned in an interval (sequence) of releases. In both cases, the intention is to overwrite any other considerations executed by the planning system (trying to optimize in the range of flexibility available).

For planning K releases ahead, three options for pre-assignment of features are considered:

5.4.2 Option 1: Fixed pre-assignment of a feature to release k

Option 1 means that the feature needs to be released in fixed release k where k is any of the possible releases 1… K+1. This convention is used to say that a feature is pre-assigned to release K+1 if it is requested to be postponed.

5.4.3 Option 2: Pre-assignment of a feature not later than release k

Option 2 means that the feature needs to be released no later than at release k where k is one out of the possible releases from 2 to K. For release K this implies that the feature cannot be postponed.

5.4.4 Option 3: Pre-assignment of a feature not earlier than release k

Option 3 means that the feature needs to be released no earlier than at release k where k is one out of the possible releases from 2 to K.

5.4.5 Illustration

The three different options for pre-assignment are illustrated in Figure 5.2. In the case of planning K = 4 releases ahead of time, the points in the grid indicate the possible assignments of features to releases. For example, if there is a pre-assignment *not later than release 3* for a feature, then this feature can be assigned to one of the releases 1, 2 or 3. This is shown in the second row of Figure 5.2. As another example, a feature can be pre-assigned to a fixed release (as shown for the top row for the assignment to release 2).

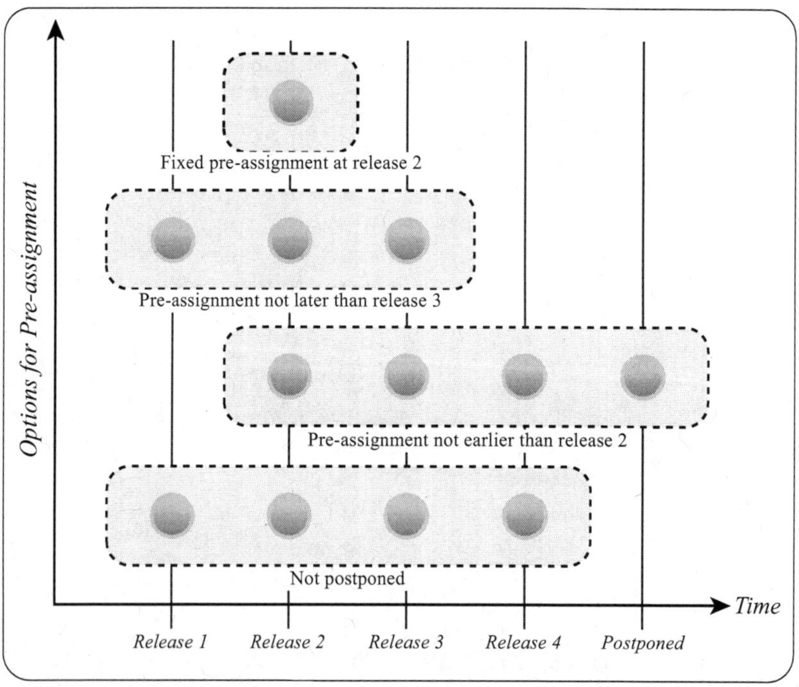

Figure 5.2 Four example options for pre-assignment of features to releases

5.5 EFFORT CONSTRAINTS

Planning without investigating the resource constraints is risky, as the resulting plans are likely to fail because of the potential lack of sufficient resources for the implementation of the features. In its simplest form, a variable called *effort* is introduced, which subsumes the estimated effort needed to implement a feature. The effort for implementing feature f(n) is denoted by *effort(n)*. It can be measured in person days or, more fine-grained, in person hours. Later in this chapter, the total effort is further differentiated according to the different roles, tools and life-cycle phases involved in feature implementation.

When planning for K subsequent releases, the consumed effort per release is not allowed to exceed a given release capacity. For release k = 1…K, this capacity is denoted by Cap(k). More formally, a feasible release plan x needs to satisfy all the constraints

(5.3) $\Sigma_{n:\, x(n)=k}\ \text{effort}(n) \leq \text{Cap}(k)$ for k = 1…K

In (5.3), for each release k, the summation is taken over all features f(n) assigned to this release.

5.6 COST CONSTRAINTS

Similar to the effort constraints as just formulated, cost constraints can be introduced. In this case, each feature f(n) is consuming a certain amount of cost denoted by cost(n). This cost estimate subsumes all the different types of resource consumptions including human and non-human constraints. The different hourly rates of human resources are then aggregated into one cost measure per feature.

Using Budget(k) for the maximum amount of cost available for release k, the corresponding cost constraints are then formulated as

(5.4) $\Sigma_{n:\, x(n)=k}\ \text{cost}(n) \leq \text{Budget}(k)$ for k = 1…K

5.7 RESOURCE CONSTRAINTS

5.7.1 Overview

Just looking into cost or effort is a first approximation of describing the resources necessary for implementation of features. This first approximation does not consider individual types of resources. In this chapter, all key resources necessary for performing the tasks assigned to this release are considered. At strategic level, only cumulative consumption per release is considered for the different resources. At a more operational level, a time-dependent allocation of human and other resources to individual tasks creating the features have to be taken into account.

The estimated consumption of resources by features is considered part of the modeling effort. Different methods are applicable for providing estimates. Most of these methods incorporate some form of learning from former projects. In addition, often these methods are hybrid in the sense that they combine formal techniques with the judgment and expertise of human domain experts. For an overview of resource estimation methods, refer to [Briand and Wieczorek '02]. For a method of hybrid estimation specific to release planning called AQUA-RP, see Section 9.2.

The definition of the actual resource types is project-specific and is done by the product manager (in collaboration with the project manager). Resources can be defined in correspondence of the product life-cycle role (for example, design, implementation, testing) or related to specific skills (for example, user interface implementation, back-end algorithms in C++).

While the granularity in the consideration of resources is flexible, the actual number of resources needs to be selected with care. The planning problem gets more complicated if more resources are involved. Often, it is well known which resources are critical for the project because they became the bottleneck in former projects. These ones are the first candidates to look at in planning.

Independent of the content of the resources, there are two different types of resources to be considered in planning. They are called *local* respectively *global* in correspondence to their mode of spending.

Definition (Local resource): A resource is called *local* if the feature-related consumption of the resource is limited to exactly the release in which the feature is offered. Resources of this class are called local based on their spending mode. □

Definition (Global resource): A resource is called *global* if the feature-related consumption of the resource can be distributed across different release periods. □

All types of human resources that are available only for a specific release period are in the category of local resources. Global resources can be spent whenever there is capacity left over. This means that there is no request to use this resource in the specific release where it is finally offered. In what follows, the constraints related to the two resource types are discussed separately.

5.7.2 Constraints for local resources

When planning for R different resource types and K releases ahead of time, each proposed product release plan needs to fulfill R·K resource constraints. The constraints for each release are formulated separately, starting with the first release. Per release and in each of the R constraints, the summation is taken over all the features f(n) assigned to the first release.

For a given plan x and all types r (r = 1…R) of resources, the total consumption called *Consumption (k,r,x)* within release period k is not allowed to exceed the respective capacity called *Capacity(k,r)*. The variable *consumption(n,r)* denotes the (estimated) consumption of resource type r by feature f(n). More specifically, the following constraints need to be satisfied for the R resource types in release period 1:

(5.5) $\text{Consumption}(1,1,x) = \Sigma_{n:x(n)=1}\ \text{consumption}(n,1) \leq \text{Capacity}(1,1)$
$\text{Consumption}(1,2,x) = \Sigma_{n:x(n)=1}\ \text{consumption}(n,2) \leq \text{Capacity}(1,2)$
...
$\text{Consumption}(1,R,x) = \Sigma_{n:\,x(n)=1}\ \text{consumption}(n,R) \leq \text{Capacity}(1,R)$

In the same way, the constraints for all subsequent releases k = 2…K are formulated. Now, summation is done for all features f(n) which are assigned to a fixed release k (k = 2…K):

(5.6) $\text{Consumption}(k,1,x) = \Sigma_{n:\,x(n)=k}\ \text{consumption}(n,1) \leq \text{Capacity}(k,1)$
$\text{Consumption}(k,2,x) = \Sigma_{n:\,x(n)=k}\ \text{consumption}(n,2) \leq \text{Capacity}(k,2)$
...
$\text{Consumption}(k,R,x) = \Sigma_{n:\,x(n)=k}\ \text{consumption}(n,R) \leq \text{Capacity}(k,R)$

5.7.3 Constraints for global resources

Resource constraints for global resources look different from those of local resources. Their formulation is given in (5.7) to (5.9). The difference to the former (local resource type) constraints is the fact that when considering a release period k, all features not yet released before k potentially can be worked on. This implies the need for a three-dimensional matrix denoted by Percentage_x, which is used to describe how implementation of the features is organized for a given release plan x. The values $\text{Percentage}_x(n,k,r)$ describe the percentage of spending in release k for resource type r when looking at feature f(n).

(5.7) $\Sigma_{n=1..N}\ \text{Percentage}_x(n,k,1)\ \text{consumption}(n,1) \leq \text{Capacity}(k,1)$ for all releases k = 1…K
$\Sigma_{n=1..N}\ \text{Percentage}_x(n,k,2)\ \text{consumption}(n,2) \leq \text{Capacity}(k,2)$ for all releases k = 1…K.
$\Sigma_{n=1..N}\ \text{Percentage}_x(n,k,R)\ \text{consumption}(n,R) \leq \text{Capacity}(k,R)$ for all releases k = 1…K

(5.8) $0 \leq \text{Percentage}_x(n,k,r) \leq 1$ for all resources r = 1…R, for all releases k = 1…K, and for all features f(n), n = 1…N

In addition to all the constraints formulated per releases, it needs to be ensured that the total of all consumptions for feature f(n) across releases equals the total demand of resource r per feature. This is illustrated in Figure 5.3. At the upper part, 100% of the resource consumption of features f(1), f(2) and f(3) is spent in exactly one release period. This is different at the lower part where the resource spending is allocated over different release periods. The related consumption constraint is formulated in (5.9).

(5.9) $\Sigma_{k=1..K}\ \text{Percentage}_x(n,k,r) = 1$ for all r = 1... R and for all n = 1…N

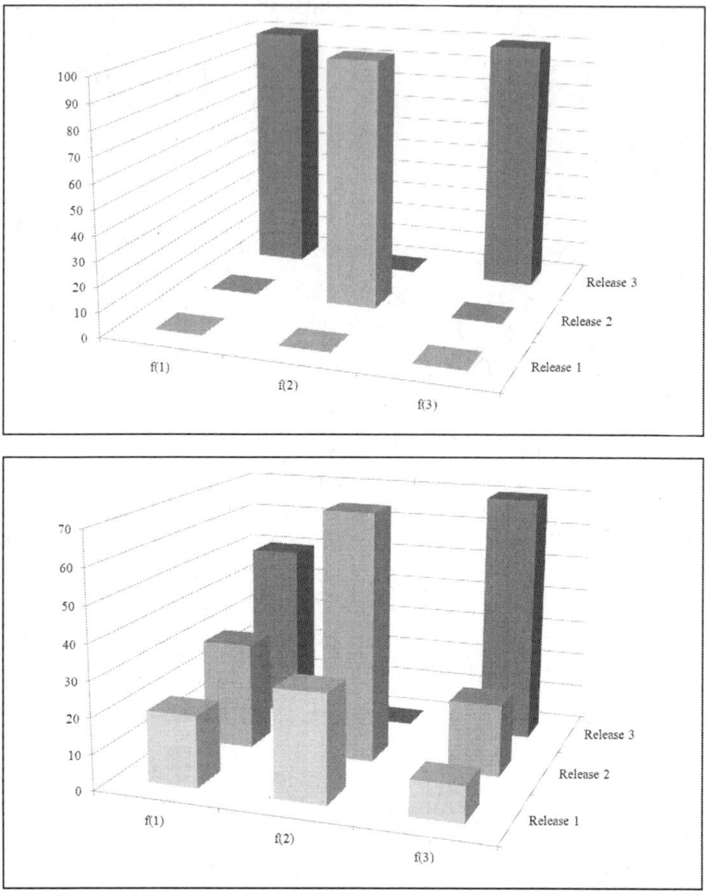

Figure 5.3 Comparison of consumption between local (top) and global (bottom) resource types

5.8 RISK CONSTRAINTS

There are different types of risk associated with a feature. For example, there is the risk of implementation, the risk of acceptance, the risk of dependency from subcontractors and the risk of maintenance. Consideration of all these risks (and maybe others) is important. However, it is difficult to treat them in a quantitative manner as part of a systematic planning method.

Besides the classification and quantification of risk, it is not clear up-front what constitutes the right way to approach risk. As part of an incremental method, does it mean that as many as possible of the higher risks should be considered in earlier releases? Or vice versa, would it make more sense to postpone the risky features to later stages? Or is a balancing of the total amount of risk per release the recommended strategy?

A simplified modeling approach introduced is intended to influence release planning strategies by at least some consideration of risk. As part of that, a classification of (one selected type) risk into a five-point scale is done. The categories are called *VERY LOW, LOW, AVERAGE, HIGH* and *VERY HIGH* risk. Each feature is assigned to one of the five categories. Consequently, risk(n) = HIGH means that the feature f(n) is classified according to the specified risk as belonging to the *HIGH* risk category.

The term #(category, k) denotes the given bound for occurrence of features assigned to release phase k and being of the specific risk category under consideration. For example, #(VERY HIGH, 1) means the number of very high risk features allowed for release 1.

Using this notation, risk related constraints can be introduced by just limiting the number of risks of a specified category per releases. Ignoring *Low* and *Very Low* risk categories, the following constraints (5.10) – (5.12) are obtained.

(5.10) $\Sigma_{n:risk(n)=VERY\ HIGH}\ 1 \quad \leq \#(VERY\ HIGH, k) \quad \text{for } k = 1\ldots K$

(5.11) $\Sigma_{n:risk(n)=HIGH}\ 1 \quad \leq \#(HIGH, k) \quad \text{for } k = 1\ldots K$

(5.12) $\Sigma_{n:risk(n)=AVERAGE}\ 1 \quad \leq \#(AVERAGE, k) \quad \text{for } k = 1\ldots K$

All release plans generated under one of these constraints would then satisfy the limit of risky features per release in each of the selected risk categories. The definition of the risk level is done by the product manager in consultation with the domain expert. It is largely based on former project and product experience.

5.9 PLANNING OBJECTIVES

5.9.1 Overview

Planning objectives give the orientation for deriving appropriate plans. Definition of the actual planning objectives is of key importance. There are a number of potential objectives, and their selection and proper balance needs careful consideration. The top-down approach for this selection starts with the strategic view of the company. From there, a projection to strategic or operational planning objectives is done. The whole process can be subdivided into three essential steps:

i. Definition of the most important planning objectives derived from business goals
ii. Selection of the most relevant objectives for the actual product planning
iii. Formalization (putting the informally stated objectives into a formalized planning function)

Business goals often vary over time and are company specific. In most cases, there is more than one objective to be pursued strategically. The *Balanced Score Card* method [Kaplan and Norton '92] is one prominent example for consideration of multiple objectives. The more specific, measurable and time-oriented the formulated goals are, the higher the chance of actually achieving them or adjusting the goals to changed conditions.

5.9.2 Candidate objectives for the evaluation of product release plans

Operational goals for requirements prioritization have been discussed by [Firesmith '04]. Most of them (listed in Section 3.5) can be extended to evaluation of product releases as well. "Good" plans are based on "good" features, but there are additional aspects related to how the features composed into one release fit together. The number of relevant criteria, the criteria themselves and the composition and weighting of the chosen criteria are very company and project specific and need to be decided based on a case-by-case analysis.

5.9.3 Stakeholder feature points

Besides the selection of planning objectives, another question is how to combine them. However, there is the additional problem of compatibility: How does one combine different criteria; for example, such criteria as the *cost of implementation* for a plan and the criterion of *urgency* of the features offered by a plan? One way to handle this problem is to provide scores to each plan for each criterion and to integrate all the scores into one overall utility value of the plan. This idea is implemented in the concept of *stakeholder feature points*.

Stakeholder feature points are a measure defined for each feature in conjunction with a release plan x. The measure describes the stakeholder satisfaction related to a plan x. The higher the number of stakeholder feature points, the higher the expected satisfaction of stakeholders with this plan.

The calculation of stakeholder feature points is based upon the scores of the stakeholder to features, the importance of the stakeholders, the importance of the criteria, and the importance of the different releases. In what follows, the key notation necessary for giving a formal definition of stakeholder feature points is introduced. The following parameters are used:

Q	—	number of independent planning criteria considered
K	—	number of releases considered for planning
P	—	number of stakeholders in the prioritization process
weight_releases(k)	—	weighting factor for the releases k (k = 1...K)
weight_stake(p)	—	weighting factor for stakeholder stake(p) (p = 1...P)
weight_criterion(q)	—	weighting factor for criterion q (q = 1...Q)
score(n,p,q)	—	score of stake(p) for feature f(n) applying criterion q

All of the weighting factors allow for the expression of relative degrees of importance. Although defined on an ordinal scale, later the weights will be treated like ratio scale measures. A pre-requisite for this interpretation is that their relative importance does not exceed one order of magnitude.

The prioritization process is the same as outlined in Chapter 3. The factors describing the level of importance for both stakeholders and criteria have already been introduced in Chapter 3 as part of the Multi-score method. The release weight factor *weight_release(k)* gives the relative importance of having a feature f(n) assigned to a release k. As a default, weight_release (k) $\geq$ weight_release(k+1) for all k = 1... K-1. What that means is that the feature contribution to the overall objective is higher the earlier the feature is delivered.

Score(n,q) is the portion of the total number of stakeholder feature points, which is provided by feature f(n) when looked at criterion q. It is formally defined as the weighted sum (5.13) from all individual stakeholder scores on this criterion. In the case of stakeholders excluded for scoring on a given feature f(n), the calculation of Score(n,q) needs to be adjusted by just looking at the active stakeholders.

$$(5.13) \quad \text{Score}(n,q) = \Sigma_{p = 1 \ldots P} \, \text{weight\_stake}(p) \cdot \text{score}(n,p,q)$$

The variable SCORE(n) defined in (5.14) is based on all the individual contributions (5.13). It combines them in consideration of the degree of importance of the different criteria.

$$(5.14) \quad \text{SCORE}(n) = \Sigma_{q = 1 \ldots Q} \, \text{weight\_criterion}(q) \cdot \text{Score}(n,q)$$

Using (5.14) allows the definition of stakeholder feature points gained from plan x for feature f(n). The *stakeholder feature points* sfp(n,x) according to plan x are a measure describing the contribution of the feature f(n) to the overall utility of plan x. The number sfp(n,x) is defined in (5.15).

$$(5.15) \quad \text{sfp}(n,x) = \Sigma_{k:\, x(n) = k} \, \text{weight\_release}(k) \cdot \text{SCORE}(n)$$

If a feature is postponed, then it does not provide any stakeholder feature points. As stakeholder feature points are determined based on stakeholder scoring, their value correlates with the conformance between stakeholder priorities and the provision of features. The better the conformance per stakeholder, the higher the number sfp(n,x) of stakeholder feature points.

The objective of planning in this model is to maximize the *total number of stakeholder feature points* (TSFP). The process of calculating TSFP(x) is based upon the concrete data for features, stakeholders, prioritization criteria and releases. The steps of the process are illustrated in Figure 5.4. For a given plan x, the number TSFP(x) is defined in (5.16).

$$(5.16) \quad \text{TSFP}(x) = \Sigma_{n = 1 \ldots N} \, \text{sfp}(n,x)$$

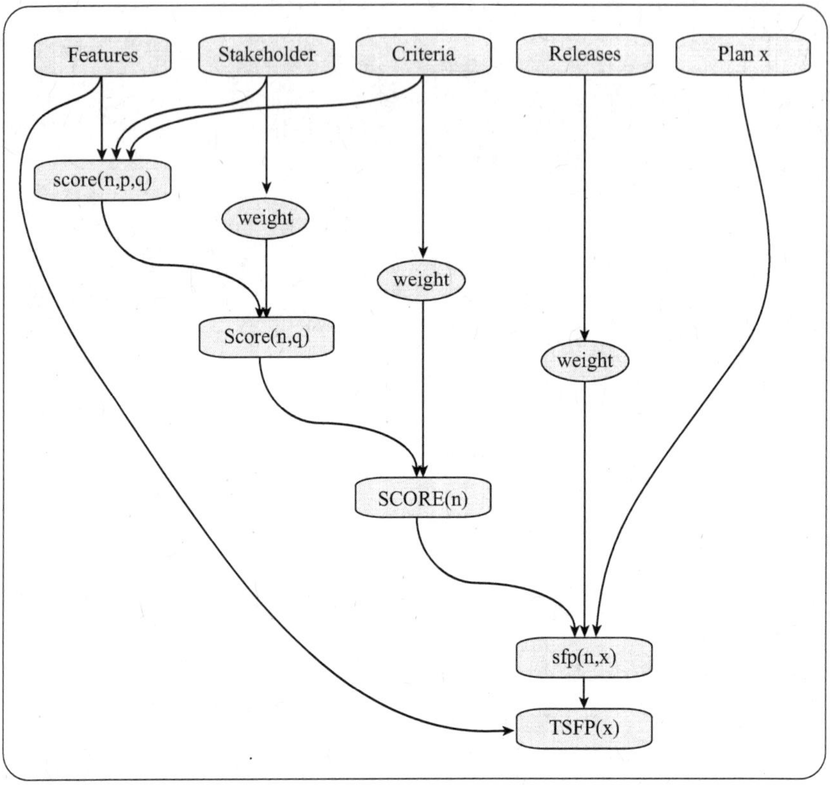

Figure 5.4 Calculation of total number of stakeholder feature points

The rationale for this function is that it reflects the objective of providing features of high stakeholder priority as early as possible. This is true the more important the stakeholder is considered. The underlying assumption is that stakeholder feature points are additive among the features, among the stakeholders and among the different criteria. The advantage of maximizing the total number of stakeholder feature points is that it is a compensational model, which allows linear combination of different criteria.

5.9.4 Non-linear objective functions

The assumption of additivity underlying the computation of TSFP(x) might not be applicable all the time, and other (non-linear) models can be considered as well. The actual composition of the planning function depends on the specific characteristics of the problem. Linear functions are easier to handle than non-linear ones.

However, in some cases it might be more appropriate to deviate from the linearity assumption. Some examples are given in (5.17) and (5.18). In these formulations, *utility(n,k)* denotes the overall utility obtained when feature f(n) is assigned to release option k. In (5.17), the results of scoring related to two criteria are multiplied. In (5.18), the minimum of the scoring results for three criteria is used for definition of overall utility of feature f(n) in release k.

(5.17) utility(n,k) = value(n,k) · urgency(n,k)

(5.18) utility(n,k) = Min {value(n,k), urgency(n,k), risk(n,k)}

In both cases, the different values are as weighted averages taken over all valid stakeholder priorities. While applied on a nine-point scale defined here, the *Min* operator and the product of values are applicable to other criteria as well.

5.9.5 Financial value maximization

The formulations (5.17) and (5.18), are still based on the compensatory model using stakeholder scores. Instead of relying on scoring of importance provided by the set of stakeholders, using one or the other form expressing the financial value of features is another alternative to formulate the objective of planning. In the spirit of value-based software engineering [Boehm and Huang '03], it is acknowledged that product development is a (financial) value creation process. What is needed for financially driven product release planning are appropriate measures to express the financial value.

The measure describing the financial value of a feature needs to be defined in dependence of time (which is the actual release date) and some assumed time horizon (which is the final release date). Consideration of time-dependent value functions in conjunction with flexible within some interval) release dates is further studied in [McElroy and Ruhe '10]. Another important consideration is that financial value is cumulative over time. Consequently, the earlier a feature is offered, the more time is available to create financial value out of this feature.

There are different financial measures that can be considered for this purpose. Two frequently used measures are:

- *Return on investment* (ROI): For each point in time, the ROI expresses the ratio between the total profit made versus the total investment done for the period of time in consideration.
- *Net present value* (NPV) gives the sum of the present values of features.

NPV assumes a given interest rate and a sequence of estimated cash flows starting from the defined release date. In this case, a feature is primarily judged based on its projected net present value assuming it will be offered at some release. This type of objective looks more accurate than stakeholder scores on a nine-point scale. However, value estimates are hard to get and uncertain in their nature.

5.10 GENERATION OF QUALIFIED ALTERNATIVE SOLUTIONS

The traditional perspective of planning is to search for just one solution, which is qualified in some specific aspect. The quality of each solution is measured by a stated utility function. In our case, this means maximizing the total number of stakeholder points. A solution is called *the best* when there is no other solution performing better. There is a good chance that more than one best solution exists. Moreover, solutions close to the best possible ones might be of strong interest as well. The concept of *K-best solutions* and the *diversification principle* both aim at further analysis of solutions close to the best ones.

5.10.1 The diversification principle

The idea of looking for *K-best solutions* instead of just one was initially applied in [Murty '68] for generating solutions of the assignment problem. A solution set of cardinality K > 1 is generated with the property that there is no feasible solution outside this set with a better objective function value than any of the K-best solutions. Computation of K-best solutions has been done (among others) for the assignment problem [Lawler '72], the perfect matching problem [Chegireddy and Hamacher '85], and the traveling salesman problem [Van Der Poort et al. '99].

The *principle of diversification* goes beyond the calculation of the K-best solutions. It considers *diversification between the solutions offered* to be an essential asset. In certain situations, when the K-best solutions chosen are very similar, the advantage provided by the set of solutions is reduced. By observing that a more diversified set of solutions provides a richer understanding and a deeper insight of the problem, the *principle of diversification* is proposed.

Informally, a qualified alternative solution subsumes two different aspects of problem solving:

i. Qualified in the sense of *solving* the *right problem*. The proposed (qualified) release plan is assumed to be meaningful for the original (real-world) problem. This can be judged by a human expert having the capability to describe the problem and to evaluate a proposed solution.
ii. Qualified in the sense of *solving* the *problem right*. The proposed (qualified) release plan is assumed to be of a guaranteed level of quality for the formalized problem. This can be achieved primarily by utilizing the strength and efficiency of computational algorithms.

Our key assumption for introducing diversification among a set of alternative solutions is as follows:

> **Principle of diversification:** A single solution of the cognitive complex problem is less likely to reflect the real-world problem solving needs when compared to a portfolio of qualified solutions that are structurally diversified. This is not changed by the formal optimality of the single solution.

What this principle suggests is to work with an approximate model and compensate the (incomplete) model by considering a structurally diversified set of (qualified) solution alternatives that are proven to be close to the optimal solution. The role of this set of solutions is not limited to just providing a short list of candidate solutions. It can also provide more insight into the problem. Through the observation and comparison of different qualified solutions, one can gain important information about the inherent structure of the problem. For the example of release planning, if a feature is consistently assigned to the same release among all the candidate plans, this is a strong argument that this assignment is strongly suggested and that this assignment is quite robust.

5.10.2 Qualified solution alternatives

In what follows, some necessary definitions are provided in order to formulate the diversification principle more precisely. The maximization of the TSFP is considered again as the objective of planning.

(5.19) $\max \{TSFP(x): x \in X\}$

In (5.19), X denotes a set of feasible release plans. A plan is called *feasible* if it fulfills all the explicitly stated constraints. The intension is to reduce the (typically large) size of the set of X based on a predefined target quality level $\alpha \in (0,1]$. With the maximum objective function value $TSFP^* = \max \{TSFP(x): x \in X\}$, α-qualified solutions are defined as follows:

Definition (α-qualified solution)**:** A solution x is called α-*qualified* if

(5.20) $TSFP(x) \geq \alpha\, TSFP^*$ and $x \in X$ □

A given set of α-qualified (release plan) solutions is abbreviated by X_α. Once α is given, all solutions in X_α are considered to be as *sufficiently good*, and differences between solutions in X_α are considered to be insignificant. The justification for that consideration is the uncertainty of the available data as well as the uncertainty of the whole problem formulation. Often, the value of α is defined by $\alpha = 0.95$ or $\alpha = 0.9$.

5.10.3 Diversified solution alternatives

In order to increase the likelihood to solve the right problem, it is expect to provide a set of alternative solutions that is not only α-qualified, but also structurally diversified. For the purpose of characterization of the degree of diversification of the selected set of solutions, the notion of *(structural) diversity* is introduced. The classical way to model the diversity (or similarity, if interpretation is changed) between two solutions x1, x2 is to define a distance measure on the solution space. The distance measure is assumed to fulfill the properties of being reflexive (the solution to itself), symmetric (between two solutions) and transitive (between three solutions) [Arkhangelskii and Pontryagin '90].

One well-known distance measure is called *Euclidean distance*. Another example measure is the *Hamming distance* between two strings of equal length, defined as the number of positions for which the corresponding symbols are different [Hamming '50]. Once the distance between two solutions of a set is defined, the diversification of a set X of solutions can be computed as the sum of all the distances between all pairs of solutions in X.

Because an absolute measure is hard to evaluate independently of the context, a relative diversification measure is introduced instead. This normalized measure relates the actual distance to the maximum distance possible. From this relative measure it is easier to judge the degree of diversification being independent of the concrete context. See [Ngo-The and Ruhe '08] for further details.

5.11 HOW ALL THE MODELING COMPONENTS COME TOGETHER

In Sections 5.2 to 5.8, different options for technological, resource, cost and risk constraints have been described. For each individual problem, the actual set of constraints needs to be defined specifically. Sections 5.9 and 5.10 have offered different options for formulating the objective of planning. The differences are in the form of the planning function as well as in the final goal of the planning procedure (one single solution versus a solution set). At the end of this chapter, three formulations (called *schemata*) of the release planning problem are given. These formulations combine the definition of constraints provided in Sections 5.2 to 5.8 with the definition of the objective of planning given in Sections 5.9 and 5.10.

Release Planning Scheme RPP1

RPP1 looks for one final planning alternative. Given a set of feasible release plans X and a utility function Utility(x) defined on X. Among a set X_α of qualified and diversified planning alternatives, determine one final plan. The selection of this plan is done by human experts and is possibly based upon the potential match of the plan with some additional implicit concerns.

Release Planning Scheme RPP2

RPP2 looks for a set of qualified planning alternatives. Given a set X of feasible release plans and a utility function Utility(x) defined on X. Among all feasible planning alternatives, the problem is to determine a set of (five) qualified and diversified planning alternatives.

Release Planning Scheme RPP3

RRP3 looks for a set of trade-off solution alternatives. Given a set X of feasible release plans and two planning criteria formulated by functions G1(x) and G2(x) defined on X. Functions G1(x) and G2(x) are assumed to be maximized.

Looking for trade-off solutions means determining all plans x with the property that there is no other plan x' fulfilling (5.21). What that means is that a plan x is a trade-off solution if there is no other plan that is better in one criterion and not worse in the other. Typically, there are several alternatives forming the set of trade-off solutions.

(5.21) $(G1(x'), G2(x')) \geq (G1(x), G2(x))$ and
$(G1(x'), G2(x')) \neq (G1(x), G2(x))$

For example, in [Saliu and Ruhe '07], the trade-off between *total feature value* and *ease of implementation* of features was studied (see also Section 9.4). Among all feasible planning alternatives, the problem is to determine a set of trade-off solutions.

Solution method EVOLVE II looks at RPP1. For that purpose, RPP2 is used as an intermediate step. Formulation RPP3 is applied in Section 14.3 for the purpose of balancing between functional and non-functional requirements. One solution method for generating the trade-off curve is to introduce one of the two objectives as an additional constraint for solving the remaining one-criterion problem. From parametric variation of the constraint level, trade-off points can be obtained from application of the one-criterion solution method. For details on solution methods for multi-criteria optimization, see [Steuer '86].

CHAPTER 6

EVOLVE II: A SYSTEMATIC METHOD FOR PLANNING PRODUCT RELEASES

6.1 INTRODUCTION

Product release planning is hard to do: It is hard to formulate, and once formulated, hard to solve. Many aspects influence the judgment of what constitutes a "good" release plan. Some of these aspects can be well defined, others are difficult to describe. The overall size of the decision problem becomes visible for a small problem with 20 features and looking three releases ahead of time. In this case, more than 10^{12} release plan possibilities exist. Intuition alone is insufficient to handle this type of complexity. Instead, a systematic method is needed combining computational strength with the creativity of the human experts to design release plans most likely to solve the actual problem.

In this chapter, a systematic decision support method for product release planning is described. Chapter 4 has made clear that neither intuition nor pure formalized methods in isolation are likely to be successful to provide meaningful results. In this chapter, a method designed to combine the strengths of both worlds is presented. The method is called EVOLVE II. The method integrates a number of new concepts and their innovative implementation, added to the initial publication of EVOLVE in [Greer and Ruhe '04]. EVOLVE II relies on the paradigm of hybrid intelligence [Ruhe and Ngo-The '04] and follows the broadly applicable idea of *evolutionary problem solving* outlined in Chapter 2. The interaction between formalized problem solving based on the application of specialized optimization algorithms and the capabilities of human experts is organized along the three phases called *Modeling*, *Exploration*, and *Consolidation* and is described in Section 6.2. This description is intended to be the underlying principle of problem solving. However, the description does not give sufficient instruction for its operational implementation.

The operational description of the whole planning process is made by a process model given in Section 6.3. Each of the 13 process steps is described by a template including the involved roles, a brief description of its main content, the input and output of the process step as well as the entry and exit criteria. The whole method is implemented by the decision support system ReleasePlanner™, which is described in more detail in Chapter 10. A comparison is made in Section 6.4 between EVOLVE II and some of the existing planning methods described in Chapter 4. Finally, practical experience from the application of the EVOLVE method is given in Section 6.5. A case study is presented as Chapter 11 to illustrate the different steps of EVOLVE II.

6.2 EVOLUTIONARY PROBLEM SOLVING FOR PRODUCT RELEASE PLANNING

6.2.1 Overview

Our formulation of the evolutionary problem-solving process contains three phases called *Modeling*, *Exploration*, and *Consolidation*. The process is supposed to be aligned with the organizational strategies and objectives such as the increase of competitiveness of products or the stronger penetration of a specific market. The planning criteria studied in Section 5.9 are considered a refinement of these global objectives. What comes out of the iterative process is a product release plan suggested for implementation.

Evolutionary problem solving refers to an effort that focuses on the process to formulate and solve the *right problem*. This capability is closely linked to a proper understanding and formulation of the problem. As this is never possible in a perfect way, we need a mechanism to evaluate the current progress in this process. Evolutionary problem solving simultaneously involves learning about the problem, its structure, the key parameters, and how things relate to each other.

6.2.2 Modeling

Modeling as part of product release planning refers to all the effort involved in the definition of the right granularity and the most appropriate constraints for describing the problem as studied in Chapter 5. Models are formulated at the level of detail and accuracy that corresponds to the understanding of the real world. This also means that certain aspects need to be intentionally left out from the model to keep it tractable.

In the process of modeling, there are problem aspects which are almost impossible to be formulated explicitly. These aspects are also called *implicit concerns*. EVOLVE II is designed to allow consideration of both explicit constraints (as formulated in Chapter 5) and implicit concerns. While explicit constraints can be handled formally, implicit concerns need the involvement of the human experts to be properly addressed. As an example of an implicit concern, the cohesiveness of the set of features offered for a specific release was introduced in Chapter 4. While is it extremely hard to model and evaluate the cohesiveness of 2^n possible combinations of n given features for one release, human experts might be able to evaluate the degree of cohesiveness of a given set of features of a specific release or to select the one being most cohesive among a given number of alternative plans.

For product release planning, *Modeling* includes the definition of a list of candidate features as well as the description of their dependencies and constraints. Modeling also includes the description of what is, or contributes to, the "goodness" of a solution and which resource or budget constraints need to be fulfilled. Other data, such as stakeholder evaluation of features, are considered part of modeling as well. It is important to also consider features from the perspective of their resource consumption. In reality, the resources necessary to implement all features within a given time frame are seldom completely available.

6.2.3 Exploration

A formalized description of the problem as obtained from Phase 1 allows the application of rigorous methods and techniques. The main goal of *Exploration* is to explore the solution space in order to obtain deeper insight into the problem and its solution structure.

At all iterations of the exploration phase, a set of the most promising alternative solutions is determined. These alternative solutions are intended to be (i) highly qualified for solving the stated problem, and (ii) diversified in relation to each other. As explained in more detail in Section 5.10, diversification among a set of qualified solutions is a mechanism for approaching the inherent uncertainty in understanding the problem and for addressing implicit concerns.

For a relatively simple problem comprising 20 features and looking at three release periods, the number of alternatives is already in the order of 10^{12}. This means that it is impossible to explore the solution space just "intuitively", without qualified computer support in place. This process, including the subsequent reduction of the space of solution alternatives, is illustrated in Figure 6.1. From the original set of 10^{12} solutions, a set of about 100 solutions is created from the associated optimization algorithms (implemented in ReleasePlanner™). All of these 100 solutions are considered *qualified* in terms of the stated objective (i.e., maximize the total number of stakeholder feature points). The diversification principle now suggests offering a subset of plans being as different as possible among each other. Analysis of the five qualified and diversified plans gives a higher chance to find one that also addresses implicit concerns. This is another formulation of saying that the plan solves *the right problem*. The number of *five* diversified plans (as described in Figure 6.1) is implementation-specific.

For performing the phase of *Exploration*, a wide range of methods and techniques exists that have proved themselves useful in very different contexts. The different optimization techniques including exact as well as heuristic approaches fit into this category. Meta-heuristics such as the ones based on genetic algorithms or simulated annealing are receiving more and more attention because of their broad application success. For complex problems, these techniques have proven to provide sufficiently good solutions in reasonable time [Harman '07]. But *Exploration* is not limited to these techniques. If appropriate, reasoning, machine learning or simulation is applicable whenever it contributes to problem solving.

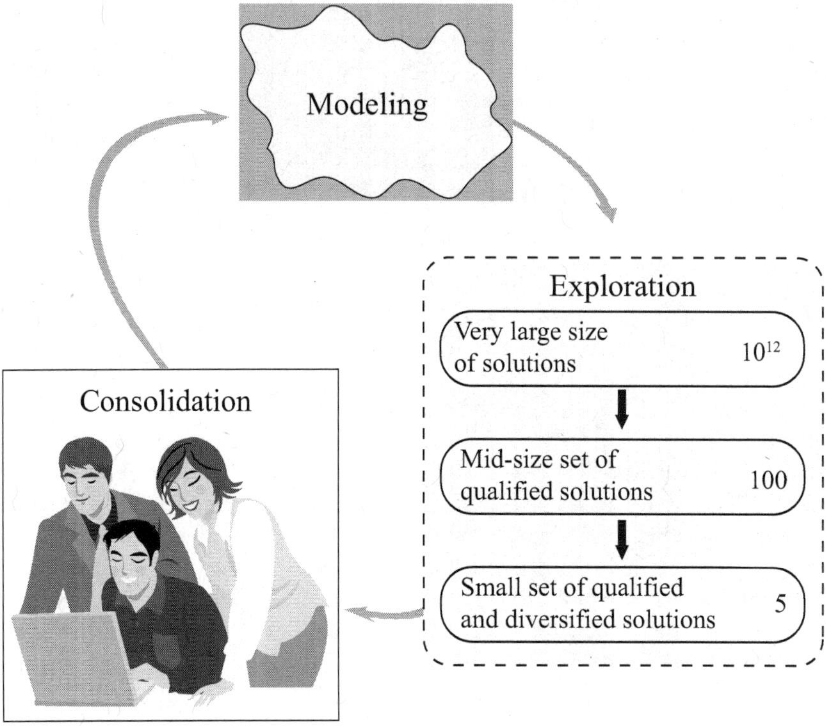

Figure 6.1 Reduction of the size of the solution space within exploration phase

6.2.4 Consolidation

In the case that proposed alternative solutions are accepted by the human expert to address *the right problem*, which one from the set of candidate solutions should finally be taken? While the emphasis of the *Consolidation* phase is on human expert involvement, there are a number of techniques and considerations that might be useful in this context.

Consolidation is relying on the knowledge and experience of the human experts. This involvement is aimed at addressing implicit concerns, which are hard or impossible to handle in a completely formalized manner. *Consolidation* refers to the process of evaluating the qualified solution alternatives, selecting the best solution or making suggestions for refinement of the underlying model.

For prioritization among plan alternative, the AHP is applicable (see Section 3.6).

Another possible method refers to ELECTRE [Figuera et al. '05]. ELECTRE is one of a family of individual methods for multi-criteria decision support. ELECTRE methods in general comprise two main procedures: (i) construction of one or several outranking relations followed by (ii) an exploitation procedure. Each individual order relation (derived from a criterion) is assigned a weight representing the relative importance of the criterion in the overall comparison. The method then aggregates these relations using their weights to achieve a final outranking relation from which one alternative can be identified as not outranked by any other one.

Facing a small set of qualified solutions, the product manager and the associated stakeholders can get further insight into the problem structure and dependencies and move to the next iteration with a refined (better) model. This is illustrated in Figure 6.1 by the link back to *Modeling*. Refinements can be related to any of the parameters, constraints and formulated objectives, in an attempt to qualify the model and to better match reality. Stakeholders can finally be asked to prioritize among the proposed (qualified) alternative solutions.

6.3 EVOLVE II: DESCRIPTION OF THE PROCESS

6.3.1 Overview

This section provides an operational description of the underlying process of the EVOLVE II method. The process is subdivided into 13 steps. Besides the product manager, stakeholders are involved in different ways at the different steps. An overview of all the steps and their dependencies is given in Figure 6.2. Some of steps are optional in the sense that their execution is not mandatory for achieving the final plan decision in Step 13. While the individual steps are largely arranged in sequential order, there are feedback links between some of them. For example, as a result of the quality and resource analysis (Step 9), it might be necessary to return to Step 7 to reformulate technology (including resource) constraints. More general, from any of the steps 9 to 12, there is the possibility to return to one of the steps 2 to 7.

In what follows, all the steps of EVOLVE II are described by applying the same template to all of them. The entries of the template are:

- **Description:** What is supposed to be done at this step?
- **Roles involved:** Which roles are involved in this process step?
- **Input:** Which artifacts are used as input for this process step?
- **Output:** Which artifacts are generated from this process step?
- **Entry criteria:** Which conditions must be satisfied for starting the step?
- **Exit criteria:** Which conditions must be satisfied to terminate the step?

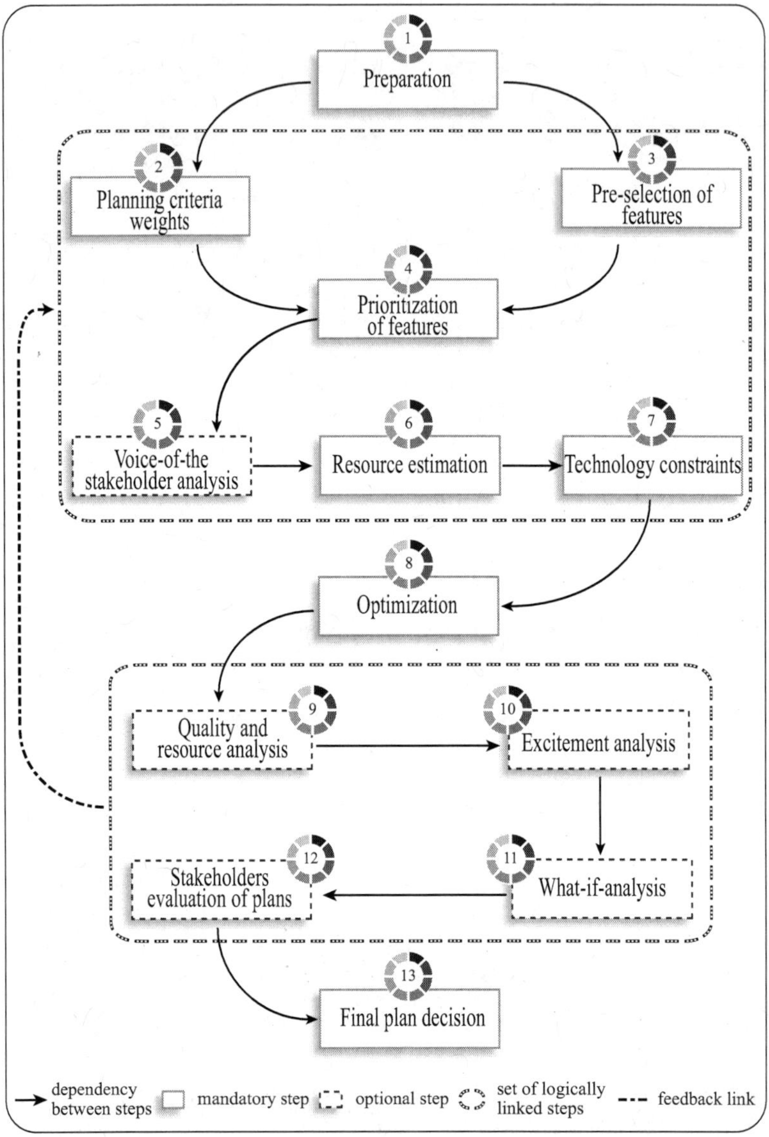

Figure 6.2 Dependency graph for process steps of EVOLVE II

6.3.2 Step 1: Preparation

The first step of the process is devoted to preparation. This step defines the actors and key parameters for the subsequent planning activities. Preparation includes the definition of planning criteria. The content of process Step 1 is shown in Table 6.1.

Table 6.1 Key information for EVOLVE II process Step 1

Description	Specification of key parameters of the planning problem based on corporate strategy and the specific project information available.
Roles involved	Product manager (decision-maker) and stakeholders.
Input	• Corporate strategy • Specific project information • Set of all candidate stakeholders
Output	• Planning criteria • Planning scope and number of releases • Selection of stakeholders involved and assignment of their roles • Specification of stakeholder weights (by product manager) • Specification of resource types relevant for planning • Resource capacities per release
Entry criteria	The project is understood well enough and is ready for planning (availability of information, people). The feature set is well defined and all the features are described to make them understandable to stakeholders.
Exit criteria	Planning criteria, planning horizon, set of stakeholders, their roles and degree of importance as well as resource types are defined.

6.3.3 Step 2: Specification of weights for planning criteria

The content of EVOLVE II process Step 2 is shown in Table 6.2. The definition of weights for the different criteria can be done by the product manager alone or as a result of a collective discussion. The latter can be achieved by prioritization performed by the selected critical stakeholders. The final weights can then be defined as the averages of this scoring, eventually followed by a subsequent discussion and negotiation of controversial issues. Alternatively AHP can be applied at this point.

Table 6.2 Key information for EVOLVE II process Step 2

Description	Prioritization of criteria and averaging of results to determine weights of relative importance.
Roles involved	Product manager and critical stakeholders assigned to this step.
Input	Planning criteria.
Output	Weights for planning criteria.

Table 6.2 (continued)

Entry criteria	Planning criteria and critical stakeholders are specified.
Exit criteria	Weights of the planning criteria are determined.

6.3.4 Step 3: Pre-selection of features

The content of EVOLVE II process Step 3 is shown in Table 6.3. In the case of a large set of candidate features (especially when including enhancements of existing features and bug fixes) it is worth performing a pre-selection of features [Heikkilä et al. '10]. This is to keep the workload for both prioritization and effort estimation focused on features that are candidates to be released. The pre-selection process is performed by a set of nominated stakeholders who are asked to provide their preference.

Table 6.3 Key information for EVOLVE II process Step 3

Description	Stakeholders with pre-selection role prioritize all features in order to select a reasonable set of candidate features for the more comprehensive, multi-criteria prioritization and subsequent planning. This step includes a validation of the understandability of the pre-selected features.
Roles involved	Stakeholders with an assigned role for pre-selection.
Input	Feature set from repository.
Output	Pre-selected features for planning.
Entry criteria	Feature set available and stakeholders nominated for pre-selection step.
Exit criteria	The set of pre-selected features is defined.

6.3.5 Step 4: Prioritization of features

Prioritization here means application of the Multi-score method described in Section 3.8. The content of process Step 4 is shown in Table 6.4. Stakeholders can be assigned to specific criteria only to reflect their specific role and background. Optionally, if features are subdivided into feature groups, the stakeholder assignment can be further differentiated by groups. That way, not all the stakeholders are supposed to prioritize all the features under consideration. This reduces their effort and allows them to focus on the features they have most competence about. In addition to the assignment to groups of features, the degree of importance of the respective scores (per criterion and per group) can be adjusted as well.

Table 6.4 Key information for EVOLVE II process Step 4

Description	Prioritization of features by stakeholders following the Multi-score method is performed for all defined criteria.
Roles involved	Product manager and all stakeholders nominated for prioritization.
Input	Project information (features, their description, stakeholders nominated for prioritization, their weights and their assignments to groups of features) is available.
Output	Priority profiles (weighted stakeholder scores per criterion and disagreement levels) for all features.
Entry criteria	Project is set-up for prioritization and stakeholder roles are defined.
Exit criteria	All stakeholders have performed prioritization of the features and criteria assigned to them.

6.3.6 Step 5: Voice-of-the-stakeholder analysis

Once all the stakeholders have provided their priority scores, analysis of the scoring can be done. This is called *voice-of-the-stakeholder analysis.* For creating optimized planning results, this is an optional process step which can or cannot be performed. It gives an overview of the ranking of features and the degree of agreement in stakeholder opinions. This has proven to be important information when individual features need to be discussed more specifically as part of the whole decision-making process. The content of Step 5 is shown in Table 6.5.

Table 6.5 Key information for EVOLVE II process Step 5

Description	Generation of priority and conformance profiles per feature and per criterion. For the detailed analysis options, see Section 3.9.
Roles involved	Product manager.
Input	Priority scores by each nominated stakeholder per feature and per criteria.
Output	Voice-of-the stakeholder report with ranking of priorities of features and level of conformance between stakeholder scores.
Entry criteria	Planning criteria and all stakeholder prioritization tasks are specified.
Exit criteria	Complete ranking results are available.

6.3.7 Step 6: Collective resource estimation

The critical task of providing reliable effort estimates is addressed in Step 6. For that purpose, collective knowledge and experience can be utilized by asking multiple experts for their opinion. For effort estimation, candidate stakeholders would be developers, domain experts or project managers. Instead of a single point-wise estimate, three-point estimation can be applied. This is defined as the optimistic, most likely, and pessimistic estimates. For feature f(n) and stakeholder stake(p), these estimates are denoted by *opt_effort(n,p)*, *likely_effort(n,p)*, and *pess_effort(n,p)*, respectively. Their integration into an overall effort estimate *effort(n,p)* per feature is done following the Program Evaluation and Review Technique (PERT) [Elmaghraby '77]:

$$(6.1) \quad \text{effort}(n,p) = [\text{opt\_effort}(n,p) + 4 \cdot \text{likely\_effort}(n,p) + \text{pess\_effort}(n,p)]/6$$

The integration of the individual stakeholder effort estimates into an overall effort estimate Effort(n) is done by calculation of the weighted average:

$$(6.2) \quad \text{Effort}(n) = \Sigma_{p=1\ldots P}\, \text{weight\_stake}(p) \cdot \text{effort}(n,p))/(\Sigma_{p=1\ldots P}\, \text{weight\_stake}(p))$$

The estimation explained for effort estimates in general is applied similarly for estimates related to specific resource types. From the integration of these multiple estimates, on average a more reliable estimate can be expected compared to estimation by just a single person. These deviations can be discussed and resolved from meetings as suggested by the Delphi-technique [Rowe and Wright '99]. The difference to the traditional techniques is that now the focus can be on the most controversial features with no obligation to look at all of them. The range of the estimation interval per single expert and the variation of intervals between experts are indicators about the (un-) certainty of the estimations. The content of Step 6 is shown in Table 6.6.

Table 6.6 Key information for EVOLVE II process Step 6

Description	Stakeholders with assigned resource-estimation role analyze the set of candidate features and available resource types. They estimate the amount of resources consumed by each feature. After that, estimates are integrated following (6.1) and (6.2).
Roles involved	Stakeholders nominated for resource estimation.
Input	Candidate features and specified resource types.
Output	(Three-point) Resource estimation per feature and their aggregation across stakeholders.
Entry criteria	All features and nominated stakeholders are available.
Exit criteria	Estimates for all features.

6.3.8 Step 7: Formulation of technology and resource constraints

The art of modeling is addressed in process Step 7. Its content is shown in Table 6.7. Modeling is done by the product manager (decision-maker) in consultation with domain experts. Pre-assignment of features in conjunction with resource and technological dependencies might create violation of feasibility. In that case, up-front analysis and resolution of the feasibility conflict needs to be done.

Table 6.7 Key information for EVOLVE II process Step 7

Description	The product manager formalizes the features' technological (dependencies, pre-assignments) as well as all other resource or risk-related constraints described in Chapter 5. A feasibility check for consistency of the constraints is done as well.
Roles involved	Product manager in consultation with domain experts.
Input	All informal planning information related to the (groups of) candidate features.
Output	Formalized planning model and feasibility check of all constraints.
Entry criteria	Results from Steps 1 to 4 and Step 6.
Exit criteria	Formal description and feasibility of the whole problem (i.e., possibility of fulfilling all constraints).

6.3.9 Step 8: Generation of qualified and diversified plan alternatives

Product release planning has been formulated in Chapter 5 as an optimization problem. On top of applying branch-and-bound and specialized integer programming procedures, a heuristic is implemented for determining upper bounds of the objective function value at each step of the branching process. See [Ngo-The and Ruhe '08] for a description of the algorithms. The content of Step 8 is shown in Table 6.8.

Table 6.8 Key information for EVOLVE II process Step 8

Description	Optimization algorithms are applied in order to obtain a portfolio of five qualified and diversified release plan alternatives.
Roles involved	Product manager.
Input	Formal problem description as a result of Steps 1, 4, 6, and 7.
Output	Optimized release plan alternatives. Each alternative plan describes for all features if they are planed for one of the future releases, and if yes, at which one.

Table 6.8 (continued)

Entry criteria	Feasibility of the formal problem description.
Exit criteria	Existence of a set of (five) diversified and optimized release plan alternatives.

6.3.10 Step 9: Quality and resource analysis of alternative plans

Step 9 is optional. It aims at the detection of differences and commonalities in resource consumption and quality between plans. Higher stability in the level of resource consumption implies higher stability in the amount of personnel needed. The quality of plans describes its (guaranteed) level of optimality for utilizing the resources in a best possible way to archive a maximum total number of stakeholder feature points. This information is a possible input for making the final release plan decision in Step 13. The content of Step 9 is shown in Table 6.9.

Table 6.9 Key information for EVOLVE II process Step 9

Description	Analysis of the optimized alternatives in terms of their quality and resource consumption.
Roles involved	Product manager.
Input	Optimized release plan alternatives.
Output	Quality evaluation (expressed by the total number of stakeholder feature points) and resource consumption report for all plans under consideration.
Entry criteria	Availability of optimized plan alternatives.
Exit criteria	Resource consumption profiles are generated and quality evaluation of plans is conducted.

6.3.11 Step 10: Stakeholder excitement analysis

In this optional process step, predictions are made on the individual excitement or disappointment reaction of stakeholders for a proposed plan. Related to a given plan, a stakeholder *excitement profile* is defined based upon the stakeholder's scoring. Excitement (or disappointment) can be defined for one specified planning criterion or as a cumulative measure over all criteria. This helps the human expert select between the set of diversified alternative solutions. The decision can be based upon different strategies such as *maximizing excitement* or *minimizing disappointment* for one or all stakeholders. The overall content of Step 10 is shown in Table 6.10.

Table 6.10 Key information for EVOLVE II process Step 10

Description	Projection of the expected reaction of the stakeholders, in terms of excitement (with the assignment of individual features), disappointments and surprises related to the assignment of all the individual features.
Roles involved	Product manager.
Input	Optimized release plans.
Output	Stakeholder excitement report.
Entry criteria	Availability of optimized plan alternatives.
Exit criteria	Excitement profiles are determined.

To describe the different possible reactions on proposed plans, seven different categories are introduced. Excitement (disappointment) of a stakeholder refers to the degree of conformance between the feature-related score of the stakeholder and the assignment of the feature to a release. Besides *excitement* and *disappointment*, there is another category called *surprise. (Very) Surprised* refers to the situation where a feature is scored (very) low, but is offered in an early (next) release. The formal notation of the excitement categories is shown in Table 6.11. This notation is then used in Tables 6.12 and 6.13 to define excitement responses to given plans.

Table 6.11 Stakeholder excitement categories and their abbreviations

Category	Meaning
VE	very excited
E	excited
N	neutral
D	disappointed
VD	very disappointed
S	surprised
VS	very surprised

The stakeholder excitement table assigns one of the seven values for each possible combination between stakeholder scores and release numbers proposed by the plan under consideration. In Table 6.12 and Table 6.13, projected excitement tables are defined for the case of two and three releases, respectively. These tables can be customized for a specific project or company context. In case of more than three releases, tables are specified accordingly.

For example, in the case of K = 2 releases (see Table 6.12), a stakeholder having scored *9* for some feature (and some criterion) will be very excited (*VE)* to see this feature in the next release (Release 1). However, the same stakeholder is likely to be very disappointed (*VD)* if this feature would be postponed, and at least disappointed (*D)* to see it in release 2. On the other hand, having scored *1* for a feature and finding it in release 1 would probably create a very surprised (*VS)* reaction, while postponing this feature is expected to result in a neutral (*N)* position.

Table 6.12 Excitement table for the case of planning for two releases

	Score								
Release	1	2	3	4	5	6	7	8	9
1	VS	VS	S	S	N	E	E	VE	VE
2	S	S	N	N	N	N	N	D	D
Postponed	N	N	N	N	N	D	D	VD	VD

Table 6.13 Excitement table for the case of planning for three releases

	Score								
Release	1	2	3	4	5	6	7	8	9
1	VS	VS	S	S	N	E	E	VE	VE
2	S	S	N	N	N	N	N	D	D
3	N	N	N	N	N	D	D	VD	VD
Postponed	N	N	N	N	D	D	VD	VD	VD

6.3.12 Step 11: What-if analysis

Proactive what-if analysis is one way to study the impact of possible scenarios of the future. This supports current decision-making because some of the projected results of the scenario runs can be taken into account. These future scenarios need a reference point (baseline) in terms of project data and a (set of) solutions generated based upon the data. Changes in the problem space can be related to a number of parameters:

- Modify planning criteria weights
- Modify stakeholder weights
- Modify resource capacities
- Modify release weights
- Add or remove feature dependencies
- Add or modify resource constraints
- Add or modify features and their resource consumption

The content of the optional Step 11 is shown in Table 6.14.

Table 6.14 Key information for EVOLVE II process Step 11

Description	The question answered by the what-if analysis is about what impact changes in the problem space will have on solutions from the changes in the solution space.
Roles involved	Product manager.
Input	Optimized release plans, scenarios for what-if analysis.
Output	What-if analysis report.
Entry criteria	A specific plan needs to be selected as a reference point to start the analysis.
Exit criteria	The impact of the parameter changes is described.

6.3.13 Step 12: Stakeholders' evaluation of alternative plans

The whole process of decision-making can be seen as a (intelligent) search in the solution space where the set of candidates is reduced more and more toward selection of the top ones. The information collected in Steps 9 through 11 was all intended to further differentiate between the five pre-selected qualified plans. In the optional Step 12, decision-critical stakeholders are explicitly asked to evaluate the proposed plans from their overall attractiveness point of view. With the same nine-point scale as applied before, the scores express the range from *Very low* to *Very high* attractiveness. For that purpose, the stakeholders can use or not use information gained from former steps. The content of Step 12 is shown in Table 6.15.

Table 6.15 Key information for EVOLVE II process Step 12

Description	Selected stakeholders are asked for their priorities related to the proposed plan alternatives.
Roles involved	Product manager and nominated stakeholders.
Input	Optimized release plans and baseline plan.
Output	Stakeholder's evaluation report of plan alternatives.
Entry criteria	Availability of optimized plan alternatives.
Exit criteria	Scoring of alternative plans.

6.3.14 Step 13: Final plan selection

Based upon all the information gained from Steps 9 through 12, the final decision needs to be made about which plan will be selected. This selected plan is the result of an evolutionary problem-solving process. Explicitly formulated constraints have been taken into account, eventually after some refinements. In addition, implicit concerns have been addressed as well. For the generation of the plan, stakeholders have played an essential role at the different stages of the process. This increases the likelihood of getting their acceptance for the implementation of the plan. The content of Step 13 is shown in Table 6.16.

Table 6.16 Key information for EVOLVE II process Step 13

Description	Final plan selection based on the previous evaluation and analysis reports.
Roles involved	Product manager.
Input	All plan alternatives (from Step 8) and their (optional) evaluation gained from Steps 9-12.
Output	Final selected plan.
Entry criteria	Availability of all alternatives and their evaluation from former steps.
Exit criteria	Final plan selected for implementation. Justification of the plan.

6.4 COMPARISON WITH OTHER METHODS

EVOLVE II is a highly flexible method that allows planning at different levels of granularity and with different modeling components involved. In Table 6.17, a comparison is made with two other planning approaches already discussed in Chapter 4. The one called *on-the-fly planning* is the planning approach applied under the assumption that the product manager can make decisions exclusively based upon intuition and some opportunistic form of communication. The second comparison is with the rigorous planning method presented by [van den Akker et al. '08]. It uses a standard optimization package but has no proven experience from its application in industry.

The comparison between methods is done using the same criteria as in Section 4.4. It can be concluded that the fact-based approaches have a lower risk of failing or providing plans missing essential opportunities. The modeling capabilities are covering most of the practical cases encountered so far. ReleasePlanner™ has already proven successful in industry. Its main strength compared to [van den Akker et al. '08] is its emphasis on holistic and web-based decision support with all the additional modeling, computational and analysis capabilities. Running different types of scenarios is supported, and the feature repository can be accessed all the time. Most importantly, EVOLVE II emphasizes the *process of planning* (not just the result) and provides support for interaction with stakeholders at the different stages.

Table 6.17 Comparison of EVOLVE II with other methods

	Method		
Characteristics	EVOLVE II	on-the-fly planning	[van den Akker et al. '08]
Time horizon	Flexible	Next release	Next release
Objectives	Flexible in the number and type of criteria	Vague and not explicitly described	Maximize financial value function
Stakeholder involvement	Strongly supported with explicitly assigned individualized tasks at the different stages	Opportunistic and by communication	Not directly supported
Solution method	Specialized integer programming with additional heuristics	Intuition and experience-based	Integer linear programming (ILP)
Quality of solutions	Five near-optimal alternative solutions with known level of optimality	Difficult to judge. The more risky, the more complex the problem	Near-optimal solutions based on ILOG
Feature dependencies	Precedence and coupling	Implicitly, hard to consider for more complex problems	Precedence, coupling, *either or* dependencies
Human resource constraints	Flexible in the number, type and granularity of the resources	Implicitly, hard to consider for more complex problems	Yes, including staffing of teams
What-if analysis (explicit support)	Yes	No	Yes
Integrated tool support	ReleasePlanner™ 2.0	No	Prototype based on usage of ILOG

6.5 APPLICABILITY

From all the 30+ industry and more than 250 research and student projects conducted so far, there are a number of factors which have been analyzed as critical for application success:

- There is an established culture in the organization that earlier investment into product planning is worthwhile and that the initial investment pays off later.
- The importance of (appropriate) product planning is well understood as a means to better satisfy customer needs and to increase competitiveness of products.
- There is (at least one) assigned role of a product manager in the company.
- There are existing stakeholders committed to participate in the planning process.
- Effort estimation needs to be an integral part of project management. Even though the estimates are not perfectly reliable, there should be some estimates in place to start with.
- Business objectives are mapped into objectives of (release) planning.
- The features under consideration can be evaluated (at least roughly) in terms of the stated objectives (for example, urgency and value).
- The higher the number of features to look at, the more attractive becomes the application of the systematic planning method. There is no need to apply EVOLVE II for small-scale projects with less than 10 features.

These criteria are necessary, but not sufficient, for planning success. Planning results can only be as good as the underlying process and the quality of the data put into the process. The main benefits the user can expect from performing product release planning in a more systematic way is to enable better product decisions. There is a higher chance to provide the most appropriate composition of features in a release. Arguably, this is one of the most important capabilities of a product development or service organization. It often increases the competitiveness of the product and subsequently the business performance and success of the organization.

Besides the higher decision quality, the efficiency of the process is expected to be improved. It becomes faster and much easier to understand the different stakeholder perspectives and to find the best possible compromise between them. Physical meetings can be focused on the most controversial issue, while there is no longer the need to waste time for things that are already quite clear. Estimation of the stakeholder excitement gives some indication toward which stakeholder might require special attention.

Optimized planning alternatives are an important input for human decision-making, but they are not assumed to be the ultimate truth. However, from running different planning scenarios, the product manager receives better insight into the key structure and dependencies of the possible problem solution. This insight is assumed to be input for making the final human decision. From having involved selected stakeholders in the key stages of the processes, the probability of addressing the right problem has been increased. As the optimization results are formally the best possible, the chances are good that the solutions provided are very meaningful related to the original product planning problem.

Besides a higher probability of making better decisions, another expected value is the increased efficiency of the whole decision-making process. Substantial time savings are possible. Finally, increased efficiency and effectiveness of decision-making is likely to result in higher attractiveness (toward customers) and higher competitiveness (toward competitors) of the products.

Planning goes hand in hand with re-planning. Once a plan is created, the changes in data, policies, capacities and competition enforce ongoing re-planning of the plan being in place. This is the content of Chapter 7.

CHAPTER 7

RE-PLANNING OF PRODUCT RELEASES

7.1 INTRODUCTION

Nothing in software development is as stable as change. Once release plans are created, business and stakeholder priorities might change afterward. Budgets are seldom stable, neither is the availability of human resources. Even features are evolving, and new features arrive. The once established plan is no longer valid and needs to be adjusted to the new circumstances. Planning requires permanent adjustment to change. The process to achieve this is called re-planning.

Changing features or requirements is considered one of the major causes for software product failure. A survey over 8000 projects undertaken by 350 US companies revealed that one third of the projects were never completed and one half succeeded only partially. The third major source of failure (11%) was changing requirements [van Lamsweerde '00].

In market-driven software development, features or requirements tend to change frequently due to many possible factors [Kotonya and Sommerville '98]:

- Requirements errors, conflicts and inconsistency
- Evolving customer/end-user knowledge of the system
- Technical, schedule or cost problems
- Changing customer priorities
- Environmental changes
- Organizational changes

Re-planning as considered in this chapter looks at the process to adjust to change. More precisely, re-planning is considered the process of modification of an existing (release) plan to accommodate new arrived features or for revised effort, value and priority estimates of already existing features. The relationship between planning and re-planning is illustrated in Figure 7.1. The status at the beginning of (strategic) planning for the next three releases of a product is illustrated in Figure 7.1(a). Features taken from a change repository are assigned to future releases of an evolving product.

Not necessarily all features from the repository need to be assigned. Instead, some features are postponed for future considerations. Figure 7.1(b) shows the assignment of features to releases as it may result from applying the (strategic) release planning method EVOLVE II. Figure 7.1(c) illustrates the occurrence of changes, either being the arrival of new features or changes in the parameter values of the existing features.

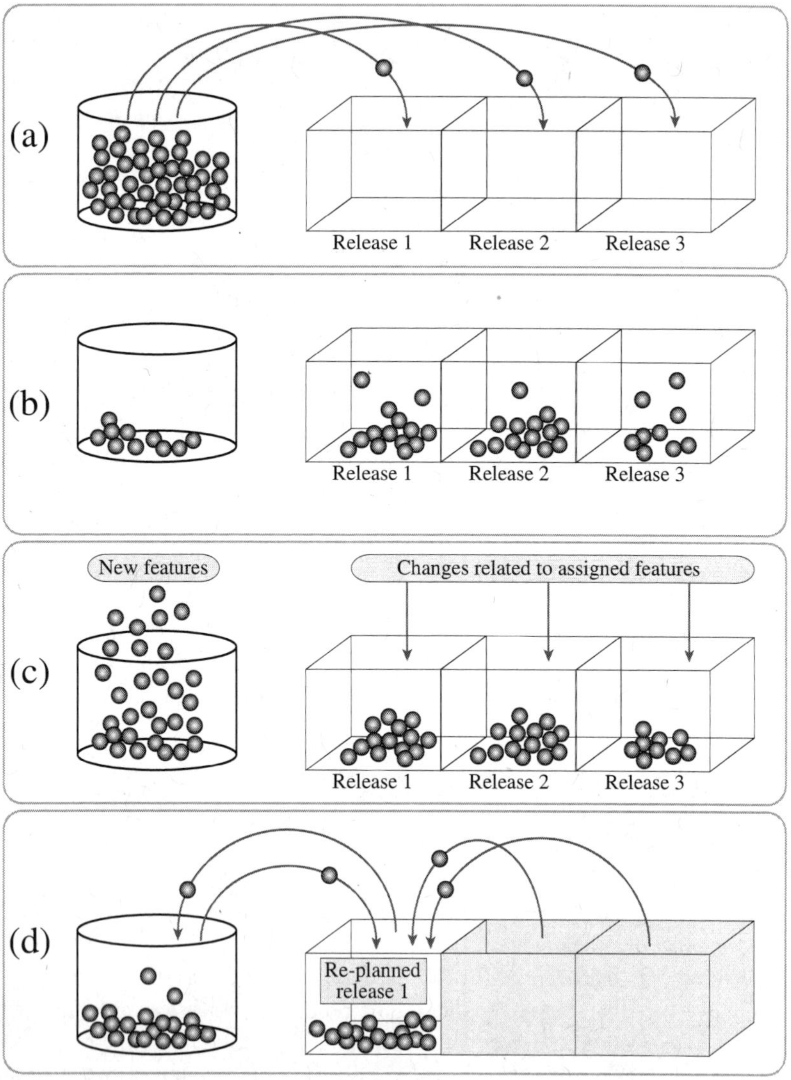

Figure 7.1 The stages of planning and re-planning

Both types of changes might be an input for the re-planning procedure illustrated in Figure 7.1(d). Re-planning just considers the next release. As the result of re-planning, new features can be assigned to the upcoming release. In correspondence to that, already assigned features might be postponed to another release.

This chapter presents a rigorous, optimization-based method for re-planning. This method is based upon the formal problem description introduced in Section 7.2. The actual re-planning method called H2W* is studied in Section 7.3. Its process steps are described in Section 7.4. The method is illustrated in Section 7.5 by a case study.

7.2 PROBLEM FORMULATION

The re-planning problem is based on different types of information related to the existing plan, the change requests, and the resource capacities and time interval of the release under investigation.

7.2.1 Existing plan

At the beginning of the re-planning process, a given (strategic) plan for assigning features to releases is considered. This given plan denoted by x describes the intended strategy for implementing the N-features. It is formally characterized by a vector x = (x(1),…,x(N)) with

(7.1) x(n) = k if feature f(n) is offered at release k (n = 1…N)

(7.2) x(n) = 0 if feature f(n) is postponed, that is, it is not offered in one of the next K product releases (n = 1…N)

The plan x can be determined by the method EVOLVE II described in Chapter 6 or (in the case of just looking at the next release) by any of the other methods mentioned in Chapter 4. In addition to the set of features F1 planned for the upcoming release, the schedule of their implementation is also needed for re-planning. The problem of scheduling and staffing for features is studied in Chapter 8. At this point, it is assumed that for a given plan x, for each feature f(n) with x(n) = 1, the start time start(n) and end time end(n) of the feature implementation are given.

7.2.2 Time period considered for re-planning

Re-planning is considered just for the next release period. While the strategic plan looks into the next K releases, the idea of accommodating most recent changes primarily makes sense for the features set selected for the upcoming release period. The assumption is that after this upcoming release has been finished, a complete new planning step needs to be performed. The implementation process of the next release starts at time t = T1. The planned release time is t = T2. The re-planning process is considered for a given time interval [T1,T2].

7.2.3 Feature sets for re-planning

It is assumed that N(t) new features have arrived since t = T1. For an existing plan x, three kinds of features sets are considered:

(7.3) F1 = {f(n): x(n) = 1 with n = 1…N} being the set of features from the original set F assigned for implementation during the upcoming release.

(7.4) F2 = {f(n): x(n) $\neq$ 1 with n = 1…N} being the set of features from the original set F not assigned for implementation in the upcoming release.

(7.5) F3(t*) = {f(n): n = N+1 … N(t*)} being the set of features having arrived until point in time t* (T1 < t* < T2).

Feature set F3(t*) varies over time, as new features (also called *change requests*) might arrive at any point in time t* within the interval [T1,T2]. To keep things conceptually easy, the initial assumption is that attribute values related to features from sets F1 and F2 have not changed at point in time t*. That means, all the values related to the feature attributes (such as effort, value and risk) remain the same for all these features as defined at t = T1. At a later stage, re-planning is considered also for the case that changes in the values have occurred.

7.2.4 Decisions to be made

With the re-planning set-up described above, three key decisions need to be made:

- *When to re-plan?* At which point in time has there been accumulated "enough reason" to consider the possibility of changing the existing set of features assigned for implementation in the next release?
- *What to re-plan?* Which features are candidates to be altered from *assigned for implementation* to *not assigned for implementation* and *vice versa*? Which criteria and which arguments are used for this decision?
- *How to re-plan?* This question refers to the procedure that helps determine re-assignment of features. To make it a rigorous process, criteria and constraints relevant for the exchange of features need to be defined. Resource capacities can be modified, and weights of criteria as well as priorities assigned by stakeholders can be changed to reflect the new project situation.

7.3 RE-PLANNING METHOD H2W*

7.3.1 Overview

The re-planning method H2W* is based on a former method called H2W [Jadallah et al. '09]. H2W is an iterative re-planning method designed to support the product manager and decision-maker. It considers the most recently created plan as a baseline for the next re-planning iteration. Re-planning may be applied repeatedly within any given interval [T1,T2]. At each re-planning iteration, the *When?*, *What?*, and *How?* questions related to the re-planning are answered. H2W* differs from H2W in its application of optimization techniques for the *How to re-plan?* question as well as in a more systematic approach to answer *When to re-plan?*

7.3.2 When to re-plan?

The decision about *when* to re-plan is critical for the overall re-planning success, which is to improve an existing plan by accommodating more attractive features having arrived after the existing plan was announced. There are two elements related to this question. The first one relates to the number and attractiveness of the newly arrived features. The second one relates to the openness of the product manager to change of an already announced plan.

Different measures could be considered to decide at which point in time there is enough reason for re-planning. One is the number of new features that have arrived. Another one is the attractiveness of the features themselves, compared to the feature being implemented according to the original plan. The results of several studies indicated that if the changes take place closer to the release date, then this has an increased impact on the density and severity of the defects (see, e.g., [Javed et al. '04]).

Openness to change is described by a function h(t) in dependence of time t in planning interval [T1, T2]. It is conceptually defined as the level of acceptance for adding new features in comparison to the amount of existing ones. Right at the beginning of the release period, changes are easier to accommodate than toward the end. The assumption is that h(t) is decreasing over time described by a linear function with negative slope. The actual function can be customized in dependence of the concrete context.

For normalization purposes (and without loss of generality), T1 is assumed to be zero (T1 = 0). T2 is then simply denoted by T. *Openness to change* h(T) is defined to be zero at the end of the interval. Parameter a with $0 < \alpha \leq 1$ allows to adjust the initial level of *openness to change*. Overall, h(t) is approximated by linear function described in (7.6).

$$(7.6) \qquad h(t) = (-\alpha/T) \cdot t + \alpha$$

The interpretation of h(t) is that, at any point in time, the value h(t) gives the percentage of features from F1, which are acceptable for replacement by new and better ones arriving after t = 0. This is illustrated in Figure 7.2 for the example of T = 40 and $\alpha = 0.25$. According to that, one fourth of the features could partially be replaced by new ones (if available) at the beginning. However, this percentage decreases as shown in Figure 7.2. For example, after 20 days, only 12.5% of the original feature set is on disposition to be replaced by more attractive features.

There are different strategies for how to decide about *When to re-plan?* One option for that is to look at the percentage of new features related to the number of all features under disposition. Another option would be to apply the same idea for value (instead of the number) of features. In either case, this function is denoted by g(t). The function g(t) needs to be compared to openness to change h(t).

Criterion for re-planning: For a given plan x with feature set F1, re-planning is considered promising at t = t*, where t* is the earliest point in time when

(7.7) $g(t^*) = \text{card}(F3(t^*))/[\text{card}(F3(t^*)) + \text{card}(F1)] \geq h(t^*)$

In (7.7), card(F) denotes the number of elements belonging to set F. Then the interpretation of this (heuristic) criterion (7.7) is that there is enough evidence for re-planning whenever (for the first time) the portion g(t) of new features (compared to all features in consideration for the ongoing release) exceeds the openness to change threshold h(t) at this point in time. The criterion serves as a guideline, and can be overwritten at any point in time by the product manager who is allowed to initiate re-planning independently of the fulfillment of (7.7). The application of the above criterion is illustrated in Section 7.5 by a case study.

For the illustrative example given in Figure 7.2, all the steps in function g(t) are indicating the arrival of new features at this point in time. At about t* = 19, there is assumed to be "enough reason" to look at re-planning while there still is enough openness to potentially accept this amount of change.

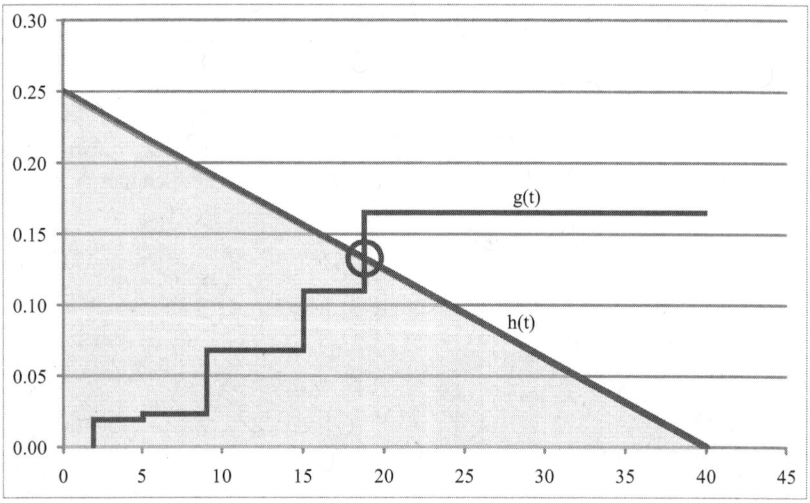

Figure 7.2 Openness to change function h(t) with a = 0.25 and T = 40.

What to re-plan?

If there is an indication that re-planning might be attractive at t = t*, further investigation needs to be done to decide which features should be considered in the process of re-planning. One (initial) assumption in the re-planning process is that the resource capacities and the release dates remain unchanged. Then, two questions have to be answered:

i. Which features should potentially be taken out of the current release?
ii. Which features should be taken into account for replacing less attractive ones?

For the first of the above questions, all features not yet started or not yet finally implemented during the ongoing release are candidates to be taken out. This information is obtained from operational planning designed as the procedure to decide which tasks of the features should be implemented at which time interval (and by whom).

For the second question, all new features F3(t*) are candidates, in conjunction with the ones formerly rejected. Although not very likely, it might happen that the replacement of a feature from F1 by a new one from F3(t*) suggests inclusion of a formerly rejected feature from F2. This becomes especially true if some of the attribute values (effort, priority) of the features from F2 have slightly changed over time.

7.3.3 How to re-plan?

Making a decision about replacing features from an ongoing release implementation is a complex process. It is hard to be performed just based on intuition. For the same reasons as provided in Chapter 6 describing the strategic planning, optimized re-planning should be applied instead of solely relying on intuition. It will be shown that re-planning can be done by applying EVOLVE II. In order to be able to do so, EVOLVE II needs to be instrumented to reflect the special nature of the (re-planning) problem:

i. Planning is only done for the next release (K = 1).
ii. The feature set for planning is constituted by the union set of F1, F2 and F3(t*).
iii. Resource estimates are needed for all new features in F3(t*).
iv. Stakeholder scoring needs to be done for all features in F3(t*), applying the same criteria as defined in the original planning process.
v. For all features from F1 or F2, stakeholder scoring or resource estimates can be revised due to improved or revised information available.
vi. It is assumed that there are no dependencies or coupling constraints for any of the new features. If this is not the case, special considerations need to be made.
vii. Pre-assignment of all features in F1 that have already been implemented or for which the implementation has sufficiently progressed.
viii. Adjustment to change (if applicable): Modified attribute values for features in F2 and modified resource capacities assumed for re-planning.

As a result of the optimization process from EVOLVE II, a new set F1* is created, which may have some features replaced by new ones as compared to the original set F1. The application of this process is illustrated in Figure 7.1(d). New features from the repository or features formerly not planned for can be included and exchanged against features already assigned for the upcoming release.

This process is illustrated in Section 7.5. for the case study project. Different scenarios for re-planning are studied including one with changed resource capacities and one with modified feature priorities assigned by stakeholders.

7.4 H2W* PROCESS DESCRIPTION

Similar to the description of the planning process in EVOLVE II, an operational description of the proposed re-planning method is given. Each step of the process is explained in more detail including the roles involved and the input and output artifacts consumed and produced, respectively.

7.4.1 Step 1: Re-planning set-up

Re-planning relies on a change request repository with all the features and the related information maintained in it. The repository needs continuous maintenance. The re-planning set-up relates to the definition of the corresponding features sets. It also includes the nomination of stakeholders and the definition of the different tasks performed by them during re-planning. The key parameters of Step 1 are summarized in Table 7.1.

Table 7.1 Re-planning process Step 1

Description	Collection of change requests. Change requests may correspond to the arrival of new features and to modifications of existing features. Their analysis includes the verification of correctness, consistency and understandability. In addition, stakeholders are nominated for participation in the different steps of the re-planning process.
Roles involved	Product manager.
Input	(Original) Plan x and its related plan of implementation of features F1 with start and end dates for all features assigned for implementation during the upcoming release.
Output	Analyzed list of change requests. List of nominated stakeholders and their roles.

7.4.2 Step 2: When to re-plan?

During the implementation of already agreed upon features, the arrival of new features might motivate re-planning. The decision about when to re-plan can be made based on quantitative arguments given in (7.7). Independently of that, there is always the possibility of overwriting this criterion. This is the case, for example, when a business-critical customer is asking for a specific new or revised feature. In this case, re-planning is initiated independent of the fulfillment of criterion (7.7). The key parameters of Step 2 are summarized in Table 7.2.

Table 7.2 Re-planning process Step 2

Description	Calibration of parameter α in equation (7.6). Decision about *when to re-plan* based on criterion (7.7). This decision may be overwritten due to other considerations.
Roles involved	Product manager.
Input	Set of new arriving features F3(t) for any point in time t during interval [0,T]. F3(t) is maintained in the change repository.
Output	*Yes* or *no* decision about re-planning at t = t*.

7.4.3 Step 3: Prioritization of new features

Prioritization corresponds to the application of the Multi-score method described in Section 3.8. The default assumption is that the same criteria are applied for re-planning as for the original planning. However, changing business needs might influence the choice of criteria, too, and provide another scenario for re-planning. The key parameters of Step 3 are summarized in Table 7.3.

Table 7.3 Re-planning process Step 3

Description	Prioritization of features by stakeholders for all defined re-planning criteria.
Roles involved	Product manager and nominated stakeholders.
Input	Set of new features F3(t). Re-planning criteria taken from the original planning process.
Output	All stakeholders have performed prioritization for the assigned features.

7.4.4 Step 4: Collective resource estimation

Estimation of resource consumption is done similarly to Step 6 of the EVOLVE II process. Instead of a point-wise estimate, nominated stakeholders can be asked to provide three estimates in the form of a best case, most likely, and a worst case estimate for resource consumption. Stakeholder estimates are integrated into one overall estimate following formulas (6.1) and (6.2). The higher the variation between estimates, the more uncertain the average estimate is expected to be. The key parameters of Step 4 are summarized in Table 7.4.

Table 7.4 Re-planning process Step 4

Description	Stakeholders with assigned resource-estimation role analyze the set of new features F3(t*) and available resource types. Then, stakeholders estimate the amount of resources that will be consumed by each feature.
Roles involved	Stakeholders nominated for resource estimation.
Input	Candidate features and specified resource types.
Output	Three-point resource estimation per feature (best case, most likely, worst case) and their aggregation across stakeholders. Uncertainty indicator per feature resource estimate.

7.4.5 Step 5: Update of planning parameters

Some of the original planning parameters such as resource capacities or degree of importance for planning criteria might have changed over time. The same is true for resource estimates and priorities assigned to features under planning. The process of updating these parameters is defined in Step 5 summarized in Table 7.5.

Table 7.5 Re-planning process Step 5

Description	Update of project or feature related planning values that have changed since the original plan was created.
Roles involved	Product manager and assigned stakeholders.
Input	Baseline plan feature set F1, and features from F2. All former planning parameters such as weight of criteria and resource capacities.
Output	Updated information for re-planning.

7.4.6 Step 6: Generation of re-planning alternatives

The same optimization algorithms as described in conjunction with EVOLVE II are applied (with specific settings such as K = 1 and pre-assignment of features that have already been implemented). Instead of just one re-planning alternative, a set of qualified and diversified (as largely as possible without lacking quality) solutions are determined. Step 6 is summarized in Table 7.6.

Table 7.6 Re-planning process Step 6

Description	Computation of optimized and diversified re-planning alternatives.
Roles involved	Product manager.
Input	All information specified in Step 5.
Output	Optimized (and diversified) re-plan alternatives.

7.4.7 Step 7: Analysis of re-planning alternatives

The different options for analyzing optimized re-planning alternatives are defined in Step 7 as shown in Table 7.7. These options refer to evaluation of the resource consumption and the quality of the re-planning alternatives as well as the analysis of their projected excitement from the perspective of the different stakeholders. The details of these analysis options are the same as described in Steps 9 through 12 of the EVOLVE II process.

Table 7.7 Re-planning process Step 7

Description	Optimized re-planning alternatives are evaluated in terms of their quality, resource consumption and projected stakeholder excitement. Stakeholders can be asked to perform scoring related to the attractiveness of the re-planning alternatives.
Roles involved	Product manager and assigned stakeholders.
Input	Optimized re-planning alternatives.
Output	Revised plan selected for implementation.

7.4.8 Step 8: Incorporation of the re-planning results into a revised baseline plan

With the decision of the most appropriate re-planning strategy, the suggested changes need to be integrated into the existing plan. Step 8 is summarized in Table 7.8.

Table 7.8 Re-planning process Step 8

Description	Update of set F1 representing the features offered in the ongoing release at time t = T.
Roles involved	Product manager.
Input	Revised plan selected as an update of the existing plan for the ongoing release.
Output	Revised sets F1 and F2 accommodating the changes suggested by the selected re-planning decision.

7.5 ILLUSTRATIVE CASE STUDY

7.5.1 Context

The method H2W* and its implementation as described in Section 7.4 are now illustrated by a case study. For that purpose, the decision scenario introduced in Section 2.2.2 is reconsidered:

> *Once the next product release features are announced, the process of their implementation is started. However, the arrival of new feature ideas and the modification of already existing features do not stop because of this. On the contrary, John, the product manager for SIP Inc., is under an ongoing demand to ensure the implementation of the already agreed upon features as well as accommodating very important requests for changes. To make his life even more challenging, the company has recently changed its business strategy, and John is expected to align with these new directions as quickly as possible.*
>
> *The situation is becoming even more complex as ideas and suggestions for new features can occur continuously. Is it advisable that a portion of the already agreed upon features become replaced by more attractive ones?*

7.5.2 Case study data

H2W* is illustrated by the above decision scenario, applied to the sample Telco project which was initially used in Chapter 3 for illustration of the Multi-score method. As a result of the application of EVOLVE II, it is assumed that an optimized release plan x has been agreed upon for the 20 features under consideration. According to this plan, a set F1 of eight features is assigned for implementation in upcoming release R14:

(7.8) $F1 = \{f(1), f(3), f(9), f(10), f(11), f(12), f(18), f(19)\}$

The set of of postponed features F2 is defined by the set of features F2 = F - F1:

(7.9) $F2 = \{f(2), f(4), f(5), f(6), f(7), f(8), f(13), f(14), f(15), f(16), f(17), f(20)\}$

The time interval considered (in working days) for re-planning is [0,82]. This is the duration of release R14. The following cumulative resource capacities are available:

- Design = 100 person days
- Software development = 75 person days
- Hardware development = 115 person days
- Testing = 80 person days
- Development cost = 200 K dollars

In addition to the strategic release plan, its operational implementation (staffing) is assumed to be done as well. In Section 8.4, a method is described for staffing to minimize overall project duration. The features are arranged according to increasing start date in Table 7.9.

Table 7.9 Features start/end dates for the operational plan for release R14

f(n)	f(3)	f(12)	f(18)	f(1)	f(10)	f(9)	f(11)	f(19)
start(n)	1	1	9	10	26	31	38	43
end(n)	12	15	40	32	52	66	82	82

Ten change requests do occur in time interval [0,82]. The features forming the set F3(82) = {f(21)...f(30)} are arriving at different points in time. The features with their arrival time, their estimated effort and cost consumption, and their priority evaluation are given in Table 7.10.

7.5.3 Re-planning scenario 1

In the first scenario, re-planning is performed under the premise that planning data (stakeholder scores, effort data, capacities) have not changed over time. For the *When to re-plan* decision, condition (7.7) is continuously checked within the time period [0, 82] (see Table 7.11). From former re-planning experience, the parameter α of function h(t) defined in (7.6) was customized to $\alpha = 0.6$. As soon as change request f(24) arrives at time t* = 38, re-planning is suggested because the percentage of new features exceeds the acceptable amount of change at this point in time.

Table 7.10 New arriving features and their attribute values

Feature	Arrival time (day)	Urgency (average score)	Frequency of use (average score)	Design effort (person days)	Software dev. effort (person days)	Hardware dev. effort (person days)	Testing effort (person days)	Cost (K dollars)
f(21)	5	6	9	15	9	11	13	18
f(22)	12	1	1	12	18	15	6	31
f(23)	29	4	2	14	10	17	8	28
f(24)	38	8	6	10	7	12	9	6
f(25)	43	7	9	9	10	17	11	21
f(26)	49	2	5	19	5	8	6	11
f(27)	57	5	4	10	15	17	9	36
f(28)	64	4	8	13	19	6	20	20
f(29)	73	7	6	7	16	8	6	7
f(30)	81	1	3	15	15	13	7	26

Table 7.11 Re-planning condition for different new change requests at different points in time

Feature	t*	g(t*)	h(t*)	g(t*) ≥ h(t*)
f(21)	5	0.11	0.56	No
f(22)	12	0.20	0.51	No
f(23)	29	0.27	0.39	No
f(24)	38	0.33	0.32	Yes

At t* = 38, some of the planned features have already been implemented (features f(1), f(3), and f(12)). Other features are in the process of implementation (features f(9), f(10), and f(18)). The features already implemented are no longer under consideration for change decisions. For the ones in progress, both their continuation and their cancellation are possible options. This is considered a human case-by-case decision which is impacted by the degree of progress in the implementation, among others. For the case study, f(18) is almost completed, while the other two features are below 50% of their implementation progress. The assumption is that there is a decision toward keeping f(18) and including the remaining features f(9) and f(10) in the re-planning process. This is considered a decision made by the human expert on a case-by-case basis. What it really means is that eventually one feature has been stopped in its implementation and os thrown away to make effort available for a new, more attractive one.

In summary, the candidate list for re-planning is constituted by

- The remaining four features f(9), f(10), f(11) and f(19) not yet (largely) implemented,
- The four new change requests available at t* = 38 (i.e., features f(21), f(22), f(23), f(24)), and
- The 12 features originally postponed.

With all these settings, planning method EVOLVE II is applied in order to create optimized re-planning alternatives. The one alternative chosen (out of the five different ones offered as a result of the planning procedure) differs from the original plan as follows:

(7.10) Features f(9), f(10) and f(19) are replaced by features f(8), f(21) and f(24).

What are the changes obtained from the suggested changes? As shown in Table 7.12, the replacement resulted in an increase of average scoring for the criterion *frequency of use*. This is the results from the comparison of the columns *Sum1* and *Sum2*. The first one refers to features f(9), f(10) and f(19), and the second one to features f(8), f(21) and f(24). Looking at the average *urgency* scoring, there is a slight decrease when moving from the original to the new set. The new feature set requires more effort for design and software development, and causes a higher total cost. However, there is resource and budget capacity left over from the original plan to accommodate these changes.

In total, the revised feature set for release R14 is defined by the new set F1 defined in (7.11).

(7.11) F1 = {f(1), f(3), f(8), f(11), f(12), f(18), f(21), f(24)}

F1 creates a total value of 4355 (measured again in terms of total number of stakeholder features points). This represents a 7.45% improvement compared to the original plan (7.8) for R14. The re-planning solution generated is the best possible for the stated objectives and constraints. This was proven as a side effect from applying EVOLVE II.

Table 7.12 Relevant data for feature exchange of scenario 1

	f(9)	f(10)	f(19)	**Sum1**	f(8)	f(21)	f(24)	**Sum2**
Average urgency	8.13	6.98	5.21	**20.32**	5.7	6	8	**19.7**
Average frequency of use	4.09	3.47	2.7	**10.26**	3.26	9	6	**18.26**
Design effort	5	6	20	**31**	45	15	10	**70**
Effort software dev.	0	1	0	**1**	0	9	7	**16**
Effort hardware dev.	25	12	15	**52**	10	11	12	**33**
Testing effort	14	12	0	**26**	5	13	9	**27**
Cost	20	19	10	**49**	40	18	16	**74**

7.5.4 Re-planning scenario 2

In this scenario, project planning data is no longer considered to be unchanged. As time has passed (i.e., after 38 time units), stakeholder priorities have changed. For the case study project, the modified stakeholder priorities related to the two planning criteria are summarized in Table 7.13. For 7 of the 20 features, the priority with respect to *urgency* and *frequency of use* is assumed to have either increased (+) or decreased (-).

Table 7.13 Modified stakeholder priorities (changes are highlighted) on average urgency and average frequency of use

	f(1)	f(2)	f(3)	f(4)	f(5)	f(6)	f(7)	f(8)	f(9)	f(10)
Average urgency	6.19	6.17	7.34	5.77	**7.28 (+)**	4.92	4.87	5.70	8.13	**3.32 (-)**
Average frequency of use	6.49	4.40	2.75	3.68	**5.92 (+)**	**6.02 (+)**	4.51	3.26	**2.21 (-)**	3.47

Table 7.13 (continued)

	f(11)	f(12)	f(13)	f(14)	f(15)	f(16)	f(17)	f(18)	f(19)	f(20)
Average urgency	**2.85** (-)	5.26	5.25	3.81	**7.15** (+)	4.79	**7.42** (+)	5.85	5.21	5.64
Average frequency of use	**2.13** (-)	3.66	4.87	4.11	**5.45** (+)	5.42	2.53	2.91	2.70	2.40

As a result of the optimization with EVOLVE II using the modified data (and with the same settings for pre-assignment of f(1), f(3), f(12) and f(18) as used in the first scenario), features f(9), f(10) and f(19) are now suggested for replacement by features f(6), f(21) and f(24). The detailed data are summarized in Table 7.14. The inclusion of feature f(6) instead of f(8) (as in the first scenario) is motivated by the increased priority of this feature in terms of its *frequency of use*.

Table 7.14 Relevant data for feature exchange of scenario 2

	f(9)	f(10)	f(19)	**Sum1**	f(6)	f(21)	f(24)	**Sum2**
Average urgency	8.13	6.98	5.21	**20.32**	4.92	6	8	**18.92**
Average frequency of use	4.09	3.47	2.7	**10.26**	6.02	9	6	**21.02**
Design effort	5	6	20	**31**	45	15	10	**70**
Effort software dev.	0	1	0	**1**	0	9	7	**16**
Effort hardware dev.	25	12	15	**52**	10	11	12	**33**
Testing effort	14	12	0	**26**	5	13	9	**27**
Cost	20	19	10	**49**	40	18	16	**74**

In total, the revised feature set for release R14 is defined by the new set F1 with

(7.12) F1 = {f(1), f(3), f(6), f(11), f(12), f(18), f(21), f(24)}

The re-planning solution generated is the best possible.

7.5.5 Re-planning scenario 3

In the final re-planning scenario, capacities are assumed to have changed. The product manager has analyzed that software development and testing were the most critical resources to implement a higher valued feature set. It was also analyzed that hardware development resources are not fully utilized. The manager evaluated the possibility to re-adjust capacities across teams by transferring some employees from the hardware development team capable of performing tasks as part of the design and testing teams instead.

In a strict sense, the re-planning model should take into account reduced productivity, since there is a learning curve for the new people and the effective time of the existing people goes to teaching the new ones. In practices, this means that the effort estimates that were originally estimated for the features do not hold. For simplicity reasons this is left out of consideration.

Also, the project manager decided to reduce the project budget (i.e., money to buy third-party software and hardware needed to implement some features) and use this money to hire more employees for the software development team. Table 7.15 summarizes the new resource capacities (in person days for human resources and K dollars for cost).

Table 7.15 Modified resource capacities for re-planning

Iteration/Resource	Design	Hardware develop-ment	Software develop-ment	Testing	Cost
Original capacities	100	75	115	80	200
Adjusted capacities	110	50	145	95	190

In total, the revised feature set for release R14 is defined by the new set F1 with

(7.13) F1 = {f(1), f(3), f(9), f(11), f(12), f(17), f(18), f(19), f(21)}

The resulting release plan achieves a higher resource utilization level. The plan is different from the original one because feature f(10) was replaced by features f(17) and f(21). The resource adjustment provided a new plan with a total value of 4680 (in terms of the total number of stakeholder features points). This is a more than 15% improvement over the original plan. The details are summarized in Table 7.16. Again, the re-planning solution generated is the best possible under the stated objectives and constraints.

7.5.6 Discussion

The systematic re-planning method H2W* is aimed at qualifying the decision-making process to finally offer the most attractive features, in consideration of the most recently arrived feature requests or changed data. For the application of the method, similar arguments as applied for the application of EVOLVE II are due. The new features arrived and considered for re-planning should be evaluated by stakeholders in terms of the stated planning criteria. Their effort estimation is another pre-requisite for the method.

Table 7.16 Relevant data for feature exchange of scenario 3

	f(10)	**Sum1**	f(17)	f(21)	**Sum2**
Average Urgency	6.98	**6.98**	6.34	6	**12.34**
Average frequency of use	3.47	**3.47**	2.53	9	**11.53**
Design effort	6	**6**	10	15	**25**
Effort software development	1	**1**	25	9	**34**
Effort hardware development	12	**12**	0	11	**11**
Testing effort	12	**12**	10	13	**23**
Cost	19	**19**	20	18	**38**

Re-planning is not limited in the frequency of its application. Although the method is formulated for one cycle of re-planning only, it easily allows its repeated application. In each (re-)application, the current plan under implementation is used as the new starting point (original plan) for re-planning. In case of replicated application of H2W*, additional constraints are imposed restricting the total amount of feature changes.

The final human decision can be impacted by additional (implicit) concerns. Even though not further highlighted in the case study, the application of EVOLVE II gives the same principal advantage of generating a set of qualified and diversified alternatives, now for the re-planning of an existing plan.

Finally, there are other possible criteria that could be considered to decide about the *when to re-plan?* Some of them can be related to the number of arriving features. Others take into account the importance of the stakeholder who issued the change request. Independent of that, there might be policies in place restricting the total amount of change related to a release decision made earlier. This applies both in case of single and replicated application of H2W*.

CHAPTER 8

STAFFING FOR PRODUCT RELEASES

8.1 INTRODUCTION

Product release plans provide the "big picture" for the evolution of a product. In order to actually implement the plan, a more fine-grained planning is needed to assign human resources to perform the individual tasks behind the selected features. Staffing for product releases relates to the question of how to organize this process. Software-based products often require very different technical and non-technical competencies ranging from communication, customization and learning to the application of the different techniques, methods and tools.

For a dynamically changing pool of human resources, the decisions to be continuously made are related to questions such as: Who is assigned to which task and why? How do we react in the case of a lack of developers? How do we react to changes in the requested effort? What are the types of human resources most critical for success? When is a good time to provide training?

The quality of these decisions strongly impacts the outcome of the project in terms of its quality and delivery date. Project managers often spend a substantial portion of their time to figure out the best assignment of people to tasks. Decision support methods described in this chapter are an important means to achieve higher effectiveness as well as better efficiency in this process.

The discipline of project management is concerned with planning, organizing, leading, staffing and controlling of projects [Wysocki '06]. As Fred Brooks stated in 1987, *today's major problems with software development are not technical problems, but management problems* [Brooks '87]. Although stated 23 years ago, things have not changed dramatically since then. [Charette '05] has analyzed factors *why software projects fail so often.* Among the 12 factors mentioned, half of them are closely related to project management:

- Unrealistic or un-articulated project goals
- Inaccurate estimates of needed resources
- Poor reporting of the project's status
- Un-managed risks
- Inability to handle the project's complexity
- Poor project management

Staffing is one of the five key major project management functions and thus belongs to the category of issues causing "major problems". Staffing takes into account the different competence levels of developers. It is well-known that there are major differences in the competencies and productivity of software developers. [Sackman et al. '68] studied professional programmers with an average of seven years experience and found that the ratio of initial coding time between the best and worst programmers was about 20 to 1. The general finding that *there is one order-of-magnitude difference among programmers* has been confirmed by other studies such as [Valett and McGarry '89], [DeMarco and Lister '99], and [Constantine '01]. Acknowledging that all developers have certain strengths in their competence profile, the question becomes identifying those people who are best suited for the different development roles. Despite its importance, currently there exists only little support for this staffing task [Acuna et al. '06].

Project management includes management of human and other resources. Human resources are often the most expensive ones. Their proper usage is of key relevance for project success. The Standish Group's report about *Solutions for Enterprise Project and Portfolio Management (PPM)* analyzed 307 surveys and 30 interviews focused on the value of features and functions of PPM solutions [Standish '09]. One of the findings was that *59% of respondents thought that project-level resource allocation could have a major effect on the success of their projects and 64% thought it to have high monetary value (ROI).*

Assigning most competent developers to appropriate tasks is a complex process. If this process is executed in an *ad hoc* manner, and solely based on intuition, then the likely results will be poor resource utilization and schedule overrun. Automated and computer-based support has been suggested as an essential component for improving efficiency and effectiveness of planning [Kapur et al. '08].

While staffing is a topic of general interest, it is studied in this chapter in the specific context of implementation of a product release. Release planning and staffing depend on each other: Each plan needs to be staffed, and staffing only makes sense in conjunction with a defined set of selected features. Staffing needs to take into account the different features, their dependencies, the tasks necessary to provide the features, the human resources available to realize the tasks, the dependencies between the tasks, and existing due dates for the release and the tasks.

In this chapter, three specific questions related to assigning human resources to tasks are investigated in more detail. Section 8.2 provides the common background and related work. The method for *staffing to achieve maximum release value* is described in Section 8.3. *Staffing for minimal project duration*, that is, the second staffing problem formulation, is investigated in Section 8.4. The third variant of staffing is called *competence-oriented staffing* and is studied in Section 8.5. It is aimed at the best assignment of developers to tasks based on requested and available competence profile. Finally, this chapter ends with an industrial case study described in Section 8.6.

A related tool for doing optimized staffing called RASORP is described in Section 10.4. Chapter 12 is devoted to a more detailed and illustrative case study for staffing. It is based upon the Telco case study project used throughout this book. It is devoted to performing and discussing a number of staffing scenarios.

8.2 BACKGROUND AND RELATED WORK

8.2.1 Key components of the staffing problem

The staffing problem means to assign the right people to the tasks to be performed. It also means to determine the right timing and sequence of task performance. The general structure of the staffing problem is summarized in Figure 8.1. The main artifacts and main operations in the staffing process are shown. Following a top-down approach, the conceptual model description starts with the formulation of the planning objectives. Dependencies can be considered both at the feature and at the task level. A pool of developers is available to assign them to sequence of tasks. Developers have a profile of competencies and related productivities for performing tasks. The general model encompasses periods of absence of the developers as well. It is assumed that each task is done by exactly one developer. This simplification makes the problem tractable. More complex assignment scenarios can be treated by refinements of either the tasks or the resources.

For the staffing problem, each feature is considered the result of performing a sequence of feature-related tasks. All of them have an estimated effort and a requested profile of competencies for performing them. Once all the tasks of a feature are implemented by the assigned developer, the features can contribute to the creation of release value. All objectives and constraints of the staffing problem are formulated in terms of features and their related tasks in conjunction with the human resources available. The solution method to the staffing problem considers the characteristics of the individual tasks and makes suggestions about the allocation of developers to tasks and the order in which tasks should be performed. Among the tasks related to the same feature, there might be different types of dependencies (see Section 8.2.3 for their categorization).

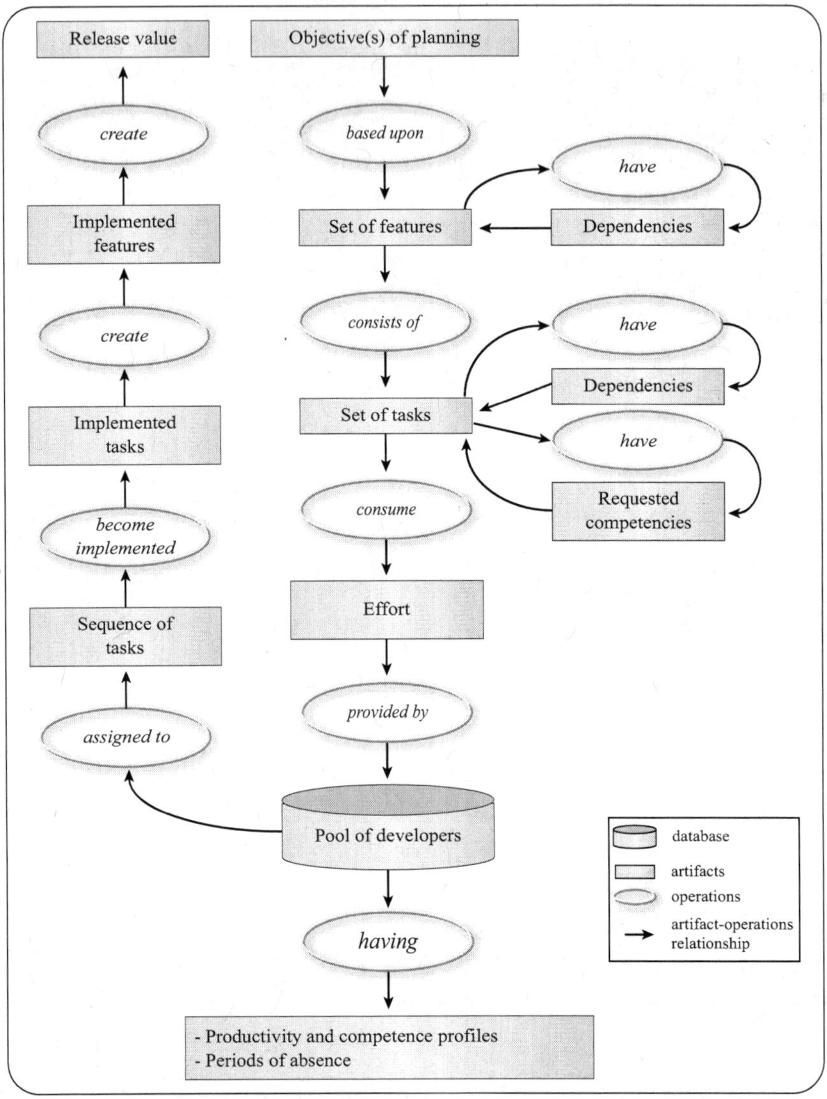

Figure 8.1 Conceptual model of the staffing problem formulation

Before providing the three variants of staffing as instances of the formulation given in Figure 8.1, an illustrative example adapted from [Kapur et al. '08] is studied in the following Subsection 8.2.2.

8.2.2 Staffing: An illustrative example

A project for implementation of six candidate features is studied. The resulting product is offered incrementally in two releases. The first one is due after four weeks and the second one after eight weeks. Implementation of a feature requires performing three tasks called *design*, *coding* and *test*. Each feature can only be offered if all the three related tasks are performed. There are dependencies between the starting dates of tasks of the same feature which need to be fulfilled: (i) Coding should not start before design starts. Similarly, (ii) testing should not start before coding starts. There are similar dependencies between the end dates: (iii) Coding should not finish before design is finished, and (iv) testing should not finish before coding is done.

Besides dependencies between tasks, there are dependencies between features as well (see Chapter 5 for further details on that). Features *Data import* and *Data export* only make sense in combination with each other. If chosen, these two features must appear in the same release. Furthermore, *Notification* cannot be released without *User administration* already being implemented.

Each feature, once made available in the market, will realize a certain value. It is assumed that this value depends on when it is released. The features f(n) (n = 1...6) and their estimated relative values called *value(n,k)* for the case of being offered in release k = 1 and k = 2 are given in Table 8.1. The values are expressed based upon a nine-point scale with *1* and *9* indicating *very low* respectively *very high* feature value. In addition, Table 8.1 contains the estimated effort (in person days) for each of the three tasks per feature. According to that, feature *Reporting* would create a value of 6 if delivered in the first release, and a value of 1 is expected if delivered in release 2. The same feature has an estimated effort of four person days for *design*, three person days for *coding*, and two person days for *testing*.

The project team consists of three developers (Anna, Dave and Ken). From analysis of their former work experience, the developers have different productivity levels for each of the tasks of design, coding and testing. The productivity evaluations are estimates and based on the performance in past projects. Average productivity is normalized to 1. A productivity value of 2 of a developer means that this developer can perform a given task twice as fast as a developer with average productivity. In Table 8.2, Anna is judged as performing about average for design, 50% above average in coding, and 100% above average developers in testing. While these assumptions are applied for all features of the same project, they might vary across varying projects.

The staffing plan also needs to look at certain periods of absence (due to training, vacation or other planned periods of absence). During the deployment of the project, Anna is not available to work during days 6 and 7. All the other developers have no predicted period of absence.

Table 8.1 Feature related data for illustrative sample project

Feature	Functionality	value v(n,k) of f(n) per release k		Effort (in person days)		
		k = 1	k = 2	Design	Coding	Test
f(1)	Reporting	6	1	4	3	2
f(2)	Billing	5	3	2	3	1
f(3)	User administration	9	2	2	3	3
f(4)	Notification	8	6	3	4	2
f(5)	Data import	9	7	5	6	4
f(6)	Data export	9	5	4	5	3

The developer-related data are summarized in Table 8.2. The general assumption is that one task can only be assigned to one developer all the time. Another assumption is that one developer can only work on one task at a time.

Table 8.2 Productivity and time windows of unavailability

Developer	Productivity			Unavailable	
	Design	Coding	Test	From day	To day
1 (Anna)	1	1.5	2	6	7
2 (Dave)	2	0.75	1	-	-
3 (Ken)	0.5	2	1	-	-

Due to the limitations in the availability of developers, it might not be possible to deliver all features within the predefined period of time. The features that cannot be implemented are postponed. The objective of the planning process is creating a staffing plan that gives the maximum total value for the two product releases. This goal can be broken down into two parts:

i. Assignment of features to releases in a manner that achieves maximal value for the product (release planning).
ii. Assignment of tasks to developers to realize the strategic release plan (staffing).

The value of a product release is additive in terms of the value of the features of that release. An example of a release and staffing plan is shown in Table 8.3. Each line of the Gantt chart represents a task of a feature. The bar shows the developer responsible for that task as well as the time allocated to it. According to this initial plan, *Reporting* is delivered in release 1 (after four days) as all the three tasks have been finished after four days. Similarly, *Billing* is offered in release 2 (after eight days). All other features f(3), f(4), f(5) and f(6) are postponed.

Developer Dave is coding all the time. However, the other two developers would have been the better choice for that as they are expected to be more productive. Ken starts with design work in the third day. However, this is the job he at which is least productive.

Table 8.3 Gantt chart of initial plan x1

Feature/task		Day							
		1	2	3	4	5	6	7	8
Reporting	Design	Anna							
	Code	Dave							
	Test			Ken					
Billing	Design					Ken			
	Code					Dave			
	Test								Anna

The value of this plan called x1 is composed by adding the value of the two proposed features, that is, value(x1) = v(1,1) + v(2,2) = 6 + 3 = 9. However, this plan is poorly designed because many of the tasks are done by developers who are not the most qualified to perform the job. For example, Ken is not doing any coding, although e is most qualified for that.

A better solution is shown in Table 8.4. In this plan, the assignment of developers is significantly improved. There is less idle time for the developers. Tasks are assigned to more productive developers. According to this plan, *User administration* is provided in release 1, and features *Reporting*, *Billing* and *Notification* are offered in release 2. The two remaining features *Data import* and *Data export* are postponed. The overall value of this plan called x2 increases to value(x2) = 19 compared to the value(x1) = 9 of the former plan x1. Looking at the plan in Table 8.4, it can be seen that the design task for the notification feature is interrupted after the end of day two. This allows Dave to start with the design for *Billing*, which allows starting with the coding for the same feature. It although becomes transparent that Anna's period of absence has been taken into account. For a final plan offered, all the originally defined dependencies are satisfied:

- Coding should not start before design starts
- Testing should not start before coding starts
- Coding is not finished before design
- Testing is not finished before coding

Table 8.4 Table of improved staffing plan x2

<table>
<tr><th rowspan="2" colspan="2">Feature/task</th><th colspan="8">Day</th></tr>
<tr><th>1</th><th>2</th><th>3</th><th>4</th><th>5</th><th>6</th><th>7</th><th>8</th></tr>
<tr><td rowspan="3">User administrator</td><td>Design</td><td>Dave</td><td></td><td></td><td></td><td></td><td></td><td></td><td></td></tr>
<tr><td>Code</td><td colspan="2">Anna</td><td></td><td></td><td></td><td></td><td></td><td></td></tr>
<tr><td>Test</td><td colspan="3">Ken</td><td></td><td></td><td></td><td></td><td></td></tr>
<tr><td rowspan="3">Notification</td><td>Design</td><td></td><td>Dave</td><td></td><td>Dave</td><td></td><td></td><td></td><td></td></tr>
<tr><td>Code</td><td></td><td></td><td></td><td colspan="2">Ken</td><td></td><td></td><td></td></tr>
<tr><td>Test</td><td></td><td></td><td></td><td></td><td>Anna</td><td></td><td></td><td></td></tr>
<tr><td rowspan="3">Reporting</td><td>Design</td><td></td><td></td><td></td><td></td><td colspan="2">Dave</td><td></td><td></td></tr>
<tr><td>Code</td><td></td><td></td><td></td><td></td><td></td><td></td><td colspan="2">Ken</td></tr>
<tr><td>Test</td><td></td><td></td><td></td><td></td><td></td><td></td><td></td><td>Anna</td></tr>
<tr><td rowspan="3">Billing</td><td>Design</td><td></td><td></td><td>Dave</td><td></td><td></td><td></td><td></td><td></td></tr>
<tr><td>Code</td><td></td><td></td><td colspan="2">Anna</td><td></td><td></td><td></td><td></td></tr>
<tr><td>Test</td><td></td><td></td><td></td><td></td><td></td><td>Ken</td><td></td><td></td></tr>
</table>

While the plan shown in Table 8.4 represents a much improved alternative to deliver features creating maximum total value, another scenario could be looked at as well. This scenario refers to the delivery of all the six pre-selected features with the objective to achieve this within minimum duration. In this scenario, the value of the features is no longer taken into account. The assumption is that this was done already in the selection of the features. For the set of features listed in Table 8.1, the overall duration to implement all features is 13 days. That means that in comparison to plan x2, the two additional features have caused five more days of implementation. The corresponding Gantt chart is shown in Table 8.5.

Comparing the staffing plans shown in Tables 8.4 and 8.5, some assignments of developers to tasks have changed. The coding for the *Billing* feature is no longer done by Anna, but has been assigned to Ken, who in that case is the better choice in terms of productivity. What the optimization delivers is the global perspective on the assignments. This implies that even non-optimal individual assignments are acceptable as long as they contribute to the global goal of minimization of the total project duration.

Table 8.5 Gantt chart of a schedule minimizing overall make-span

Feature/task		Day 1	2	3	4	5	6	7	8	9	10	11	12	13
Reporting	Design		Dave	Dave										
	Code			Anna	Anna									
	Test					Anna								
Billing	Design				Dave									
	Code				Ken	Ken								
	Test					Dave								
User administrator	Design	Dave												
	Code	Ken	Ken											
	Test	Anna	Anna											
Notification	Design						Dave	Dave						
	Code						Ken	Ken						
	Test								Anna					
Data import	Design								Dave	Dave	Dave			
	Code								Ken	Ken	Ken			
	Test									Anna	Anna			
Data export	Design											Dave	Dave	
	Code											Ken	Ken	Ken
	Test												Anna	Anna

8.2.3 Description of dependencies between tasks

In the illustrative example given in Subsection 8.2.2, there was a request for begin-begin as well as for end-end precedence relationship between tasks. In reality, an even more fine-grained overlap of tasks might be requested. For example, modeling the dependency between start of design and start of coding can be considered in dependence of the duration of the design task. This would avoid that design and coding are done completely concurrently. Instead, a certain progress of initial design work is supposed to be done before entering the coding stage.

In the following, different types of dependencies are described. For that purpose, the following notation defined for the q-th task task(n,q) of feature f(n) is used:

(8.1)	Begin_task(n,q):	Begin time for task(n,q) of to feature f(n)
(8.2)	End_task(n,q):	End time for task(n,q) of to feature f(n)
(8.3)	Duration_task(n,q):	Duration of task(n,q) of to feature f(n)

In total, 12 types of dependencies between tasks related to the same feature are considered. The types differ by the way the dependencies are expressed. The first four types (8.4) to (8.7) correspond to the four possible combinations of start and end dates of a pair of two tasks in consideration. For the other types of dependencies, there is an additional impact of the duration of the reference task. What that means is that for these more complex types of dependencies, a certain degree of the duration of a task needs to be executed before the other task could be started.

For two sample tasks task(n,q1) and task(n,q2), coefficients α are used in (8.8) to (8.15) expressing the portion of a task which needs to be executed before the dependent follow-up task can be started. In addition to that, some fixed time period β needs to be waited. To keep notation simple, the dependency of α and β from n and q is left out. Using these coefficients, the dependencies can be stated as follows:

(8.4) $\text{Begin\_task}(n,q1) \leq \text{Begin\_task}(n,q2)$

(8.5) $\text{Begin\_task}(n,q1) \leq \text{End\_task}(n,q2)$

(8.6) $\text{End\_task}(n,q1) \leq \text{End\_task}(n,q2)$

(8.7) $\text{End\_task}(n,q1) \leq \text{Begin\_task}(n,q2)$

(8.8) $\text{Begin\_task}(n,q1) + \alpha 1\ \text{Duration\_task}(n,q1) + \beta 1 \leq \text{Begin\_task}(n,q2)$

(8.9) $\text{Begin\_task}(n,q1) + \alpha 2\ \text{Duration\_task}(n,q1) + \beta 2 \geq \text{Begin\_task}(n,q2)$

(8.10) $\text{Begin\_task}(n,q1) + \alpha 3\ \text{Duration\_task}(n,q1) + \beta 3 \leq \text{End\_task}(n,q2)$

(8.11) $\text{Begin\_task}(n,q1) + \alpha 4\ \text{Duration\_task}(n,q1) + \beta 4 \geq \text{End\_task}(n,q2)$

(8.12) $\text{End\_task}(n,q1) + \alpha 5\ \text{Duration\_task}(n,q1) + \beta 5 \leq \text{End\_task}(n,q2)$

(8.13) $\text{End\_task}(n,q1) + \alpha 6\ \text{Duration\_task}(n,q1) + \beta 6 \geq \text{End\_task}(n,q2)$

(8.14) $\text{End\_task}(n,q1) + \alpha 7\ \text{Duration\_task}(n,q1) + \beta 7 \leq \text{Begin\_task}(n,q2)$

(8.15) $\text{End\_task}(n,q1) + \alpha 8\ \text{Duration\_task}(n,q1) + \beta 8 \geq \text{Begin\_task}(n,q2)$

Dependency types (8.4) to (8.9) are illustrated in Figure 8.2. For any two tasks of the same feature, end-end, begin-begin, begin-end, as well as end-begin relationships are visualized. Moreover, the degree of execution of a task is taken into account for the generalized begin-begin and the generalized begin-end dependency. This means that task(n,q2) can only be started after task(n,q1) is done to a certain degree (say 70%, i.e., $\alpha 1 = 0.7$) and some additional time $\beta 1$ has been passed.

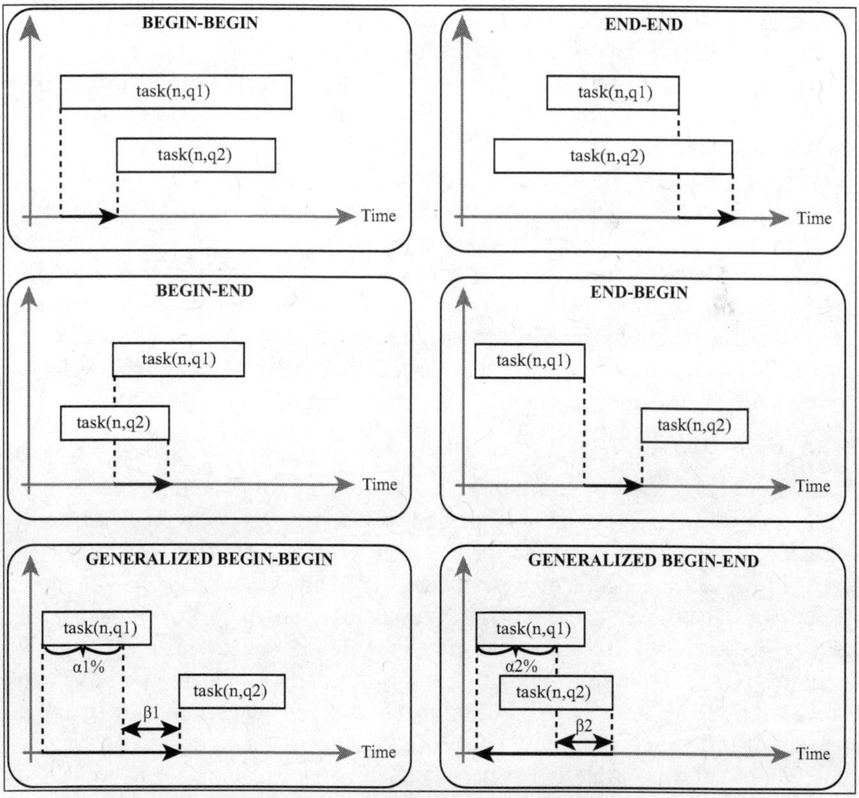

Figure 8.2 Illustration of dependencies (8.4) to (8.9) between tasks

Similarly, the bottom right figure describes a situation that task(n,q2) should not start later than some point in time given by the portion execution $\alpha 2\%$ of task(n,q1) plus some additional period $\beta 2$. The remaining dependency types can be treated analogously.

8.2.4 Three variants of the staffing problem

In this chapter, three variants of the staffing problem are formulated. Each of them is studied in further detail in subsequent Sections 8.3, 8.4, and 8.5.

Staffing problem 1: Staffing for maximum total release value

Release due dates are fixed. For a given set of features requested for implementation, the objective is to find a subset of features that results in maximum total feature value. This is achieved by the best staffing plan. Objects of investigation are features with their related tasks and developers with their individual productivity profiles. All staffing plans are in conformance to the stated availability constraints of developers.

Staffing problem 2: Staffing for minimum make-span

For a given set of features requested for implementation, the objective is to implement all the proposed features in minimum overall project duration. This is also called *make-span minimization.* Objects of investigation are features with their related tasks and developers with their productivity profile. Given release due dates can be exceeded. All staffing plans are in conformance to the stated availability constraints of developers.

Staffing problem 3: Staffing for maximum competence match

For a given set of tasks to be performed, the objective of the third staffing problem is to find the best assignment of developers to tasks. Each task has a specified requested profile of competencies. Each task is executed by exactly one developer. Each developer has a specific competence profile which reflects former work experience. The staffing problem is to assign developers to tasks such that there is a best possible total match between requested and offered (by the assigned developers) competencies. This is independent of any consideration of features.

8.2.5 Related Work

The different variants of staffing are closely related to scheduling and resource allocation problems. There is a large body of knowledge in project scheduling [Blazewicz et al. '07] and project management [Wysocki '06]. Project scheduling as part of project management was studied, for example, in [Alba and Francisco Chicano '07]. In order to decide (i) which resources are used to perform which tasks and (ii) when each task should be performed, the authors suggested applying genetic algorithms (GAs). The application of GAs for project management was initiated by [Chang et al. '01]. The proposed method focused on schedule minimization and did not examine different productivity levels of developers.

Staffing of software projects has been studied with other methods as well. As an earlier effort, [Abdel-Hamid '89] investigated staffing of software projects based on a comprehensive system dynamics model of the software development process.

Bayesian belief networks were used by [Fenton et al. '04] as a means to circumvent the inherent uncertainty in estimating effort for resource decisions. Their causal model (using a Bayesian network) incorporates empirical data. The authors showed how this model can be used in a practical decision-support tool, allowing a project manager to trade-off the resources used against the outputs (delivered functionality, quality achieved) in a software project.

Different search-based techniques (genetic algorithms, hill climbing and simulated annealing) were used for planning resource allocation in large massive maintenance projects [Antoniol et al. '05]. The approach was validated by an empirical study of a large, commercial Y2K massive maintenance project, which compared these techniques with each other. According to the authors, the best search technique reduces the project duration by as much as 50% compared to the application of baseline random search.

Staffing of software projects was modeled and solved as a constraint satisfaction problem in [Barreto et al. '08]. Their approach takes into account the characteristics of the project activities and their demand on individual competencies. Different types of utility functions are examined. However, the scalability of the method to mid- or even large-scale real-world staffing problems was not addressed. In summary, existing methods and techniques either were not applicable to the general staffing formulation presented in this chapter, or their applicability was just shown for small scale examples without demonstrating their scalability.

8.3 STAFFING FOR MAXIMUM TOTAL RELEASE VALUE

8.3.1 Problem description

Staffing problem 1 aims at the maximization of the total release value for the case of fixed release dates. Staffing in general requires more detailed information than the strategic release planning problem considered in Chapters 5 and 6, where resources are taken into account just on a cumulative basis with the total amount available over the whole release period. In correspondence to the higher level of detail in data and planning, the time horizon for staffing is shorter than for the case of strategic planning. Because of the uncertainty of data and processes, it does not make sense to perform detailed staffing for a longer period of time advance.

More precisely, the following parameters and related constraints are considered as part of a more formal description of constraints given in [Ngo-The and Ruhe '09] and [Kapur et al. '08]:

1. Number K1 ($\leq$ K) of releases considered for staffing.
2. Existence of fixed release dates rd(k) for k = 1…K1 for subsequent releases.
3. Features offered in release k need to have all their tasks completed not later than at rd(k) (k = 1…K1).

4. The effort of task q of feature n, that is, task(n,q), is defined as the *amount of time units (e.g. person days) needed to fulfill the task q of feature n by an average developer* and denoted by effort(n,q). For example, effort(1,3) = 2 means that an average developer can perform task 3 of feature f(3) in 2 time units (such as days).
5. Productivity of developer d with regard to task q is defined as *effort of task q realized by a developer d in one time unit* and is denoted by prod(d,q).
6. Dependencies between tasks of the same feature are of the same type. They can be any of the types as formulated in (8.1), (8.3) and (8.4).
7. Dependencies between features (coupling, precedence) as formulated in Chapter 5 for strategic release planning.
8. A pool of developers with productivity profiles for performing the different types of tasks.
9. Availability constraints related to developers, defined by periods of absence describing the period of time a developer is not available.
10. Each task is considered pre-emptive. It is executed by just one developer. Each developer is working on no more than one task at the same time.

The Boolean variable x(n,k) indicates whether feature f(n) is provided at release k (x(n,k) = 1) or not (x(n,k) = 0). In the formulation of the problem, all the individual Boolean variables are aggregated into a vector x describing the assignment of all features to releases. The value of having feature f(n) provided at release k is denoted by value(n.k).

The features can only be offered if all the related tasks are done. The tasks themselves are performed by developers. The vector u is to describe the assignment of developers to tasks. The objective of planning is to maximize the overall utility function F(x) defined in (8.16). This is an additive function expressing the total value out of assigning the different features to the possible releases. F(x) solely depends on x, while the staffing vector u is important to formulate the feasibility of release plan x. The term *staffing* is used here as a synonym for assigning developers to tasks. All the feasible alternatives of assigning developers to tasks and performing the tasks fulfilling all the dependency constraints is abbreviated by UX.

(8.16) $\text{Maximize } \{ F(x) = \Sigma_{n=1 \ldots N} \Sigma_{k=1 \ldots K} \text{value}(n,k) \cdot x(n,k) \text{ subject to } (u,x) \in UX \}$

8.3.2 Solution method

In our approach, the *staffing for maximum release plan value* problem is modeled as a combination of a scheduling problem called the *job shop scheduling problem* and a variant of the *knapsack problem*. Both problems in isolation have been extensively studied and are known to be NP-complete [Garey and Johnson '79]. A comprehensive survey of job shop scheduling techniques can be found in [Blazewicz et al. '07]. For knapsack problems and all its variants, see [Kellerer et al. '04].

A two-phased solution method presented in [Ngo-The and Ruhe '09] combines the strength of special structure integer programming (Phase 1) with the power of genetic algorithms (Phase 2). In Phase 1, a simplified version of the original problem is solved. This simplification is done by ignoring some of the constraints. As a result, a solution is received which serves as a quality measure for the subsequent solution in consideration of all the remaining constraints of the problem. The plan received from Phase 1 is not necessarily feasible in terms of the dependencies between tasks. The plan, however, is taken as a starting solution for the subsequent search procedures executed in Phase 2.

The advantage of this solution method is twofold. First, an upper bound for the maximum value achievable can be generated from Phase 1. This allows a quality evaluation of the solution generated in Phase 2. The ratio between the solutions obtained in Phase 2 and the one obtained in Phase 1 give the guaranteed degree of optimality of the final plan. Second, the solution obtained from Phase 1 is utilized to restrict the search space elaborated in Phase 2. The set $\prod$ of all permutations of N features is reduced to the set $\prod^* \subset \prod$ used in the genetic algorithm of Phase 2. This reduction can significantly reduce the computational effort.

Phase 2 can be applied without application of Phase 1, but the search space would be substantially larger in this case. The restriction provided by Phase 1 is heuristic in its nature. That means it is likely that Π^* (reduced search space) contains a good solution. However, there is no guarantee that it necessarily contains the optimal solution. For further details of the method, see [Ngo-The and Ruhe '09].

8.3.3 Empirical validation

An initial empirical validation of the solution method is reported in [Ngo-The and Ruhe '09]. For a series of randomly generated problems, a comparison was done between the results of unfocused search (UFS) (just performing Phase 2 of the method outlined above without running Phase 1) and focused search (FS) (running Phase 1 and subsequently Phase 2 as described above). The results of the comparison from varying the number N of features between 5 and 204 and simultaneously varying the number K of releases between 1 and 4, are shown in Figure 8.3. With the exception of very small problems, the focused search performs better. The improvement is measured by the relative improvement ratio Improve(FS, UFS) based upon the solution x_{FS} and x_{UFS} obtained from FS and UFS, respectively. It is defined by (8.17).

(8.17) $\text{Improve(FS, UFS)} = [F(x_{FS}) - F(x_{UFS})] / F(x_{UFS})$

It is observed that the relative improvement ratio (8.17) is the more in favor of the focused search option, and thus, the bigger the problem (measured by $N \cdot K$). In some cases, the relative improvement achieved by focused search becomes more than 50%.

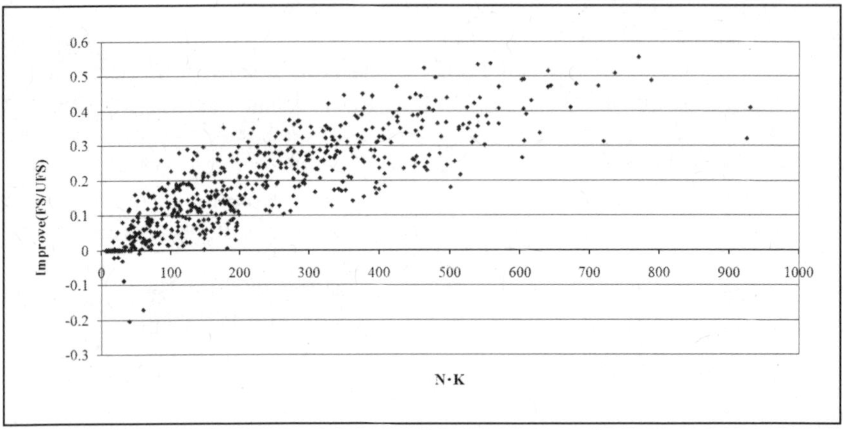

Figure 8.3 Comparison of the results between focused and unfocused search for staffing with the objective of maximum total release value [Ngo-The and Ruhe '09]

8.4 STAFFING FOR MINIMUM PROJECT DURATION

8.4.1 Problem description

Another important instance of the general staffing problem formulation relates to finding good plans under the premise that all features need to be processed. The best plan here is the one implementing all the features in the shortest period of time. Make-span minimization differs from the maximum release value problem by its objective: Instead of maximizing the value achievable from features for given release periods, the goal becomes to minimize the maximum finishing time among all tasks corresponding to features.

This formulation of staffing is related to the classical job shop scheduling problem (JSSP), which asks for the scheduling of n jobs job(1) ... job(n) on m identical machines. The objective is to minimize the total length of the schedule. Our problem is more general than the JSSP problem because it allows different productivity levels for the different machines (developers).

More precisely, the problem formulation is composed by the following parts:

i. The effort of task q of feature n is defined as *the amount of time units needed to fulfill the task q of feature n by an average developer* and is denoted by effort(n,q).
ii. The productivity of developer d with regards to task q is defined as *effort of task q realized by developer d in one time unit* and is denoted by prod(d,q).
iii. Dependencies between tasks of the same feature are of the same type. They can be any of the types as formulated in (8.1), (8.3) and (8.4).

iv. A pool of developers with different levels of productivity for the different types of tasks.
v. Up-front known periods of absence of developers.
vi. Each task is considered preemptive. It is executed by just one developer. Each developer is working on no more than one task at the same time.

8.4.2 Solution method

The staffing for minimum make-span does not consider releases and release values, just the maximum of the end-times of all tasks, which is aimed to be minimal. Because of its similarity to the JSSP, any method applicable to a general JSSP can be adapted to this problem. Our solution approach is a variant of the RASORP solution method described in [Ngo-The and Ruhe '09] with only Phase 2 being executed. For that, a special implementation of the genetic algorithm of [Hartmann '98] was used. A detailed case study going through various staffing and re-staffing scenarios is presented in Chapter 12.

8.5 STAFFING FOR MAXIMUM COMPETENCE MATCH

8.5.1 Problem description

The third staffing problem is directed toward perfect matching of requested and available competencies for performing a sequence of tasks. The tasks are partially ordered based upon priority. Each task has specific competence requests. The underlying assumption here is that the better the match of the competencies, the faster the tasks can be executed. For a given period of time, the objective is to find a matching that allows the maximum number of tasks being executed.

One prominent representative of this class of problems is fixing bugs as part of software development and maintenance projects. Looking at scenarios of having hundreds (if not thousands) of bugs in a repository, a proper assignment of developers to bug fixing tasks becomes a tremendous challenge. A comparison of various greedy-based solution methods and a case study conducted with open source data is available from [Rahman et al. '09].

A process of fixing a given set of individual tasks in a given time interval is considered with M tasks under consideration. The time interval of the project is defined as [0, T], that is, a planning horizon of T time units (e.g., days) is looked at. The question studied is: Who should perform which task and when? For that, a pool of developers DEV = {dev(1), ..., dev(D)} consisting of D individuals is assumed to be available during the given time interval.

In the context of a specific organization or a specific project, there is a set of competencies that have been observed to be relevant for performing the tasks. All these competencies are summarized into a vector having R components. For example, task related competencies in consideration of a project context can be related to

- Java programming (r = 1)
- MySQL (r = 2)
- Code review (r = 3)
- Testing (r = 4)
- PHP (r = 5)

For optimized assignment of developers to tasks, requested competencies of task(m) and available competencies of developer dev(d) to be assigned to execute the task are defined. The vector of requested competencies is called *Request(m)* and has R components. The individual components are denoted by request(m,r). Each component expresses the (estimated) portion of the total task effort devoted to the r-th competence type. Both the number and the content of these competencies are context-specific.

The requested competence levels per task(m) are formulated by numbers from interval [0,1] expressing the percentages of the respective competence levels related to the total amount of competence. The vectors Request(m) are normalized to 1:

(8.18) $\sum_{r=1...R} \text{request}(m,r) = 1$ for all m = 1...M

For the example stated above, in consideration of a task(m), the corresponding vector Request(m) has R = 5 components. Request(m) = (0.50, 0, 0.20, 0.30, 0) then means that for performing task(m), 50% of the effort is expected to be on Java programming, 20% is expected to be code review and another 30% for testing. No competencies are expected for both *my SQL* and *PHP.*

In order to find optimized assignments of developers to tasks, the competence levels of the developers need to be known as well. Similar to the formulation of the *staffing for maximum release value* problem, the average competence of a developer dev(d) related to competence r is expressed as a ratio measure defined by (8.19) and (8.20).

(8.19) dcomp(d,r) = 1 if dev(d) has average level of competence of type r

(8.20) dcomp(d,r) > 1 (<1) if dev(d) has above (below) level of competence of type r

The individual competencies of developer dev(d) are summarized into a vector Dcomp(d). It is assumed that a developer's competence is directly correlated with productivity. That implies that a competence level of comp(d,r) allows performing a task in 1/dcomp(d,r) units of time when compared to a developer having average competence for that task.

Each task(m) is further characterized by its (estimated) effort called *effort(m)*. The total effort is allocated proportionally to the different required competencies given in (8.18). This means that the effort related to a competence type r is given as the product of effort(m) and request(m,r). Finally, it is assumed that each task has an assigned priority called *prio(m)*. This priority is defined on an ordinal 5-point scale with prio(m) = 5 (= 1) being the highest (lowest) priority.

More precisely, the problem for maximum competence match is composed by the following parts:

i. All given tasks need to be executed.
ii. Each task is considered preemptive. It is executed by just one developer.
iii. Each developer is working on no more than one task at the same time.
iv. A lower priority task cannot be executed before a higher priority task.
v. The duration needed to execute a task is composed by the time needed for all of its competence-related parts.
vi. The time needed for a competence-related part requesting competency request(m,r) is indirectly proportional to the competence level dcomp(d,r) of the developer dev(d) assigned to this task.

The objective of planning is to find an assignment of developers to tasks such that the overall duration of executing all tasks is minimized.

8.5.2 Solution method

The problem formulated in Section 8.5.1 is a special case of the *resource-constraint project scheduling problem* known to be NP-complete. Our proposed heuristic solution method is applying *greedy search* [Cormen et al. '06]. Greedy search is based on some given order of the objects under consideration. The ordering is given by the priority of the tasks. At each step when a new task is assigned to an idle developer, the selection is done based upon the match of fitness between the requested competence profile and the competence profiles of available developers.

To overcome the limitations of making local decisions, which eventually prevents assignment of more capable developers to a task at a later stage, an additional look-ahead time for the search is introduced. That means, for a given point in time, not only idle developers at this time are considered, but also developers becoming available within the given look-ahead-time are looked at. This is called *greedy-X*, where X is the look-ahead time in days. Further details related to the algorithm and initial empirical results for nine milestones of the Eclipse open source project can be found in [Rahman et al. '09].

8.5.3 Illustrative example

The problem formulation and the proposed solution method are illustrated by an example with 10 tasks. In total, five competencies are taken into account for all these tasks. The competencies are related to Java, mySQL, review, testing and PHP. The requested competence profiles for the 10 tasks are given in Table 8.6.

Table 8.6 Competence profiles (in percentages) for the 10 tasks of the example

Tasks	Java	mySQL	Review	Testing	PHP
task(1)	45	20	0	15	20
task(2)	56	20	0	0	24

Table 8.6 (continued)

Tasks	Java	mySQL	Review	Testing	PHP
task(3)	65	12	0	10	13
task(4)	60	0	40	0	0
task(5)	80	15	0	5	0
task(6)	55	0	18	15	12
task(7)	65	10	25	0	0
task(8)	70	7	23	0	0
task(9)	70	20	0	10	0
task(10)	60	25	3	0	12

For example, task(1) is expected to require 45% of its effort related to Java programming, 20% to mySQL database development, 15% to testing and 20% to PHP. It becomes clear as well that not all competencies are requested for all tasks. Projecting the requested portions to the overall effort results in the effort profiles for the different tasks as presented in Figure 8.4.

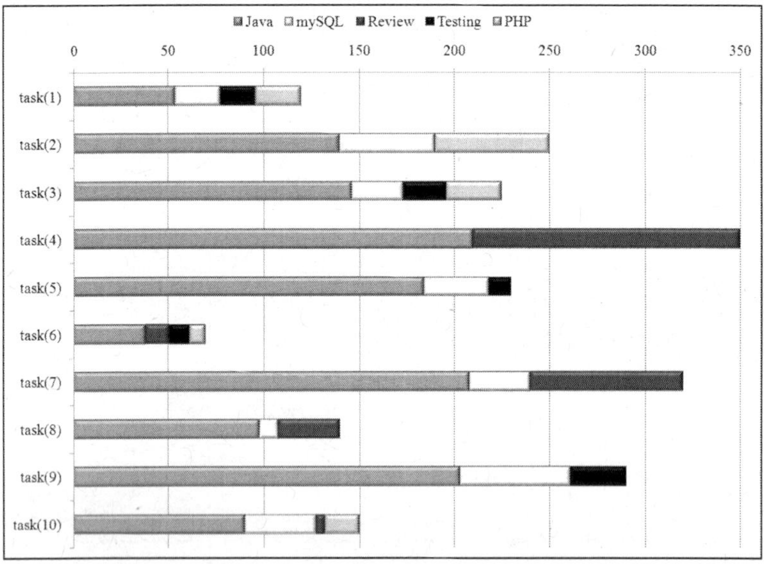

Figure 8.4 Effort profile for the 10 tasks of the example (in person days)

For completing the 10 tasks, a pool of three developers is assumed to be available. Their competence profiles are summarized in Figure 8.5.

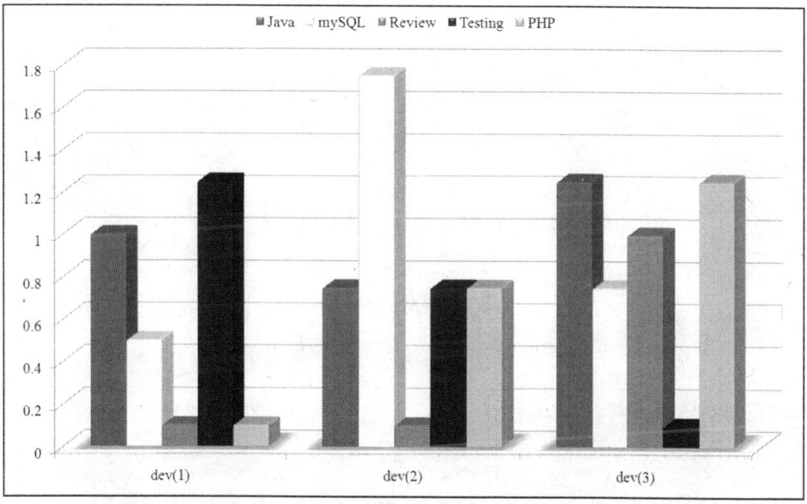

Figure 8.5 Competence profiles for the three developers available

For example, developer dev(1) has an above average productivity in testing, but only very low competencies in terms of both *Reviews* and *PHP*. Solution procedure greedy-X always tries to assign the most competent available developer to the next task in the sequence. This principle is applied from the very beginning until the end (when there are no tasks remaining). In case of no look-ahead time, if no developer is available, than it will assign the task to the developer who is available next, independent of qualification. This might create poor assignments in some cases. To overcome the limited choice of developers, the concept of *look-ahead time X* is introduced.

The Gantt chart in Figure 8.6 shows how different tasks are performed by different developers when staffing is done without look-ahead time. In this case, all tasks will be completed after 227 days. The long duration primarily results from the assignment of the developer being the least appropriate (dev(2)) to the most comprehensive task (task(4)).

Instead of always looking at the best developer available, greedy-15 applies a 15-day look-ahead time. As a result and shown in Figure 8.7, assignments have changed (when compared to Figure 8.6). For example, after finishing task(1), developer dev(2) is not immediately assigned to the next task being task(4). Instead, after a break of 12 days, dev(2) is assigned to task(5) and task(4) is assigned to dev(3), who is more qualified for this task. In total, these re-assignments result in a total duration of 201 days.

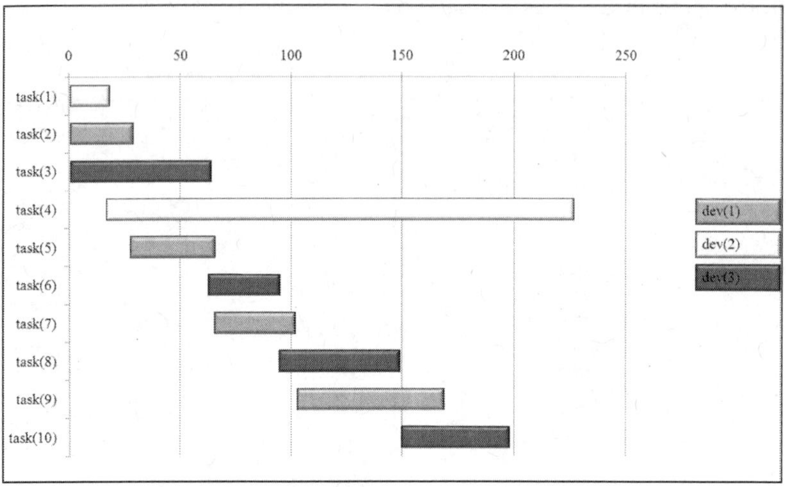

Figure 8.6 Gantt chart for schedule of task implementation from greedy-0

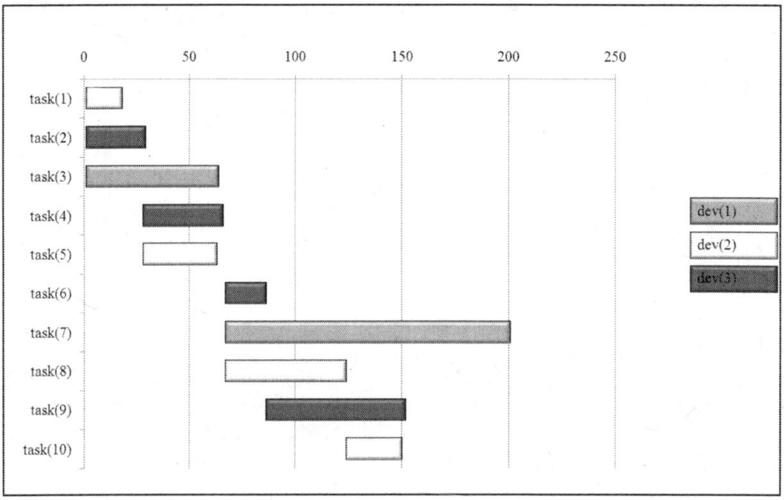

Figure 8.7 Gantt chart resulting from the application of greedy-15

Similar arguments can be made when further increasing the look-ahead time. The results of the application of greedy-30 can be seen in Figure 8.8. dev(1) is used the first time after 30 days for task(5). The total duration is now reduced to 141 days. It can be seen that task(4) now is assigned to dev(3), who is the better choice in terms of the match between requested and available competence profile.

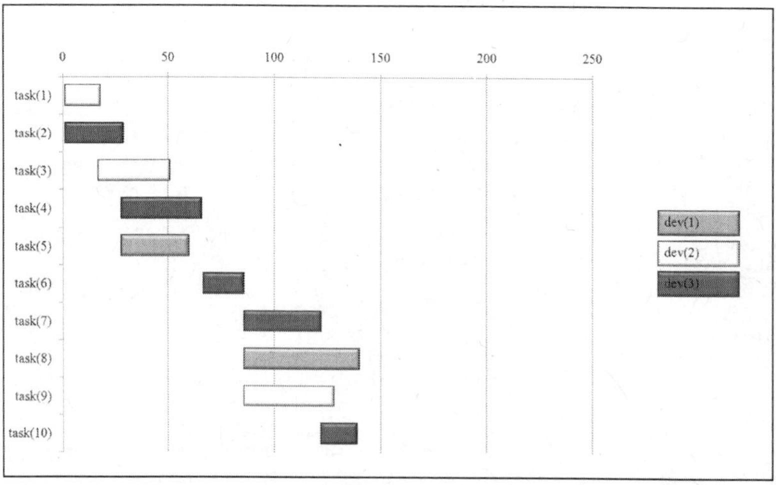

Figure 8.8 Gantt chart resulting from the application of greedy-30

8.6 INDUSTRIAL CASE STUDY

8.6.1 Context and project data

This case study reports about the experience and insights gained from applying staffing for maximum total release value (cf. Section 8.3) at Chartwell Technology [Kapur et al. '08]. Chartwell provides software and services to more then 60 clients who operate in multiple markets, with multiple languages and differing legal jurisdictions. As a result, customer opinions on new features and new requirements often vary widely.

The case study project looked at staffing for two releases ahead of time. The first release period was 8 weeks, the second was 7 weeks. A set of 75 candidate features were considered. These requirements came from the change repository where new or to be modified requirements are stored. Among them, 15 coupling constraints and 1 precedence constraint were taken into account.

The requirements were evaluated by 20 stakeholders. Most of them were sales representatives and able to judge the importance of features for business success. For staffing, a pool of 15 developers was available. Their estimated capabilities for four types of tasks are presented in Table 8.7. Three levels of productivity were defined related to the four types of tasks related to *Flash*, *Action Script*, *Java*, and *DBA*. Although not completely precise, this is a first step to overcome the limitations of considering all developers having the same productivity. Further maturity in productivity measurement is needed to be able to work with more accurate productivity profiles [Kitchenham and Mendes '04].

Table 8.7 Productivity of developers dev(d) for the different types of tasks

Developer ID	Flash	Action Script	Java	DBA
dev(1)	0.75	0.75	1.25	1
dev(2)	0	0	1	1.25
dev(3)	0.75	0	1	1.25
dev(4)	0.75	0	1.25	1.25
dev(5)	0.75	1	1.25	1.25
dev(6)	0	0.75	1.25	1.25
dev(7)	0	0	0.75	1
dev(8)	0	0	1.25	1
dev(9)	1.25	1.25	0.75	0.75
dev(10)	0.75	0.75	1.25	1.25
dev(11)	0.75	0.75	1.25	1.25
dev(12)	0	0	1.25	1.25
dev(13)	0	0	1.25	0
dev(14)	0.75	0	1.25	1.25
dev(15)	0	0	1.25	1

8.6.2 Main findings

The main findings of the case study project are related to a comparison between manual planning based upon intuition and experience and optimized planning applying the method described in Section 8.3. The resulting solutions are called *x-manual* and *x-optimized*, respectively. Three main findings were gained. They are described in the following.

Finding 1: Quality of plans

A formal comparison of the two plans indicated that the optimized plan was about 43.5% better in terms of the stated quality criteria (satisfaction of stakeholders). Another indicator of the improved quality is the number of features provided according to both plans. While the optimized plan offers 52 features with the two releases, it offers only 42 features for the manual plan.

Finding 2: Quality of staffing

An assignment of a developer to a task is classified as as *good, average* or *bad* if the competence level of the developer for this task is above average (prod(d,q) = 1.25), average (prod(d,q) = 1), or below average (prod(d,q) = 0.75), respectively.

A formal comparison of the two plans indicates that the optimized plan has more (in total) assignments of developers to tasks. The total number of assignments has increased from 161 to 203 with an increase of the good assignments from 136 to 155 when moving from manual to optimized planning.

Figure 8.9 presents the comparison of the assignments for each of the 15 individual developers. At the horizontal axis, all the 15 developers under consideration are listed. For each of them, the task assignment between *manual* and *optimized* is compared. The comparison itself is done in terms of counting how often each developer is assigned to tasks in the respective plans. The count is done for each productivity category, that is, counting when a developer has above average (*good*), average (*average*) or below average (*bad*) competencies for an assigned task. In most of the cases, the number and quality of the assignments in the optimal staffing plan are better than in the manual staffing plan. The main improvement over the manual plan is the increase of the absolute number of assignments to tasks. This increase corresponds to more effective utilization of developer resources.

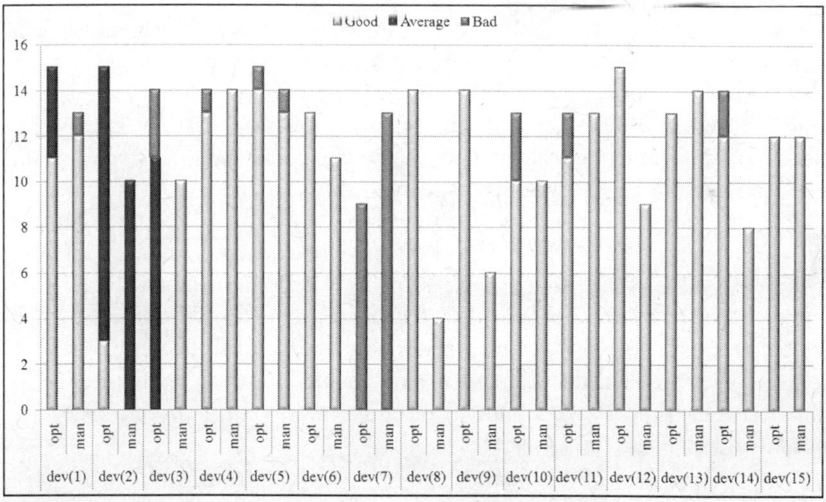

Figure 8.9 Quality of assignment: Comparison between manual (man) and optimized (opt) task assignments for each of the 15 developers [Kapur et al. '08]

Finding 3: Effort required

Besides the improved quality, the comparison also reveals a significant advantage for the optimized staffing plan in terms of effort needed. The time savings becomes more significant the more additional re-planning or proactive what-if analysis is conducted. In reality, this is happening quite often, in order to adjust to change or to run possible planning scenarios.

On average, experienced project managers spend one third of their time to handle the planning process manually. This substantial amount of effort compares with seconds of running the algorithms plus the initial effort to set-up the formalized planning process, which is in the order of two to three hours.

8.6.3 Discussion

Staffing for product releases is an extremely complex endeavor. Any ad hoc assignment would likely be deemed a waste of time and/or resources. Since human resources are typically the most critical resources for project success, any support for managers to perform staffing based on computer support looks promising [Kapur et al '08].

To provide meaningful staffing results, project and product managers need to consider a variety of factors. Not all of them are included in the proposed model (for example, organizational factors, process factors, or human factors related to staffing were not taken into account). The main argument is that a good solution to a reasonable approximation of the real-world problem already is a step forward in determining a practically applicable solution.

The same arguments are applicable to address the inherent uncertainty of data. Effort and productivity estimates are approximations and prone to errors. From running different scenarios (instantiations of the problem with varying parameter settings) of the given problem, the impact of parameter variations can be better understood. This proactive analysis is considered to be an essential step to facilitate better and more objective decisions made by the product and project manager.

The main practical benefits of qualifying the staffing and resource allocation process can be expected in terms of more effective resource utilization and improved (higher) total value of the proposed release plans. This value can be seen in financial terms or in terms of a better overall stakeholder satisfaction. In order to achieve these benefits, processes for planning and road-mapping of software releases, effort and resource estimation, definition of the values of features in relation to time and evaluation of the productivity of human resources need to be in place and need to be constantly qualified.

CHAPTER 9

ADVANCED TOPICS

9.1 INTRODUCTION

The main content of this book so far has been devoted to processes and methods directly applicable to decision-making for product releases. Making good decisions is not a release planning issue in isolation. Instead, there are a number of enabling technologies having direct impact on results and their acceptance. Two of them are studied in this chapter as an advanced topic or research:

- How to qualify effort estimation in the context of release planning?
- How to increase acceptance of decision support provided to users?

In some decision scenarios, the scope needs to be enlarged to cover the more complex reality. Two of these advanced models are studied in this chapter as well:

- How to make release decisions in the presence of design considerations?
- How to evaluate proactively the impact of uncertainty on the overall duration of implementation of a set of features?

These four topics are areas of recent and ongoing research. They are studied by explaining their main content and in highlighting their practical value. The commonality between all of them is that they are designed to qualify and support the product release planning process.

In this chapter, four advanced topics, closely related to making release decisions, are considered. In the order of the sections, the content covers part of the PhD work done by Jingzhou Li [Li '07], Gengshen Du [Du '09], Omolade Saliu [Saliu '07] and Ahmed Al-Emran [Al-Emran et al. '10]. The content of each section is presented in close relationship to some former chapters and examples given there. The emphasis is to describe key aspects of the approach and to provide some illustrative examples. In all cases, potential application scenarios are outlined.

9.2 EFFORT ESTIMATION FOR RELEASE PLANNING

9.2.1 Motivation

One of the pre-requisites for product release planning is knowledge of effort consumption for implementing the features. Therefore, the effort for each individual feature needs to be estimated before release planning can be conducted. Different from the effort estimation for a single project, effort estimation for a set of features of a product is more challenging in that there may be tens or even hundreds of features of a product involved in the release planning process. Although manual estimation is always an option, techniques for automated or at least semi-automated effort estimation are considered more efficient. While the problem and the solution approach are formulated in terms of effort estimation, it can be applied in the same way to cost and resource estimation.

The principle of *estimation by analogy* (EBA) is to derive effort estimates for new objects from analogous ones from a historical database (DB). For effort estimation in the context of release planning, the historical DB is composed of a set of features and a set of attributes characterizing the features. DB is arranged as a table with features and attributes corresponding to rows and columns, respectively. The set of features in DB is denoted by HF = {hf(m)} (m=1...M).These features are taken from former product releases with their actual effort values known. The values for all selected attributes are assumed to be given for all features. However, some estimation methods such as AQUA [Li '07] may tolerate missing values.

For a given feature f(n), the principal solution approach is to find the top similar features from HF denoted by HF(n) and combine their (actual) efforts to a prediction for effort(n). The estimation using the effort information from the analogs is called *analogy adaptation*. The set HF(n) of the L(n) most similar features is called the *top L(n) analogs* related to feature f f(n).

The effort to be estimated for implementing a new feature f(n) from the set of candidate features CF for the next releases is denoted by effort(n) (n = 1...N), The problem of *EBA-based effort estimation for product release planning* is formulated as follows:

(9.1) Estimate effort(n) for all candidate features f(n) of CF based on the knowledge about effort of top L(n) analogs of F(n)

9.2.2 Estimation by analogy method AQUA$^+$

One of the key issues for EBA is that it is unknown up front which value for the number of analogs works best in which situation. Some researchers proposed using a certain fixed number of analogs, for example, L(n) = 3 for all n. Estimation method AQUA$^+$ [Li et al. '07] is an EBA method that overcomes this limitation by up-front application of a learning process to determine L(n) and the related set of historical features HF(n) for a given feature f(n). The learning process is executed against the historical database DB. In AQUA$^+$, the concept of the historical database is applicable to objects that may be requirements, features of a product or even complete projects. In what follows, a feature of a product in the context of release planning is referred to as object in AQUA$^+$.

AQUA$^+$ employs local and global similarity measures and a set of accuracy and acceptance criteria to determine the sets HF(n) of features f(n). In general terms, *local similarity* measures the similarity between two objects over a single attribute; while *global similarity* measures the similarity between two objects over a given set of attributes. Global similarity is an aggregation of local similarity measures. For two objects *a* and *b*, its global similarity is denoted by Gsim(a, b).

One of the strengths of the AQUA$^+$ method is that it can tolerate missing values in DB, when calculating local and global similarity measures. While missing values do not prevent the application of the method, it is only possible at the cost of estimation accuracy, that is, the more missing values are in the DB, the less accurate the estimation will be. Examples of accuracy criteria used in AQUA$^+$ are *MMRE* (Mean Magnitude of Relative Error) and *Pred(α)* (Prediction at a certain level α of accuracy). Detailed definitions and discussions about missing values, similarity measures, and accuracy criteria can be found in [Li '07].

The main process of AQUA$^+$ consists of four phases called *preprocessing*, *attribute weighting*, *learning*, and *estimation*. During preprocessing, erroneous values are filtered and missing values are dealt with. The phase of attribute weighting addresses the question: Which are the most critical attributes in their contribution to the final estimate? In principle, any method for attribute weighting can be used in this phase. Example heuristics for attribute weighting can be found in [Tosun et al. '09] and [Li and Ruhe '08].

The key idea of AQUA$^+$ is to perform some learning for the purpose of making a recommendation on the number L(n) of similar objects (features) to be considered for estimation of effort(n). Learning is performed in the historical feature DB. Leave-one-out (or jack-knife, see [Efron and Gong '83]) cross-validation is applied by varying the number L of analogs and the threshold T for their global similarity. The result is the *accuracy distribution database,* which is then used to make suggestions for the actual values of parameters L(n) and T(n) for effort estimation of a new feature f(n).

The process to determine effort(n) is illustrated in Figure 9.1. Initially, the new feature is compared with all the features in the historical DB and the corresponding similarity measures are determined. In the illustrative example, the historical feature hf(3) has been found to be the most similar, and hf(8) the second most similar to the new feature f(n).

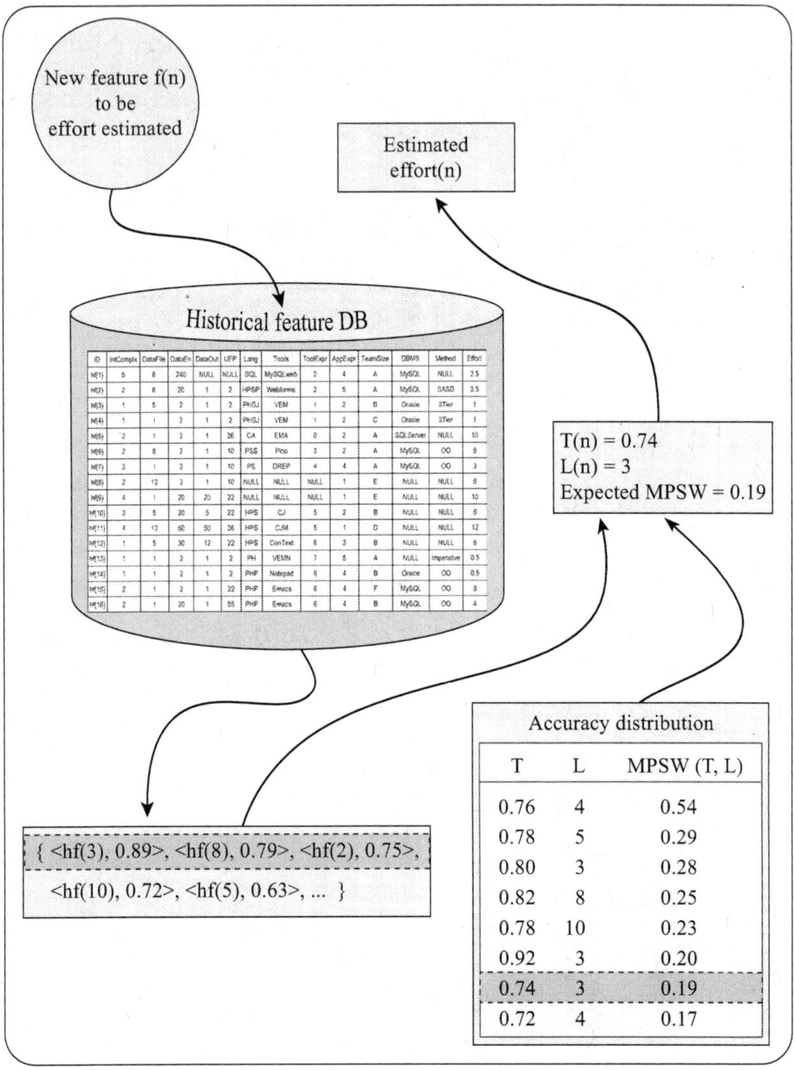

Figure 9.1 Effort estimation by retrieving and combining closest analogs

For answering the question how many similar features should be taken into account for effort estimation of the new feature f(n), the accuracy distribution database AccuDistr(DB) needs to be retrieved. AccuDistr(DB) has been obtained from the learning phase. The entries in the table represent all learned combinations of T, L and the resulting value MPSW(T, L), which is defined as a weighted linear combination of three atomic measures *MMRE*, *Pred*, and *Strength* [Li '07]. The higher the value is, the higher the assumed prediction accuracy. All the entries in the table are ordered decreasingly according to MPSW and (in case of equal values) ordered increasingly according to T and L. It can be seen that best prediction results were obtained for L(n) = 3 objects with a similarity threshold of T(n) = 0.74.

The next step finds the matched T(n) and L(n) in AccuDistr(DB): T(n) = 0.74 and L(n) = 3, with expected prediction accuracy MPSW(0.74, 3) = 0.19, because this is the first row satisfying the condition that there are three analogs in the vectors with global similarities equal to or greater than 0.74. Therefore, the top analogs and their corresponding global similarity measures are determined as shown in (9.2):

(9.2) <hf(3), 0.89>, <hf(8), 0.79>, <hf(2), 0.75>

Consequently, the set of similar features related to f(n) is defined as HF(n) = {hf(3), hf(8), hf(2)}. Finally, the estimated effort for a given object under estimation is calculated as the weighted average of the efforts of the top analogous. For that, their corresponding global similarity measures are applied as weighting factors.

9.2.3 AQUA-RP: A method for integration between release planning and effort estimation

The integration between the process of release planning (following EVOLVE II described in Chapter 6) and the continuous application of learning and prediction as suggested by AQUA^{+} (see Section 9.2.2) is outlined in Figure 9.2.

The set of candidate features has been pre-selected from the feature repository to become the input for the planning process. Attribute values characterizing the features are prepared as input for the later estimation process. Stakeholders are involved in this process as long as estimates need to be made. Stakeholder participation is continued until the final steps of balancing between (i) the estimates generated automatically from applying the learning-based estimation and (ii) applying expert judgment. This combination is called *hybrid estimation* in Figure 9.2.

The result of this hybrid estimation is the input for the estimation-based release planning process. The integration of EBA method AQUA^{+} into the process of ongoing release planning and organizational learning is called *AQUA-RP*. The stakeholder participation at the hybrid estimation process is seen as an effective means for collecting expert knowledge for the purpose of organizational learning [Ruhe '01]. The continuous update of the historical feature DB by the features implemented for each release is part of this organizational learning process.

9.2.4 Discussion of applicability

In addition to the strengths and weaknesses of EBA in general [Li et al. '07], the applicability of AQUA-RP is discussed below. Main advantages are:

- Flexibility in terms of granularity: AQUA-RP provides effort estimation at levels of requirement, feature and project, other than only project level as in previous EBA methods. Therefore, product release planning at different levels can be supported by this method.

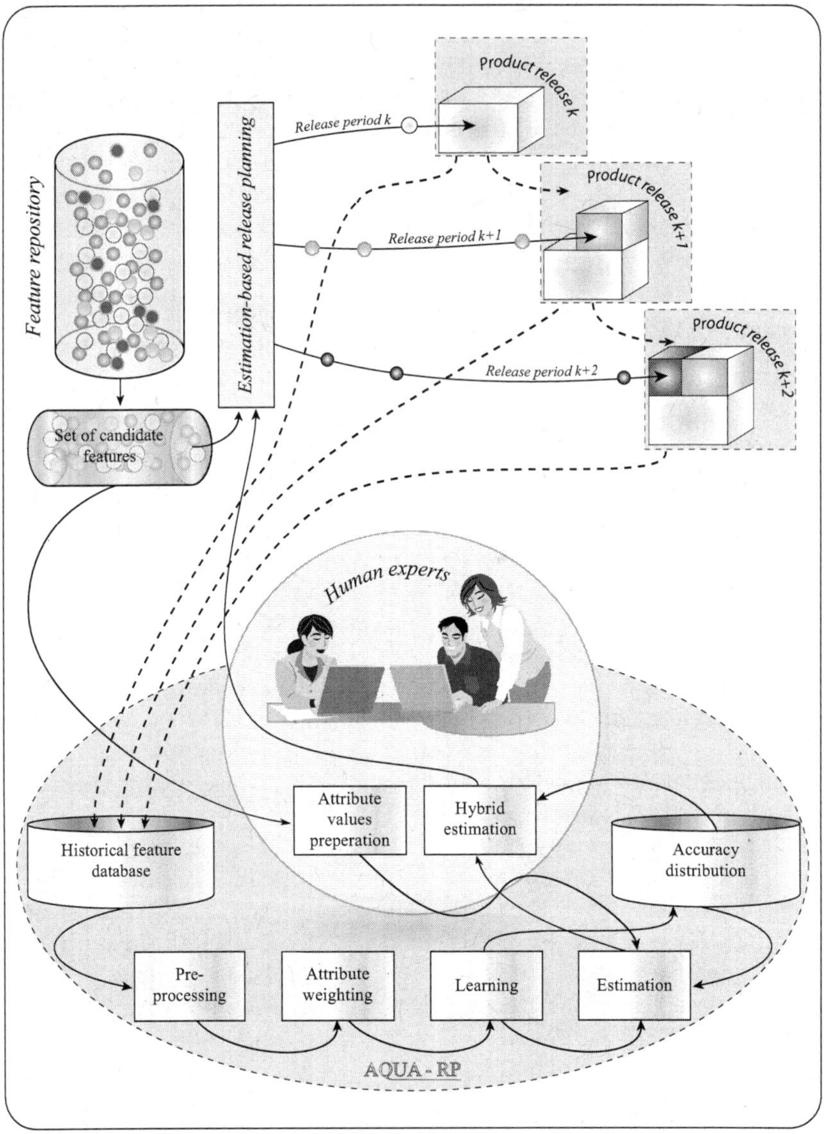

Figure 9.2 Workflow of estimation-based release planning method AQUA-RP

- Flexibility in terms of attribute types: Set, nominal, fuzzy-set and interval attributes are supported, not only numerical attributes as used in most previous methods. This extends the applicability of analogy-based effort estimation methods.

- Using experience and expert judgment: Since the context in which the analogous were implemented might be different from that of the object under planning, conditions and constraints about the analogous are taken into consideration in the method.
- Expert judgment from various stakeholders being involved in the effort estimation is aggregated instead of using the result from a single stakeholder. This is part of the automated estimation process.

Despite the advantages mentioned above, there are limitations as well. First, since EBA is a data-driven approach, the quality of data affects the quality of estimation and the applicability of the method. Second, compared to former EBA methods, the learning phase for AQUA$^+$ requires extra effort to get the set of closest analogous in order to determine the top analogs. Third, the total effort of AQUA-RP is substantial. It will vary in dependence of the number of stakeholders involved, the number of attributes used, and the number of estimates needed per feature. Careful considerations have to be made on *how much accuracy is enough* and which stakeholders, attributes and estimates contribute most to the quality of the results.

9.3 DECISION SUPPORT BY EXPLANATION OF RESULTS

9.3.1 Motivation

A decision support system (DSS) is a computer-based solution used to support complex decision making and problem solving. Research in this area typically focuses on how information technology can improve the efficiency, effectiveness and transparency of the decision-making process. By analyzing the last decade of existence of these systems, within and beyond the domain of software engineering, hesitation of decision makers to trust the computer-based solutions has been analyzed. This tendency was evaluated and confirmed for ReleasePlanner™, the decision support tool for product release planning, as well.

A series of controlled experiments was conducted to explore the user's *confidence* in this tool's solutions and *trust* of the tool itself [Du et al. '06]. A major finding revealed that the tool's user acceptance was not very high, even though the tool's solutions were more accurate and were generated more efficiently compared to the manual approach. Similar results were received by [Lethola et al. '04]. They compared a manual versus a more formalized procedure for pair-wise comparison of requirements. One of the main findings was that participants mistrusted the results they got from the more formalized method.

In [Carlsson and Turban '02] it was concluded that the main barriers for broader acceptance of solutions offered by decision support systems are not technology-related, but *people problems*:

i. People have cognitive constraints in adopting intelligent systems;
ii. People do not really understand the support they get and disregard it in favor of past experience and visions;

iii. People cannot really handle large amounts of information and knowledge;
iv. People are frustrated by theories they do not really understand; and
v. People believe that they get more support by talking to other people.

For decision problems that involve complex trade-offs or optimization, such as product release planning problems, the advice or solutions generated by the DSS may be difficult to be accepted by the users because they do not understand the reasons why these solutions were suggested.

This section provides the outline of a method to create explanation for solutions offered by ReleasePlanner™ (which is discussed in more detail in Section 10.3). The method is based on combining results from machine learning. In particular, it applies three specific techniques called *rough set analysis* (RSA), *dependency network analysis* (DNA), and *concept analysis* (CA). In what follows, a brief overview of these techniques is given.

9.3.2 Explanation generated by the application of machine learning algorithms

Machine learning is a well-established method which has been successfully applied in various areas of science and engineering. [Menzies '01] has outlined various applications of machine learning in the area of software engineering and knowledge engineering. They include prediction, classification, diagnosis, planning and monitoring.

Explanation as part of decision support is some form of diagnosis. Three machine learning techniques have been studied and evaluated in terms of their capability to provide explanation for better acceptance of results. All these techniques assume that data is represented by a decision table with rows and columns corresponding to objects and attributes describing the objects, respectively. The values of the attributes are assumed to be on nominal or ordinal scale. If this is not naturally the case, some form of discretization is applied.

Rough set analysis [Pawlak '91] is a machine learning technique aiming to characterize objects by means of lower and upper approximations by means of information provided from a set of condition and decision attributes'. Knowledge obtained from rough set-based analysis of experimental data is represented by means of production rules that describe the relationships between premises (related to condition attributes) and conclusions (related to decision attributes). The objects in the data set are partitioned into subsets such that all the objects of one subset have the same values for the explanatory variables. It might be the case that these subsets do not change even after a few independent variables are discarded. Some explanatory variables may be redundant and thus can be removed without affecting the accuracy of classification of the objects in the data set. On the other side, some of the explanatory variables are core attributes, which means that their elimination would decrease the accuracy of classification.

Dependency network analysis [Heckerman et al. '00] is a machine learning technique aimed to build graphical models of probabilistic relationships. Explanatory knowledge derived from this type of analysis is represented in the form of dependency networks to highlight the subset of premises that influence the conclusions the most. In addition, decision trees are also generated to describe the detailed causal relationships between the most influencing premises and conclusions, along with the probabilistic distributions of all the possible values of the decision attribute. This technique starts with independently performing a probabilistic inference for each premise. Once the estimates on the local distributions of all premises are available, the structure of the dependency network from the estimated distributions is constructed and a joint probabilistic distribution for the domain is calculated and represented by dependency networks and decision trees.

Concept analysis [Wille '82] is a machine learning technique to identify conceptual structures among a set of data. This technique investigates the relations between objects and their attributes in a decision table. A *formal concept* demonstrates a common pattern, that is, a relationship, among a subset of premises for a subset of the objects. All formal concepts identified from a decision table are called a *complete concept lattice*, based upon which a subset of premises having the most impact on conclusions can be identified. Unlike the relationships identified by RSA and DNA, which are independent from each other, the relationships identified by CA can be generalized or specialized to other relationships in the same complete concept lattice.

Various tools implementing these machine learning techniques have been developed, such as ROSE2 [ROSE2] for RSA, the WinMine toolkit [WinMine] for DNA, and the open source library Colibri/Java [Colibri/Java] for CA.

9.3.3 The approach *EXPLAIN-RP*

The explanation approach called *EXPLAIN-RP* is aimed to provide two types of explanations out of a sequence of learning examples. Once generated, both forms of explanation are not intended to be valid in general, but just for a specific problem context.

- *Explanation type 1:* A subset of the most important condition attributes in terms of their impact on the decision attributes.
- *Explanation type 2:* Formulation of if-then rules between combinations of condition attributes with their values and corresponding decision attribute values.

Figure 9.3 shows the roles of these explanations for ReleasePlanner™. The underlying hypothesis is that more insights into the justification of specific solutions are provided by both types of explanation.

To generate these explanations, a three-step procedure is involved. The first step called *preparation* is to specify and prepare the decision table. In the context of product release planning, the rows in this table correspond to the features defined for the project under investigation. The columns correspond to the planning attributes or to a combination of attributes. In addition, one column corresponds to the decision variable being the release assignment of the feature (specific to the explanations generated in this section).

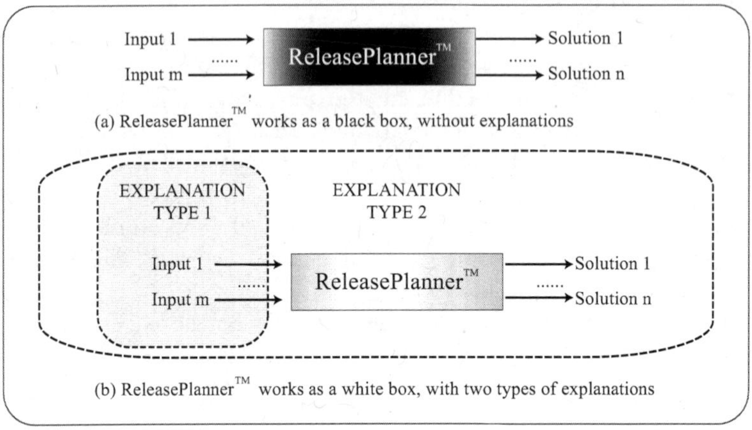

Figure 9.3 Usage of ReleasePlanner™ with and without EXPLAIN-RP

In the second step called *generation*, the three machine learning techniques RSA, DNA and CA are applied to analyze the decision table prepared in the first step. Two types of results can be generated from these three techniques: (i) a subset of planning attributes that have the greatest impact on output solutions (Explanation type 1), and (ii) if-then rules between planning attributes and output solutions (Explanation type 2).

In the third step called *integration,* the individual results generated from the three techniques are analyzed and integrated for each explanation type. As a result, the integrated results are based on multiple techniques. Therefore, they are expected to be more reliable than just having the individual results of each technique in isolation.

9.3.4 Explanation for the Telco case study project

In what follows, the application of RSA is presented as an example instantiation of the proposed procedure. For this purpose, the Telco sample project (introduced in Chapter 3) is reconsidered. Two instances (set of all parameter settings) of this sample project were analyzed in this example.

Preparation: The various condition attributes (related to premises) and decision attributes (related to conclusions) are defined. Score(n,Frequency) and Score(n,Urgency) are condition attributes that indicate the weighted average of individual stakeholder scores for the criteria *frequency of use* and *urgency*, respectively. Another condition attribute is called *ResRatio(n,Design)*, which is defined as the resource consumption ratio for feature f(n) related to the capacity of the *Design* resource. Similar attributes are defined for the other four resources:

- ResRatio(n,SWDevelop),
- ResRatio(n,HWDevelop),
- ResRatio(n,Testing), and
- ResRatio(n,Cost).

A formal definition of the attributes is left out here, but can be found in [Du and Ruhe '09a]. The values of the above condition attributes are transformed to ordinal scale. In our case, the values of the condition attributes are discretized to *high*, *medium* and *low*. The value of the decision attribute indicates the release number for the feature of that row. This is defined on an ordinal scale. The decision table used for RSA contains 200 objects. These learning objects result from 20 features under investigation, all of them part of the five generated release plans for each of the two project instances investigated. The term *project instance* refers to a complete set of values for all project parameters.

Generation: The decision table determined above is input to the ROSE2 tool for RSA. Two parts of explanation results are generated for the Telco project under investigation. In the first part of the results, in total five condition attributes are identified by ROSE2 as the most important among all the defined condition attributes. They are Score(n, Frequency), ResRatio(n, Design), ResRatio(n, SWDevelop), ResRatio(n, HWDevelop) and ResRatio(n, Cost).

As the second part of RSA results, ROSE2 generates 18 if-then decision rules. They highlight the relations between the condition and decision attributes defined in the context of the Telco project. Table 9.1 shows two example rules derived. The first rule indicates that if there is a feature f(n), with *high* weighted average of stakeholder scores on the criterion *frequency of use*, and *low* level of consumption on the resource type *testing*, then this feature is assigned to release R14. This rule has a strength of 10%. That means that for 20 out of the total 200 objects this rule is applicable.

Table 9.1 Example relationships between the condition and decision attribute

Rule 1 (strength: 10%)	
IF	Score(n,Frequency) = *high* AND ResRatio(n,Testing) = *low*
THEN	x(n) = R14
Rule 2 (strength: 5%)	
IF	ResRatio(n,Design) = *high* AND ResRatio(n,Cost) = *high*
THEN	x(n) = PP

In general the expectation is that, the more problem-solution pairs exist, the higher the chance to generate meaningful explanation results. All the problem-solution pairs should come from the same context.

Integration: To make this example simple, only one machine learning technique was applied for explanation generation. Therefore, integration of results from different techniques is not applicable. For further details on the process of integration see [Du and Ruhe '09a].

9.3.5 Applicability of Results

To evaluate the usefulness of the above explanations for the overall acceptance of the release planning tool, a controlled experiment was conducted [Du and Ruhe '09b]. Subjects from both academia and IT industry evaluated the usefulness of the explanation generated from the application of RSA, DNA and CA. The acceptance of the tool was measured in terms of the users' *degrees of confidence* in the tool solutions and in terms of the *trust* in the tool itself.

The results indicated that the confidence and trust levels of a majority of the users were improved after they were provided with the explanations generated. Figure 9.4 provides further details on that. At least 40.0% of the users in the experiment had *some increase* with the three types of explanations, and at least another 26.7% had *significant increase*. This increase was confirmed in a similar way for all of the three techniques.

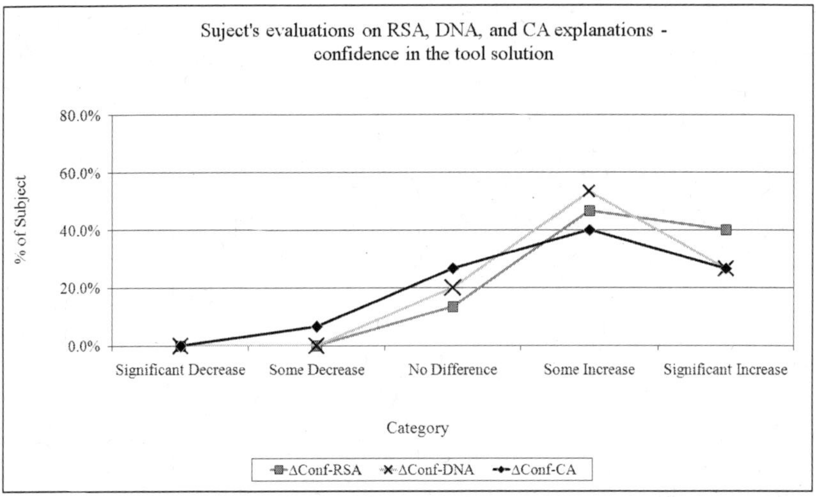

Figure 9.4 Improvement of user confidence in tool solutions with the explanations [Du and Ruhe '09b]

To improve the efficiency of the process, a software tool was developed to automatically generate explanations based on the given planning data. Figure 9.5 shows a sample screenshot for generation of the second type of explanation discussed in this section. A more detailed description of the tool is available at [EXPLAIN-RP].

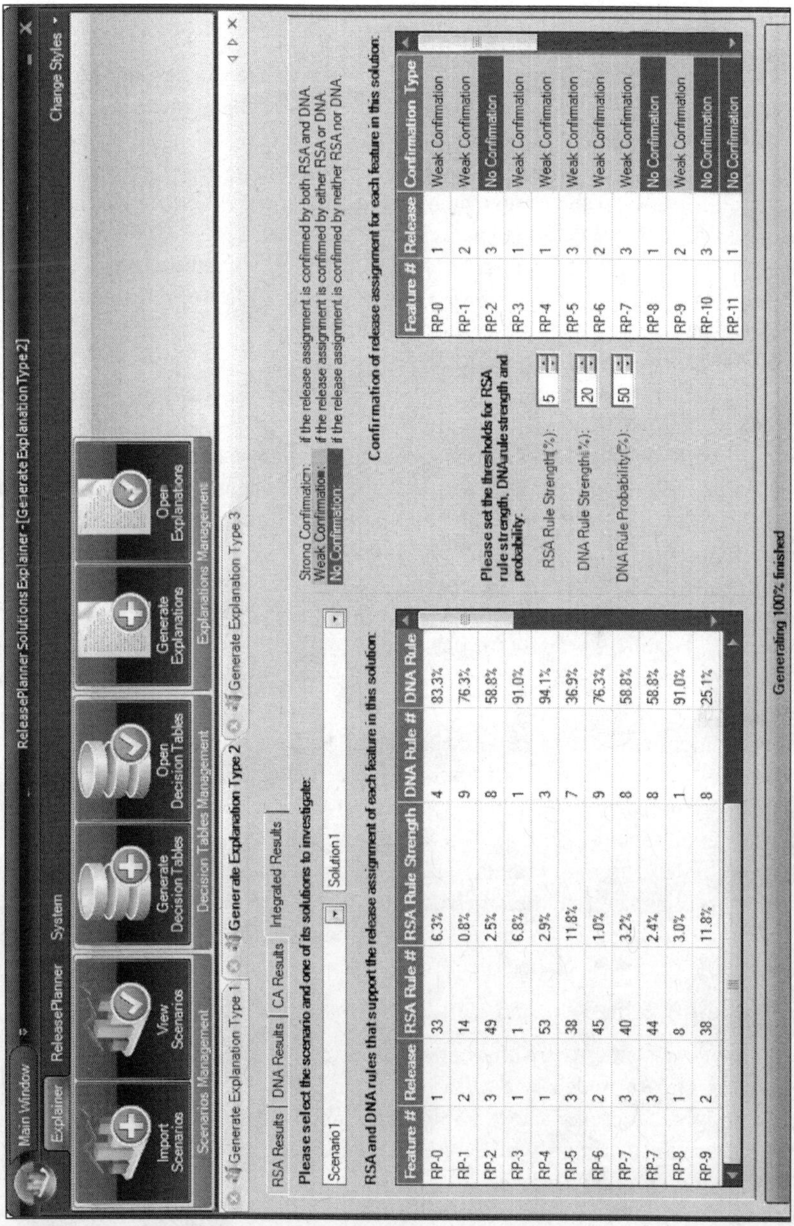

Figure 9.5 Sample screenshot from EXPLAIN-RP for explanation type 2

9.4 RELEASE PLANNING IN CONSIDERATION OF DESIGN CONSTRAINTS

9.4.1 Motivation

Software systems have the tendency to evolve because of the ongoing need to extend functionality of the system by adding new features or removing defects [Lehman '96]. Release planning for large software systems is complex from a business perspective. The *business perspective* on release planning captures the concerns of business stakeholders, which include users, customers, management and marketing departments (in case of market-driven products).

However, system constraints might have a substantial impact on time and cost of feature implementation [Lindgren et al. '08]. This relates to dependencies between features and the existing code base, and potential reuse of code. This is called the *technical perspective* on release planning. Work studied in this section is motivated by the importance of simultaneously addressing the business and the technical perspective.

In evolutionary product development, release planning needs to consider design decisions already implemented in the existing architecture of the system. This eventually restricts its ability to easily accommodate future sequences of releases. In addition, some of the features to be implemented overlap in the components that would implement them in the existing system. If there exist overlaps in the components that would implement two or more features in the existing system, the features are said to be *interdependent*. At this point, the granularity of considerations is not pre-defined. Components could be subsystems, modules, files, classes or packages.

From a technical perspective, it would be desirable to cluster interdependent features together in the same release. This could help to reduce the cognitive complexity associated with understanding the implementation of features, thereby resulting in reduced development effort. By implementing interrelated features together, it may be possible also to avoid unplanned dependency among code elements, which could result from haphazard implementation of features [Giroux and Robillard '06]. However, this clustering is not necessarily the best choice of sequencing features when taking the business perspective.

9.4.2 Modeling feature dependencies in the solution domain

Modeling of the business concerns of release planning has been provided in Chapter 5. The functionality provided by a software system is derived from the domain of the problem through collection of new features or change requests or both. The users of a software system are primarily interested in the functionality that the system offers. This is called the *problem domain*.

Software developers, on the other hand, examine features and change requests in terms of the development activities that are required to implement the features.

This is called the *solution domain*. Features potentially depend on each other both in the problem domain (because they share requirements or depend on each other for services), and in the solution domain (because they share subsystems or modules) [Turner et al. '99].

The focus of this analysis is on feature dependency in the solution domain. It is modeled as the intersection of the components impacted by the implementation of the feature. The existence of solution domain dependency between features is equivalent with the non-zero overlap of their set of impacted components.

Definition (SD-dependency)**:** Given two features f(n) and f(m) with their impacted components Impact(n) and Impact(m), respectively. The two features are called *SD-dependent* if the intersection of Impact(n) and Impact(m) is non-empty. □

A feature could share impacted components with one or more other features, but the number of such shared components could vary. The strength of SD-dependency between any pair of features refers to the degree of dependency that exists between the two features.

Definition (Strength of SD-dependency)**:** Given a pair of features f(n) and f(m) with corresponding sets of impacted components Impact(n) and Impact(m). Suppose Com(n,m) is the set of common components between Impact(n) and Impact(m). Then the *strength of SD-dependency* SSD(n,m) between f(n) and f(m) is defined as:

(9.3) SSD(n,m) = [card(Com(n,m))]·[card(Impact(n)) + card(Impact(m))]/ 2·card(Impact(n)·card(Impact(m)) □

Metric (9.3) is based on the cardinality card() of the set of common components, and the cardinalities of the set of impacted components for each pair of features being considered. This metric is normalized to allow for meaningful comparisons. The higher the strength of SD-dependency, the more the two features are assumed to be interrelated. A complete dependency (SSD(n,m) = 1) between a pair of features f(n) and f(m) exists if and only if the two features are realized by exactly the same set of components.

For a feature f(n), a system value *Svalue(n)* is defined based on the number of features with which the feature shares impacted components. For a more formal definition of Svalue(n), the set of components Adjacent(n) is introduced in (9.4).

(9.4) Adjacent(Impact(n)) = {Impact(m): Impact(n) and Impact(m) have non-empty intersection}

Definition (System value)**:** Let f(n) be a feature with a set of impacted components Impact(n) and let *Adjacent(n)* be the set of adjacent components of Impact(n) defined in (9.4). Then the system value Svalue(n) of a feature f(n) is defined as:

(9.5) $\text{Svalue}(n) = \Sigma_{m:\ \text{Impact}(m) \in \text{Adjacent}(\text{Impact}(n))}\ \text{SSD}(n,m)$ □

It is desirable to implement the highest system-valued features in early releases because they have the highest potential implementation synergy with other features. This is based on the assumption that implementing features that share a high number of implementation components together would result in reuse of implemented components.

9.4.3 Solution method

The *stakeholder feature points* sfp(n,x) for a feature f(n) according to plan x are a measure describing the total number of feature points collected from the different stakeholders and considering all (business) planning criteria.

To keep the description simple and because data become more uncertain for later releases, planning is considered for just the next release (K = 1). Then the (business) objective of planning F1(x) is to maximize the *total number of stakeholder feature points* achieved in the next release among all feasible plans x.

$$(9.6) \qquad F1(x) = \Sigma_{n:\, x(n) = 1}\ sfp(n,x)$$

The formulation of objective F2(x) is motivated by the objective to maximize the assignment of features with high interrelatedness as well as high strength of SD-dependency into the same release. F2(x) is defined as:

$$(9.7) \qquad F2(x) = \Sigma_{n:\, x(n) = 1}\ Svalue(n)$$

Among all feasible planning alternatives, the problem is to determine a set of trade-off solutions x*. Looking for trade-off solutions means determining all plans x* with the property that there is no other plan x' with

$$(9.8) \qquad (F1(x'), F2(x')) \geq (F1(x^*), F2(x^*)) \text{ and } (F1(x'), F2(x')) \neq (F1(x^*), F2(x^*))$$

A detailed discussion of the solution methodology is not the purpose of this section and can be found in [Saliu '07]. The key constituents of the solution method are:

- Handling the business concerns using priorities of features specified by the stakeholders for all business planning criteria.
- Modeling of technical concerns of implementing features in the existing system.
- Quantifying the potential synergy in the implementation of features as a result of their dependency analysis.
- Calculation of alternative plans constituting trade-off solutions between the business and technical implementation objectives.

9.4.4 Applicability of the Model

To investigate the applicability of the proposed release planning approach, a case study was conducted using real-world data collected on the evolving ReleasePlanner™ system. The system is structured into eight main components, and the challenge was to select feasible release alternatives, which look at both their business impact and the potential synergies in the stage of implementation.

N = 33 candidate features were considered for the next release of the product. Three stakeholders have been involved in the prioritization of the features from the perspective of their value. Five types of resources were taken into account related to performing analysis, implementation, quality assurance, user interface design and research. Details of the data can be found in [Saliu '07].

The list of all features f(n) with their impacted components Impact(n) is given in Table 9.2. What can be seen is that the implementation of the feature f(1) described as *Comparative analysis with manual solutions* impacts six out of the eight components C1…C8 of the system. This components are related to the functionality of Reporting, Validator, IP component, Java brokers, Import/export component, Stakeholder voting analysis, DB connectivity, and Alternative analysis wizard, respectively.

Table 9.2 Features f(n) and impacted components Impact(n)

Feature		Impacted components							
ID	Description	C1	C2	C3	C4	C5	C6	C7	C8
1	Comparative analysis with manual solutions	X		X	X	X		X	X
2	Record of history of sets of alternative solutions	X			X	X		X	X
3	Conformance across alternative solutions	X			X			X	X
4	Comparison within one set and across sets	X			X			X	X
5	MS excel advanced compatibility				X	X		X	
6	MS Project compatibility				X	X		X	
7	Compatibility with requirement management tools				X	X		X	
8	Generation of solutions based on selected criteria	X		X	X			X	
9	Planning across projects	X	X	X	X		X	X	X
10	Re-planning capabilities	X							X
11	Allowing splitting of features over two releases	X	X	X	X			X	X
12	Accommodation of different skill sets	X	X	X	X	X	X	X	X
13	Fuzzy boundaries	X			X			X	X
14	Value-risk trade-off	X						X	X
15	Multiple windows							X	

Table 9.2 (continued)

Feature		Impacted components							
ID	Feature description	C1	C2	C3	C4	C5	C6	C7	C8
16	Integrated Excel sheet					X		X	
17	Dashboard to show user actual study of project planning				X			X	
18	UI redevelopment	X					X		X
19	Extending reporting component	X						X	
20	Explanation component							X	
21	Visualization of output	X					X	X	X
22	Context-sensitive explanation of terms							X	
23	Further development of the feasibility validator		X	X	X			X	
24	Fine-tuning optimization			X	X				
25	Re-factoring			X					
26	Caching mechanisms			X	X				
27	Stakeholder requirements	X						X	
28	Stakeholder to enter resource estimates	X						X	
29	Weighted stakeholder permissions	X				X	X	X	
30	Stakeholder conformance	X		X	X			X	X
31	Individual stakeholder voting feedback	X					X	X	
32	Competitor stakeholder voting	X					X	X	
33	Stakeholder voting analysis extensions	X					X	X	

Table 9.3 gives the structure of the three optimized release plans and their values for the two objective functions. All the release plan alternatives are structurally different in terms of which features are assigned to the next release and which ones are postponed. Plan x1 is more biased toward the business perspective, while the plan whose objective values are given by the point x3 is biased toward the technical perspective.

Table 9.3 Alternative release plans

Plans	Features assigned to the next release	F1(x)	F2(x)
x1	f(1), f(3), f(7), f(8), f(9), f(15), f(17), f(18), f(19), f(22), f(24), f(25), f(26), f(29), f(30), f(31), f(33)	11370	1467
x2	f(1), f(3), f(7), f(9), f(13), f(14), f(15), f(17), f(18), f(19), f(22), f(24), f(25), f(26), f(29), f(30), f(31), f(33)	11320	1627
x3	f(1), f(3), f(7), f(8), f(13), f(14), f(15), f(18), f(19), f(22), f(24), f(25), f(26), f(29), f(30), f(31), f(33)	11315	1657

The sample results are intended to support human decision-making, and not being intended to be prescriptive. Independent of the actual values of the objective function, some suggestions can be immediately made. For example, feature f(1) is contained in all three plans and thus is a strong candidate for inclusion in the next release. On the other hand, feature f(2) is never suggested. Consequently, it is a strong candidate to not be considered for the next release. Further in-depth analysis and re-running the problem under different data scenarios would be easy to do and could provide additional insights and recommendations.

9.5 THE IMPACT OF UNCERTAINTY IN OPERATIONAL RELEASE PLANNING

9.5.1 Motivation

Since many planning parameters and features are under continuous change [Stark et al. '99], release planning becomes a very dynamic endeavor. Managers would like to have an estimate in advance how much deviation from the originally proposed release plan may arise due to an anticipated range of uncertainty. Based on this information, managers could evaluate associated risks of implementing the proposed plan and to take a *go* or *no go* decision.

[Zhang et al. '08] stated that *more attempts are needed to effectively tackle the uncertainty of software process in practice*. Among the existing research related to product release planning, [Yang et al. '08] studied the impact of uncertainty on software release time. However, their focus is solely on variability of actual cost, whereas the study approach discussed in this section is extendable to a wide variety of estimation uncertainties involving, for example, task effort and developer productivity.

9.5.2 Operational release planning

Staffing for minimum project duration was studied in Section 8.4 of this book. While the focus of staffing is on assigning the right people to perform tasks, the perspective of operational release planning (ORP) is different. It is considered as being a follow-up topic to strategic release planning aimed at scheduling of individual tasks to achieve minimum project duration. In this section, a simulation-based approach is outlined, which is applicable to the study of the impact of various uncertain input parameters on the overall project duration.

Different tasks (e.g., related to design, code or test) must be carried out in order to implement the features. For each of the tasks, there is an associated estimated effort. There are dependency constraints between tasks of the same feature. For implementation of all the tasks, a pool of developers is needed. Each developer has estimated productivity rates per task (such as productivity per design, coding or testing).

In summary, the following parameters and constraints are relevant to describe an ORP problem: Features, feature related tasks, effort for performing the tasks, dependencies between tasks, developers for performing the tasks and productivity of the developers for performing the tasks. A graph describing the semantic relationship between the parameters of the ORP problem is shown in Figure 9.6. The dashed rectangles are ORP input parameters that are two possible sources of uncertainty and, hence, referred as *uncertainty factors* for the rest of the section. This, of course, does not mean that these are the only uncertainty factors. Release *make-span* (the total duration for implementing a release) is the only output parameter shown in the figure which is affected by uncertainty factors and is referred to as *response factor* for the rest of the section.

9.5.3 Analysis of the impact of uncertainty

Based on the formulation of the operational release planning problem, the problem studied in this section is: *Analyze the impact of uncertainty on make-span related to the estimated efforts and the productivity of developers.*

More precisely, four analysis questions are studied:

Analysis question AQ1: Stochastic analysis of the impact of a change ΔEffort of the vector of estimated efforts on the project make-span when compared to a given baseline plan.

Analysis question AQ2: Stochastic analysis of the impact of a change ΔProductivity of the vector of estimated productivity on the project make-span when compared to a given baseline plan.

Analysis question AQ3: Stochastic analysis of the combined impact of changes ΔEffort and ΔProductivity on the project make-span when compared to a given baseline plan.

Analysis question AQ4: For two proposed operational plans, which one likely is more robust against changes ΔEffort and ΔProductivity coming from the input parameters.

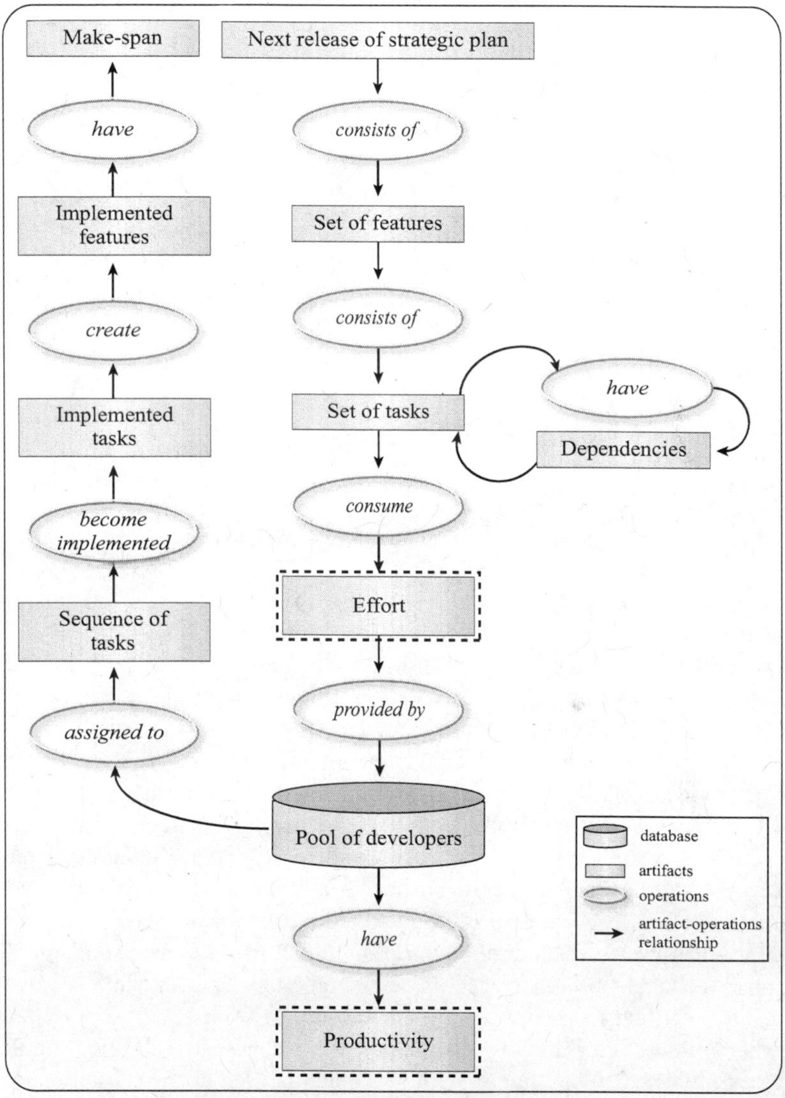

Figure 9.6 Structure of the ORP problem

9.5.4 Solution approach

Simulation models are often used in proactive analysis that involves stochastic parameters. Uncertainty is described by a probability function with a minimum and maximum value range (typically obtained from past project experience) to each vulnerable planning parameter. A sample probability function for effort distribution is given in Figure 9.7. In this case, a triangular function is defined between the best-case and worst-case estimates for effort.

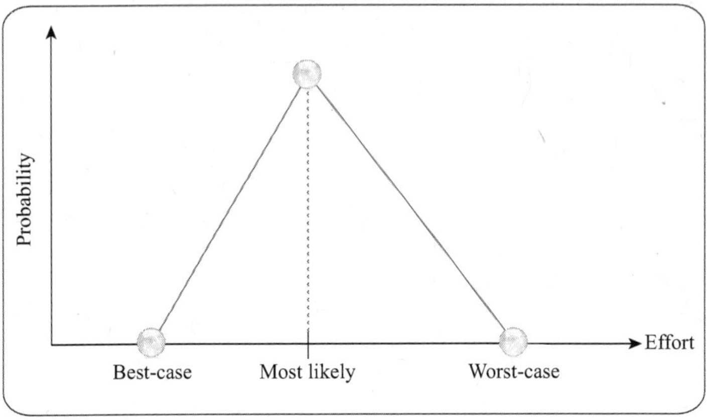

Figure 9.7 Sample triangular probability distribution function for effort

Each simulation run samples a value from the input distributions and determines the related output value. This technique is commonly known as *Monte-Carlo simulation* [Rubinstein and Kroese'07]. Multiple simulation runs sample different values from the distributions to model uncertainty involved in the respective planning parameters. The corresponding project outcome, for example, make-span, is obtained from running a process simulation model.

The proposed solution approach is an integrated method called ProSim/ORP (Project Simulation for Operational Release Planning) that combines Monte-Carlo simulation (to simulate uncertainty) with process simulation (to simulate the execution of the ORP process). Further details on this approach are given in [Al-Emran et al. '10]. For a given baseline plan, it asks for the specification of the probability distribution related to the uncertainty factors under investigation. Then it performs a Monte-Carlo enhanced process simulation. The simulation results are analyzed and verified.

In what follows, ProSim/ORP is illustrated for a baseline plan for the Telco case study project. The baseline (operational) plan is used as the starting point for investigation of analysis questions AQ1 to AQ4. The objective is to analyze the impact of uncertainty resulting from effort and productivity estimates on the make-span of the project. Details of the plan and its relationship to strategic planning are given in Chapter 12. For the eight features to be implemented according to this plan, the total duration (make-span) is 82 working days.

Since the method involves varying uncertainty factors and observing their effects in response factors, the ranges and structure of the variation needs to be specified. There are two common ways of constructing such distribution functions [Pfahl '05]:

(i) collecting and analyzing data as part of an organizational experience database, and (ii) expert opinion. Construction of experience-based distribution functions is done by fitting one of the existing generic probability functions (e.g., triangle distribution, normal distribution) to available data from (similar) past projects. If empirical data is not available an expert-based distribution function is constructed by interviewing experts.

In an effort to study the impact of uncertainty in the context of operational release planning, probability distributions are introduced to express the range and profile of uncertainty. For the case study, triangular functions were considered with minimum, maximum and peak values specified in Table 9.4. A sample triangular probability function for effort distribution has been shown in Figure 9.7. The position of best case and worst case would be switched for the case of a probability distribution related to productivity. Typically, experts are asked to estimate the most likely value (Peak), the best-case value (Min) and the worst-case value (Max) [Al-Emran et al. '10].

Table 9.4 Definition of uncertainty distribution

Analysis question	Uncertainty factors	Triangular distribution		
		Min	Peak	Max
AQ 1	Effort	0%	0%	50%
AQ 2	Productivity	-50%	0%	0%
AQ 3 and AQ 4	Effort	0%	0%	50%
	Productivity	-50%	0%	0%

Monte-Carlo simulation is applied to the uncertainty factors in order to sample values. These changes are expressed as percentages of change from the original values being used for baseline planning. The varied values are used by the process simulator, which can execute the modeled ORP process to determine the estimated make-span. A total of 1000 simulation runs were conducted to produce the results for this analysis.

After conducting simulation runs, results were analyzed and interpreted. Descriptive statistics such as mean or standard deviation were used as a starting point. For that, the following notation is used:

(9.9) *make-span(0)* is the make-span of the baseline release plan

(9.10) *make-span(r)* is the make-span from the rth simulation run based on the rth-random variation of parameters

(9.11) *Δmake-span(r)* denotes the relative change in make-span due to r[th] variation of uncertainty factors when compared to the baseline

The relative change in the make-span value is defined in (9.12). A positive (negative) value indicates an increase (decrease) in make-span.

(9.12) Δmake-span(r) = [make-span(r) – make-span(0)]/make-span(0)

Standard descriptive statistics measures can be calculated to analyze the results of all simulation runs. Results related to analysis question AQ1, AQ2 and AQ3 are shown in Figure 9.8, Figure 9.9 and Figure 9.10, respectively. For example, from Figure 9.10 it can be seen that the impact of combined variation of effort and productivity within the defined intervals results in 68 to 70% make-span increase. This result corresponds to a 95% confidence level.

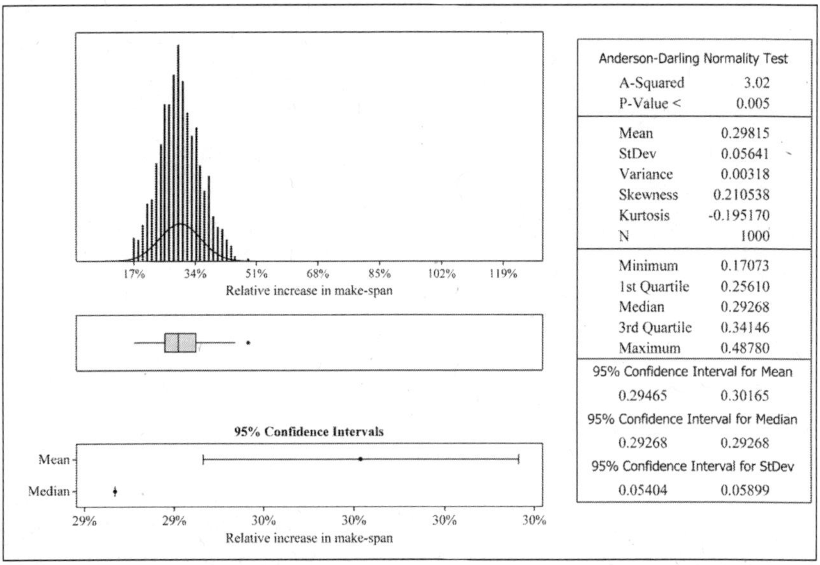

Figure 9.8 Descriptive statistics for effort variation (AQ1)

To better compare the three analysis cases, Figure 9.11 provides the approximation curves (fit to normal distribution) plotted in an overlaid graph. In summary, the different forms of descriptive statistics convey a twofold message:

i. *Effort* and *Productivity* uncertainty factors have a significant impact on *make-span*;

ii. The impact becomes considerably higher when looking at the combined impact.

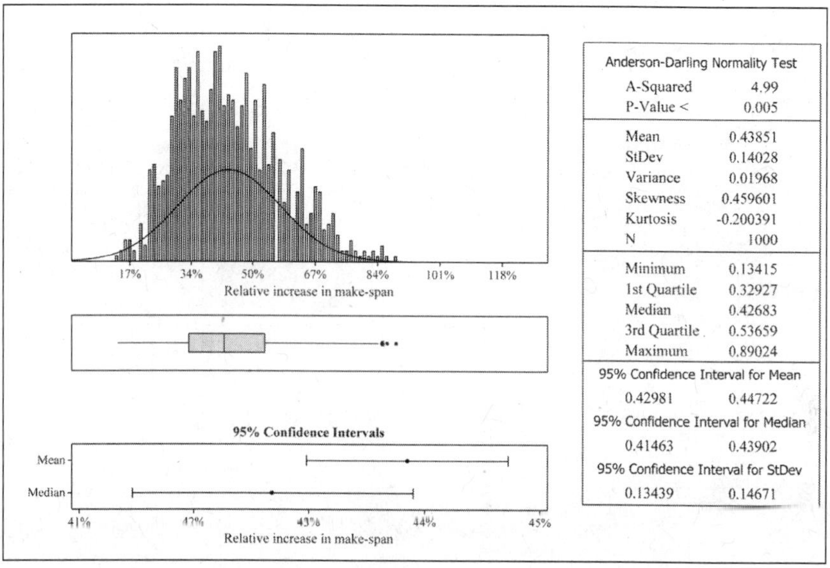

Figure 9.9 Descriptive statistics for productivity variation (AQ2)

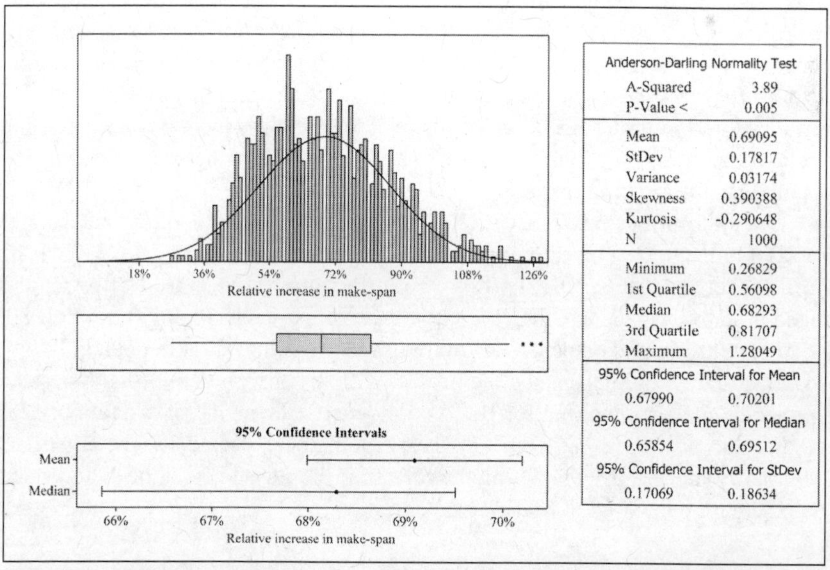

Figure 9.10 Descriptive statistics for combined effort and productivity variation (AQ3)

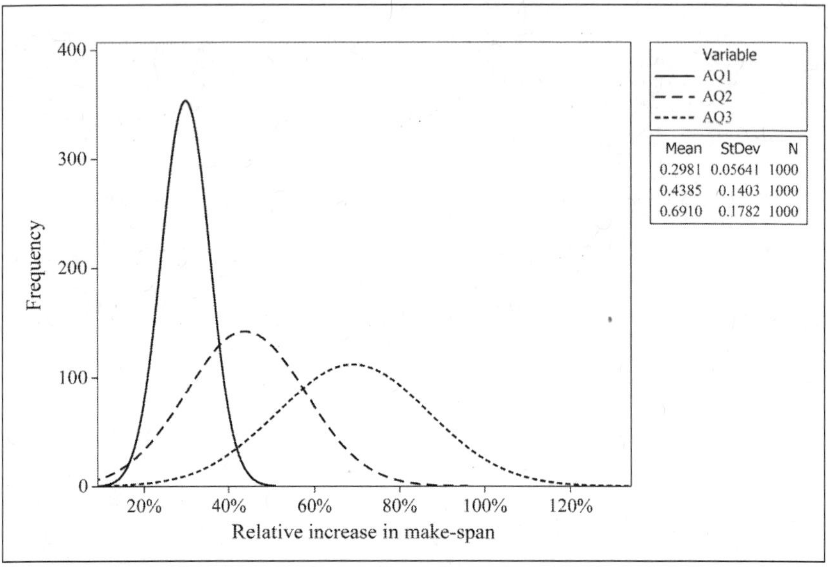

Figure 9.11 Distribution fit for histograms of make-span increase for AQ1 to AQ3

The above analysis results can be applied for predicting the likelihood of exceeding a given level of increase in total project duration. Figure 9.12 shows cumulative probabilities for make-span extensions as a result from the combined impact of uncertainty factors. The first information which can be gained from the graph is that for the given variations, there is no hope that all the features of the release can be implemented in time (this corresponds to 0% of relative increase in make-span). Therefore, a contingency plan is needed to accommodate an increase in make-span.

As another information, for any given level of probability (e.g., 25%, 50%, 75% and 100%), the projected relative delay in make-span can be retrieved from the curve of Figure 9.12. For example, if the project manager wants to be 75% sure for the expected make-span extension resulting from the increased effort and the reduced productivity values, then the curve provides a value slightly above an 80% relative increase in make-span. With the original (baseline) duration being 82 days, this means that with 75% chance the project will be finished about 65 days later. If the project manager is looking for 100% confidence, then an increase of about 128% (total duration of 187 instead of just 82 days) should be expected. On the other hand, there is a 50% chance of completing the release if the revised deadline is adjusted to a 68% increase compared to Make-span(0).

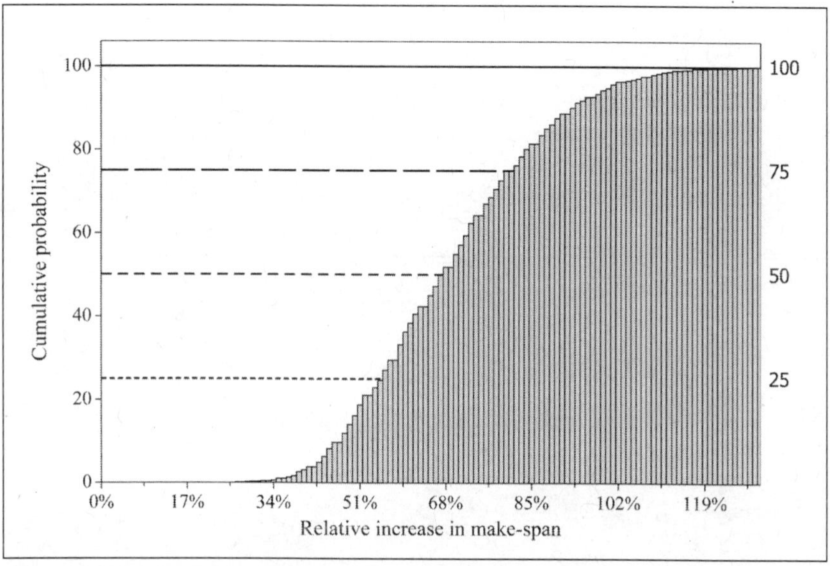

Figure 9.12 Cumulative probabilities for the occurrence of increase in make-span (AQ3)

9.5.5 Applicability of results

The Standish Group's investigation on solutions for enterprise project and portfolio management revealed that *resource management, with the ability to do project-level resource allocation, is among the most predominant concerns with regard to achieving project success* [Standish '09]. Proactive evaluation of the possible impact of changes in parameters is a means to improve planning quality. It allows providing early adjustments to accommodate for changes in project parameters. Simulation-based uncertainty analysis is a means to better predict and control the impact of changes. The above example was kept simple for illustrative purpose. In reality, more than two uncertainty factors need to be taken into account. The principal approach remains the same and can even be extended to response factors other than make-span. For example, this can be the relative degree of change in the assignment of developers to tasks compared to the baseline assignment or the relative change of the time intervals for implementation of the tasks. For each simulation run, the respective response value would be determined, and similar types of analysis as for make-span could be conducted. This information could be used to compare to different baseline plan alternatives in terms of their robustness toward likely changes of parameters. This was defined as analysis question AQ4.

In Figure 9.13, a sample comparison is made for operational plans of two release plan alternatives 1 and 5 obtained from strategic planning resulting from the application of the EVOLVE II method described in Chapter 6. In this case, only variation of productivity is considered. The robustness of both plans is roughly the same in terms of changes in make-span and in terms of the assignment of developers to tasks. However, the operational plan related to alternative 5 seems to be significantly more robust (less variation) in terms of the actual task implementation intervals. If this aspect is important for decision-making, strategic planning alternative 5 might be preferable to alternative 1 as its operational implementation is likely to be more robust against possible parameter changes in the productivity of developers.

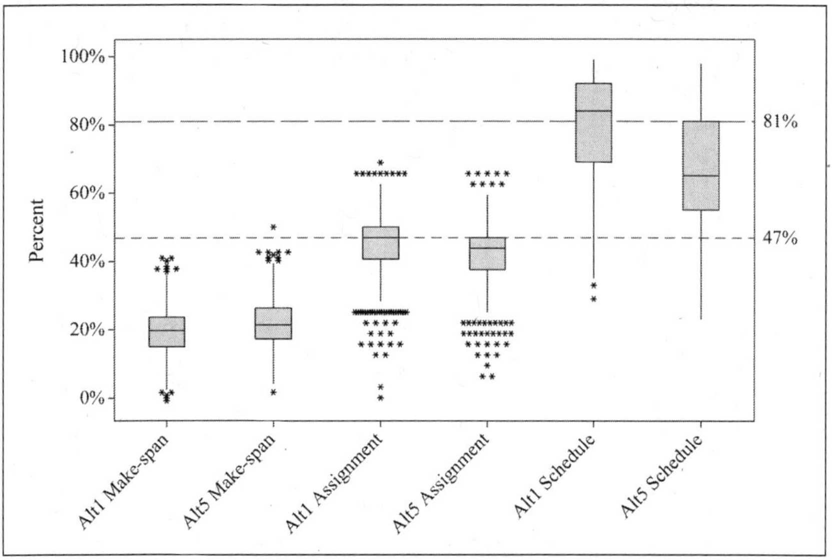

Figure 9.13 Impact of variation on make-span, assignment and schedule in operational plans related to alternatives 1 and 5

Part C: Tools

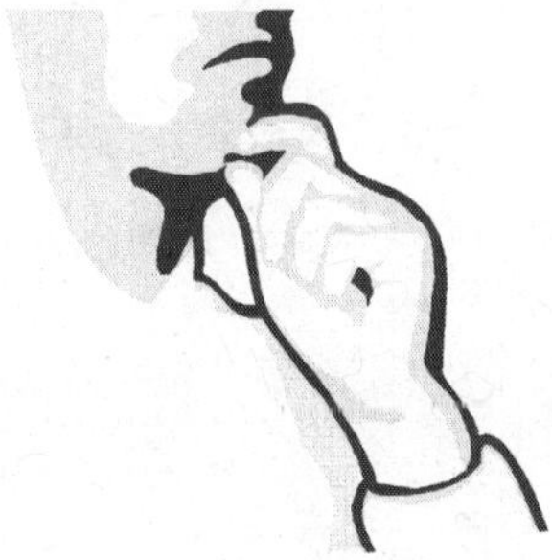

CHAPTER 10

TOOL SUPPORT

10.1 INTRODUCTION

Tools have always been the object of promises and expectations. As in any other discipline, tools can play an essential role in making processes better and faster. But is this automatically the case? And what needs to be done to provide the right expectations and to make them happen? With emphasis on the main topic of this book the question becomes: What could be expected from tools in the context of product release decisions?

In this chapter, three decision support systems with different foci and levels of planning detail are described. They are devoted to prioritization of features, planning of product releases and staffing for implementation of features plans. All of them are designed to support the product or project manager in the process of planning. The idea is not to let the tools make the decisions, but to provide valuable input to the human expert to make the right decision, thus increasing the quality of the decision-making process.

Tools in isolation are doomed to failure. Any tool usage needs a careful evaluation of processes, effort, time and capabilities of the people involved. Before presenting the three tools relevant in the context of this book, some comments about tools in general, and about planning tools in particular, are due. To allow a tool to provide efficient support, a number of factors need to be fulfilled.

First, the tool needs to be properly synchronized with the underlying process. It is not the tool that determines the process, but vice versa. The actual process is the key reference point, and the tool needs to fit properly into this. From a tool vendor perspective, this means to provide tools that are helpful but still generic enough to be adapted to different kinds of processes.

Second, the tool usage needs to match the purpose for which it was originally planned. Tools are designed for specific tasks, and so is their usage. A good tool has clearly stated assumptions, which need to be fulfilled for its successful application. Outside the intended usage scenario, there is a risk that the tool becomes distracting.

Third, a tool requires competence and skills for its proper execution. Training for usage of the tool is an essential investment when introducing tools. The tool provider is expected to have proper training material in place. This is an upfront investment, which might initially slow down existing processes. However, the potential benefits of a tool will become visible when users are familiar with it.

Fourth, the results gained from the tools can only be as good as the input provided to them. Even the best tool in the world is likely to fail if the data entered into it is not reliable. Consequently, tools can only provide effective and efficient support if there is some level of maturity in data collection and measurement.

It is worth mentioning that the above conditions are in a logical *and* relationship. Consequently, it is not enough that one of them is fulfilled. In fact, if one of them fails, the whole benefit of introducing a tool might be in jeopardy.

In what follows, three planning tools of different focus are presented. Each of them is studied in one section:

- *VeryBestChoice*^{Light} for multi-criteria stakeholder prioritization done by multiple stakeholders and subsequent analysis of results (Section 10.2)
- *ReleasePlanner*™ decision support system for generating optimized product release planning alternatives (Section 10.3)
- *RASORP* for staffing of the task-based implementation of features defined for the next release (Section 10.4).

The primary user of the tools is a product manager or a project manager of a product or service company. While the three tools can be used completely independently from each other, there is a logical sequence for using and combining them. At the first level, support is provided by *VeryBestChoice*^{Light} for performing prioritization of features. From the different analysis results, the product manager is supported in the decision of which features should come next.

At the next level, application of *ReleasePlanner*™ goes beyond prioritization. A more comprehensive approach including optimization is done, taking into account available resources and trying to achieve the best possible total stakeholder satisfaction. To better mitigate the influence of uncertainty, running various what-if scenarios allows us to make an impact analysis of possible parameter changes.

At the third level, more detailed staffing is done for the different tasks providing the features. For a pool of developers with specific competencies, *RASORP* creates optimized staffing plans. Different types of dependencies between the feature creating tasks can be taken into account. Following these plans allows us to achieve minimum total duration of the whole implementation project. The resulting Gantt charts can be exported into MS Project® to facilitate monitoring and control of the implementation of the plans.

10.2 SUPPORT FOR PRIORITIZATION: THE TOOL VERYBESTCHOICE^{LIGHT}

10.2.1 Overview

VeryBestChoice^{Light} (VBC^{Light}) is a Web-based system for supporting priority decisions. Priority decision-making based upon stakeholder scoring is described in Section 3.7. VBC^{Light} is the implementation of the method called Multi-score with all the analysis capabilities described in Section 3.7.

VBC^{Light} is an easy to use system. The main goals of the tool are to

- Facilitate proper priority decision-making by human experts based upon the input of a number of nominated stakeholders;
- Allow active participation of stakeholders in the process of discussing the content and value of the priority items and suggesting new ones;
- Maintain the necessary priority information in a related repository;
- Provide comprehensive survey functionality by allowing stakeholders to articulate their preferences at any time and anywhere (just requiring Internet access);
- Allow proactive what-if scenarios by changing parameters such as importance of criteria, importance of stakeholders, or capacities available; and
- Provide a variety of analysis options with charts and diagrams used for human decision-making.

10.2.2 Process steps

Usage of VBC^{Light} is guided by an underlying process structure. The five steps of the process are called DEFINE, ESTIMATE, PRIORITIZE, DISCUSS and ANALYZE. Their respective content is described below. These process steps are not in conflict with existing application processes, but independent and on top of them.

Step 1: DEFINE

In this step, the key parameters and data of a prioritization project are defined. This includes features and their grouping, stakeholders and their grouping, prioritization criteria and their weights, as well as the definition of access rights of stakeholders (called *permissions*). Permissions define which stakeholder is supposed to score for which group of features and related to which prioritization criteria. A screenshot with the different options for the tool's process steps 1 is presented in Figure 10.1.

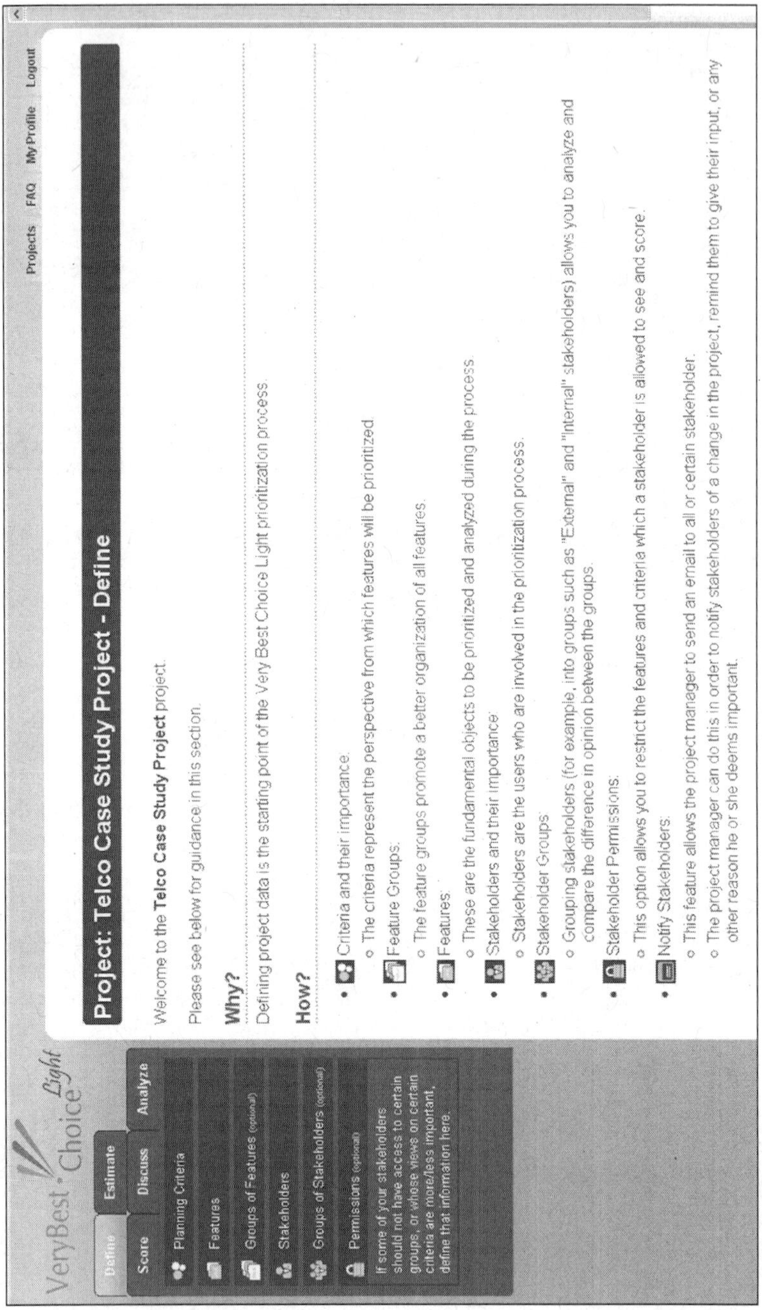

Figure 10.1 Process step DEFINE in VBC^{Light}

STEP 2: ESTIMATE

Estimation of the effort expected to complete the features is essential for subsequent decision-making. This process step is organized as collective estimation, in the sense that different stakeholders will be asked to provide their input. The input itself can consist of three types of estimates: Best-case, most likely, and worst-case estimate. The most likely case is a required input, the best and worst cases are optional. A sample screenshot for the three estimates related to features f(9) and f(10) is shown in Figure 10.2. The variation between best and worst case estimate per stakeholder can be considered an indicator of the degree of certainty into the most likely estimate. The variation between the most likely estimates of all stakeholders can be used as an indicator of the overall certainty into the effort estimate.

STEP 3: PRIORITIZE

For a selected criterion, prioritization refers to the process of assigning features to pre-defined categories of importance. VBC^{Light} offers a nine-point scale which allows sufficient differentiation between importance of features (or, more generally, between prioritization items). The process is facilitated by an easy to use drag and drop functionality.

A sample screenshot for prioritization of features for the criterion of urgency is given in Figure 10.3. A short description of the features is available to allow the stakeholder the understanding of the main content of the feature. The same applies for the definition of the prioritization criteria. On demand, further explanation can be made available using attachments and Web links. The user performs prioritization by simply dragging the next feature to be scored into one of the boxes corresponding to its perceived level of priority.

Prioritization is a prerequisite process to understand stakeholder priorities and commonalities and differences in their opinions. The quality of this understanding depends on the quality of the input provided by the stakeholders. In VBC^{Light}, there are two modes of prioritization: cumulative and free prioritization. For *cumulative* prioritization, the total number of points used is limited to five times the number of features to be prioritized. This is the default mechanism. Alternatively, no limitation is given (called *free prioritization*).

STEP 4: DISCUSS

Communication with and between stakeholders facilitates proper understanding and better quality of prioritization results. The tool also includes a Web-based discussion forum, in which stakeholders and the product manager are allowed to create topics of discussion and reply to existing topics, thereby participating in online discussions with other stakeholders. The product manager has the additional option to

- Make a topic sticky (sticky topics always stay at the top of the topic list);
- Make a topic locked (stakeholders may not add replies to locked topics); and
- Hide a post (stakeholders cannot see hidden posts, but they remain visible to the product manager).

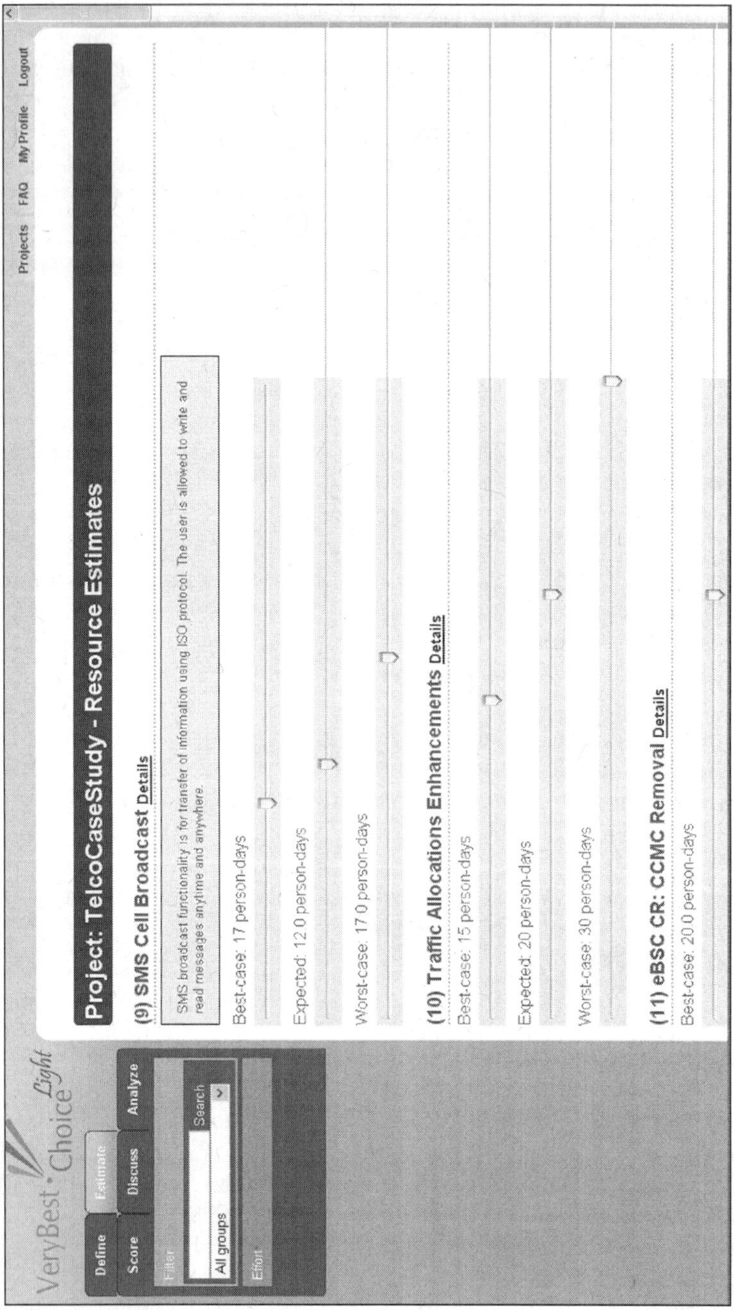

Figure 10.2 Sample screenshot of effort estimation for features f(9) and f(10)

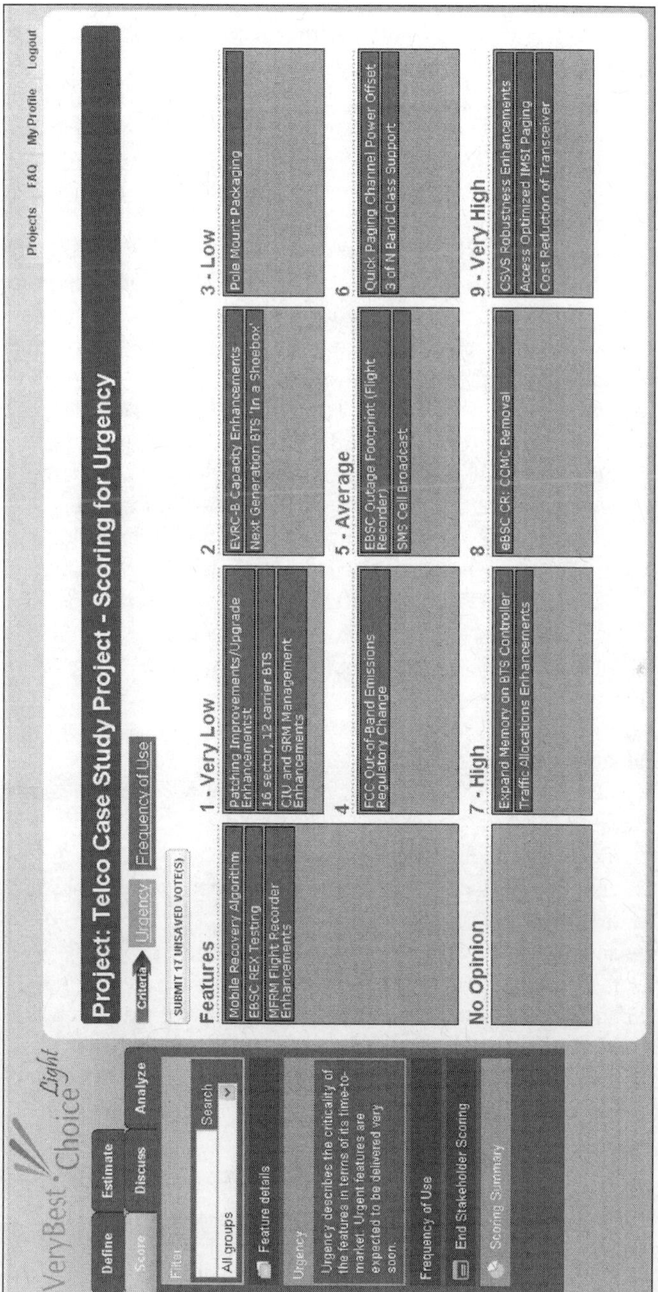

Figure 10.3 Sample screenshot for performing prioritization

STEP 5: ANALYZE

Once stakeholders have given their scores, data analysis tries to provide insight into the overall preference structure between features. In this *voice-of-the-stakeholder analysis*, differences and commonalities in the scoring between stakeholders or between the different criteria are detected, and different forms of ranking are done. VBC^{Light} allows 10 different analysis options (besides showing all the baseline data). The opening screen with thumbnails of all analysis options is shown in Figure 10.4.

10.2.3 Applications

In Chapter 13, the usage of VBC^{Light} in the context of adaptable project management is described. In that case, for each of the next iterations, decision support is provided for selection of the right features to be accomplished during the next iteration.

To allow getting some direct experience with the system, a trial login with *user name* = *book* and *password* = *trial* is available at the login page of the tool at http://edi.lite.verybestchoice.com/login [Trial_VeryBestChoice '09]. This is a reading account, allowing retrieval of the different stages of the prioritization process for the sample Telco case study project introduced in Chapter 3.

In general, import of data and export of results can be done using Microsoft Excel®. This helps to get easy compatibility with existing information systems and to edit the data for the specific purposes needed. Based on comprehensive stakeholder evaluation of candidate features against different prioritization criteria, the following questions can be answered by the VBC^{Light} analysis options:

i. Ranking of features based on their (weighted average) stakeholder scores for one criterion.
ii. Ranking of features based on their (weighted average) stakeholder scores for a combination of (weighted) criteria.
iii. How all the stakeholder scores for one criterion are distributed in the levels *high*, *medium* and *low*?
iv. How is the comparison in the frequency scores in the categories of *high*, *medium* and *low* when comparing between groups of stakeholders?
v. How is the comparison in the frequency scores in the categories of *high*, *medium* and *low* when comparing between criteria?
vi. How is the comparison in the frequency scores in the categories of *high*, *medium* and *low* when comparing between groups of features?
vii. How is the comparison in the frequency scores per features in the categories *high*, *medium* and *low* scores when comparing between groups of stakeholders?
viii. For one specific feature, how is the ranking among stakeholders based on their scores for one specific criterion?

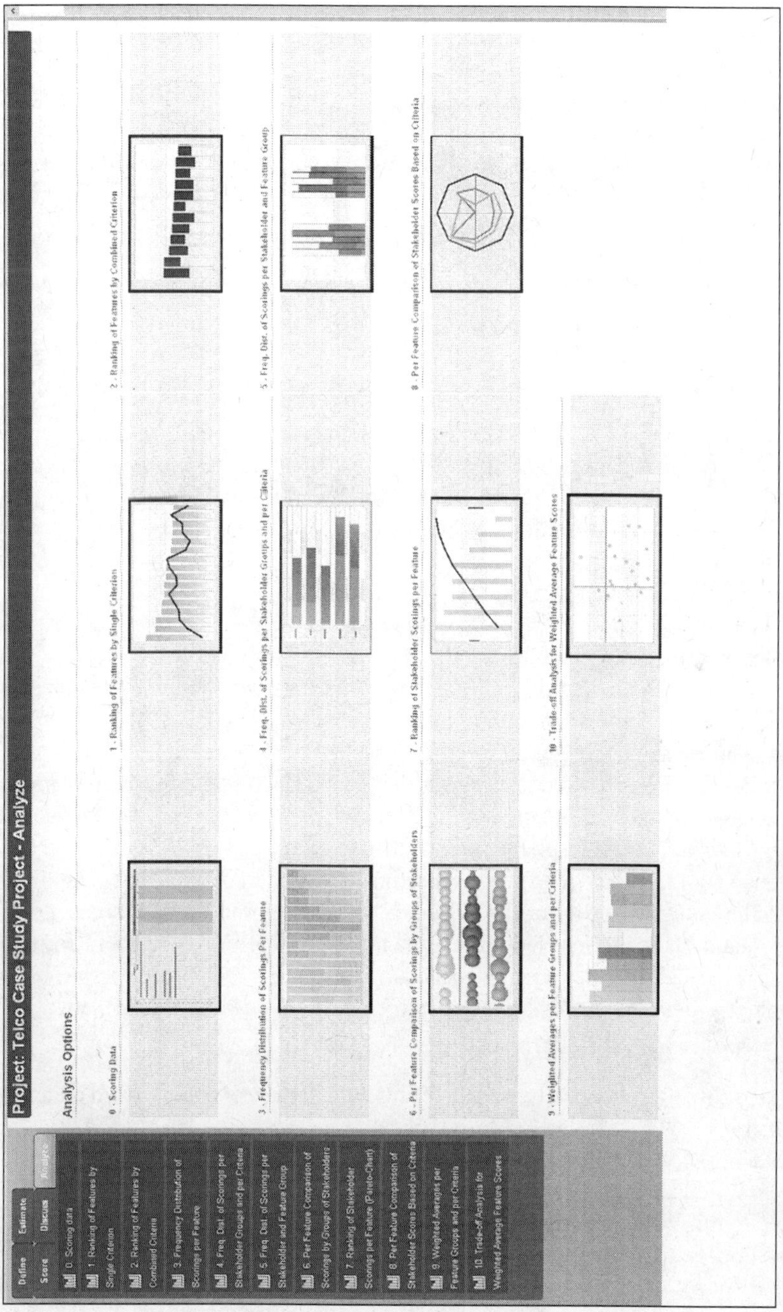

Figure 10.4 Analysis options for VBC^{Light}

ix. Compare among all stakeholder scores applied to all criteria when considering one specific feature.
x. How is the comparison of weighted average stakeholder scores when looked at different groups of features?
xi. How is the comparison of weighted average stakeholder scores when looked at different criteria?
xii. Which features are most (least) interesting in terms of a trade-off analysis for two selected criteria?

10.3 PRODUCT RELEASE PLANNING: THE RELEASEPLANNER™ TOOL

10.3.1 Overview

ReleasePlanner™ is a Web-based system supporting product release decisions. However, the application is by no means limited to that. As further explained in Chapter 14, there is a much broader range of applications including

- Road-mapping for multiple products
- Release planning with consideration of quality demands
- Agile project management following Scrum
- Planning for competitiveness of products
- Project portfolio planning

All of these problems are highly complex. The ReleasePlanner™ tool presented in this chapter directly or indirectly supports all the 13 steps of the EVOLVE II method. The main difference between ReleasePlanner™ and some of the existing commercial requirements and project management tools is related to the fundamental difference between *administration of objects* and *intelligent search for best possible decision alternatives*. ReleasePlanner™ includes various administrative functions (maintenance of a feature repository, reporting, import and export), but is not limited to that. The main capability of the system is to conduct intelligent search as part of various planning scenarios. Optimized planning alternatives are generated, which serve as a guideline for human decisions. The plans are optimized toward best stakeholder satisfaction utilizing the resources available in a best possible way.

10.3.2 Main functionality

In the following subsections, the main functionality of the tool is listed and briefly explained:

- Generation of optimized release plan alternatives
- Maintenance of a feature repository
- Flexible modeling capabilities
- Support of active stakeholder involvement in the different stages of the process

- Comprehensive analysis capabilities
- Support for proactive what-if-analysis
- Reporting

Generation of optimized release plan alternatives

Release decisions are hard to be completely formalized. A single solution of the cognitively complex problem is less likely to reflect the real-world problem-solving needs as well as a portfolio of qualified solutions. This is especially true if these qualified solutions are structurally different. The tool suggests working with an approximate model of reality to compensate for the uncertainty of the model. Instead of just one solution, a small set of (qualified) solution alternatives is considered. The role of this set of solutions is not limited to just providing a short list of candidates with a proven degree of optimality. It can also provide more insight into the problem, that is, through the observation and comparison of different qualified solutions one can recognize new aspects of the problem.

Based upon stakeholder priorities and the estimated resource consumption of the candidate features, the system generates a set of optimized release plan alternatives. Specialized integer programming algorithms exploiting the special structure of the problem are applied. These algorithms are applied in combination with heuristics to speed up the process. Different runtime options are offered to balance between computational time and accuracy of results. The algorithms are able to provide a guaranteed level of optimality.

Maintenance of a feature repository

All the features relevant for the planning and implementation of the release plans need to be maintained in a repository. This repository changes dynamically and always contains the information about the actual content and the status of the features. The information maintained includes the description of the features, any annotations made in the life-cycle of the feature, as well as existing resource or cost estimations. The tool allows feature-related attachments or Web links to offer stakeholders further details in the description of the features. The repository also maintains all the history of plans generated based upon the different data input configurations.

Flexible modeling capabilities

The tool provides a variety of modeling options. The user can decide which of these options are appropriate for the specific project under consideration. The formal definition of the modeling components is given in Chapter 5. In brief, the modeling options are:

- Definition of the planning objects (such as features, requirements, services or use cases)
- Definition of the planning horizon (from planning just for the next release to a more mid-term or even long-term perspective)

- Definition of the number of criteria, the content of the criteria, and their degree of relative importance
- Definition of dependencies between the planning objects (coupling and precedence)
- Definition of resources considered for planning. The number, content and type of resources (local versus global) is decided by the user
- Definition of pre-assignments of features to releases or sets of consecutive releases
- Definition of stakeholders and their relative importance
- Definition of groups of features
- Definition of specific access rights of stakeholders to feature groups, criteria, and process steps
- Definition of criterion-dependent scoring mode for stakeholders

Support of active stakeholder involvement in the different stages of the process

Stakeholders play a pivotal role in the process of pre-evaluation, prioritization, estimation and final decision-making [Heikkilae et al. '10]. Based upon their role in the organization and in the actual product development process, their roles in the planning process need to be specified explicitly. The tool allows specific assignments depending on the process step.

Allowing stakeholders anywhere, anytime access not only provides more flexibility in the actual prioritization process, but is likely to provide more objectivity in general. The only requirement for doing this is the availability of a computer with access to the Internet.

Critical stakeholders can be invited to pre-evaluate candidate features before asking a broader group of users, customers and other stakeholders for their more detailed prioritization scores. In the prioritization step, stakeholders can be assigned to look at pre-specified groups of features or look at feature prioritization only from the perspective of a specific criterion. Likewise, effort estimation of features can be performed based on expert stakeholder opinion, instead of just relying on the expertise of a single person. Finally, a group of critical stakeholders can be included in the process step of evaluating the generated planning alternatives to allow for a final decision about which release plan finally should be implemented.

Comprehensive analysis capabilities

The system offers different options for analyzing stakeholder scores and the analysis of optimized release plan alternatives. Some of the analysis capabilities will be illustrated further by the case study in Chapter 11.

- ***Voice-of-the-stakeholder analysis***

A sample screenshot is given in Figure 10.5. This analysis gives criteria-based ranking of features based upon their weighted average stakeholder scores.

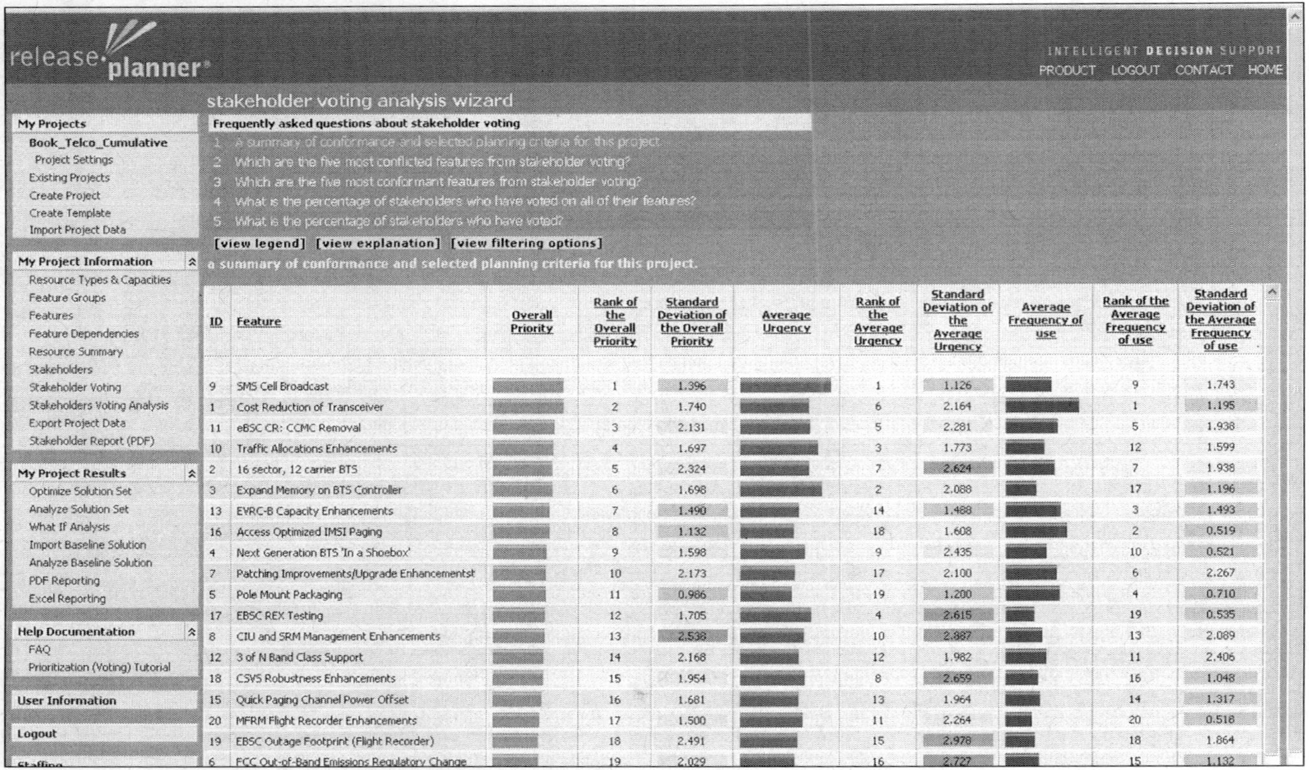

Figure 10.5 Screenshot of voice-of-the-stakeholder analysis

In addition, the level of disagreement (measured by the standard deviation) is given per feature and criterion.

- ***Quality evaluation of plan alternatives***

For the set of optimized alternative plans, their degree of quality is given. This is measured as the degree of formal optimality. As an absolute measure, the total number of stakeholder feature points of each solution is presented. In Figure 10.6, five optimized planning alternatives are compared with a manual baseline solution. Besides the degree of optimality and the total number of stakeholder feature points, the number of features offered per release in each of the alternatives is listed. It can be seen that alternative 1 is the best possibility when just relying on stakeholder feature points. While all optimized solutions provide eight features in the next release R14, alternatives 1 and 2 are the only ones offering six additional features in R15.

- ***Stakeholder excitement analysis***

The idea of pre-evaluation of plans by looking at the expected level of excitement of the stakeholders was introduced in Section 6.3. Depending on the importance of the stakeholders and the overall product development strategy of the organization, this analysis helps in selecting the best plan among the optimized candidate plans. Excitement can be measured per stakeholder, per criterion and per plan.

A sample screenshot is given in Figure 10.7. Therein, planning alternative 1 is analyzed. It can be seen that the CEO stakeholder is not very disappointed with any of the assignments, while being excited or very excited with five of the feature assignments. This situation is different for the CTO, who is one time very disappointed and just two times excited or very excited.

For excitement analysis, three principal options are provided:

i. Per stakeholders analysis for alternative plans (per single criterion)
ii. Per plan analysis for alternative stakeholders (per single criterion)
iii. Per stakeholder and per plan analysis for combined criteria

- ***Resource consumption***

Another analysis option provides resource consumption for all the alternatives and their respective releases. This information can be utilized to determine the bottleneck resources for the different plan alternatives.

- ***Comparison of structural commonalities between alternative plans***

This kind of analysis compares the optimized (and optionally an imported manual baseline) plans in terms of their structural commonalities. Some features might be assigned to the same release in all alternatives. In this case, the human decision-maker is likely to follow that proposal. For other features, there are differences in the assignments. In that case, the recommendation is not that obvious and eventually needs further discussion.

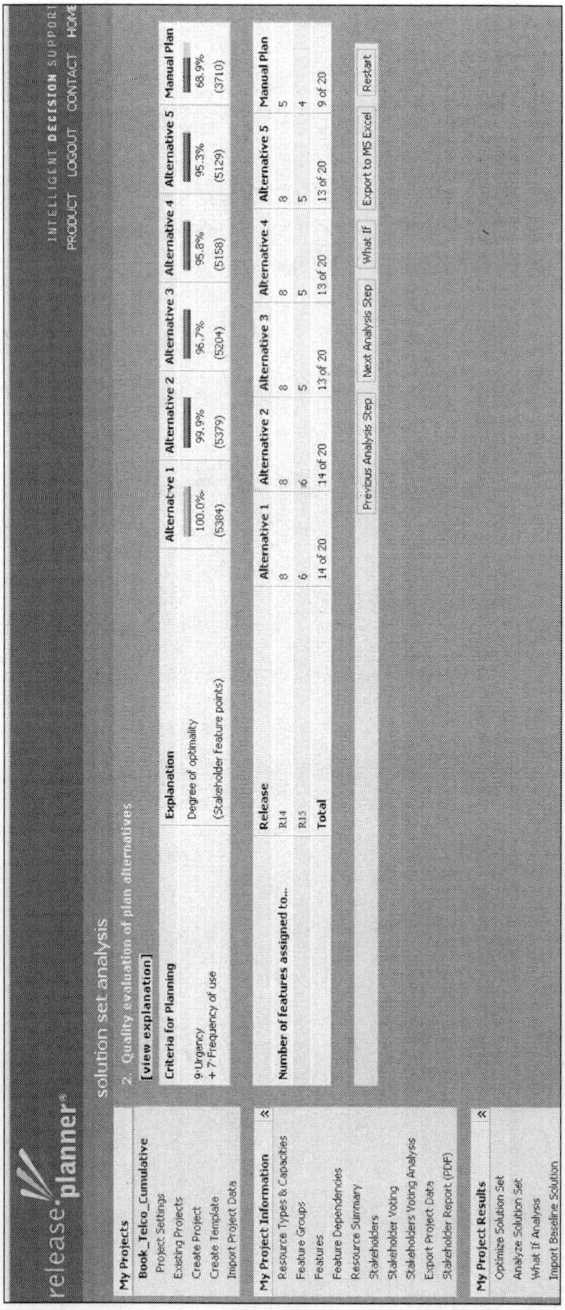

Figure 10.6 Quality evaluation of plan alternatives

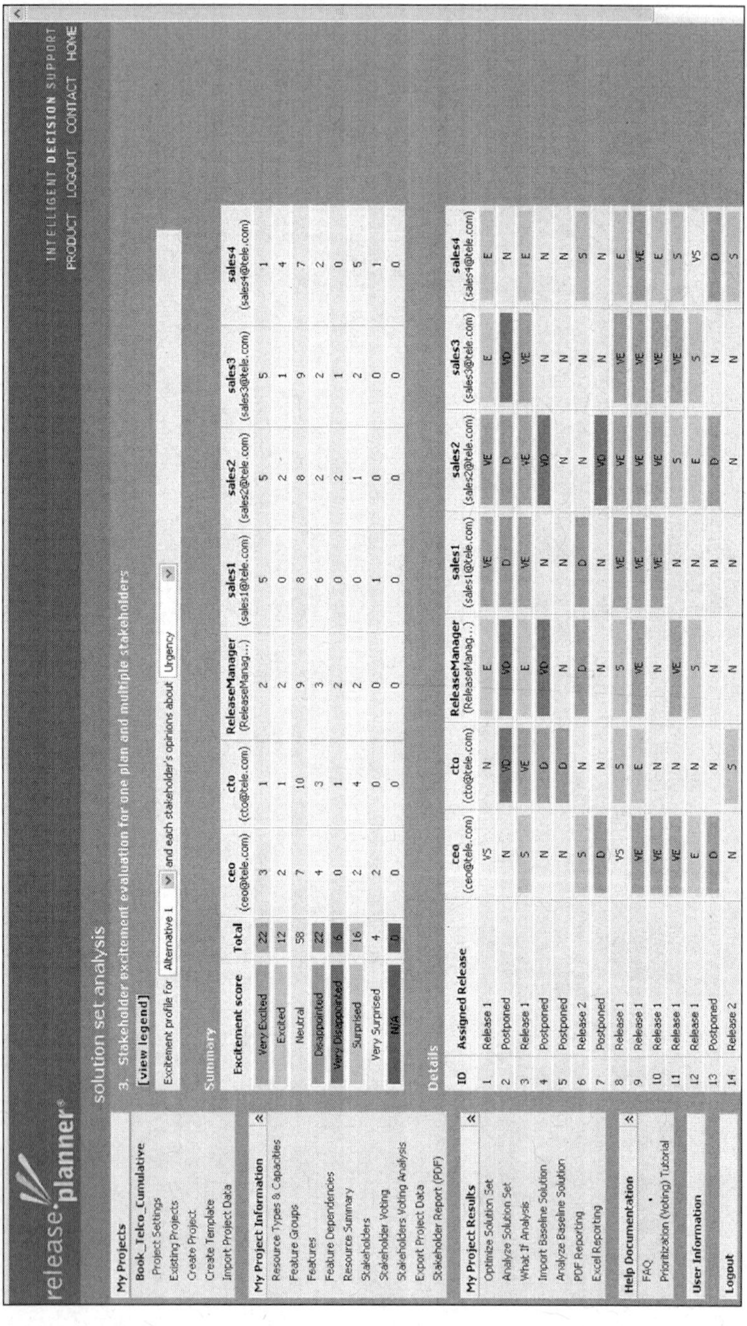

Figure 10.7 Sample screenshot for stakeholder excitement analysis for alternative 1

Import and export of project data and results

The ReleasePlanner™ system uses simple Microsoft Excel® templates to import data and results. The first worksheet of the import template is shown in Figure 10.8. The template is organized according to worksheets following the main structures of the problem definition:

- *Project information*: Key parameters for the project set-up
- *Resources*: List of all resources and their capacities per release period.
- *Features*: Groupings, pre-assignments, dependencies and resource consumptions of product features
- *Stakeholders*: List of all stakeholders and their access rights
- Scoring sheets per criterion (optional)

The export template is the same as the import template with one additional worksheet devoted to all the generated alternative plans and their structure. In the case of minor changes in data, the modifications can be done online within the system. In the case of more comprehensive updates, the changes can be more efficiently done by updating the project import file and re-importing the revised data.

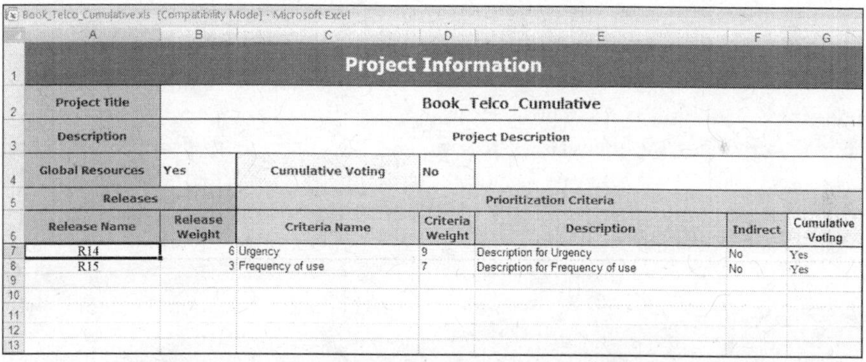

Book_Telco_Cumulative.xls [Compatibility Mode] - Microsoft Excel

Project Information						
Project Title	Book_Telco_Cumulative					
Description	Project Description					
Global Resources	Yes	Cumulative Voting	No			
Releases		Prioritization Criteria				
Release Name	Release Weight	Criteria Name	Criteria Weight	Description	Indirect	Cumulative Voting
R14	6	Urgency	9	Description for Urgency	No	Yes
R15	3	Frequency of use	7	Description for Frequency of use	No	Yes

Figure 10.8 Template for import of project information

What-if analysis

ReleasePlanner™ offers comprehensive support to conduct different forms of what-if analyses. What-if analysis is a means to perform proactive scenarios to better understand the impact of parameter changes. Often, it is important to know how changes in parameters influence the solution structure of a problem. This can be helpful in the context of risk mitigation or the investment of additional resources to increase the quality of planning results.

In the tool, there are different options for conducting what-if analysis:

- Modify planning criteria weights
- Modify stakeholder weights
- Modify resource capacities

- Modify release weights
- Add or remove feature dependencies
- Add or modify resource constraints
- Add or modify features and their resource consumption

For running a what-if analysis one has to decide which parameters are intended to be changed, how they are changed, and what is the reference (baseline) one wants to relate the changes to. For each of the possible changes listed above, the user needs to select a reference problem instance and its related solution. The reference problem serves as the baseline for the subsequent comparison.

Figure 10.9 shows a screenshot for the selection of the reference problem (baseline scenario) to get the what-if analysis started. In the above scenario, changes of the relative importance of the planning criteria were studied. In Table 10.1, it is shown how the change of the perspectives of planning (criteria) impact the structure of the (best) solution. It can be seen that there are substantial differences in between the solution created for a weighted combination of all criteria (being *time-to-market*, *alignment to business objectives* and *certainty of implementation*) and just looking at *time-to-market* in isolation. The three releases considered are at Jan-11, May-11 and Oct-11.

Reporting

The user can generate customized PDF reports, which present key project data and results. A summary of the project settings is given in the report. The stakeholder report summarizes the analysis results from stakeholder scoring of features. The report also provides the list of features ranked according to their overall priority. In addition, the performance of the features with respect to the individual criteria is listed. Besides the rank, the average priority and their standard deviation value (as an indicator of the level of disagreement) are shown.

The project results report lists all the participating stakeholders and their assignments to groups and criteria, the original resource baseline (consumption versus capacities available) as well as the plans actually generated. In addition to the PDF format report, the project data and results can be exported into Microsoft Excel®. This allows us to generate customized charts and diagrams.

10.3.3 Applications

The development of the decision support tool has strongly been impacted by a number of industrial projects. ReleasePlanner™ has proven successful in about 30^{+} industry and more than 250 academic and student projects. Running these projects and incorporating all the feedback has provided a number of important insights. From running real-world road-mapping projects with several hundred features, experience was gained about the computational performance and the need to improve the optimization algorithms to provide sufficient usability. Three of the industry collaboration projects are briefly discussed below.

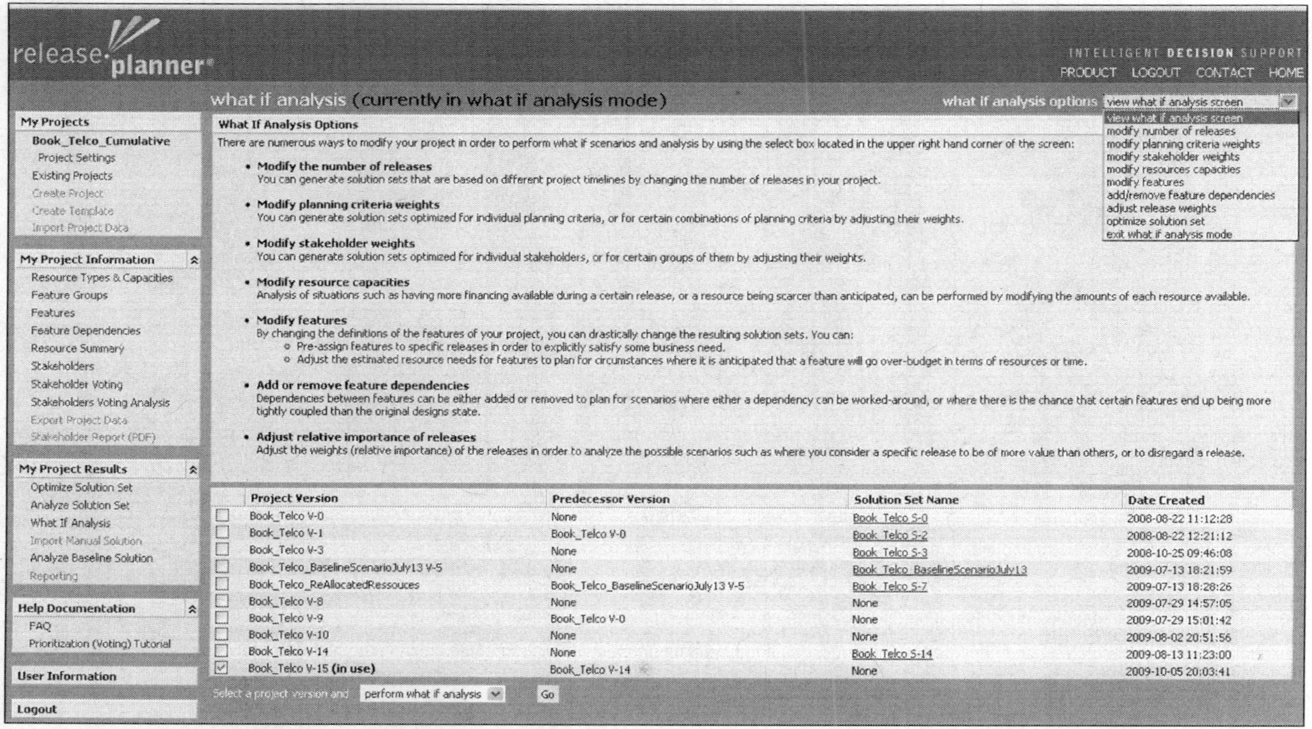

Figure 10.9 Sample screenshot of what-if analysis for studying the importance of planning criteria

Table 10.1 Structure of plans in dependence of criteria

Service	Weighted combination of all criteria	Time-to-market
Backlog management	Jan-11	Jan-11
MOSSE upgrade	Oct-11	Oct-11
Safety plan	May-11	Oct-11
Server upgrade	Postponed	Postponed
Business information system upgrade	Postponed	Postponed
SAP Phase 1	Jan-11	Jan-11
SAP Phase 2	Postponed	May-11
MMAP Performance measures	Jan-11	Jan-11
DP Standard conditions	May-11	Jan-11
Matrix reporting	Jan-11	Jan-11
Field technology deployment	May-11	May-11
Motion and directive tracking	Jan-11	Jan-11
DBL Planner reference database	Jan-11	Jan-11
DBL Training program	Oct-11	May-11
Base mapping Geodatabase project	Jan-11	Jan-11
Corporate building repository	Jan-11	May-11
CRM Implementation	Jan-11	Jan-11
UD Core service streamlining	Jan-11	Jan-11
Security review	Oct-11	Oct-11
Client data migration	Jan-11	Jan-11

[Amandeep et al. '04] reports about an application at iGrafx, a product group of Corel Inc. Before using ReleasePlanner™, iGrafx releases were planned in an informal fashion using a Lotus Notes® database of collated customer requirements. Records in the database were created for each distinct requirement received from customers (existing and prospective) and internal sources. Prioritization was refined into different criteria (urgency and value). For about 250 features, the company was able to plan three releases into the future instead of only one release, which was the usual former practice. Stakeholders participating in this process were providing earlier and more valuable feedback.

[Momoh and Ruhe '06] presented the results of a case study at Trema Group, a provider of strategic software solutions for the financial industry. Requirements were added to the product incrementally. The features for the next releases of the suite of products came from different sources such as contractual commitments, market positioning, technology opportunities, sales analysis, customer needs and existing functionality enhancements.

The inventory of features from which strategic release plans were developed contained over 500 features requested by customers to be in future releases. There were five stakeholders with varying interests on each of the features participating in prioritizing these features. The stakeholders were located in different places around the world. The process of ranking and agreeing on the content of the releases has formerly taken several days using spreadsheets to calculate and collate the results.

[Bhawnani et al. '06] report about the experience of introducing systematic processes for roadmapping of products and services at Siemens Corporate Technology. The main experience gained from these projects has been the increase in the efficiency of the planning process and the (higher) quality of the results.

The reader of this book is invited to look into the tool as well. For that purpose, a (read only) trial account with *user name* = *book* and *password* = *trial* is prepared at https://www.releaseplanner.com/rpApp/ [Trial_ReleasePlanner '09].

10.4 STAFFING: THE TOOL RASORP

10.4.1 Overview

Once strategic roadmaps are generated as a result of the application of ReleasePlanner™, the follow-up question is about if and how these plans can be implemented operationally. In Chapter 8, staffing and operational planning was studied in more depth. Staffing here refers to just human resources, and operational planning includes all resources. Both terms are defined by the premise that each feature to be offered is the result of performing a sequence of specified tasks.

In this chapter, the focus is on a tool called RASORP designed to support the staffing process. RASORP is an implementation of the two-staged staffing procedure described in [Ngo-The and Ruhe '09]. In Chapter 12, a case study is performed for the Telco project used throughout the book. This will provide further illustration of the process and the support of the tool in its different stages.

10.4.2 Functionality

The usage of the tool is organized in three main sections:

i. *My plans to be staffed*: Allows for the selection or definition of a strategic plan to be staffed.
ii. *My staffing information*: Allows for entering and editing of all the parameters and data necessary for running the staffing procedure.

iii. *My staffing results*: Allows for generating Gantt charts for visualizing the results. That means it gives the sequence of tasks to be performed by each developer according to the optimized plan.

My staffing plans

The starting point for using RASORP is a (strategic) release plan generated from ReleasePlanner™. For a given release planning project, this plan can be selected from one of the optimized strategic plans generated. RASORP also works independent of a plan generated in ReleasePlanner™ as a stand-alone tool. In that case, the planning data is entered by a Microsoft Excel® sheet. This includes the features with all their related tasks.

My staffing information

To perform detailed staffing, more detailed information needs to be provided. RASORP takes the resource types related to human effort defined at the strategic level as a default assumption for defining the same types of tasks for the staffing and operational planning. For example, if there was a resource type *design*, the tool will look into the same task type as part of staffing. The difference, though, is that now individual developers are assigned to specific tasks at different time intervals, as opposed to the cumulative view taken at the strategic planning level. The tool maintains detailed information on each employee, including skills, intervals of absence, schedule and assigned tasks.

The default task type setting defined for strategic planning can also be overwritten. In that case, however, all the estimates for the new task types need to be entered. For example, a task can be related to the usage of a specific tool or a specific programming language, thus refining a former task type *implementation*.

Similar to ReleasePlanner™, the data for planning can be entered via a Microsoft Excel® sheet. The tool also allows maintaining different types of precedence relationships between tasks. The relation *task A precedes task B* can have four different interpretations:

i. *End-Start*: Task B can only start after task A is finished.
ii. *Start-Start*: Task B can only start after task A has started.
iii. *End-End*: Task B can only be finished after task A is finished.
iv. *Start-Start/End-End*: Task B can only start after task A has started and task B can only be finished after task A has finished.

The different tasks can be performed by the given set of developers. RASORP makes the (simplifying) assumption that a task is performed by just one developer. Switching developers within a task can only be done through up-front specification of assignments (thus fixing the assignments that way). Each developer has an associated productivity profile vector, which is of the same dimension as the number of different task types. The productivity profile gives the (best possible) information about the assumed productivity level for performing the different tasks.

My staffing results

The results of the optimization done in RASORP can be represented as a Gantt chart or can be exported in Microsoft Excel® format. A sample Gantt chart is shown in Figure 10.10. The results give an easy to understand visual description of which tasks of which features are performed by which developers, and at which time interval. For example, the implementation of the *Cost Reduction of Transceiver* feature starts at the beginning with concurrent *Design* and *HardwareDevelopment*, which are done by developers dev(1) and dev(3), respectively. *SoftwareDevelopment* is done by developer dev(4). It starts March 11, 2010 and is finished March 25, 2010.

The plan generated from RASORP can be exported to Microsoft Project®. Once a staffing plan is in place (either taken directly from RASORP or after having performed a customization), the capabilities of this professional tool can be used for monitoring and control purposes. This capability is further illustrated in the case study presented in Chapter 12.

10.4.3 Applicability

In order to perform staffing in the context of release planning, a rigorous planning process needs to be in place. Synchronized tool support is an important component in this process. The complexity of the planning process, especially for mid- or even large-scale problems, by far exceeds the capabilities of the human product or project manager when looking for optimized schedules and staffing.

RASOPR is a research prototype tool and has been applied primarily for academic purposes so far. There are several potential advantages of using the optimization-based tool. First of all, it is able to determine better schedules resulting in (shorter) project duration. Second, from the staffing perspective, better assignments of the most qualified people to jobs requesting specific skills can be expected. These improved assignments have an impact on the duration of the tasks to be performed, but also on the quality coming out of this improved assignment.

The whole planning and re-planning can be done more efficiently with RASORP when compared to manual planning. Project managers spend considerable effort creating staffing plans and often an equal amount of time altering the plan in response to changes resulting from the unavailability of developers or changed market conditions [Kapur et al. '08]. RASORP has inherited the ReleasePlanner™ capability of maintaining essential planning information, which allows running and re-running different scenarios whenever requested.

The applicability is intended to support human decision-makers in their effort to find the most appropriate staffing plans. The modeling assumptions are simplifications of reality, and the estimates on effort and productivity are uncertain in their nature. Consequently, the results from RASORP serve as a guideline, to provide a direction to go for, but not as a prescriptive instruction.

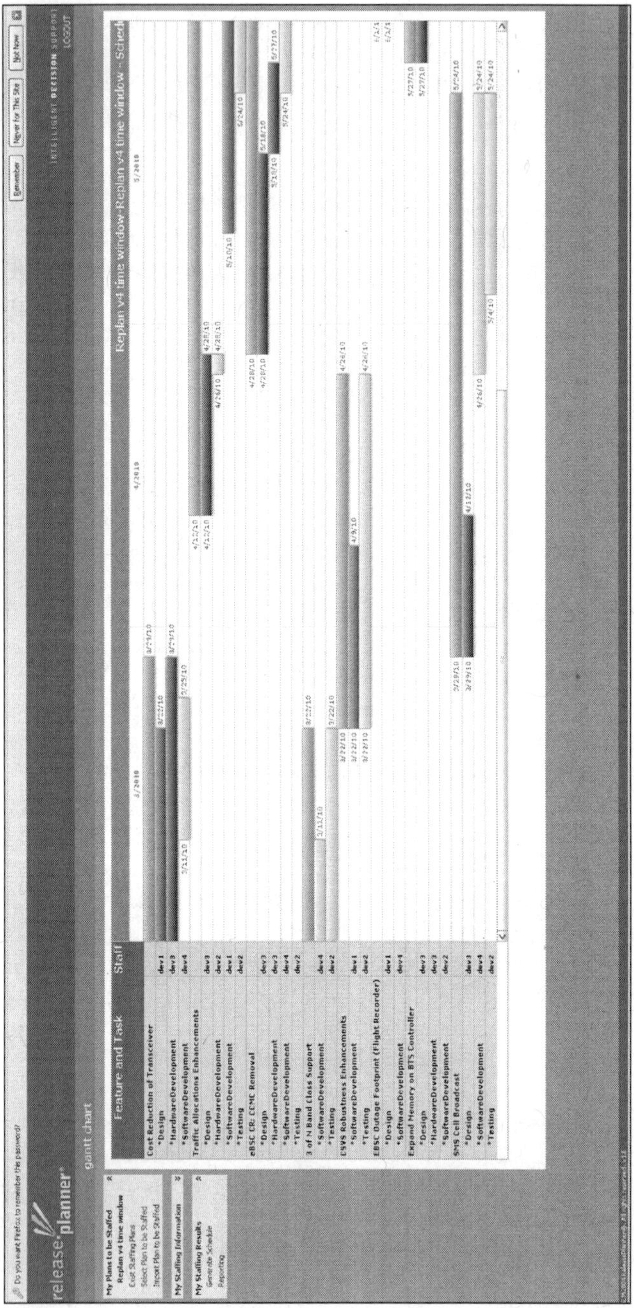

Figure 10.10 Sample Gantt chart generated from RASORP

Part D: Applications

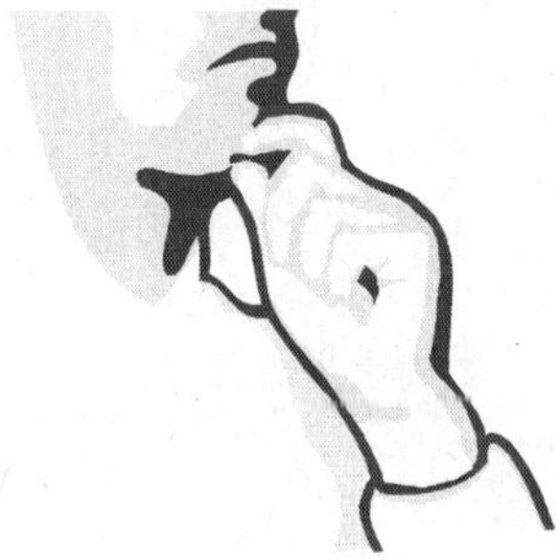

CHAPTER 11

CASE STUDY: PRODUCT ROADMAPPING

11.1 INTRODUCTION

One of the decision-making scenarios given in the early chapters was related to John and his job as the product manager for a mid-size Telco company called SIP Inc. His key challenge is how to select the right features. Providing features never to be used is as business critical as missing features being expected by the majority of the customers. A second challenge is how to react to last-minute changes. The resources available are largely fixed, with limited flexibility for re-organization. Finally, quality is of key concern for the company in order to maintain and extend their market position.

How do the methods and tools presented in this book support John in making the best possible decisions? Or at least help him to avoid major pitfalls? This chapter aims to go through the Telco case study and demonstrate the kind of support John can expect in making decisions about his product roadmap.

Release planning is a complex and ongoing process relying on different pieces of information and incorporating the opinions of different stakeholders. The systematic method outlined in Chapter 6 integrates the experience and intuition of the human experts with the computational strength of optimization algorithms. A (proper) tool could play the role of a catalyst in this whole process. It could maintain all the data with all the ongoing updates needed. A tool could also facilitate communication between stakeholders as well as encourage active participation at different stages of the process. It could support the final release decision by generating promising alternatives.

This chapter describes how to perform a systematic release planning process as specified by the EVOLVE II method using ReleasePlanner™ as a supporting tool.

The case study project involves planning for releases R14 and R15 as part of an ongoing product development process. The case study presented in this chapter is based on the Telco sample project used throughout this book. Besides going through the proposed process, further discussion is included at the different steps and for the results achieved. This case study is intended for all readers to better understand the proposed method and its potential benefits. In particular, it is aimed at practitioners to allow them to run the process themselves.

11.2 PREPARATION FOR PLANNING

11.2.1 Planning objectives

Planning does not happen in isolation from all the other information processes of a company. Before starting the prioritization and planning process, the company needs to decide about the key planning criteria they want to look at. In a strict sense, there are four related decisions to be made at the beginning:

i. Who is involved in deciding about the planning objectives?
ii. How many key planning objectives does the company want to look at?
iii. What are these objectives?
iv. What is their relative importance?

Planning objectives should be aligned as much as possible to the company's business strategy. For that purpose, John has included the CEO, CTO and the chief architect to become stakeholders in this process and to help answer questions (ii) and (iii) as stated above. As a result, they have proposed five candidate criteria (with reference to the perspective mainly relevant):

- Criterion 1: Urgency (to address time-to-market of the product)
- Criterion 2: Financial value ROI (to improve financial success)
- Criterion 3: Frequency of use (to achieve higher customer satisfaction)
- Criterion 4: Risk of implementation (to reflect aspects of implementation)
- Criterion 5: Impact on competitiveness (in increase market share)

From running the systematic prioritization process AHP described in Section 3.6, the normalized vector of weights related to the five criteria is determined. These weights are the result of determining the importance of the above five criteria from performing pair-wise comparisons. This is done by John in collaboration with the CEO, the CTO and the company's chief architect. The four internal stakeholders in this product release planning process have different perspectives of the five criteria. All the local (individual stakeholder related) priorities obtained that way are integrated into one (normalized) vector of global priorities (0.45, 0.10, 0.35, 0.05, 0.05). The i-th component of this vector corresponds to the i-th criterion mentioned above.

The results of the AHP process indicate that there are two criteria of greatest importance to the company: *Urgency* and *frequency of use*. Their degree of importance is substantially higher than the other three criteria. Each accepted criterion implies that each nominated stakeholder performs prioritization of all features. To balance between the overall effort to score the candidate features and the resulting benefit out of this process, John decided to concentrate just on the two top criteria.

The main stages of the study are the preparation for planning (Section 11.2), prioritization of features by stakeholders (Section 11.3), planning without tool support (Section 11.4), generation of optimized release plan alternatives (Section 11.5) and re-running the process (Section 11.6).

11.2.2 Stakeholders and their degree of importance

Stakeholders play a prominent role in the EVOLVE II planning method. Their selection is critical for achieving the best possible results. Different views of the process and the product under investigation need to be harmonized. To cover a broad range of customer groups and locations, four customer representatives were selected by John to participate in the process. They are called *Key customer East, West, North,* and *South*, respectively. All the customer representatives are considered equally important. The relative level of importance of the eight stakeholders has been defined as shown in Table 3.4, Chapter 3.

11.2.3 Candidate features and their dependencies

The case study company maintains a repository of feature requests. These requests can be for new features and revisions or enhancements of existing features. The definition of what constitutes a *feature* is flexible. The appropriate granularity needs to be defined. It does not make sense to have very large (in terms of their effort consumption) nor to look at very small features. One of the fundamental modeling assumptions of EVOLVE II is that the size of the features does not vary by more than one order of magnitude.

The size of the repository is large, and some of the features are not in consideration for the next two releases but are planned for later releases. John, supported by the CTO and some of the internal stakeholders, performs some pre-selection of features which are considered candidates for the next two product releases. This is a subset of all the features maintained in the repository. However, even this set is not likely to be implemented completely because of the existing resource and time constraints. The process of pre-selection of features for subsequent road-mapping for releases R14 and R15 is illustrated in Figure 11.1.

The 20 features of the project pre-selected for the actual release planning process were already introduced in Chapter 3 when illustrating the prioritization method Multi-score. Three dependencies between features are defined:

- *Mobile Recovery Algorithm* must not be released later than *Quick Paging Channel Power Offset*
- *SMS Cell Broadcast* must not be released later than *Traffic Allocations Enhancements*
- *eBSC CR*: *CCMC Removal* needs to be in the same release as *3 of N Band Class Support*

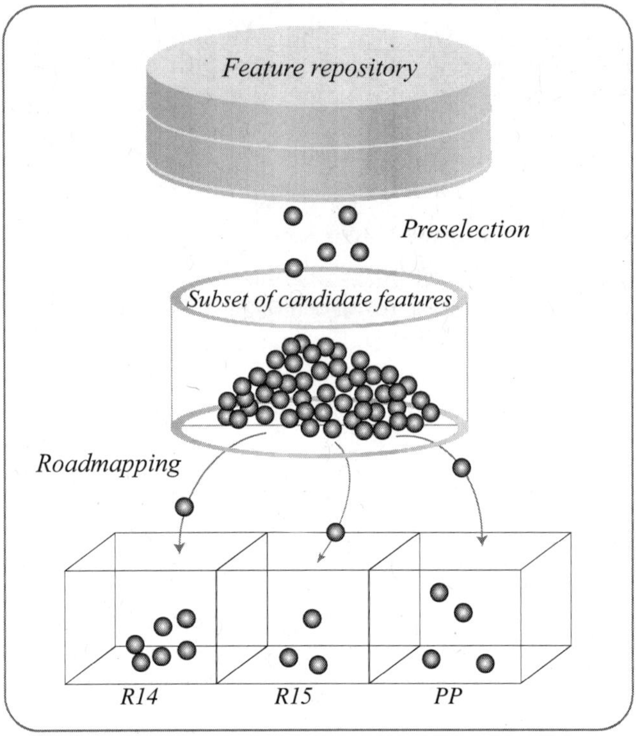

Figure 11.1 Preselection of features for roadmapping

11.2.4 Resources and their capacities

The considered product development for releases R14 and R15 is part of an evolutionary process. It is well known from past product releases which key resources are needed for feature development. As the release dates are fixed up-front, the cumulative capacities of the different resource types can be estimated as the product of the average number of people available per person day multiplied by the duration (in working days) of the release period.

Resource types and their capacities available for releases R14 and R15 are summarized in Table 11.1. What can be seen, for example, is that the total *design* effort available is expressed in person days and is limited to 120 person days for both release R14 and R15. Related to the different resources relevant for consideration in planning, there is consideration of *cost* in addition to human resources. Cost here refers to all the necessary expenditures which can be directly related to the development of that feature. Cost may or may not include all the expenditures for human resources. In case that it does, then the cost figure serves as an aggregation of all expenses for human and non-human resources.

Table 11.1 Resource capacities per release

Resource	Resource Capacities		
	Resource Units	Releasc R14	Release R15
Design	Effort in person days	120	120
Hardware development	Effort in person days	80	80
Software development	Effort in person days	90	90
Testing	Effort in person days	80	80
Cost	Effort in K dollars	200	200

11.2.5 Features and their resource consumptions

In order to balance the attractiveness of the features as articulated by stakeholders with the necessary effort to develop them, estimation of effort consumption is a required input. Among the informal methods for effort estimation, expert judgment is most prominent. However, there is no need to rely exclusively on one expert. Instead, different experts can be taken into consideration. With this input, weighted averages can be computed. A meeting for consolidation and discussion of the different estimates can be set up. The consolidation effort should be focused on the most essential estimates, as in total there is a need to perform N·R estimations. For the case study having N = 20 features and considering R = 5 different resources, this would mean conducting 100 estimations.

In case there is a well-documented record of the effort of former feature development, *estimation by analogy* [Shepperd and Schofield '97] can be applied. The main idea is to consider the effort consumed by similar features implemented in the past. In order to estimate the effort for a new feature, the estimation by analogy procedure looks for similar features from the past with recorded effort. Further details of the process of estimation by analogy and its application for release planning are described in Section 9.2.

For our case study project, all resources can be consumed globally. This means that even if a feature is released in R15, its (partial) implementation can already be started in R14. The feature-related resource consumptions for the 20 features are summarized in Table 11.2. For example, implementation of feature f(1) consumes 15 person days for design, 20 person days for software development and 12 person days for hardware development. The total cost of this feature is estimated to be $20,000.

Table 11.2 Resource consumption per feature (same units as in Table 11.1)

Feature ID	Resource Consumption				
	Design	Hardware development	Software development	Testing	Cost
1	15	20	12	0	20
2	40	30	15	15	20
3	7	12	1	0	7
4	45	35	37	12	50
5	40	18	30	5	40
6	40	12	10	0	20
7	57	42	40	20	25
8	45	0	10	5	40
9	5	0	25	14	20
10	6	1	12	12	19
11	7	7	30	12	45
12	0	0	10	15	10
13	25	10	40	40	40
14	20	10	25	25	25
15	0	0	30	25	25
16	10	10	15	10	30
17	10	0	25	10	20
18	0	0	10	25	15
19	20	0	15	0	10
20	10	0	30	20	20

11.3 PRIORITIZATION OF FEATURES BY STAKEHOLDERS

Eight stakeholders have been selected to be part of the product release planning process. Their names, roles and the assigned weights for relative importance are the same as described in Table 3.4, Chapter 3. The prioritization of features is done from the perspectives of both *urgency* and *frequency of use.*

The result of release planning can only be as meaningful as the quality of the data used for this process. It is important to motivate stakeholders to actively participate and to provide meaningful input. Using ReleasePlanner™, all nominated stakeholders get notified, which includes the secure login information to perform scoring. A sample screenshot from performing the scoring is shown in Figure 11.2.

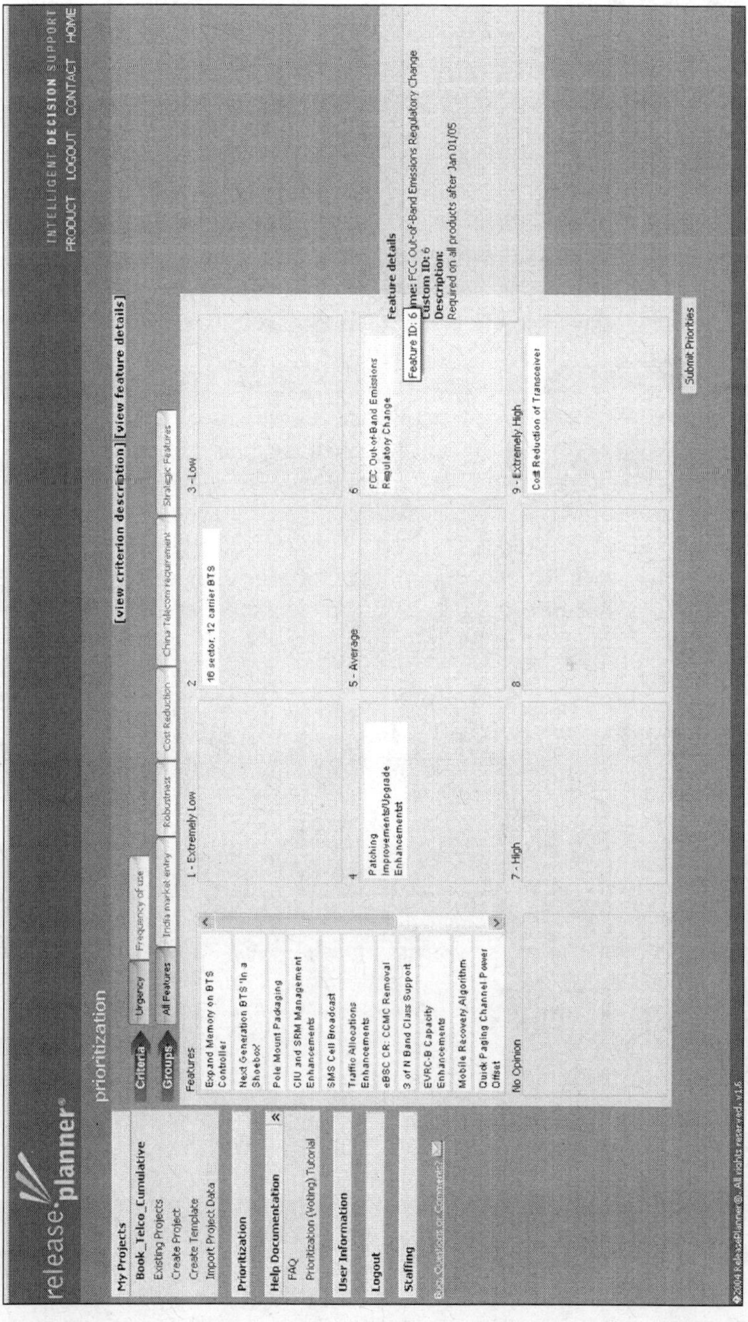

Figure 11.2 Sample screenshot from *urgency* prioritization of all features

The complete results of scoring for *urgency* and *frequency of use* are shown in Figure 11.3. Although all stakeholders have been asked to provide a priority for all features, this does not always need to be the case. Especially for larger projects and for different levels of familiarity with sets of features, it might be useful to assign just certain groups of the whole feature set to a specific stakeholder. The same idea applies for the different criteria: Some stakeholders might be asked to provide their opinion just from the perspective of a specific criterion.

Although not used by John in this project, specification of access rights (or *permissions*) is illustrated in Figure 11.4. In this tentative scenario, *Key customer East* is assigned just to prioritize three (out of the five existing) groups of features. These active groups are being check-marked. The assignment is made from the perspective of the *urgency* criterion. John has decided not to ask this stakeholder to look at the groups of features called *India market entry* and *China Telecom requirement.* In addition, this stakeholder is not requested to consider *frequency of use* for prioritization of features. It can be seen as well that the importance of the input of the stakeholder varies among the three assigned groups of features. The input is most important for group *Cost reduction* and least important for *Robustness*.

As a result of the scoring process, the ranking of the features based on a combination of the two criteria can be seen at Figure 11.5. In total, feature f(1) appears to be the most attractive when just looking at the priorities, followed by f(9) and f(11). In the next section, this ordering based on combined criteria is used as the input for simulating a prototypical real-world planning process primarily relying on the priority of features.

11.4 PLANNING WITHOUT TOOL SUPPORT

Before performing tool-supported planning, John's traditional approach (without tool support) is illustrated. Following that, a plan is created from always looking at the highest prioritized features still available. This is done as long as none of the capacities is exceeded. The result of this process is summarized in Table 11.3. This includes the cumulative resource consumption. For each subsequent set of features, the cumulative resource consumption is provided. After adding the third ranked feature f(11), the coupled feature f(12) needs to added, too. When adding the next ranked feature f(2), the capacity of software development would be exceeded. The same would happen in case of inclusion of f(16) or f(13). However, feature f(10) is still possible to add. After that, no more features can be added without violation of capacity constraints.

The same process is applied for the remaining features to plan for release R15. The process starts with the highest ranked feature not assigned to release R14. The results of this process (including cumulative resource consumption at the different stages of the process) are summarized in Table 11.4.

Explanation

Scoring data

Criteria: Urgency (1), Frequency of Use (2)

Feature		CEO		CTO		Release manager		Key customer East		Key customer South		Key customer North		Key customer West		Architect	
ID	Name	1	2	1	2	1	2	1	2	1	2	1	2	1	2	1	2
1	Cost Reduction of Transceiver	2	6	5	7	7	6	9	9	7	5	7	6	8	7	7	6
2	16 sector, 12 carrier BTS	1	1	8	4	9	4	6	7	5	5	9	5	6	7	7	4
3	Expand Memory on BTS Controller	3	5	8	2	7	2	9	3	7	2	9	3	9	3	9	1
4	Next Generation BTS 'In a Shoebox'	4	4	7	4	9	4	5	4	2	3	5	3	9	4	5	3
5	Pole Mount Packaging	5	6	6	4	5	5	5	5	4	4	2	5	5	5	4	4
6	FCC Out-of-Band Emissions Regulatory Change	2	5	5	3	9	3	9	2	2	2	4	2	5	2	4	4
7	Patching Improvements/Upgrade Enhancementst	6	1	2	3	5	5	5	7	5	5	4	7	9	7	3	3
8	CIU and SRM Management Enhancements	1	8	4	2	4	3	9	3	7	2	8	2	9	2	7	2
9	SMS Cell Broadcast	8	8	7	4	9	3	9	3	8	3	9	3	9	3	6	4
10	Traffic Allocations Enhancements	8	7	5	3	5	3	9	3	7	3	8	3	9	2	5	2
11	eBSC CR: CCMC Removal	9	9	5	3	9	4	5	4	4	4	8	4	4	4	4	3
12	3 of N Band Class Support	7	9	5	3	4	3	5	2	2	2	4	2	7	2	8	4
13	EVRC-B Capacity Enhancements	7	8	3	4	5	4	4	4	6	4	4	4	7	4	6	6
14	Mobile Recovery Algorithm	6	7	2	3	4	3	3	4	2	4	4	3	5	4	4	4
15	Quick Paging Channel Power Offset	9	6	4	2	4	3	3	2	5	3	4	2	5	3	7	3
16	Access Optimized IMSI Paging	7	6	5	5	5	6	2	5	3	6	5	5	6	5	4	5
17	EBSC REX Testing	5	3	6	3	9	2	9	2	1	2	8	3	7	2	6	3
18	CSVS Robustness Enhancements	3	5	2	3	9	3	9	2	5	2	8	3	7	2	6	2
19	EBSC Outage Footprint (Flight Recorder)	6	7	2	1	5	2	9	2	7	2	1	2	4	2	9	2
20	MFRM Flight Recorder Enhancements	7	3	6	2	5	3	6	2	6	2	1	2	5	2	9	3

Figure 11.3 Overview of scoring results

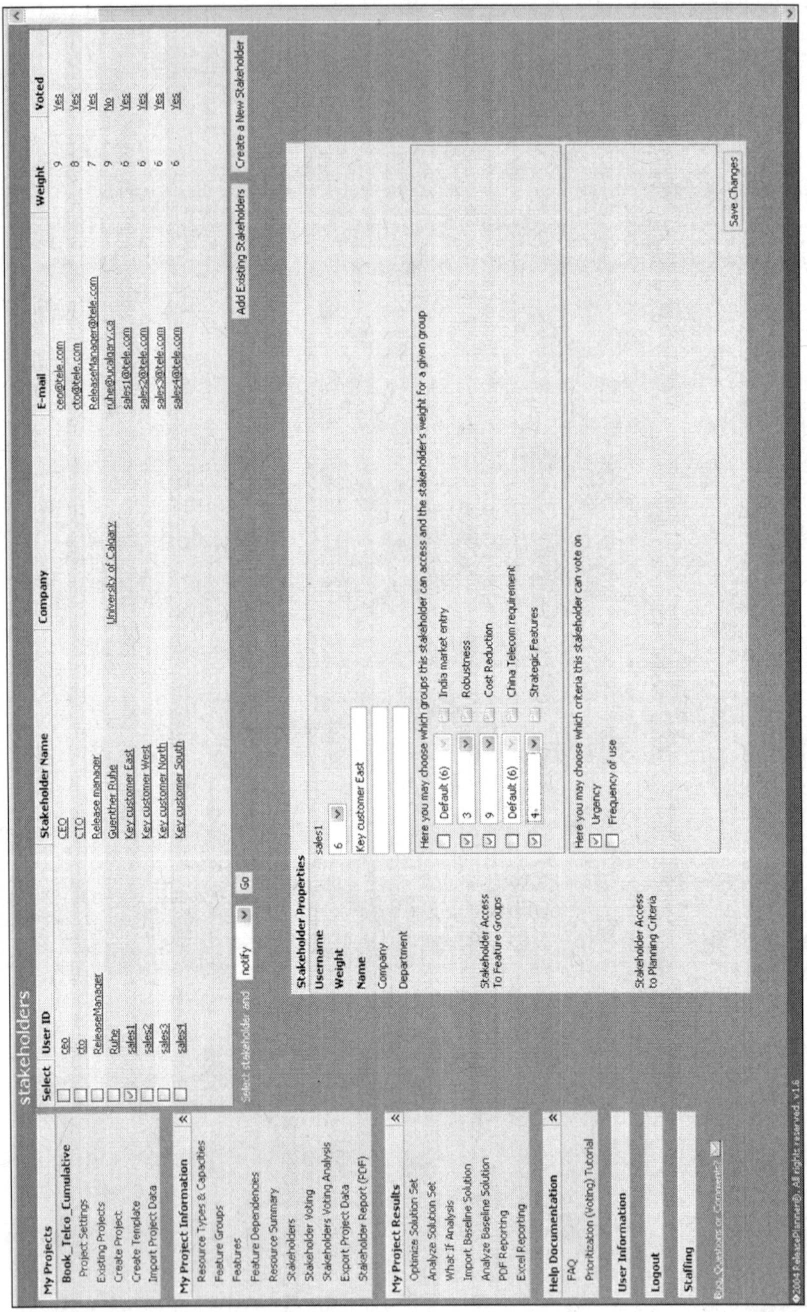

Figure 11.4 Definition of permission rights for *Key customer East*

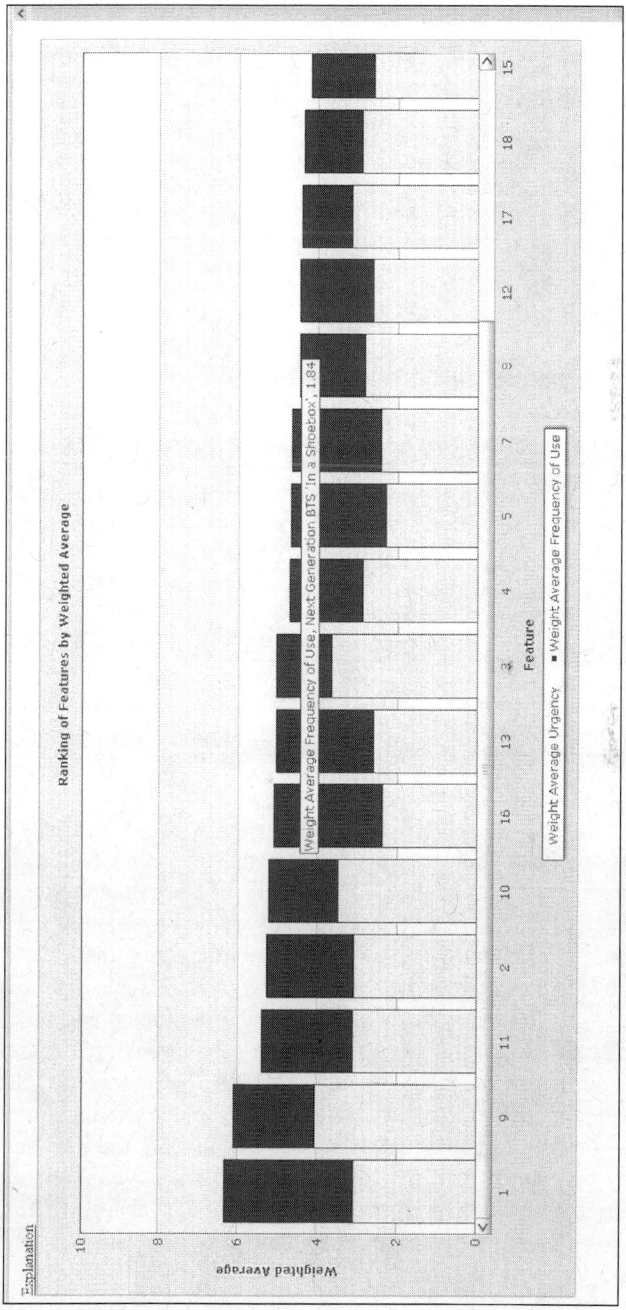

Figure 11.5 Ranking of features for combination of both criteria

Table 11.3 Greedy-based selection of features for R14

Feature set	Design	Hardware	Software	Testing	Cost
f(1)	15	20	12	0	20
f(1),f(9)	20	20	37	14	40
f(1),f(9),f(11)	27	27	67	26	85
f(1),f(9),f(11),f(12)	27	27	77	41	95
f(1),f(9),f(11),f(12),f(2) ✗	67	57	92	56	115
f(1),f(9),f(11),f(12),f(10)	33	28	89	53	114
Capacity	120	80	90	80	200

Table 11.4 Greedy-based selection of features for R15

Feature set	Design	Hardware	Software	Testing	Cost
f(2)	40	30	15	15	20
f(2),f(16)	50	40	30	25	50
f(2),f(16),f(13)	75	50	70	65	90
f(2),f(16),f(13),f(3)	82	62	71	65	97
f(2),f(16),f(13),f(3),f(4) ✗	127	97	108	77	147
Capacity	120	80	90	80	200

After having assigned four features to R15, the next one (feature f(4)) would violate software capacity constraints. In fact, none of the remaining features can be added, as for each of them, one of the constraints would be violated.

In total, running the manual planning process by applying the greedy algorithm described in Chapter 4 provides a plan with offering five features in R14 and another four features in R15. In the subsequent section, the same planning process will be conducted tool-supported using the optimization capabilities of ReleasePlanner™. As a result, a solution is generated which is about 30% better than the manual one in terms of the stated objective to maximize total stakeholder satisfaction. Besides the higher quality, the time to generate this solution is just a portion of what John has spent to create the manual plan. This advantage becomes even more substantial if ongoing re-planning has to be performed to accommodate changed priorities of the planning criteria or modified resource capacities.

11.5 GENERATION OF OPTIMIZED RELEASE PLAN ALTERNATIVES

With all the information introduced above, release planning is now conducted using ReleasePlanner™. For performing optimization, the weights of the releases need to be specified. This information gives the relative value of assigning features in R14 versus in R15. If the feature is not assigned to either of them, it does not contribute to the total stakeholder satisfaction (measured in the total number of stakeholder feature points as defined in Chapter 6).

For the case study, weight_release(R14) = 6 and weight_release(R15) = 3. What that means is that the feature contribution to overall objective is twice as high for being assigned to R14 as compared to assignment to R15. As a result of the optimization, a set of five highly qualified plans is received. The structure of the plans (including the manual plan generated in the previous section) is shown in Figure 11.6. Therein, all feature-to-release assignments labeled by *1,2* or *3* refer to the assignment to R14 and R15, respectively, to postpone the feature.

It becomes clear that some of the features are consistently assigned to the same release for all five plans. For example,

- f(1), f(9) and f(10) are consistently assigned to R14.
- f(4), f(14), f(15) and f(20) are consistently postponed.

On the other hand, there are features such as f(11) and f(12), for which each of the three possible assignments are suggested by at least one of the alternative plans. This means that additional flexibility can be offered in the human decision-making process by following that alternative which is best in terms of the fulfillment of implicit concerns.

In addition to the structure of the alternative plans, formal quality evaluation is of interest. The quality of a plan is measured by the total number of stakeholder feature points achieved. Another measure refers to the degree of optimality. If a plan has achieved 100% optimality, then this means that, under the given resource and technology constraints, there is no better plan possible in the sense of achieving a higher total number of stakeholder feature points. Often, plans above 95% of optimality are considered by John as being *good enough* for practical purposes.

In Figure 11.7, the degree of optimality of the plans, the total number of stakeholder feature points and the number of features per release are shown for the five optimized alternative plans as well as for the manual (greedy) plan. All the optimized alternatives offer seven features in the next release R14 and four or five more features in R15. In all five cases, there are eight (nine in case of alternative 5) features which are suggested to be postponed. While the number of features is largely the same in each release, the features themselves slightly differ from each other. What is remarkable for this case study is that there are even three different optimal solutions. This case also shows that the greedy algorithm (typically) comes up with a plan (being 76.9% optimal in this case) which is a long way from utilizing resources in the best possible way.

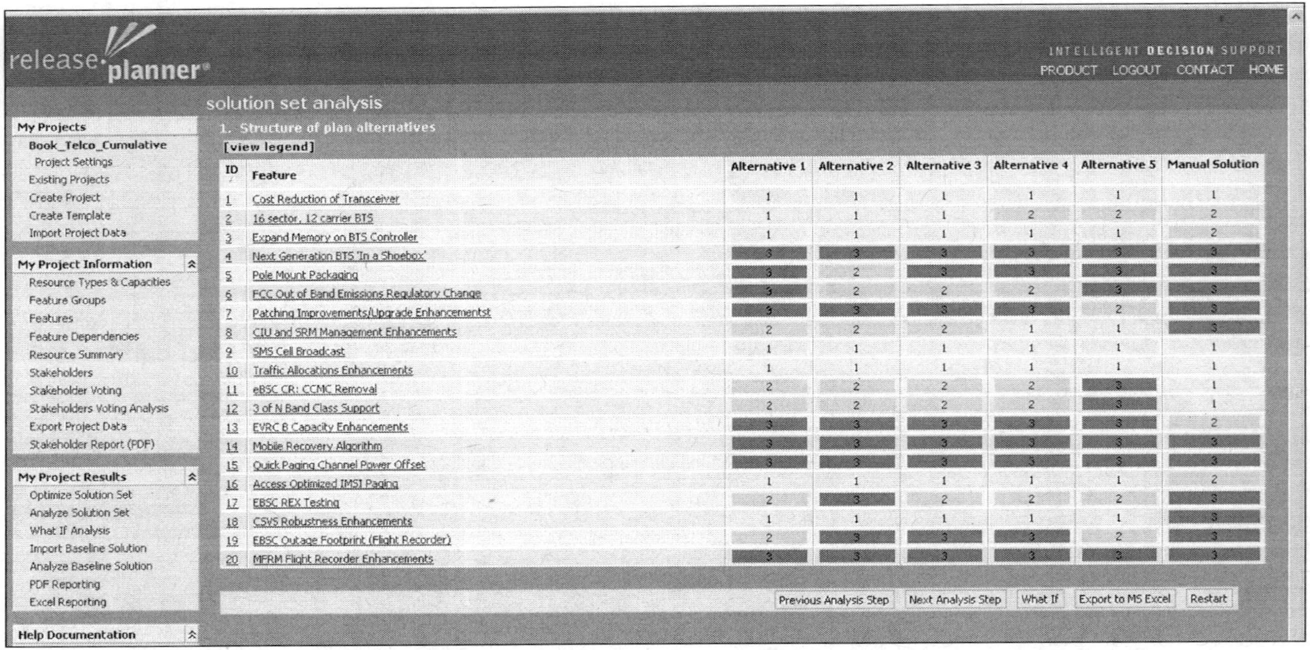

Figure 11.6 Structural comparison of optimized and manual plan alternatives

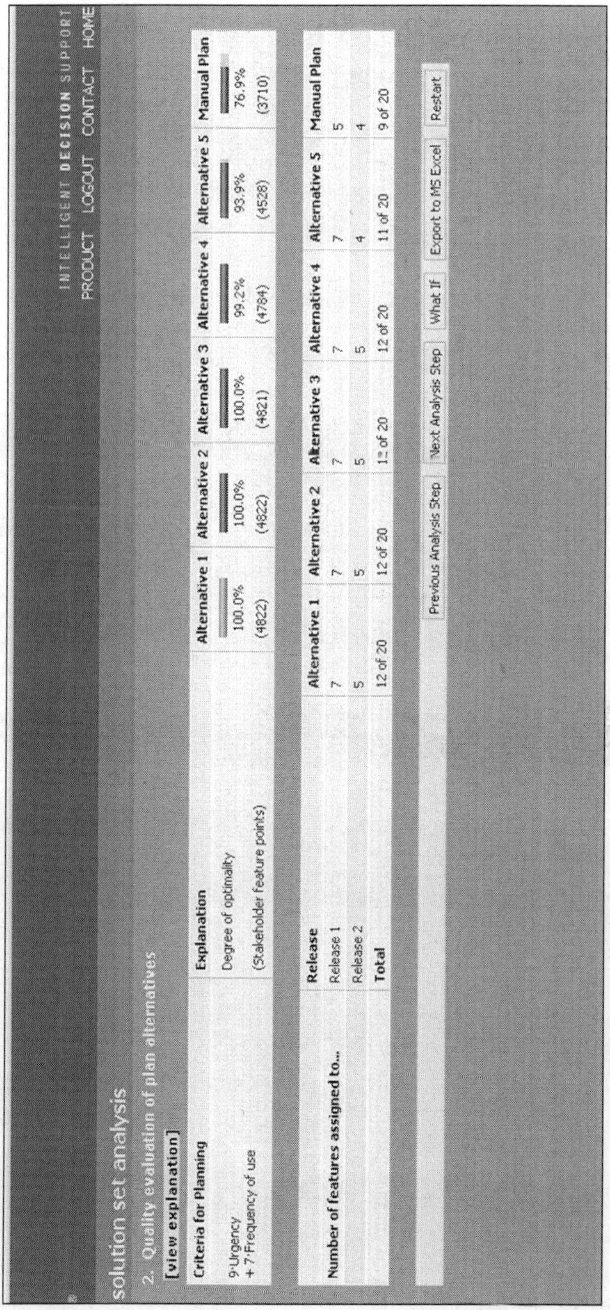

Figure 11.7 Quality evaluation of the optimized alternatives and the manual plan

Besides structural and quality considerations, John also takes a look at the tool's resource utilization analysis. The selection of the final planning solution is also influenced by the different levels of resource consumption. Table 11.5 provides the details on that. The table shows the percentage of resource consumption (related to the capacity available) for all resources and for both release periods. What can be seen is that there are substantial differences between the plans when looking at how resources are spent. For example, the effort for *hardware development* for release R14 varies between 91.3% (Alternative x1) to 53.8% (Alternative x4) of the total capacity available for this release period.

Table 11.5 Relative resource consumption in R14 and R15 for the alternative plans

Resource	Release	Alternatives					
		x1	x2	x3	x4	x5	Manual solution
Design	R14	69.2%	79.2%	69.2%	73.3%	79.2%	27.5
	R15	68.3%	100.0%	85.0%	80.8%	100.0%	68.3
	Difference	0.9%	20.8%	15.8%	7.5%	20.8%	40.8
Hardware development	R14	91.3%	91.3%	91.3%	53.8%	53.8%	35.0
	R15	8.8%	46.3%	23.8%	61.3%	90.0%	77.5
	Difference	82.5%	45.0%	67.5%	7.5%	36.2%	42.5
Software development	R14	100.0%	100.0%	100.0%	94.4%	100.0%	98.9
	R15	100.0%	100.0%	94.4%	100.0%	100.0%	78.9
	Difference	0.0%	0.0%	5.6%	5.6%	0.0%	20.0
Testing	R14	95.0%	95.0%	95.0%	82.5%	82.5%	66.3
	R15	52.5%	46.3%	52.5%	65.0%	56.3%	81.3
	Difference	42.5%	48.7%	42.5%	17.5%	26.2%	15.0
Cost	R14	65.5%	65.5%	65.5%	75.5%	75.5%	75.0
	R15	62.5%	77.5%	67.5%	57.5%	37.5%	48.5
	Difference	3.0%	12.0%	2.0%	18.0%	38.0%	8.5

Besides the level of resource consumption, there is also a substantial difference in the stability of the amount of resource consumption when comparing between two releases. When comparing alternatives x1 and x2, the absolute difference in resource consumption is 0.9% versus 20.8% for design and 82.5% versus 45.0% for hardware development. This implies quite substantial change in the amount of usage of the resources. At this point, John does not consider this to be a problem.

The resource consumption analysis also gives a snapshot of the criticality of the different resources. As can be seen in Table 11.5, there is consistency between all five alternatives in the fact that software development is a bottleneck resource. Bottleneck resources are those that limit the further expansion of the plans (adding more features). For all of the alternatives in both releases R14 and R15, the *software development* capacity is either fully or mostly consumed. As a consequence, any unexpected shortages in this resource type immediately result in shortages in the amount of functionality that can be offered in this release (assuming there is a fixed release date scenario). Looking at the manual plan, it looks (as a tendency) that resource utilization is lower than for the other plans. But this is exactly where the better results are based upon: more comprehensive and more effective usage of the resources available.

With all the plans generated and evaluated so far, it would be interesting to be able to predict the likely reactions of the stakeholders to the proposed plans. This prediction, as well, would help John to decide if one of the plans should be implemented or if, eventually, some further re-planning needs to be done with adjusted problem parameters. To perform this prediction, stakeholder excitement analysis is executed (Step 10 of the EVOLVE II process model, see Chapter 6).

Some sample results on this analysis are shown in Figure 11.8. It is the projected excitement for the stakeholder *Key customer East* with respect to the articulated priorities of the features in terms of their urgency. The stakeholder considers feature f(1) as extremely urgent (score = 9). As this feature is proposed in all solutions to be delivered in R14 (see Figure 11.6), the stakeholder is expected to be very excited. The perception becomes different when looking at feature f(8). This feature was considered by the same stakeholder as urgent as feature f(1). However, according to the manual plan, it will be provided in neither R14 nor in R15. This is likely to create a strong disappointment if this plan were followed. On the other hand, alternatives 4 and 5 are suggesting to offer this feature in R14, which would create strong excitement again.

The summary (called *excitement profile*) as well as the detailed excitement information presented in Figure 11.8, are available for all stakeholders and for all planning criteria. The information is intended to predict the likely reaction of a stakeholder in response to a proposed plan. This information can be used to argue in favor or against a proposed plan (depending on the level of excitement it creates). Once a plan is finally committed to, this information can be used to contact stakeholders up-front (before announcing which feature will be provided and as part of which release) and to explain to them why things have been decided in that way. In most of these cases, this has to do with the inherent conflict between the local view of a specific stakeholder and the global view of the company, where the set of *all* (potentially contradicting) stakeholder views need to be integrated into one action.

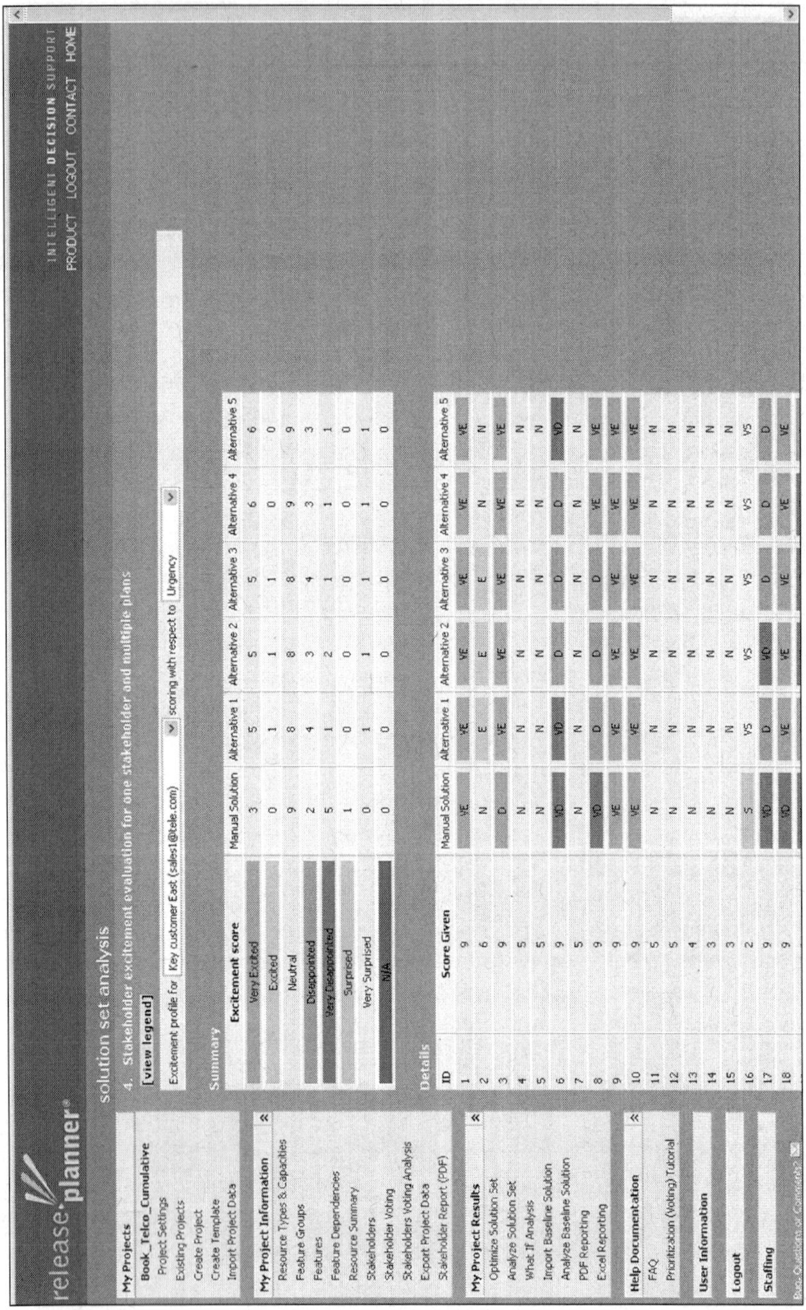

Figure 11.8 Excitement analysis sample screenshot from ReleasePlanner™

At this point of the planning process, John looks at the attractiveness of the current plans (their "fitness for purpose"). This re-consideration of the computed plans is very important to ensure their practical validity. Validity evaluation also means looking at possible implicit concerns, this not having been part of the formalized planning model looked at so far.

The main conclusion drawn from the analysis of the proposed plan is that the CTO and John concur in their ambition to increase the amount of functionality offered in the next two releases. From the resource analysis performed, John concludes that software development is a bottleneck resource in achieving this goal. He looks for possibilities to provide additional resources for software development. This could be done by either hiring new people or finding people within SIP who are able to switch smoothly to software development.

Another conclusion of the discussion between John and the CTO was that features f(1) and f(9) were considered so important that they should be made mandatory in the upcoming release R14. Technically speaking, this means pre-assigning these two features for any follow-up planning iteration. In addition, f(10) is pre-assigned to not being postponed, that is, being delivered at either R14 or R15.

11.6 RE-RUNNING THE PROCESS

Entering a second iteration of planning, software development capacities are adjusted by John. John knows that some hardware developers are capable of conducting software development as well. As a result, 15 person days of hardware development capacity have been re-allocated to software development. The resulting capacities used for the second iteration of planning are summarized in Table 11.6.

Table 11.6 Modified resource capacities for the Telco sample project

Resources			Resource capacities	
Resource name	Resource type	Resource units	Release R14	Release R15
Design	Effort	Person days	100	100
Software development	Effort	Person days	115	115
Hardware development	Effort	Person days	75	75
Testing	Effort	Person days	80	80
Cost	Budget	K dollars	200	200

Compared to the initial capacities, software development now has 115 person days available for both releases. With this new capacity profile, optimized alternative plans are generated again. The structure of the alternative x1 to x5 plans with the individual assignments of features to releases and their quality evaluation are shown in Table 11.7.

Just considering the comparison of the numerically best plans (in terms of the total number of stakeholder feature points achieved) from iterations 1 and 2, it becomes clear that re-shifting capacities has paid off. The total number of stakeholder feature points has increased from 4822 to 5384. This is an improvement of 11.7 %. Simultaneously, the number of features offered in either R14 or R15 has increased from 12 to 14.

At this point, the motivation behind creating a portfolio of five plans instead of just looking for the one numerically best plan is reiterated. With the uncertainty of data and the incompleteness of the underlying planning model, it is unclear up-front which plan among the five is the best fit with the actual real-world problem. While the difference in the formally defined quality — determined by the difference in the total number of stakeholder feature points (TNSFP) between the five alternative plans — is marginal, John is looking at additional concerns that would qualify one solution over another. The assumption here is these concerns are more relevant than the marginal differences in TNSFP.

In EVOLVE II, there are two principal ways to derive the final planning decisions. The first one (as suggested in Step 12) is to ask selected stakeholders to score the planning alternatives in terms of their overall attractiveness (between *very low* and *very high*). According to that, the final plan is obtained from the one having the highest (weighted) average score. In other words, the same process as defined for prioritization of features is applied for prioritization among the optimized candidate release planning alternatives.

The second option (following Steps 9 to 11) is to evaluate the alternatives in terms of the additional concerns. An overview of the relative (in % of the capacity available) resource consumption for all candidate alternatives and all resource types is shown in Figure 11.9. What can be seen is that software development still represents the bottleneck resource in R14 for most of the alternatives.

John performs an overall excitement analysis and considers this result as the key indicator for the preference of an alternative. The aggregated stakeholder excitement profile for all criteria and all the five final alternatives is presented in Table 11.8. What can be seen, for example, is that alternative 3 in total has 30 *very excited* ratings from the eight stakeholders under consideration. On the other hand, alternative 5 is expected to create in total 12 times a reaction of *very disappointed.*

Table 11.7 Structure of alternative solutions generated in iteration 2 (Step 9 of the EVOLVE II process)

Features		Alternatives				
ID	Name	x1	x2	x3	x4	x5
1	Cost Reduction of Transceiver	R14	R14	R14	R14	R14
2	16 sector, 12 carrier BTS	PP	PP	R15	R15	PP
3	Expand Memory on BTS Controller	R14	R14	R14	R14	R14
4	Next Generation BTS 'In a Shoebox'	PP	PP	PP	PP	PP
5	Pole Mount Packaging	PP	PP	PP	R15	PP
6	FCC Out-of-Band Emissions Regulatory Change	R15	R15	PP	R14	R14
7	Patching Improvements/Upgrade Enhance-ments	PP	PP	PP	PP	R15
8	CIU and SRM Management Enhancements	R14	R14	R15	PP	PP
9	SMS Cell Broadcast	R14	R14	R14	R14	R14
10	Traffic Allocations Enhancements	R14	R14	R14	R15	R14
11	eBSC CR: CCMC Removal	R14	R14	R14	R14	R14
12	3 of N Band Class Support	R14	R14	R14	R14	R14
13	EVRC-B Capacity Enhancements	PP	PP	PP	PP	PP
14	Mobile Recovery Algorithm	R15	R15	PP	PP	R15
15	Quick Paging Channel Power Offset	R15	PP	PP	PP	PP
16	Access Optimized IMSI Paging	R14	R14	R15	R14	R15
17	EBSC REX Testing	R15	R15	R15	PP	R15
18	CSVS Robustness Enhancements	R15	R15	R14	R14	R14
19	EBSC Outage Footprint (Flight Recorder)	R15	R15	R14	R15	R15
20	MFRM Flight Recorder Enhancements	PP	R15	R15	R15	PP
	Degree of optimality of the plan (in %)	100	99.9	96.7	95.8	95.3
	Total number of stakeholder feature points	5384	5379	5204	5158	5129

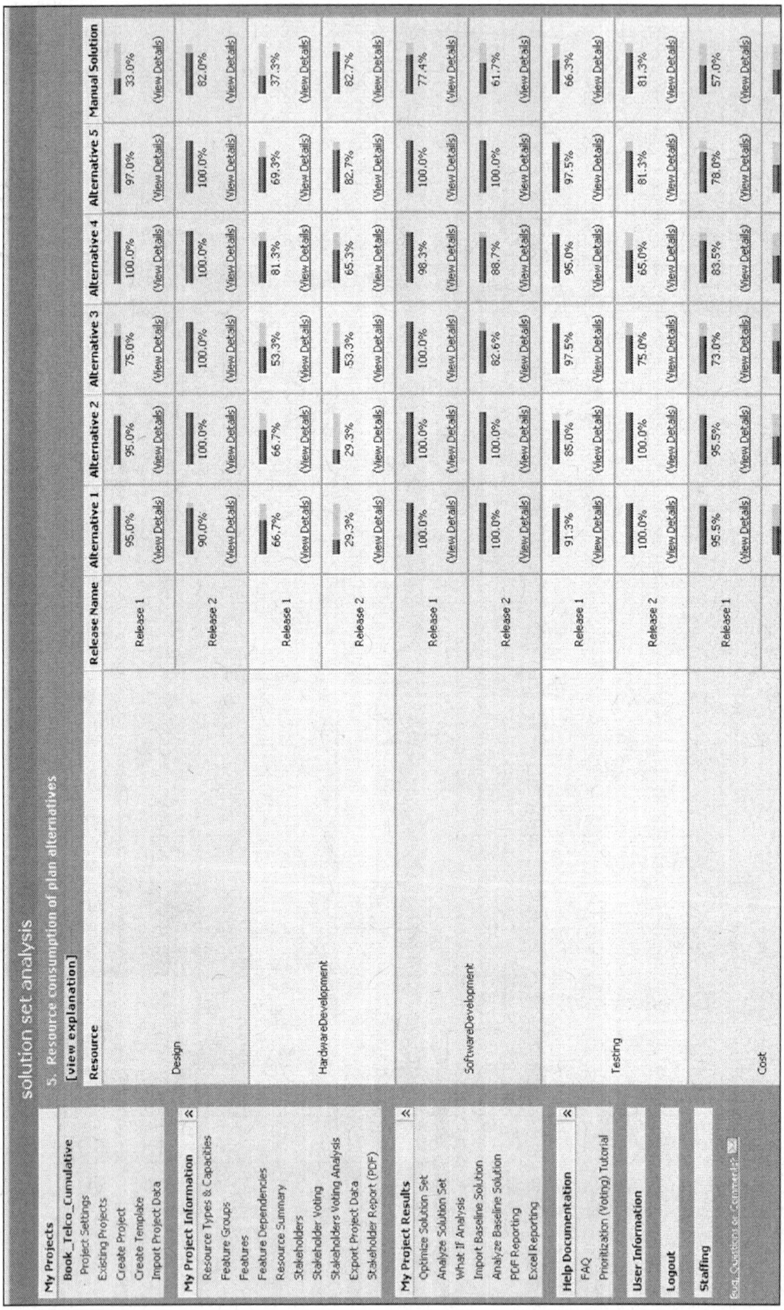

Figure 11.9 Resource consumption profile

Table 11.8 Aggregated stakeholder excitement profiles related to final planning alternatives

	Alternative 1	Alternative 2	Alternative 3	Alternative 4	Alternative 5
Very Excited	29	29	30	26	30
Excited	25	25	23	23	20
Neutral	140	139	151	151	149
Disappointed	32	30	27	29	27
Very disappointed	8	8	7	12	12

Looking at the projected excitement, John and the involved stakeholders consider alternative 3 as the most attractive. It generates the third highest total stakeholder satisfaction, the highest number of strong excitements and the least number of strong disappointments. From running the excitement analysis, John also understands with which stakeholder he needs to talk to explain the final decision despite some individual disappointments. In total, John is now able to make an informed decision about which features should be offered in R14 and R15. Moreover, he is able to achieve an increase in the expected total stakeholder satisfaction. Finally, John has the commitment of the stakeholders having been involved in the process and is able to explain and justify his proposed roadmap plan to them.

CHAPTER 12

CASE STUDY: STAFFING FOR PRODUCT RELEASES

12.1 INTRODUCTION

With all the knowledge gained about methods for staffing, the question becomes: How does all this apply in a concrete case study project? John, the product manager at our sample telecommunications company SIP Inc., is working closely with Jane, one of the project managers of the company. Jane's responsibility is to ensure that the plans created and revised by John are properly scheduled, and that the assignment of developers to perform the individual tasks is feasible and efficient. Staffing for product releases needs to be done almost continuously. Jane has to make weekly staffing decisions related to the following questions:

- Which features will be implemented next?
- Which tasks are assigned to whom?
- In which order should the tasks be performed?
- How do we react to changed plans?
- How do we react to changes on the availability of personnel?

The main interest in this chapter is on staffing of plans that have been obtained as the result of strategic planning. At the strategic level, resources were considered in a cumulative way, without looking into the details of an individual task to be done at a specific interval. The different levels of skill of the developers have been left out of consideration as well.

Hiring and staffing decisions have a strong impact on project performance and success. Because of their importance, there is a growing interest in providing rigorous support. In [Choi et al. '08], continuous simulation based on *system dynamics* [Abdel-Hamid '89] is studied. As discussed by [Malinowski et al. '08], there are two difficulties in this decision-making process. The first difficulty refers to the proper evaluation of the degree of fitness of a single candidate with a required profile. The second difficulty is related to the decision of how well a given candidate would fit into an existing team when looking at the sum of the team competencies. Both questions are addressed in this chapter.

Different scenarios for operational staffing are studied. Although inspired by staffing for product releases, the scenarios are applicable more broadly. Starting with a baseline staffing plan, five scenarios for proactive and reactive staffing are studied in this chapter. *Proactive staffing* tries to go through different scenarios up-front to better understand their possible impact and to come up with actions for risk mitigation. *Re-active staffing* refers to the need to change things in the course of ongoing development. More specifically, the scenarios are devoted to the following topics:

Scenario 1: Study the impact of modified productivity of developers
Scenario 2: Study the impact of periods of absence of developers
Scenario 3: Study the impact of revised effort estimates
Scenario 4: Study the impact of adding a new feature
Scenario 5: Decision support for finding the best new hire for joining a given pool of developers.

The baseline for all these scenarios is explained in Section 12.2. Main solution steps, their results and their applicability are described for all five scenarios in Sections 12.3 to 12.7.

12.2 BASELINE

12.2.1 The baseline scenario data

Most of the project information related to the Telco case study project has already been given in previous chapters. As described in the product roadmapping case study of Chapter 11, five optimized strategic plans were created. The structure of the five plans was given in Section 11.6. In consideration of all the implicit concerns, alternative x3 was considered to be the most attractive one among the five plans generated. Consequently, it is taken as the starting point for staffing.

The goal of this case study is to go through the process of implementing all the tasks related to the features assigned to R14 of the final release planning alternative x3 from Chapter 11. These are the tasks related to the features f(1), f(3), f(9), f(10), f(11), f(12), f(18) and f(19). The four types of tasks relevant for the features are called *design, hardware development*, *software development* and *testing*.

There are eight tasks-related dependencies per feature:

- The *design* task of a feature should never start later than the two development tasks.
- The *hardware development* and *software development* should not start later than testing.
- The *design* task of a feature should never end later than the two development tasks.

- The *hardware development* and *software development* should not end later than testing.

The features and their estimated effort (measured in person days) for the different resource types are given in Table 12.1. What can be seen is that not all features require the performance of all the four tasks. For example, f(1) does not require testing and f(9) has no hardware development. Similarly, features f(12) and f(18) only require software development and testing.

Table 12.1 Features and their effort consumptions considered for staffing

ID	Feature	Design	Hardware develop-ment	Software develop-ment	Testing
1	Cost Reduction of Trans-ceiver Expand Memory on BTS	15	20	12	0
3	Controller	7	12	1	0
9	SMS Cell Broadcast Traffic Allocations	5	0	25	14
10	Enhancements	6	1	12	12
11	eBSC CR: CCMC Removal	7	7	30	12
12	3 of N Band Class Support CSVS Robustness	0	0	10	15
18	Enhancements	0	0	10	25
19	EB SC Outage Footprint (Flight recorder)	20	0	15	0

For implementation of the tasks, a pool of four developers is available. The productivity profile of the developers is shown in Table 12.2. Initially, the developers are assumed to be available without any interruptions (periods of absence).

Estimation of productivity of developers is a difficult ask. It can be based upon former work experience. One method determining the relative productivity levels would be the application of pair-wise comparison between developers as done by the Analytic Hierarchy Process AHP described in Section 3.6.

As introduced in previous chapters, average productivity is expressed by a factor equal to 1. Productivity above average is described by a factor > 1. Correspondingly, productivity below average is described by a factor < 1. Overall productivity is defined on a ratio scale, that is, the ratio prod(1)/prod(2) of two measures prod(1) and prod(2) describes how much (in %) more (> 1) or less (< 1) productive prod(1) is compared to prod(2).

Table 12.2 Productivity profile of the four available developers

Name	Design	Hardware development	Software development	Testing
dev1	1	0	0.75	0.5
dev2	0	0.5	0.75	1
dev3	0.5	1	0	0.5
dev4	0.75	0.5	1.25	0

12.2.2 Baseline scenario plans — manual versus optimized

The staffing problem for make-span minimization is to find an assignment of developers to tasks such that the overall duration for completing all tasks is minimized. For any feasible plan, all precedence relationships between tasks need to be fulfilled. Initially, the application of the manual planning procedure is simulated. Jane has used a spreadsheet to calculate and maintain all the data. For any task of consideration, Jane is always trying to assign the developer being most productive in this type of task. Features are ordered decreasingly according to their perceived value. The ones with the highest value are implemented first. Following this process, Jane provides a manual staffing plan, which takes 96 days. In total, this process has taken her about five hours of time.

What is shown next is the result of the application of the intelligent planning tool RASORP for the same problem. In general, the results generated from RASORP can be exported in such a way that they allow subsequent representation in Microsoft Project®. The Gantt chart displayed is using the project management tool Microsoft Project®. As a result of running RASORP for the baseline planning scenario, the plan shown in the Gantt chart in Figure 12.1 is generated. As opposed to manual generation of plans, the optimized plan can be generated in a few seconds. This advantage becomes more significant the more scenarios for re-planning are conducted.

What can be seen is that implementation of the feature f(1) called *cost reduction of transceiver* starts March 12, 2010 with work on the design task. This job is assigned to developer dev(1). The task ends April 1, and the whole feature is implemented until April 13, which is determined by the hardware development. The assignment of dev(1) to the design task looks reasonable, as this is the developer most capable in design. The same is true for assignment of dev(3) and dev(4) to hardware and software development, respectively.

From looking at the tasks associated with the same feature, all the precedence relationships formulated above are fulfilled. For example, for *cost reduction of transceiver*, design starts before the two development tasks, and is also finished not later than the development tasks. The design effort for the same feature is 15 person days. As the assigned developer dev(1) has an average productivity, the duration of the whole task is 15 working days. The whole project requires 82 working days.

ID	Task Name	Duration	Start	Finish
1	**Cost Reduction of Transceive**	**23 days**	**Fri 3/12/10**	**Tue 4/13/10**
2	Design	15 days	Fri 3/12/10	Thu 4/1/10
3	HardwareDevelopment	20 days	Wed 3/17/10	Tue 4/13/10
4	SoftwareDevelopment	10 days	Tue 3/23/10	Mon 4/5/10
5	**Traffic Allocations Enhancem**	**28 days**	**Fri 4/2/10**	**Tue 5/11/10**
6	Design	6 days	Fri 4/2/10	Fri 4/9/10
7	HardwareDevelopment	2 days	Thu 4/8/10	Fri 4/9/10
8	SoftwareDevelopment	10 days	Mon 4/12/10	Fri 4/23/10
9	Testing	12 days	Mon 4/26/10	Tue 5/11/10
10	**eBSC CR: CCMC Removal**	**47 days**	**Mon 4/19/10**	**Tue 6/22/10**
11	Design	7 days	Mon 4/19/10	Tue 4/27/10
12	HardwareDevelopment	7 days	Mon 4/19/10	Tue 4/27/10
13	SoftwareDevelopment	40 days	Wed 4/28/10	Tue 6/22/10
14	Testing	12 days	Mon 6/7/10	Tue 6/22/10
15	**3 of N Band Class Support**	**15 days**	**Mon 3/1/10**	**Fri 3/19/10**
16	SoftwareDevelopment	8 days	Mon 3/1/10	Wed 3/10/10
17	Testing	15 days	Mon 3/1/10	Fri 3/19/10
18	**CSVS Robustness Enhancem**	**32 days**	**Thu 3/11/10**	**Fri 4/23/10**
19	SoftwareDevelopment	8 days	Thu 3/11/10	Mon 3/22/10
20	Testing	25 days	Mon 3/22/10	Fri 4/23/10
21	**EBSC Outage Footprint (Fligh**	**40 days**	**Wed 4/28/10**	**Tue 6/22/10**
22	Design	40 days	Wed 4/28/10	Tue 6/22/10
23	SoftwareDevelopment	12 days	Mon 6/7/10	Tue 6/22/10
24	**Expand Memory on BTS Cont**	**12 days**	**Mon 3/1/10**	**Tue 3/16/10**
25	Design	7 days	Mon 3/1/10	Tue 3/9/10
26	HardwareDevelopment	12 days	Mon 3/1/10	Tue 3/16/10
27	SoftwareDevelopment	2 days	Wed 3/10/10	Thu 3/11/10
28	**SMS Cell Broadcast**	**36 days**	**Mon 4/12/10**	**Mon 5/31/10**
29	Design	5 days	Mon 4/12/10	Fri 4/16/10
30	SoftwareDevelopment	20 days	Mon 4/26/10	Fri 5/21/10
31	Testing	14 days	Wed 5/12/10	Mon 5/31/10

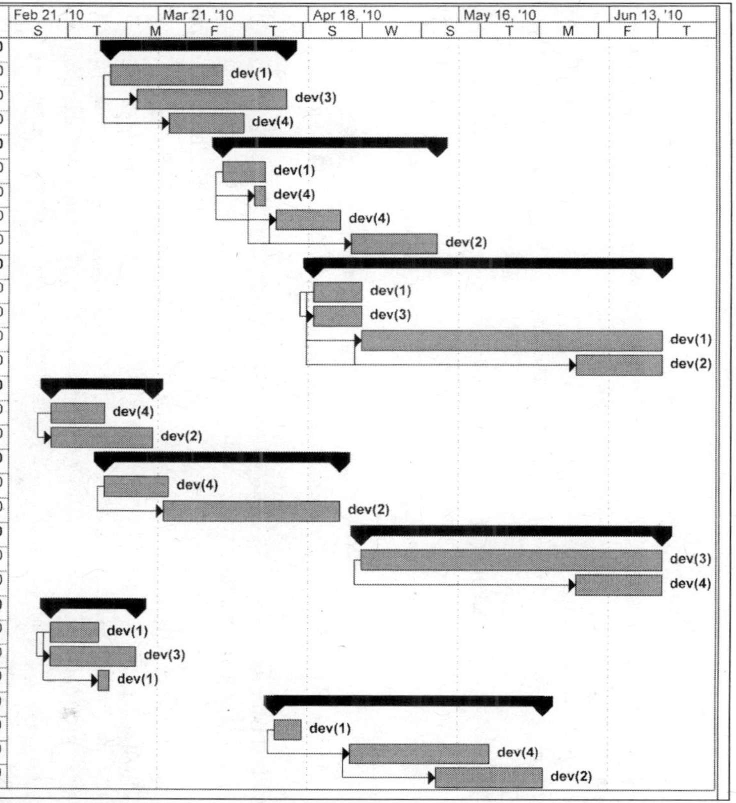

Figure 12.1 Optimized baseline staffing plan

The project is expected to be finished on June 22, 2010. That means that the make-span has been reduced from 96 (manual plan) to 82 (optimized plan) days. For better comparison, the results of the manual and optimized plan are shown in Figure 12.2. The first number in each segment refers to the feature number, the second one to the task number. A comparison between the two plans reveals that the optimized one creates less idle time for developers. This has been achieved by assigning tasks to developers other than the top one (in terms of productivity). As a result, the total amount of idle times is reduced. Idle times for dev(1), dev(2), dev(3) and dev(4) according to the manual plan are 6, 31, 29 and 23 days, respectively. These periods are substantially reduced by the optimization, resulting in 0, 4, 3 and 12 days of idle time, respectively. While reducing idle time is not the primary goal, it is a good indicator of the quality of the plan, especially if developers are assigned mainly to tasks in which they are most productive.

12.3 THE IMPACT OF IMPROVED PRODUCTIVITY

Staffing is an ongoing effort. Computer-based tools such as RASORP can be used to explore scenarios proactively as well as to re-plan a once established staffing agenda. The first scenario is devoted to better understanding of the impact of having improved productivity of the developers. This is motivated by the question whether investment into training of personnel or hiring of new personnel pays off. It is assumed that the productivity in testing of dev(1) has been improved from 0.5 to 1.0. Similarly, productivity of dev(2) in terms of software development has increased from formerly 0.75 to now 1.0. Both increases can be the result of training or hiring better skilled developers.

How do these two improvements impact the staffing plan created in the baseline scenario? The Gantt chart resulting from this planning scenario is shown in Figure 12.3. Looking at the developers dev(1) and dev(2), it becomes clear that their assignments to tasks have changed. In the baseline plan, dev(2) was exclusively working on tasks devoted to testing. With the increased productivity in software development, the optimized plan assigns this developer to five tasks, where three of them are devoted to testing and two to software development. This increased flexibility in properly assigning the developer to different tasks contributes to better results for the overall make-span of the schedule. The same arguments apply for developer dev(1).

As a consequence of the more flexible usage of developers dev(1) and dev(2), the remaining two developers are assigned differently as well. The total duration of implementing all tasks has been reduced from 82 to 74 working (or 12 calendar) days. The project is predicted to be finished on June 10, 2010.

The scenario gives some principal insight into the impact of changed (improved) performance of developers. More detailed models could look into the performance in dependence of different tasks and into the effect of learning within the same project.

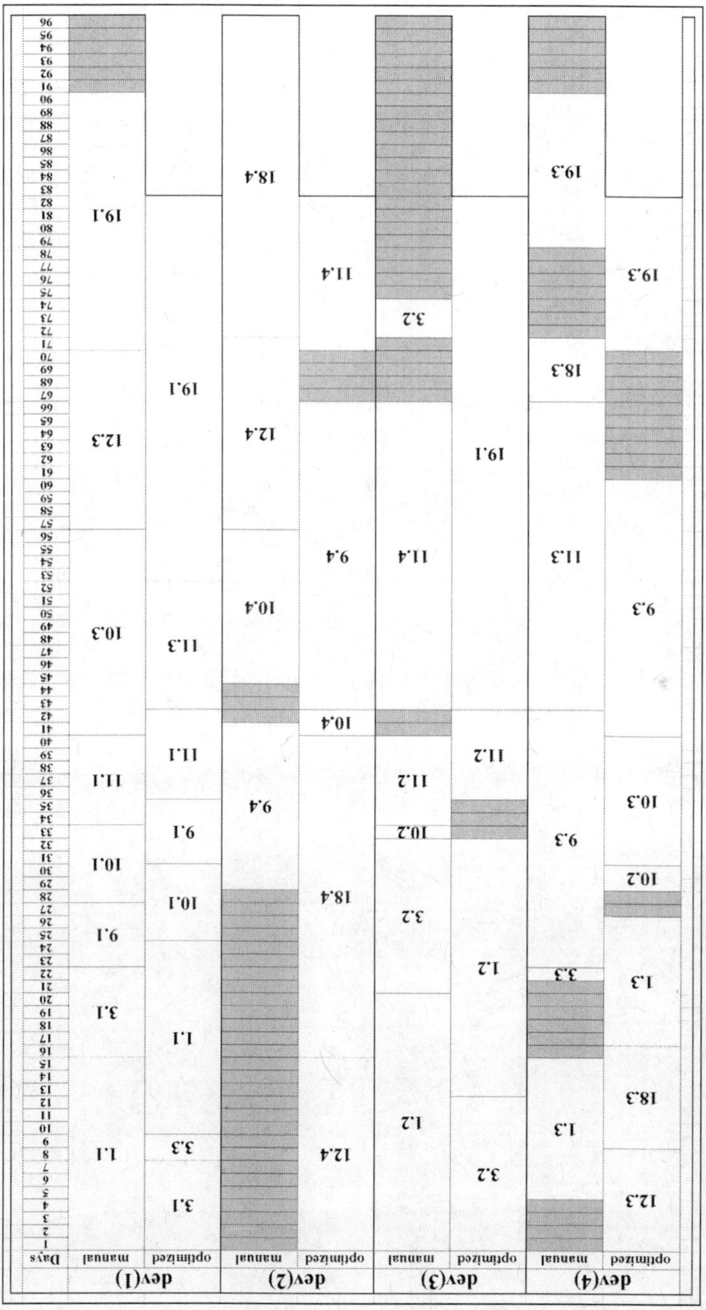

Figure 12.2 Comparison of manual versus optimized baseline staffing plan. Grey boxes refer to idle times

ID	Task Name	Duration	Start	Finish
1	**Cost Reduction of Transceive**	**50 days**	**Wed 3/10/10**	**Tue 5/18/10**
2	Design	30 days	Wed 3/10/10	Tue 4/20/10
3	HardwareDevelopment	20 days	Wed 4/21/10	Tue 5/18/10
4	SoftwareDevelopment	10 days	Fri 4/30/10	Thu 5/13/10
5	**Traffic Allocations Enhancem**	**30 days**	**Fri 4/30/10**	**Thu 6/10/10**
6	Design	6 days	Fri 4/30/10	Fri 5/7/10
7	HardwareDevelopment	1 day	Wed 5/19/10	Wed 5/19/10
8	SoftwareDevelopment	12 days	Mon 5/10/10	Tue 5/25/10
9	Testing	12 days	Wed 5/26/10	Thu 6/10/10
10	**eBSC CR: CCMC Removal**	**24 days**	**Mon 3/1/10**	**Thu 4/1/10**
11	Design	7 days	Mon 3/1/10	Tue 3/9/10
12	HardwareDevelopment	7 days	Mon 3/1/10	Tue 3/9/10
13	SoftwareDevelopment	24 days	Mon 3/1/10	Thu 4/1/10
14	Testing	12 days	Wed 3/17/10	Thu 4/1/10
15	**3 of N Band Class Support**	**26 days**	**Fri 4/2/10**	**Fri 5/7/10**
16	SoftwareDevelopment	8 days	Fri 4/2/10	Tue 4/13/10
17	Testing	15 days	Mon 4/19/10	Fri 5/7/10
18	**CSVS Robustness Enhancem**	**35 days**	**Mon 3/1/10**	**Fri 4/16/10**
19	SoftwareDevelopment	10 days	Mon 3/1/10	Fri 3/12/10
20	Testing	25 days	Mon 3/15/10	Fri 4/16/10
21	**EBSC Outage Footprint (Fligh**	**20 days**	**Fri 4/2/10**	**Thu 4/29/10**
22	Design	20 days	Fri 4/2/10	Thu 4/29/10
23	SoftwareDevelopment	12 days	Wed 4/14/10	Thu 4/29/10
24	**Expand Memory on BTS Cont**	**20 days**	**Mon 5/10/10**	**Fri 6/4/10**
25	Design	7 days	Mon 5/10/10	Tue 5/18/10
26	HardwareDevelopment	12 days	Thu 5/20/10	Fri 6/4/10
27	SoftwareDevelopment	2 days	Wed 5/19/10	Thu 5/20/10
28	**SMS Cell Broadcast**	**67 days**	**Wed 3/10/10**	**Thu 6/10/10**
29	Design	5 days	Wed 3/10/10	Tue 3/16/10
30	SoftwareDevelopment	20 days	Fri 5/14/10	Thu 6/10/10
31	Testing	14 days	Mon 5/24/10	Thu 6/10/10

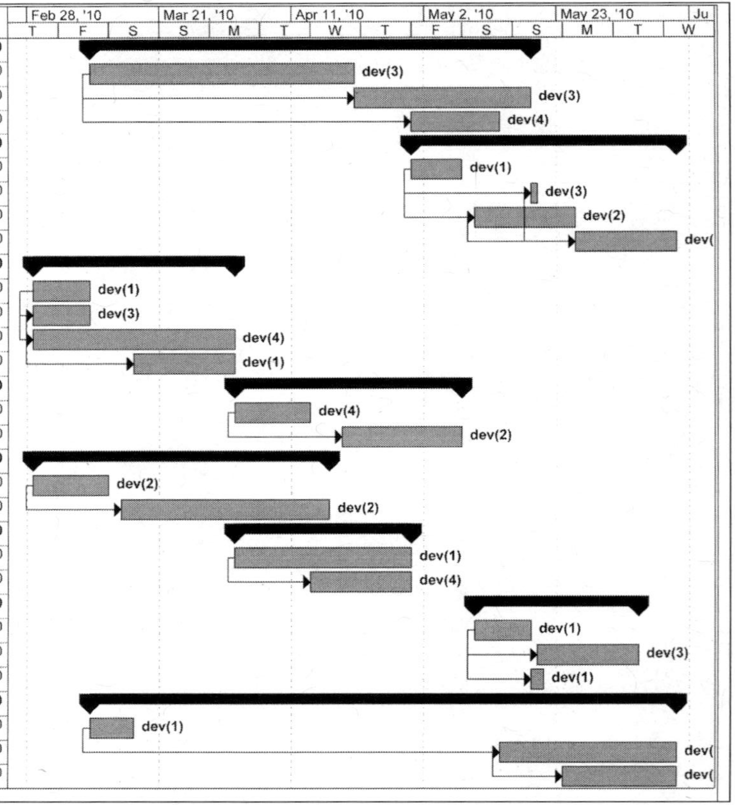

Figure 12.3 Staffing plan for increased productivity of dev(1) and dev(2)

12.4 THE IMPACT OF PREDICTED AND UNPREDICTED ABSENCE OF DEVELOPERS

As the second scenario, the impact of periods of absence is studied. Again, the baseline staffing plan serves as a reference point. Another assumption is that no additional developer would be available at this point in time for replacement. For the scenario studied here, dev(1) is assumed to be absent during time interval [40,60]. Similarly, dev(4) is away during [17,40]. These absences will certainly delay the whole plan, especially with considering the dependencies between tasks. For this case study the computation shows the plan will be delayed by 30 days and finished in 112 days, if the project manager sticks to the baseline plan.

Assume the project manager knows about these absence periods in advance. This is called *predicted absence*. Correspondingly, if the absence occurs unpredicted, this is called *unpredicted absence*. It will be shown in this section that (i) RASORP can be very helpful in reducing the effort for accommodating both types of changes, and (ii) provides clearly better options as manual re-staffing. The two arguments are illustrated for the two periods of absence introduced above.

Figure 12.4 shows the Gantt chart of the plan generated from RASORP (in conjunction with MS Project®) for the case of predicted absence. Compared to the baseline plan, the assignment and timing of the tasks have been changed dramatically. For example, designing feature f(1) is done by dev(1) in the baseline plan while it's done by dev(3) in the revised plan. Similarly software development of feature f(19), which was supposed to be done by dev(4) at t = 71 in the baseline plan, is now be done by dev(2) at t = 26. Overall, the staffing optimization tool has been able to accommodate predicted changes in the availability of the developers.

The case of making the same periods of absence for developers dev(1) and dev(4) being unpredicted is now assumed to be treated manually, applying the same idea of greedy planning as demonstrated in Section 12.2 for the baseline plan. As a result, project duration of 131 days is obtained. Although there some changes in the assignments, e.g., testing of feature f(11), which is done by dev(1) in the new plan vs. dev(2) in the baseline plan, these changes still cannot mitigate the absence of developers in the same way as the optimization method does.

The above scenario is intended to be illustrative. The expectation is that the impact of optimized staffing and re-staffing becomes the more severe, the larger and the more complex the problem. Size here is measured by the number of tasks, the number of features and the number of developers. Complexity refers to constraints between tasks and the number of periods of absence. The more difficult case of unpredicted absence in reality has the additional difficulty of being eventually unknown in its duration.

ID	Task Name	Duration	Start
1	**Cost Reduction of Transceive**	**67 days**	**Wed 3/10/10**
2	Design	30 days	Wed 3/10/10
3	HardwareDevelopment	20 days	Wed 4/21/10
4	SoftwareDevelopment	10 days	Fri 5/28/10
5	**Traffic Allocations Enhancem**	**30 days**	**Mon 5/31/10**
6	Design	6 days	Mon 5/31/10
7	HardwareDevelopment	1 day	Mon 6/7/10
8	SoftwareDevelopment	16 days	Tue 6/8/10
9	Testing	24 days	Tue 6/8/10
10	**eBSC CR: CCMC Removal**	**64 days**	**Mon 3/1/10**
11	Design	7 days	Mon 3/1/10
12	HardwareDevelopment	7 days	Mon 3/1/10
13	SoftwareDevelopment	24 days	Mon 4/26/10
14	Testing	12 days	Wed 5/12/10
15	**3 of N Band Class Support**	**71 days**	**Thu 3/11/10**
16	SoftwareDevelopment	8 days	Thu 3/11/10
17	Testing	15 days	Fri 5/28/10
18	**CSVS Robustness Enhancem**	**25 days**	**Mon 3/1/10**
19	SoftwareDevelopment	8 days	Mon 3/1/10
20	Testing	25 days	Mon 3/1/10
21	**EBSC Outage Footprint (Fligh**	**38 days**	**Wed 3/10/10**
22	Design	20 days	Wed 3/10/10
23	SoftwareDevelopment	20 days	Mon 4/5/10
24	**Expand Memory on BTS Con**	**42 days**	**Wed 4/7/10**
25	Design	7 days	Wed 4/7/10
26	HardwareDevelopment	12 days	Wed 5/19/10
27	SoftwareDevelopment	2 days	Fri 4/16/10
28	**SMS Cell Broadcast**	**34 days**	**Mon 5/24/10**
29	Design	5 days	Mon 5/24/10
30	SoftwareDevelopment	20 days	Fri 6/11/10
31	Testing	14 days	Mon 6/21/10

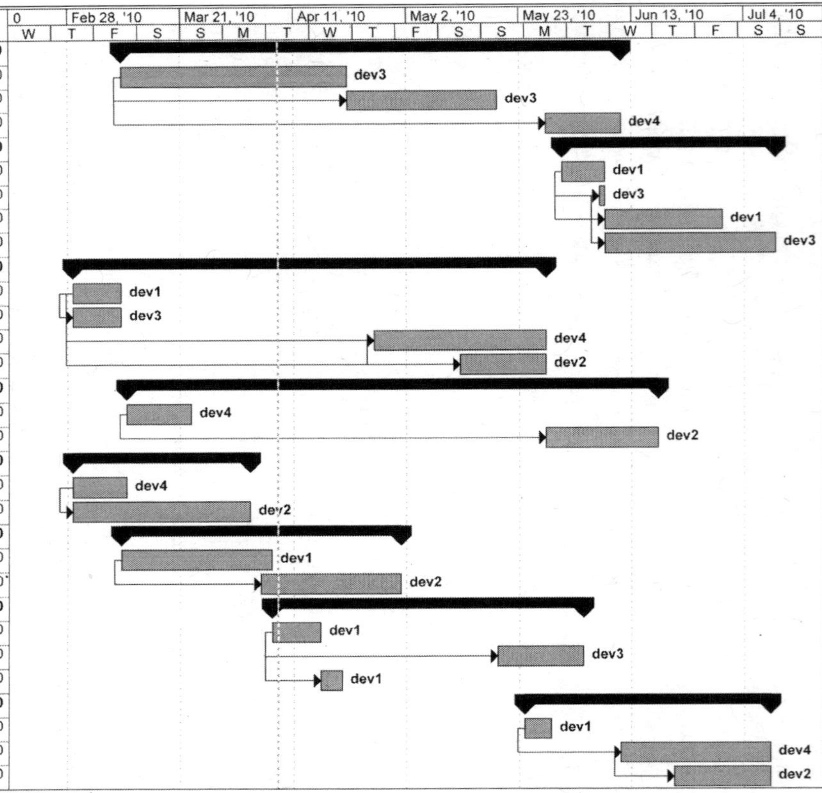

Figure 12.4 Gantt chart for the scenario of *unpredicted absence*

12.5 THE IMPACT OF UNPREDICTED CHANGE OF EFFORT ESTIMATES

The third scenario investigates the impact of encountering higher than estimated actual efforts for some tasks. Uncertainty in effort estimation among others results from the lack of knowledge about the tasks to be done. This is especially true at an early stage of the development (e.g., during design). Consequently, it is quite common that effort estimates need to be adjusted in the course of the project.

At point in time t = 40, a re-estimation of the former effort estimates has been made (called *unpredicted change*). The following adjustments of the original effort estimates have been made:

- Feature f(9): Effort for software development needs to be increased from originally 25 to now 37 person days
- Feature f(11): Effort for software development needs to be increased from originally 30 to now 45 person days
- Feature f(12): Effort for testing needs to be increased from originally 15 to now 22 person days
- Feature f(18): Effort for testing needs to be increased from originally 25 to now 37 person days

The question becomes how strong the impact of these modified efforts on the overall project duration will be. From Figure 12.5 it can be seen that the overall project duration has substantially increased. The project now takes until July 20, 2010, which corresponds to an overall duration of 102 (working) days. This is a delay of 20 days. What can be seen from that is that it is very important to re-plan and re-staff immediately when changes become transparent.

12.6 THE IMPACT OF ADDING NEW FEATURES DURING DEVELOPMENT

Another possible scenario refers to the situation that in the course of implementation of all tasks related to the agreed upon features, one of the key customers strongly requests an additional feature. Different from the re-planning process described in Chapter 7 (where release time and resource capacities remained unchanged), the question becomes, how much would this additional feature delay the established schedule?

For our case study project, it is assumed that the additional feature is f(20) with the following (estimated) effort consumptions:

- Design: 10 person days
- Software development: 30 person days
- Testing: 20 person days

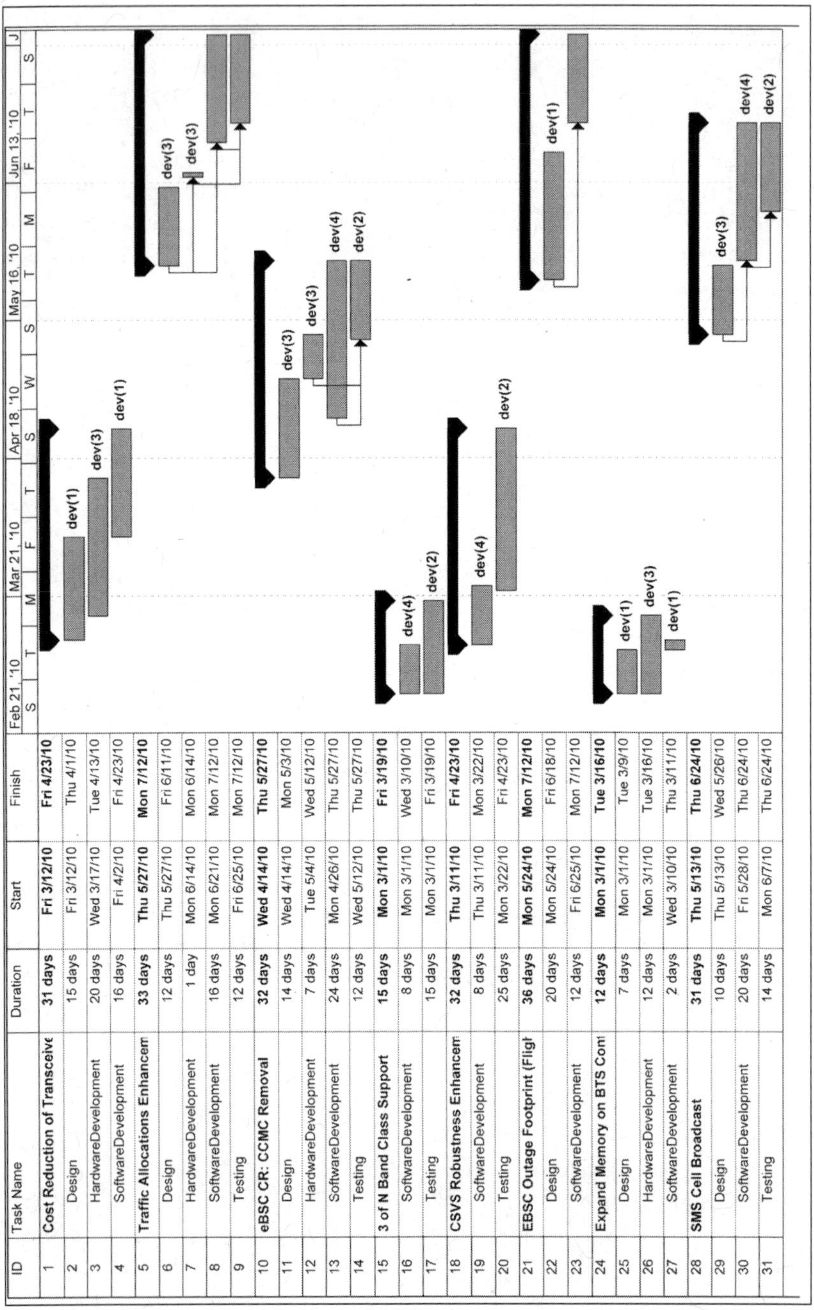

Figure 12.5 Gantt chart for the scenario *dynamic increase of effort*

The feature request arrives at t = 40. At this point in time, some features have already been developed or are in progress of development. That means for the optimized re-planning, all assignments and scheduling made until this point in time need to be fixed in the same way for the re-planning. As a result of running the staffing and scheduling optimization including the additional feature, the overall schedule would be delayed by 18 (working) days, which is more than three calendar weeks. The project and product manager need to decide if this is acceptable and they need to inform all the involved customers and stakeholders about the delay.

12.7 DECISION SUPPORT FOR HIRING

Decision support for the selection and the subsequent job assignment process is rare. Existing approaches are mainly based on standard database queries that do not appropriately tackle the complexity of the task. The reason for this is that they focus solely on the fitness of the person with the job, neglecting the fitness of the person with the team — which is important as well [West and Allen '97].

The final scenario considers the case that for reducing the duration of the project, the company considers hiring a new developer to joint the team. There are four possible candidates who have been taken into consideration. All of them can be assigned to three of the four types of tasks in consideration. Their related productivity profile is summarized in Table 12.3.

Table 12.3 Productivity profile of the four hiring candidates

	Design	Software development	Hardware development	Testing
Hire1	0.75	0.75	0.75	0
Hire2	0.75	0.75	0	0.75
Hire3	0.75	0	0.75	0.75
Hire4	0	0.75	0.75	0.75

In a simplified manner, all of the four candidates are similar in the sense that their sum of all their productivity assessments is the same. However, from looking at the specific team profile and the needs of the project, there are substantial differences in how much the different candidates would help to reduce the project duration. The assumption here is that all candidates would equally well and quickly integrate into the team to achieve their estimated productivity from the very beginning. Differences in salary are left out from consideration here for simplicity reasons.

Application of RASORP allows proactive evaluation of the impact of hiring one of the four developers. The primary decision criterion is the amount of reduction achieved from hiring this person. From running all four scenarios, the results are:

- When deciding for hire 1, the projected new project duration is 69 days
- When deciding for hire 2, the projected new project duration is 70 days
- When deciding for hire 3, the projected new project duration is 64 days
- When deciding for hire 4, the projected new project duration is 68 days

According to this information, the (likely) decision would be in favor of hire 3. This developer would not contribute to *software development*, but in this capability the team is already strongest (measured, in a simplified manner, by the column sums in Table 12.2). Consequently, this developer could potentially contribute to all the remaining competencies and this has been confirmed having the strongest impact on overall project duration. Although a simplified model, it gives at least some guidance on whom to select among the four candidates. For the final human decision-making, this is considered to be one out of several relevant inputs.

12.8 DISCUSSION

The five scenarios give insight into the possibilities to proactively or reactively adjust to changed project situations. This was respectively called predicted and unpredicted change. The analysis was done from the perspective of staffing for shortest overall project duration (or minimizing make-span). Running the scenarios using a computer-based support system such as RASORP is effective and efficient. It allows easy change of the data and re-running scenarios with changed parameters.

The underlying model is a simplification of reality. Productivity of developers is difficult to estimate. It might change in the course of the project and might vary from feature to feature. There are also additional effects such as getting some benefit from assigning the same developer to more than one task of the same project. These are additional constraints and considerations which are left out initially to keep the model tractable.

Decision support for project staffing is still in its infancy. First attempts have been made to make decisions based upon more solid grounds [Smith et al. '04], [Malinowski et al. '08]. The results obtained from such decision support are meant to guide, not to prescribe a solution (or decision) to the product or project manager.

The possibility of exporting plans into Microsoft Project® allows usage of this standard software for all the monitoring and tracking objectives it is designed for. Even though certain aspects of the whole process cannot be formalized and are intentionally left out, the optimized staffing plans are likely be very good in terms of the formalized planning criteria. In the same way, they are likely to be superior to any manual plans created, especially if the number of tasks and features becomes larger. This was initially shown for the case of creating the manual plan and for creating a plan for unpredicted re-estimation of resource consumptions. In all scenarios, another benefit comes from early understanding of critical project parameters and the possibility to initiate mitigating actions.

CHAPTER 13

CASE STUDY: ADAPTABLE PROJECT MANAGEMENT

13.1 INTRODUCTION

Naturally, the purpose of all project management activities is to perform processes in a cost-effective manner in order to achieve their stated objectives. However, what is considered "just enough" for the moment may become "not enough" at a later stage. There is a trade-off between the uncertainty of information on the one hand, and the need to look ahead to achieve the stated project goals.

A short-term, iterative planning and project management approach has the advantage of relying on higher certainty of information and of being able to react more quickly on requested changes. However, there is substantial risk to achieve mid-term release planning goals from just applying a local and short-term perspective. The question becomes if there is a "sweet spot", the right balance between uncertainty of information and looking at the right scope, which is beyond just the next iteration? The answer might be different depending on the characteristics and target objective of the specific project and organization.

This case study looks at release and iteration planning for the next release of the VeryBestChoice*Light* product. Instead of advocating one specific method being the ultimate truth, adaptability to stated specific needs is emphasized. The main purpose of the case study is to (i) facilitate a process of balancing uncertainty and scope, and to (ii) demonstrate alternative options of tool support at the different stages of the overall process.

Adaptability in general refers to the possibility to customize methods, tools and techniques toward specific requirements. Following the planning onion [Cohn '06], an iteration is the next refinement of a release period. For example, the Rational Unified Process [Kruchten '00] recommends a release to be subdivided into 2 to 4 iterations. The conceptual assumption is that during an iteration, no changes are made in terms of the feature set being implemented. This does not contradict the need to re-plan within a release (as studied in Chapter 7).

Both release and iteration planning are considered in this case study. The process is designed to be adaptable. This may provide the opportunity to find the right trade-off between the scope of planning (short-term versus mid-term) and the accuracy of results (accurate versus tentative). As part of this planning process, emphasis is on a reasonable effort to keep information updated.

The content of the case study project is the implementation of release v1.2 of the VeryBestChoice*Light* tool. In Section 13.2, the adaptable project management approach is outlined. The case study project and the different stages of project management are presented in Section 13.3. Finally, the results and their applicability in a broader context are discussed in Section 13.4.

13.2 AN ADAPTABLE PROJECT MANAGEMENT APPROACH

13.2.1 Trade-off between accuracy and time horizon of planning

It is well known from cost estimation fidelity that higher accuracy can be expected from shorter time horizons of estimation [Boehm et al. '00]. The principal trade-off relationship between accuracy of information and results on the one hand and scope and look-ahead time of planning on the other hand is illustrated in Figure 13.1. Four planning activities are compared in the figure: (Strategic) release planning, iterative planning, weekly and daily planning. The decrease of accuracy over a given time horizon is assumed to be non-linear. On the other hand, the impact of "good" decisions during the planning activities becomes stronger the wider the scope and the time horizon are. This is illustrated by the second curve of the figure. Because the exact form of the curve is hard to determine, the increase of impact is assumed to be linear.

As this is a trade-off relationship, it does not make too much sense to advocate advantages of one planning activity over the other. Instead, an effective interplay among the four perspectives is necessary to achieve overall good results. How this interplay can be organized and how this can even be supported by appropriate tools is the main content of this case study.

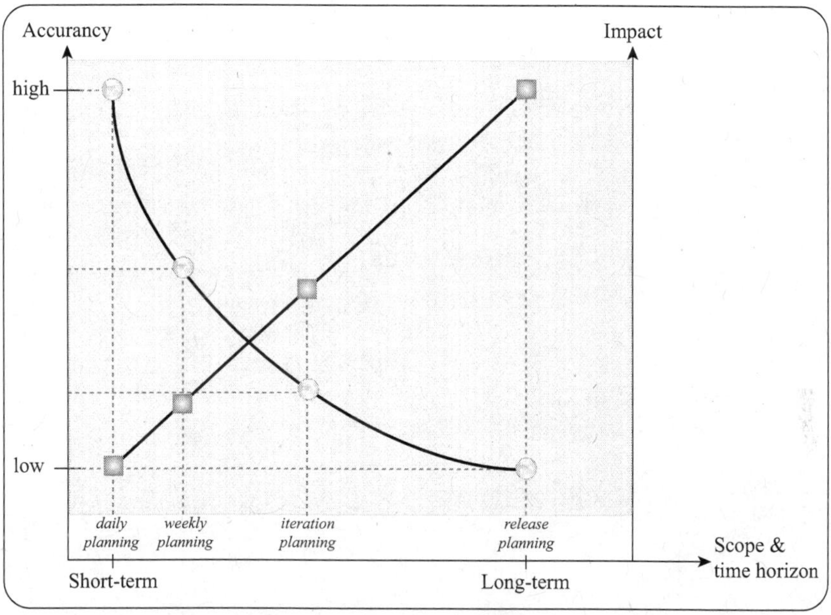

Figure 13.1 Trade-off curves between accuracy and impact versus scope and time horizon of planning

13.2.2 The effort-risk trade-off for the next release decision

The adaptable project management approach for product development starts with a decision about which features should be implemented in the next release. Features from the repository are evaluated, prioritized and finally selected. Depending on the size and complexity of this selection problem, different levels of *effort* and *risk* can be applied. Utilizing the content of Chapters 3, 4, 5, 6 and 10, a classification into five levels of effort-risk trade-off situations is given.

(13.1) *Level 1:* Ad hoc decision about what should be considered for the next release. This option follows the premise that intuition and communication are sufficient for making these decisions.

(13.2) *Level 2:* Prioritization of the features based on one criterion (often this is business value) just by the project or product manager.

(13.3) *Level 3:* Same as Level 2, but assigned stakeholders participate in the prioritization process.

(13.4) *Level 4:* Same as Level 3, but applied for several criteria (such as value and urgency).

(13.5) *Level 5:* Same as Level 4, but now applying resource optimization on top of this prioritization process. This is the process as described for EVOLVE II.

Level 5 is the most powerful approach, as it allows proactive investigation of the impact of uncertainty by running what-if scenarios. At the other end of the spectrum are ad hoc decisions, which are risky and hard to predict in their ramifications. The assumed principal trade-off relationship between (i) effort spent on decision-making and (ii) the inherent risk of not making appropriate decisions (e.g., missing essential features or offering features not needed) is shown in Figure 13.2. Both attributes are defined on a ordinal five-point scale. Effort subsumes all the contributions in collecting, analyzing and interpreting data, as well as the contributions necessary for making the decisions. Risk here refers to possible impact of not making "good" decisions. The content of "goodness" is context-specific, but could, for example, relate to the degree of customer satisfaction.

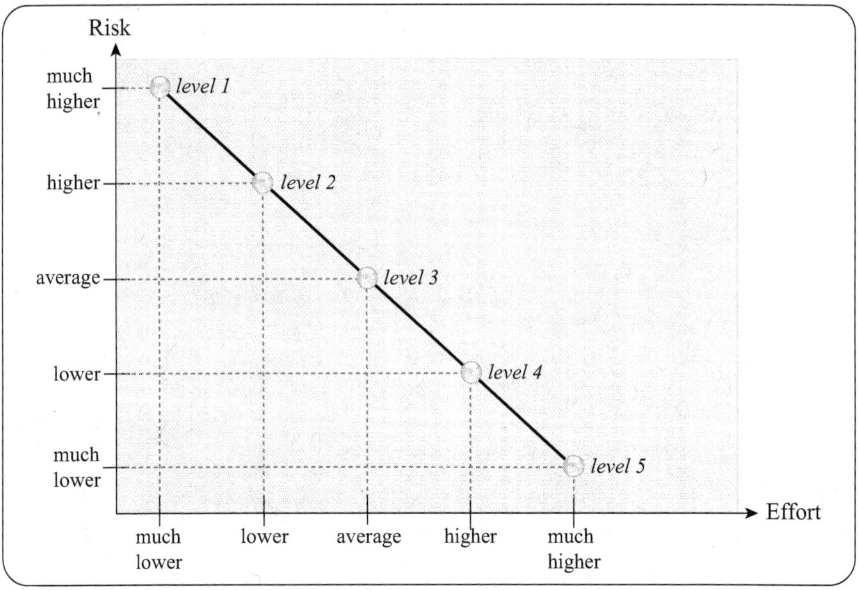

Figure 13.2 Trade-off between effort and risk of priority and release decisions

13.2.3 Three phases of the adaptable approach

The adaptable project management approach studied in this chapter has three layers. The main idea of the approach is to consider the sequence of release, iteration and weekly planning as an integrated process. As part of that an appropriate level of effort and risk can be selected at each layer.

The first layer refers to (next) release planning. One of the five possible options (levels) as outlined in (13.1) to (13.5) are applicable. The tool support includes VeryBestChoice*Light* for Levels 2 to 4 and ReleasePlanner™ for Level 5.

The second layer refers to iteration planning. Similar levels as above can be defined for this layer, covering the spectrum from ad hoc (level 1) to optimized (level 5) decisions.

In any case, the decisions are about what should be developed in the next iteration. As part of this phase, re-estimation of effort and re-prioritization of features is important to base decisions on the most up-to-date information. For tool support, the same arguments apply as used for the first phase.

The third layer is devoted to weekly planning. Now, the question becomes more operational: Who should work on what and in which order of sequence? In principle, this again is possible to be done ad hoc or with different levels of supporting techniques. Optimization-based staffing as supported by RASORP is most powerful, but also most ambitious in terms of data demands. The impact of not making "good" decisions becomes lower compared to the two previous layers. The three fundamental phases of the method are illustrated by the case study presented in the next section.

13.3 CASE STUDY

13.3.1 Project context

The adaptable project management approach is applied to the case study. The case study project analyzes the process of planning for release 1.2 of the VeryBestChoice*Light* tool. From an existing repository, a number of features are selected to be added to the existing release 1.1.

From running in total 75 prioritization and planning projects with release 1.1 of the same tool, a comprehensive list of suggestions for new, revised or corrected features has been proposed. The list includes 95 features. It would not have been practical to consider all of them for planning right away. Instead, a pre-selection process has been performed. This pre-selection included all the stakeholders presented later in Table 13.2. Their initial task was to prioritize 95 feature entries in terms of their *overall attractiveness*.

Overall attractiveness of a feature is a combination of its urgency (in the case of features defined as bug fixes or for requests from business-critical customers), their estimated effort (a rough estimation of the implementation effort), and the inherent risk of the feature (which itself is an aggregation of different types of risk). The stakeholders were performing the scoring process which resulted in a list of 21 features considered for release 1.2. For that purpose, either VeryBestChoice*Light* or ReleasePlanner™ could be used. For the case study, the former one was selected.

The 21 features include improvements of existing features as well as new features suggested by existing or former users. The features are grouped into six different areas called *analysis*, *estimation*, *messaging*, *project creation*, *reporting* and *scoring*. The features and their grouping are summarized in Table 13.1.

Table 13.1 Case study features and their group classification

ID	Group	Feature name
1	Reporting	Print/report individual chart
2	Reporting	Automated reports
3	Reporting	Generate report
4	Analysis	Weighted criteria for ranking of features
5	Analysis	Specify default analysis options
6	Analysis	Monitoring
7	Analysis	Visualization of analysis alternatives
8	Analysis	Disable empty rows or columns from display of stakeholder scoring
9	Analysis	Warning: Empty data set
10	Estimation	Include effort in analysis options
11	Estimation	Effort estimation
12	Estimation	Compatibility of estimates
13	Messaging	Confirmation of stakeholder notification
14	Messaging	Terminate voting
15	Messaging	Stakeholder login
16	Project creation	User manual
17	Project creation	Stakeholder permissions
18	Project creation	Import failure messaging
19	Project creation	Group permissions for stakeholders
20	Scoring	Attachments
21	Scoring	Better visibility of the different prioritization criteria

13.3.2 The case study process

The three-staged approach outlined in Section 13.2.3 is used to perform release, iteration and weekly planning for the case study project. The process flow is shown in Figure 13.3. It can be seen that the initial planning for the next release can be supported by VeryBestChoice*Light* or ReleasePlanner™. The result of this process is the evaluation of the attractiveness of the 95 candidate features from the repository.

Once the release has been decided upon, more qualified data are used to plan for iterations and weekly work plans. For that purpose, ReleasePlanner™ is applied to determine the features for each iteration. Subsequently, RASORP optimizes the assignments of developers to tasks.

13.3.3 The stakeholders

For this case study, three different types of stakeholders are included in the process: Four developers, five customers and one project manager. Each of the nominated stakeholders has specific permissions to participate in the process. The permissions relate to the involvement in effort estimation and the involvement of feature prioritization. The product development process is investigated with focus on the business value of the features and their risk of implementation. The list of stakeholders and their assigned permissions are summarized in Table 13.2.

Table 13.2 Stakeholders with their groups and scoring permissions

Stake-holder ID	Group	Pre-selection of features	Effort estimation	Prioritiza-tion for value	Prioritiza-tion for risk
1	Developer	yes	yes	yes	yes
2	Developer	yes	yes	yes	yes
3	Developer	yes	yes	yes	yes
4	Developer	yes	yes	yes	yes
5	Customer	yes		yes	
6	Customer	yes		yes	
7	Customer	yes		yes	
8	Customer	yes		yes	
9	Customer	yes		yes	
10	Project manager	yes	yes	yes	yes

Four developers were available for the actual implementation of features. They have specialized expertise for implementation of features for specific groups only:

- Developer 1: Reporting, Analysis, Estimation, Messaging
- Developer 2: Analysis, Estimation, Messaging, Project creation
- Developer 3: Estimation, Messaging, Project creation, Scoring
- Developer 4: Reporting, Analysis, Project creation, Scoring

Developers are assumed to work five hours per day and five days a week exclusively on implementation of the features. This is the direct effort only, not counting additional time needed for communication, installations, learning or reporting. One iteration lasts two weeks or 50 hours. With four developers available, the effort capacity per iteration is 200 person hours.

13.3.4 Collective estimation and prioritization

Stakeholder involvement has been emphasized to be one of the critical success factors for product development [Heikkilae et al. '10]. The process of collective estimation and prioritization is supported by VeryBestChoice*Light* in two different ways. The first way is to allow a number of selected stakeholders to provide their individual estimation, which can be even a three-point estimation which is later integrated into one. In addition, stakeholders can articulate their priority of the features by scoring them based on the defined prioritization criteria.

The second way in which VeryBestChoice*Light* supports collective estimation and prioritization is the possibility to communicate and discuss opinions and arguments. A discussion forum can be used to balance controversial cases of estimation or priority. Figure 13.4 shows a screenshot from a discussion, which is related to the communicated average effort estimate of features f(1) and f(2). At any point in time, it can be seen by all stakeholders, for which features any comments have been provided. This facilitates understanding and eventually justifies adjustment of existing estimates.

13.3.5 Which features to consider for the next iteration?

The decision about which features should come into the next iteration is based upon the stakeholder evaluation of feature's effort and risk. The individual ranking of the features based on both criteria is shown in Figure 13.5 and Figure 13.6, respectively. Each of the two dual charts presents the ranking of features and the level of disagreement between stakeholders in terms of their scoring for effort estimate and risk, respectively.

Looking at the (collective) effort estimates in Figure 13.5, the highest disagreement is for the *Monitoring* feature f(6) and the *Import failure messaging* feature f(18). It can also be seen from Figure 13.6, for example, that the *User manual* f(16) feature has the highest risk disagreement. For all these and maybe other feature estimates or scores, the project manager would probably initiate a discussion between involved stakeholders to better understand and eventually reduce the variation of assigned values.

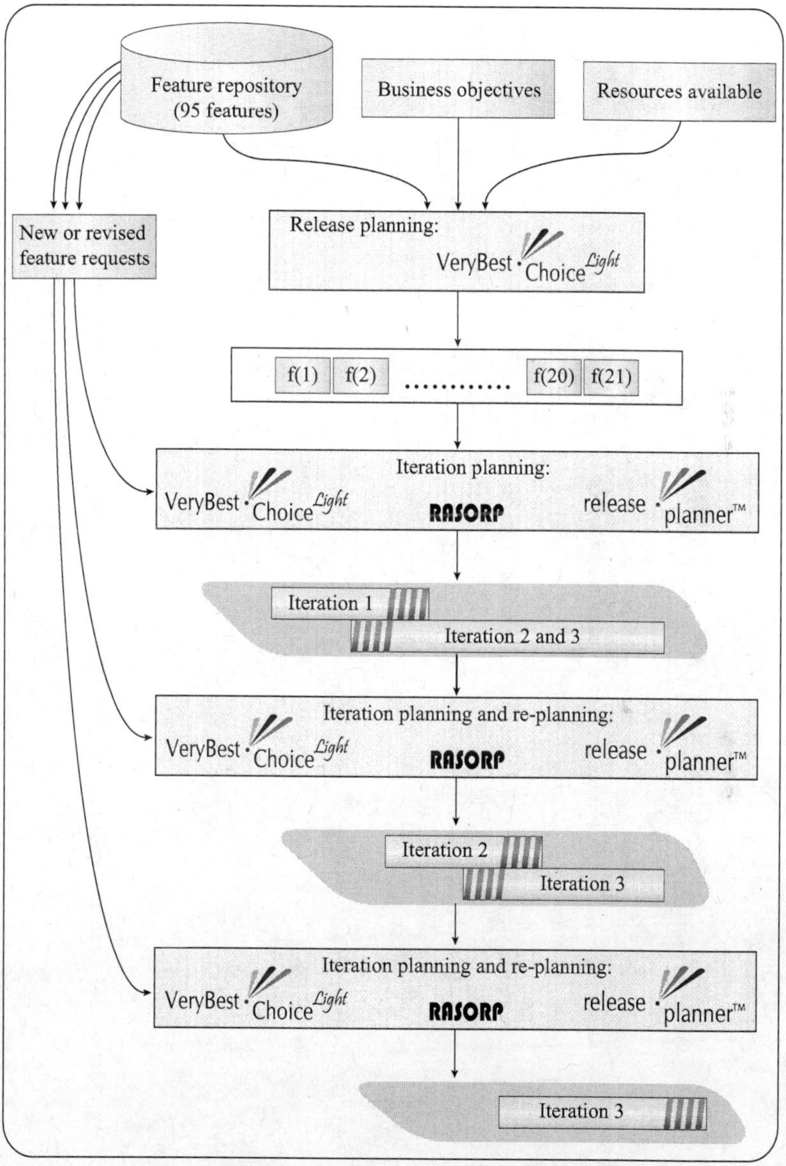

Figure 13.3 Process flow of the case study project

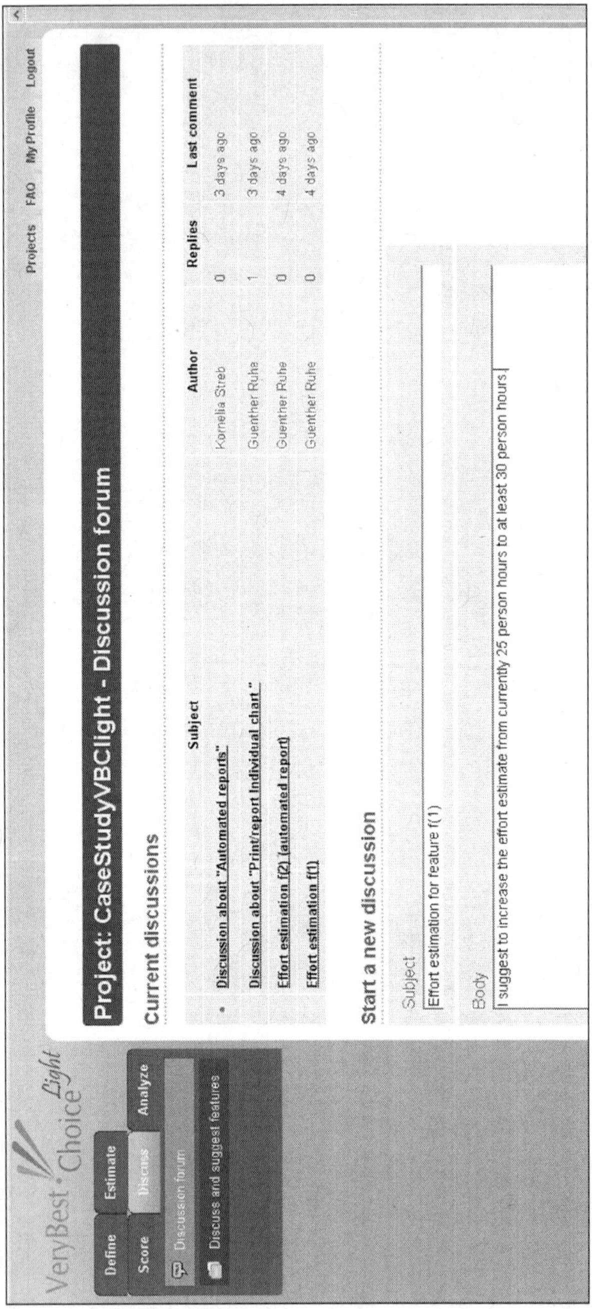

Figure 13.4 Screenshot from the (effort) discussion forum of VeryBestChoice^{Light}

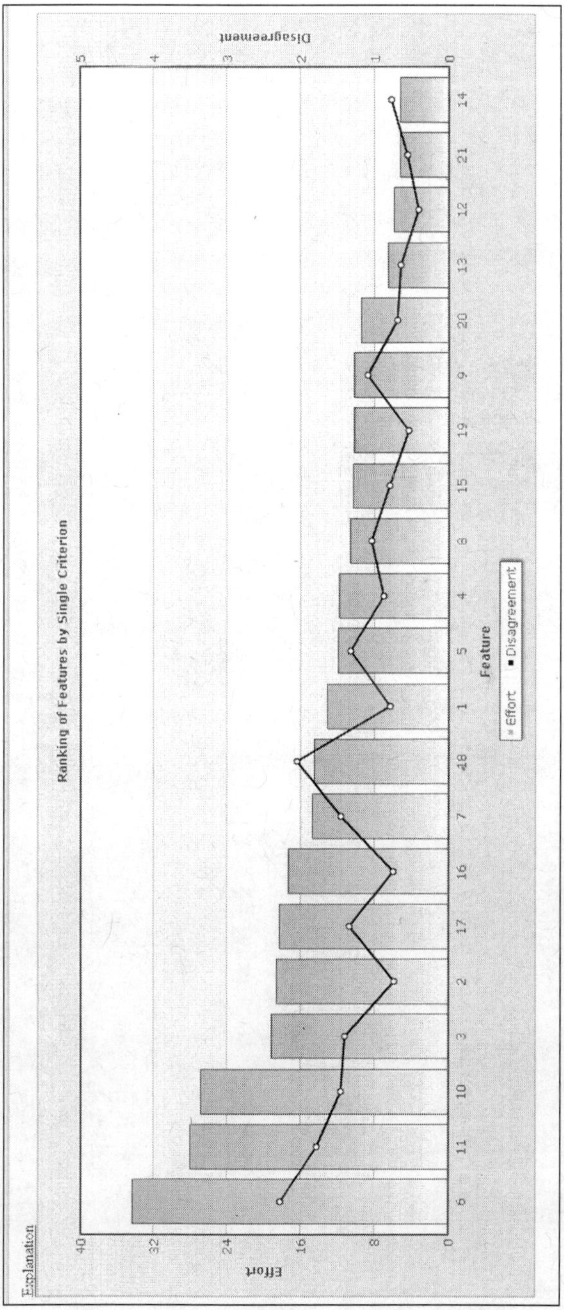

Figure 13.5 Ranking of case study features based on their weighted average effort

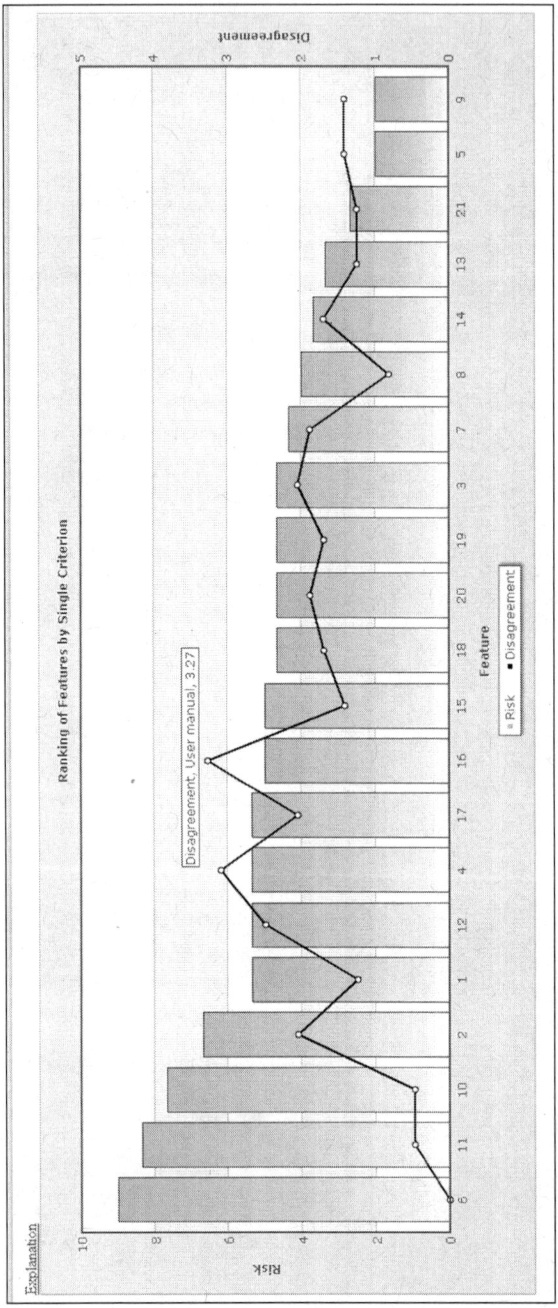

Figure 13.6 Ranking of case study features based on risk

The decision about which feature should be implemented when depends on the given project context. Is it better to start with risky features? Or selecting the features having the highest value? Or selecting them based upon a combination of the two criteria? All of the suggested policies have arguments for and against their implementation. Their commonality is that it is hard to oversee which combination of features is most attractive for the next iteration.

Following the workflow structure given in Figure 13.3, optimization-based selection is applied to determine the most attractive combination of features for the next iteration. This is one of the possible options to perform the adaptable project management approach. For the case study, this means to define iteration capacity of 200 person hours. In addition, the feature's value and risk evaluation are taken into account. The results are an optimized collection of feature sets.

Once features are assigned to the next iteration from running ReleasePlanner™, RASORP is applied (both tools are directly linked to each other) to determine the actual staffing for implementing these features. The algorithm takes care of the restriction that each developer is familiar with four out of the six different feature groups only.

At each iteration, a re-estimation of the effort for the outstanding features is done. Applying this process and applying the adjusted effort estimation results in the delivery of the following features for the three iteration originally planned for:

(13.6) Iteration 1: Features f(4), f(8), f(12), f(13), f(14), f(15), f(20), f(21)

(13.7) Iteration 2: Features f(1), f(5), f(9), f(10), f(19)

(13.8) Iteration 3: Features f(2), f(11), f(16), f(18)

An overview of the implementation stages of these features is provided in Figure 13.7. For example, it can be seen that feature f(1) is implemented during the second iteration by developer dev(2) during time interval [11, 50]. The original estimate of 25 person hours was quite inaccurate because the actual effort ended up being 40 person hours. It can also be seen that all reporting features are implemented by the same developer. Some of the features take longer than originally planned. Because of that, features f(15) and f(19) cannot be finished in the first, but during the second iteration.

From looking at the trend of the *backlog size* (backlog size is defined as in Scrum [Schwaber and Beedle '02] being the total effort of all features left at the backlog) reduction as shown in Figure 13.8, it becomes clear that an increase of most of the original effort estimates has contributed to an increase of the backlog size for the original 21 features when adjusted to the new estimates. This is shown by the growing size of the grey bars over the course of iterations.

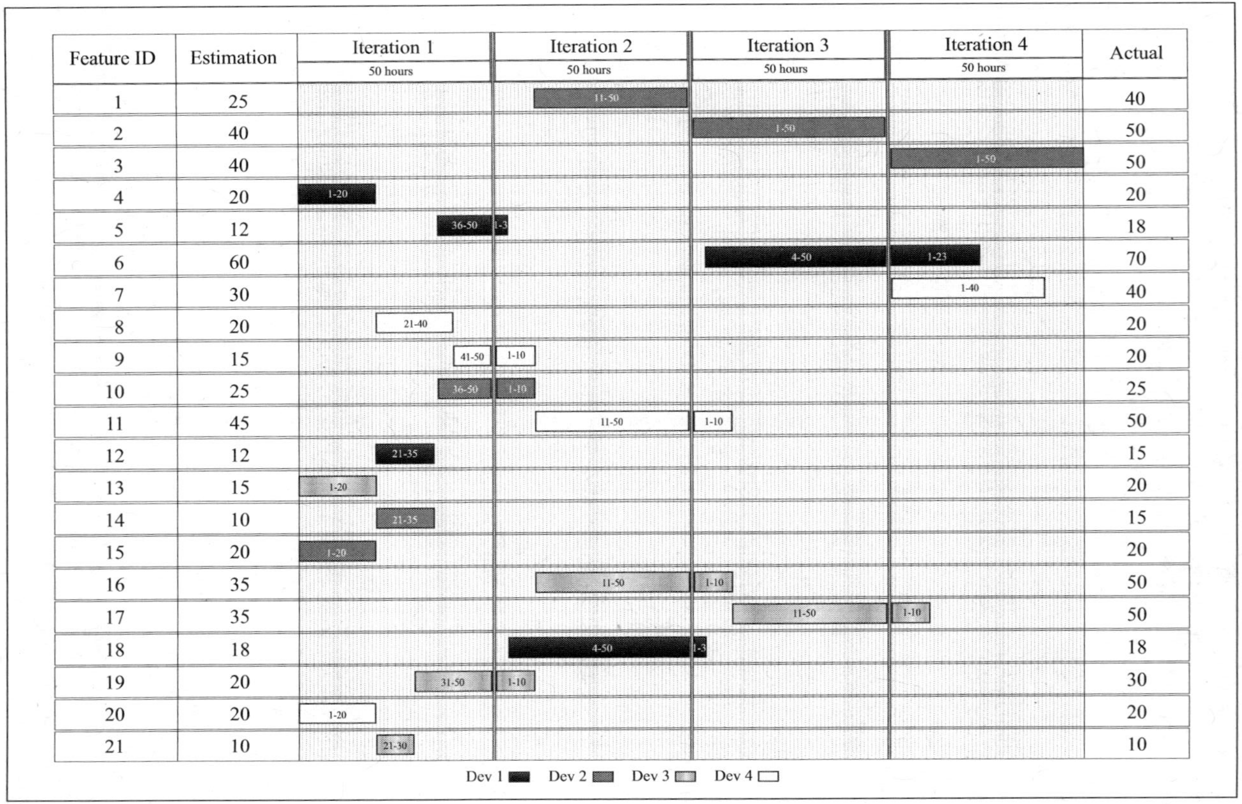

Figure 13.7 Overview of feature implementation per iterations as a result of applying RASORP

As a consequence, another iteration is needed to offer the pre-selected features for the next release of the product. The iterative reduction of the actual backlog size is illustrated by the dark grey bars. The backlog gets to zero after the fourth iteration (13.9).

(13.9) Iteration 4: Features f(3), f(6), f(7) and f(17).

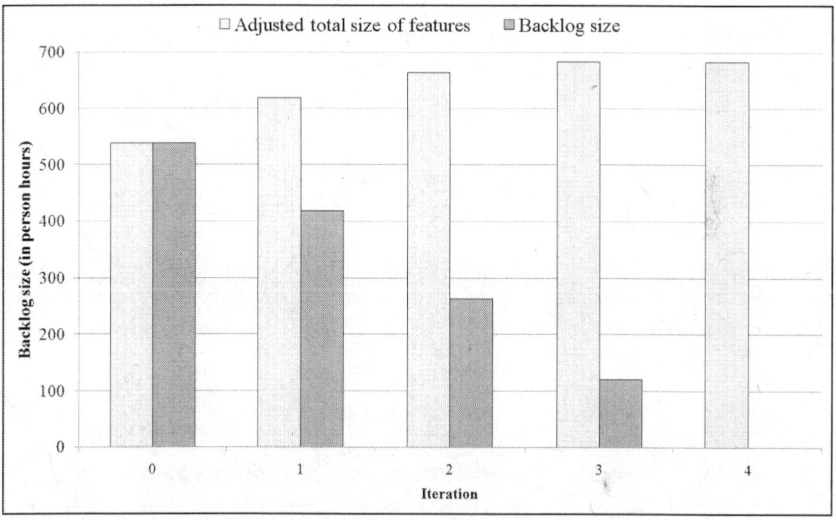

Figure 13.8 Trend of backlog size reduction

The attractiveness of the features selected for the first iteration is confirmed when looking at the value-risk-effort profile of the 21 features shown in Figure 13.9. The features proposed by the optimization algorithms are among the most promising ones, having high expected value, low estimated effort and low predicted risk. For example, f(21) looks very attractive from this perspective. The first iteration provides eight features, which is a recommended strategy to receive early feedback from trial users.

13.4 DISCUSSION OF RESULTS

An adaptable project management approach was illustrated for release, iterative and weekly planning for a case study project. Among the possible options to perform the three phases, easy-to-use tool support was selected. Adaptability is another form of flexibility. Following the positive experience obtained by Scrum [Schwaber and Beedle '02], flexibility in the sense of constant accommodation of change has been complemented by flexibility in terms of the rigor of the method used at the different stages. This is a continuation of the work proposed in [Heikkilae et al. '10].

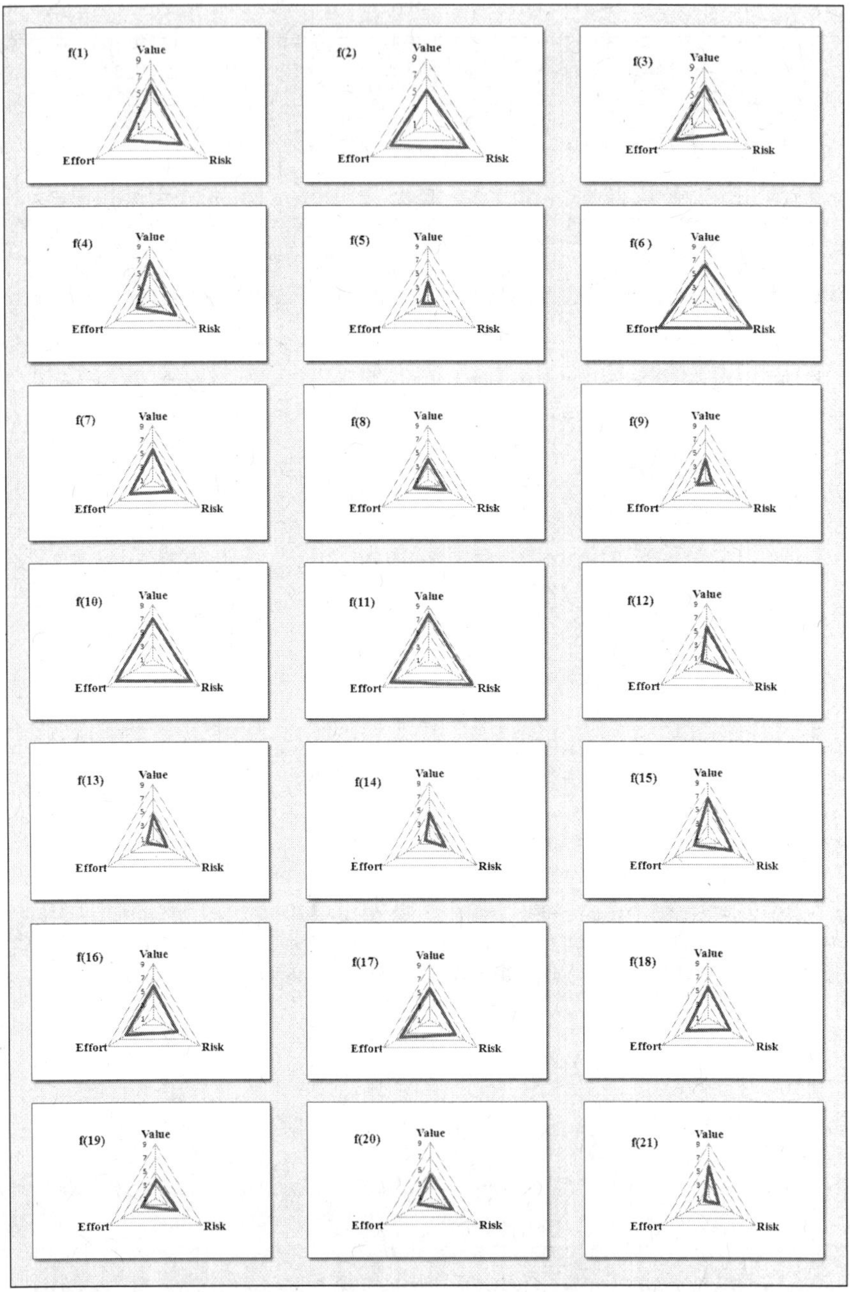

Figure 13.9 Value, risk and effort evaluation for the 21 features of the case study

In our case study, all the tools described in this book have been applied. This not only helps in more complex planning scenarios to develop quality plans, but also it is likely a useful way of reducing the daily or weekly effort spent for planning and re-planning. Looking at the Gantt charts and allocation plans for a small team of developers on a daily base already confirms that such an assignment is not easy to make. In the case study presented in Chapter 12, it was illustrated how significant the difference can be between results from manual versus optimized planning. This becomes especially true for unpredicted changes requiring quick and smooth adjustment of plans.

Although not further explored in this case study, the same idea of adaptability toward the context can be used for effort estimation. The range here is the same going from individual expert estimates to more advanced estimation techniques as described in Section 9.2.

Adaptable project management also might imply that for small scale problems, approaches at level 2 and 3 can already be "good enough". This is exactly the flexibility the project manager has to decide upon what is needed and to adjust the approach correspondingly.

CHAPTER 14

APPLICATION SCENARIOS

14.1 INTRODUCTION

This book is primarily about decisions for product release planning. This chapter is intended to extend this view and to demonstrate that the models, methods and tools presented are not limited to release planning, but applicable more broadly. More precisely, what is demonstrated is that a range of seemingly different problems can be reformulated to allow for the application of the same methods and tools presented for release planning. The problem classes considered for this purpose are:

- Road-mapping for multiple products
- Release planning with consideration of quality demands
- Agile project management following Scrum
- Planning for competitiveness of products
- Project portfolio planning

In all previous chapters, a methodology for prioritization of objects and optimization of business performance against stated criteria and resource constraints was described. This chapter is intended to demonstrate that the existing modeling framework outlined in Chapter 5 is general enough to address an even broader range of problems. The key idea behind all of this is illustrated in Figure 14.1. For all the problems listed, it will be shown how to reduce the formulation of the "new" problem into one that can be expressed within the modeling framework behind EVOLVE II. Once this mapping has been done, it allows the usage of the tools for multi-criteria prioritization (VeryBestChoice^{Light}), optimization of resources in iterative development (ReleasePlanner™) and operational planning and staffing (RASORP).

The commonality of all of these problems listed in Figure 14.1 is that they have a similar basic structure. What that means is that all of them can be described by some instantiation of the following problem template:

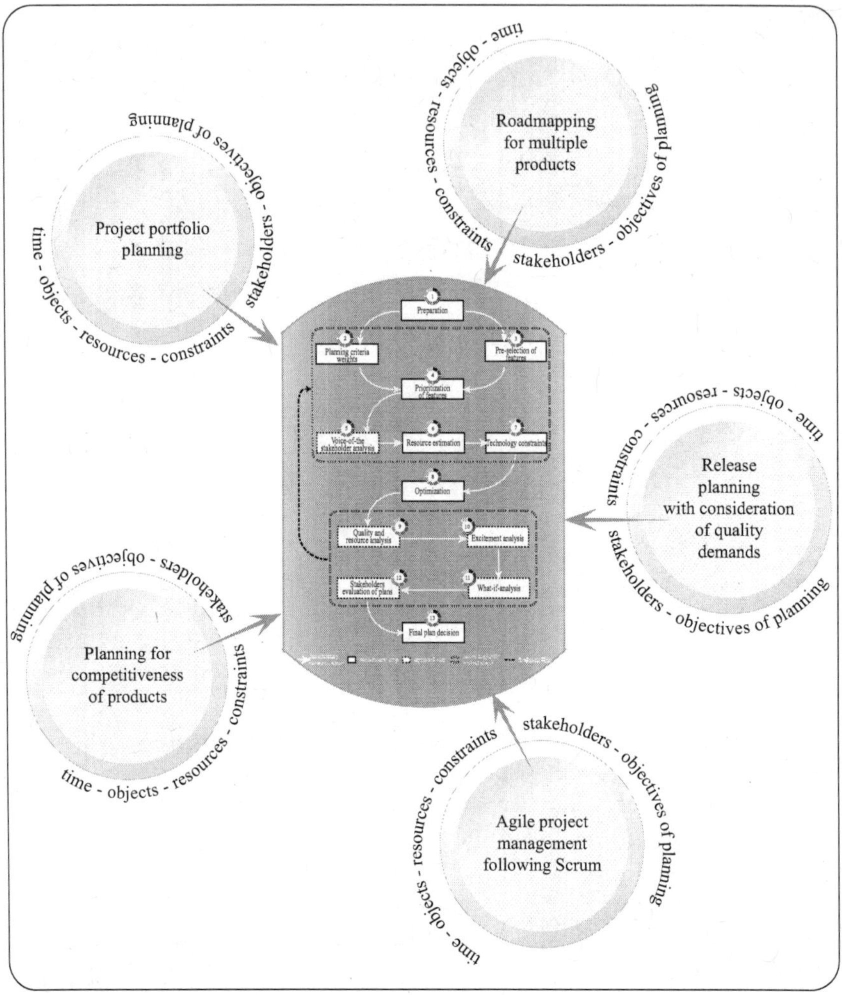

Figure 14.1 Application scenarios transferable to EVOLVE II

Objects:	A set of objects (e.g., features, services, projects).
Stakeholders:	A set of stakeholders involved at different stages of the decision-making process.
Time:	Number and length of time intervals (e.g., releases) considered for planning.

Resources:	One or more resources are in consideration (human or non-human). Each object consumes certain amounts of resources. The total amount of resources consumed by objects is limited per time intervals.
Constraints:	Technological or business conditions related to the design and implementation of objects.
Objectives of planning:	Set of criteria considered for planning. The criteria are combined into a utility function formulated in dependence of the objects. This is an additive function of the values of individual objects, which are determined by stakeholder prioritization.

In what follows, each of the five problem classes is studied in more detail. For all of them, their background is given as well as the instantiation of the problem template outlined above.

14.2 ROADMAPPING FOR MULTIPLE PRODUCTS

14.2.1 Background

Instead of looking into the planning of just one product, often a suite of related products is offered. This increases not only the functionality, but also allows for better customization and selection of the most appropriate products of the suite. As the development of a product suite typically follows the same paradigm of staged development, the problem of release planning for one product can naturally be generalized into a problem with multiple products. At this point, a product suite can be either software or hardware related or a mixture of both.

The higher complexity of planning for a product suite results from the demand that the individual products of the suite should be offered simultaneously. If this cannot be achieved, then a substantial part of the overall value expected from offering a product as a suite is jeopardized, and the release of the suite needs to be delayed until the last product is finished.

The process of synchronization of individual release cycles is illustrated in Figure 14.2 for the case of three products P1, P2 and P3. The planning process considers the next three releases. These release dates of the suite are called R1, R2 and R3, respectively. Without synchronization, the release dates for each product are expected to be different. Consequently, if the products of the suite are to be offered in conjunction for each release, the latest release date among the products determines the release date of the suite.

This situation is assumed to change after synchronization has been applied. As a consequence, for each release, the individual product's release dates become the same and the overall release date of the suite is expected to be earlier than without synchronization. This can be achieved by better allocation and utilization of the resources needed for the three products. Instead of a local perspective (just looking at the individual products), a global perspective ensures that the best result for the whole suite is achieved.

In addition to synchronization, additional complexity in the case of planning for multiple products results from more complex structures of resource utilization. Some of the (human or non-human) resources can be specifically assigned to one product only, while others might be used across products. This creates additional complexity in the planning process. The ability to manage this additional complexity adds to the advantages of more systematic planning for the case of one product as described in Chapters 5 and 6.

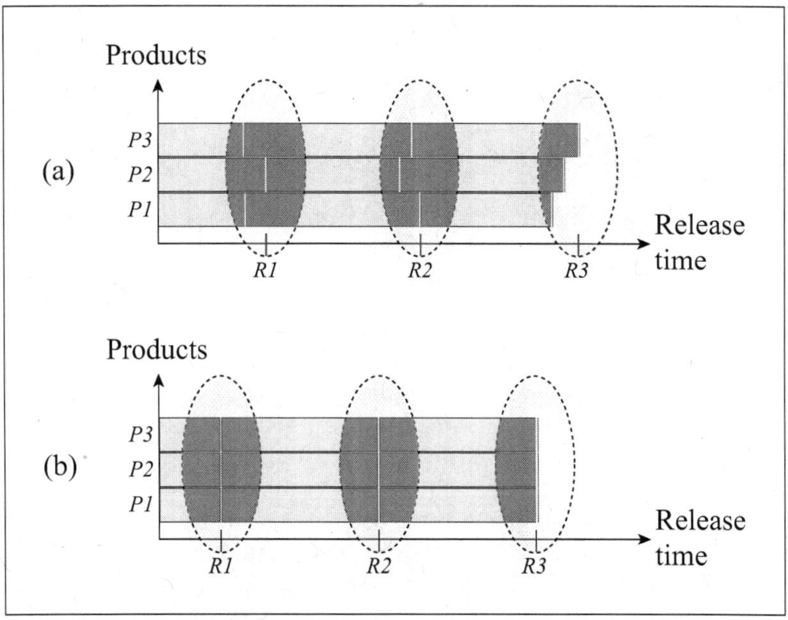

Figure 14.2 Illustration of release planning of multiple products (a) without and (b) with synchronization between products

14.2.2 Re-formulation of the problem

In what follows, the key ideas of reducing the *roadmapping for multiple products* problem to the modeling assumptions of solution method EVOLVE II are described. Applying the problem template, the problem is characterized as follows:

Objects:	Candidate features of products belonging to a product suite. All features of one product of the suite are considered to be a group of features from the perspective of planning for one product.
Stakeholders:	A set of stakeholders involved in road-mapping decisions. The stakeholders can be assigned to different groups of features or to different planning criteria when they prioritize features.
Time:	Number of time intervals (release periods) for the product suite.
Resources:	All resources (cost, effort or more specific human resource types) relevant for the planning of product development. All objects consume an estimated amount of the different resources.
Constraints:	Total amount of resource consumption is limited per resource type by fixed capacities defined per release. In addition, dependencies between features are considered (coupling, precedence).
Objectives of planning:	The goal is to maximize (a measure of) total stakeholder satisfaction based upon assigned priorities to features (same as for one product).

In order to avoid additional and complex notation, the idea of the re-formulation is illustrated by a simple example. For that, a set of 12 different candidate features is considered. Utilizing the modeling capability of defining groups of features, the features are arranged linearly in correspondence to their grouping. That means, with N1, N2 and N3 being the number of candidate features for products P1, P2 and P3, respectively, there are in total N = N1 + N2 + N3 candidate features in consideration. Features f(1) … f(N1) correspond to the first product, features f(N1+1) … f(N1+N2) to the second and f(N1+N2+1) … f(N1+N2+N3) to the third product.

If there are features that occur in more than one product, this can be easily modeled using the coupling relationship. As the feature in fact is implemented only once, the effort is shared in equal portions between the products where it is included. Even though this is a simplification of the truth, it could serve as a reasonable initial approximation.

The whole transformation approach is illustrated in Table 14.1 for the case of planning with three products. For simplicity, the three products are assumed to have N1 = 3, N2 = 4 and N3 = 5 features, respectively. There is one (core) feature which is supposed to be the same for all three products. The case of one joint feature for all three products is modeled by introducing coupling relationships. As shown in Table 14.1, features f(1), f(4) and f(8) are coupled to express the fact that the features are actually the same. Applying ReleasePlanner™, this whole process is supported by the option to edit coupling and resource constraints by using Microsoft Excel®. As a result of this process, globally optimized feature sets are obtained.

From Table 14.1 it also becomes clear that resource types 1, 2 and 3 are specific to products P1, P2 and P3, respectively. Resource type 4, however, is used across the individual products. Its proper allocation is of key importance to achieve proper synchronization between release dates and to achieve maximum stakeholder satisfaction from the proposed product-suite roadmap.

Table 14.1 Planning for three products with three product-specific resources and one resource type used across products

Product	Groups of features	Coupling	Resources			
			Type 1	Type 2	Type 3	Type 4
P1	f(1)	f(4)	x			x
	f(2)		x			x
	f(3)		x			x
P2	f(4)	f(8)		x		x
	f(5)			x		x
	f(6)			x		x
	f(7)			x		x
P3	f(8)	f(1)			x	x
	f(9)				x	x
	f(10)				x	x
	f(11)				x	x
	f(12)				x	x

14.3 PLANNING WITH CONSIDERATION OF QUALITY DEMANDS

14.3.1 Background

The traditional view of release planning favors delivery of added or revised pieces of functionality (called features or requirements) on top of an evolving product in the best possible way. For a feature to become part of a product release, it needs to be implemented and thus consumes resources. The core question at this point is how to utilize the resources to provide the best (in terms of total stakeholder satisfaction) combination of pieces of functionality. What is completely lacking in this view is the quality aspect of the resulting release product(s). *Quality* here refers to one or more of the non-functional requirements such as reliability, security, performance or maintainability.

While there is the implicit assumption that effort is related to a fixed level of (standard) quality, it is also assumed that increasing this level of quality results in the increase of the related effort to achieve this quality (under the premise that there are no changes in the process or the technology applied). [Regnell et al. '08] have studied this question for the case of mobile-phone development. In their approach, they combine cost and benefit views into a roadmap of each important quality indicator for the particular domain.

Independent of how precisely quality is defined, there is a quality-effort dependency as illustrated in Figure 14.3. The curve indicates how much more effort is expected for achieving a higher than standard level of quality. In general, the increase in the total effort for implementation is expected to grow stronger than just linearly, eventually even exponentially. To determine the specific function, goal-oriented measurement programs [Basili et al. '01] need to be set-up collecting the data related to effort and the quality aspect under consideration. Of course, the overall assumption at this point is that the defined standard quality measure is not yet the maximum achievable.

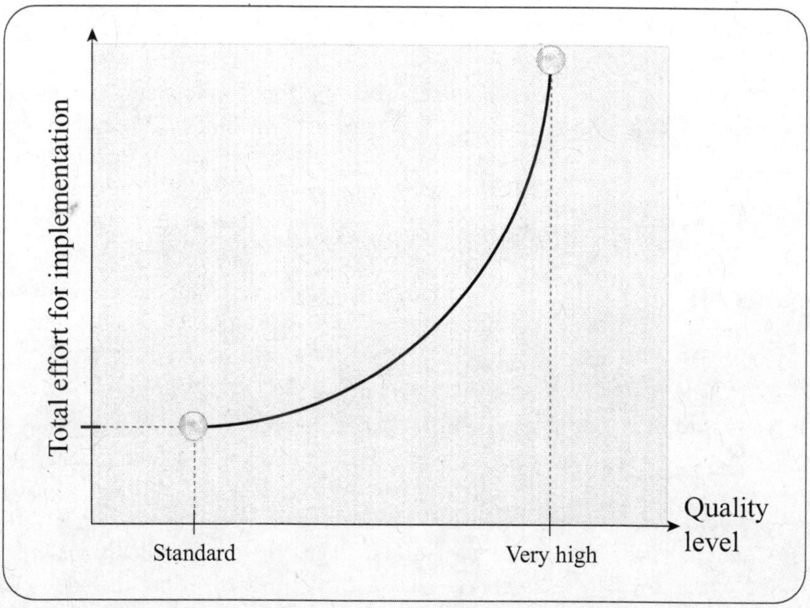

Figure 14.3 Total implementation effort of a feature in dependence of the quality level

Depending on the granularity of the planning, the specific effort attributed to higher target levels of quality can be feature-related or can be related to the whole product release (as a form of cross-cutting concern). The latter case can be modeled by introduction of a dummy feature, which consumes effort but has no direct contribution to functionality.

With this formulation given, the problem no longer is just to find a plan implementing the most comprehensive and attractive set of features. Instead, the problem now becomes a trade-off analysis where the balance needs to be found between providing the most comprehensive and attractive functionality and the level of target quality of the product release. In consideration of the additional amount of uncertainty resulting from determining the quality-effort dependency, just the next release is considered for planning.

14.3.2 Re-formulation of the problem

Applying the problem template introduced in this section again, the problem can be characterized as follows:

Objects:	Candidate features of a product
Stakeholders:	A set of stakeholders involved in roadmapping decisions
Time:	The time period for the next release
Resources:	All resources (cost, effort or more specific human resources devoted, e.g., to testing or design) relevant for the planning of product development. All objects consume an estimated amount of the different resources. There is an assumed known dependency between feature and release dependent additional effort necessary to achieve higher than standard level of quality.
Constraints:	Total amount of resource consumption is limited per resource type by fixed capacities defined per release time period. In addition, dependencies between objects (coupling, precedence) are considered.
Objectives of planning:	Quality-effort trade-off analysis between levels of (target) quality and total amount of functionality.

The problem can be approached by a two-staged process. Both stages follow the EVOLVE II process structure. At the first stage, quality considerations are not addressed explicitly. The assumption is that the estimated effort includes effort devoted to achieve the "standard" level of quality. As a result of this phase, a release plan x1 is received with specific sets of features in each release. Following the first stage, increased target levels of quality are considered in the second stage. Under the premise that the total capacities are not changed, higher levels of target quality imply a reduction in the amount of resources available for feature development, consequently reducing the number of features that can be offered.

As an illustrative example, five different alternatives for allocation of cost between generating functionality (for new or revised features) of standard quality and cost devoted to achieve higher than standard target quality levels are considered. In Figure 14.4, the left-most bar represents the traditional view of allocation. This means ignoring cost spent for additional quality, that is, the view of just looking at functionality of standard quality. With each increase in the amount of effort exclusively devoted to improve quality of the release product, this effort is no longer available for providing the original amount of functionality. Consequently, less functionality can be offered. The resulting trade-off curve with the five points G1, G2, G3, G4 and G5 generated from the five different effort allocation scenarios from Figure 14.4 is shown in Figure 14.5.

The five alternative points are non-comparable in the sense that an improvement along one criterion can only be made by getting worse in terms of the other. G1 represents the alternative incorporating the highest amount of functionality. However, the (estimated) quality level is lowest among the five alternatives. On the other hand, G5 (corresponding to alternative 5) is best when just looking at quality, but lowest in the amount of functionality offered. In total, the different alternatives provide an important input to the human decision-maker who can now better balance between the two competing criteria and select the alternative representing the most appropriate compromise under the given circumstances.

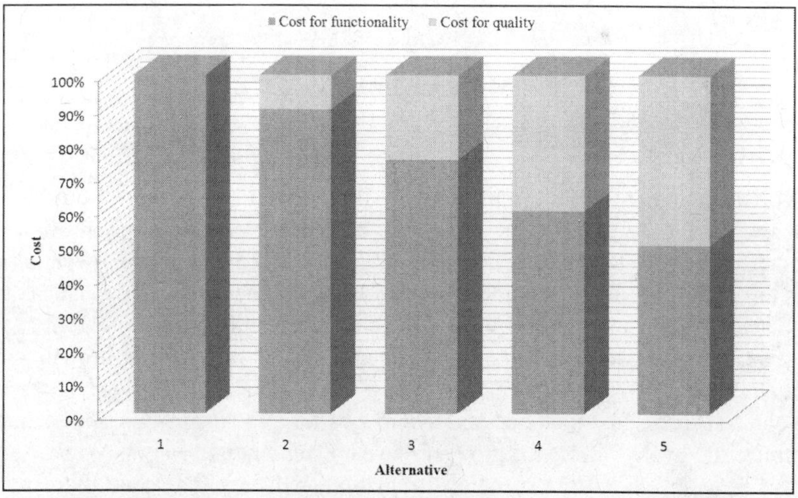

Figure 14.4 Five alternatives for cost spending devoted to functionality versus additional quality

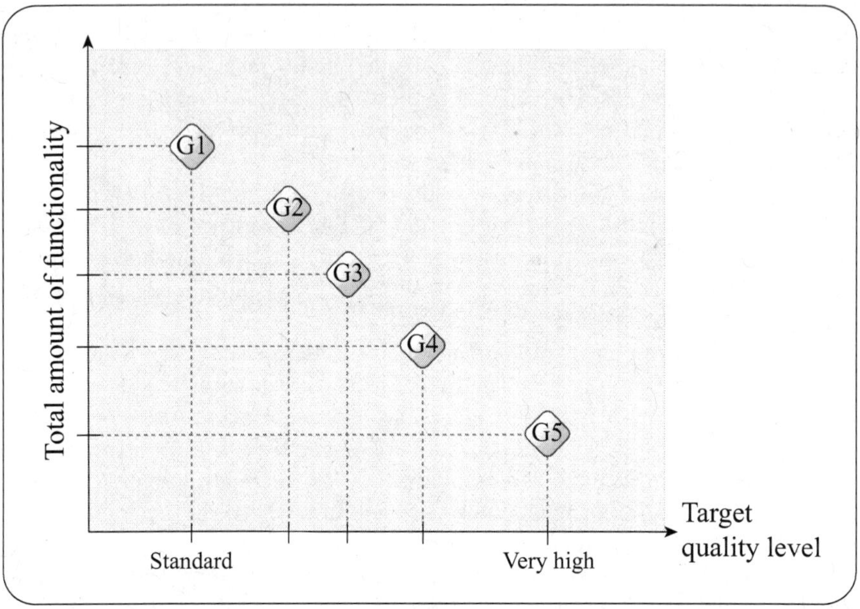

Figure 14.5 Trade-off curve for (next) release planning with consideration of quality demands

14.4 AGILE PROJECT MANAGEMENT FOLLOWING SCRUM

14.4.1 Background

Agile development differs from the more plan-driven approaches in putting less emphasis on up-front plans and strict plan-based control, while relying more on mechanisms for change management during the project [Nerur and Balijepally '07]. Does this mean that the suggestion is to make planning obsolete? No, the idea is *not* to replace planning completely by communication and self-organization, but to plan *just as much as needed.* While this sounds very reasonable, the most difficult part is to find out *how much is needed.*

[Cohn '06] presented methods and techniques for agile estimation and planning. To reduce the overall effort for product release planning, one can do several things such as reducing the effort spent on estimation, reducing the scope of planning, reducing the number of people involved, or reducing the level of detail. While all these considerations will likely contribute to an overall effort reduction, it will eventually also reduce the quality of the results. But where is the "sweet spot", the best compromise between effort invested and quality of results gained out of it?

One of the most frequently used agile methods is called *Scrum* [Schwaber and Beedle '02]. Originating from the early work of [Takeuchi and Nonaka '86], Scrum has matured into a project management technique for iterative development. It consists of three phases: (a) pre-sprint planning, (b) sprint and (c) post-sprint meeting [Cohen et al. '04]. During the *pre-sprint planning* phase, features and functionality are selected from the release backlog and placed into what is called the *sprint backlog* (a prioritized collection of tasks to be completed during the next sprint). During the *sprint* phase, the Scrum team implements a working version of software that meets a small set of high-priority customer needs. Finally, during the *post-sprint meeting*, developers demonstrate working software to their customers, adjust their priorities and repeat the cycle. The proposed decision support is for the phase of *pre-sprint planning*.

14.4.2 Re-formulation of the problem

The Scrum phase of pre-sprint planning is considered for reformulation applying the problem template again. The decisions to be made are related to prioritization and selection of features considered for implementation during the next sprint.

Objects:	Features are organized, respectively, as the release and iteration product backlog list.
Stakeholders:	The Scrum master is responsible for running the process. The product owner primarily looks at the backlog list, which can include new or revised features. The project team organizes itself for achieving the goals of the iteration. The role of the customer and the management are the same as defined for non-Scrum projects.
Time:	Planning is done in iterations (called sprints). Just the next iteration is considered all the time. Each iteration provides new (additional) pieces of functionality. An iteration typically has a duration between one and six weeks.
Resources:	All resources relevant for product development can be considered. All objects in the backlog list consume estimated amounts of the different resources in consideration. In the simplest case, focus is just on effort.
Constraints:	The total amount of resource consumption is limited per resource type and per iteration. In addition, possible technological or business dependencies between objects are considered.
Objectives of planning:	Maximize usefulness of the functionality added to the product as the result of the iteration.

Agile development is associated with many claims such as the achievement of higher job satisfaction, higher productivity and increased customer satisfaction. A rigorous empirical analysis revealed that, so far, there is insufficient evidence for these claims [Dyba and Dingsoyr '08]. Most of them are not confirmed yet and are relying on explorative case studies or even anecdotal evidence. [Moe and Aurum '08] study the decision-making process in Scrum. The authors found that *a prerequisite for introducing Scrum is the alignment of decisions on a strategic, tactical and operational level*.

In [Heikkilae et al. '10], a method is described trying to combine the strengths of Scrum with a stakeholder-centric decision-making process exploiting fact-based decision-making wherever appropriate. The same idea was applied in this section when complementing Srum by the modeling capabilities given in EVOLVE II. As described in detail in Chapter 6, the systematic planning method gives a lot of flexibility in how to instantiate the process (granularity in terms of objects, type and number of stakeholders, time intervals, type and number of resources considered, number and type of constraints, type and depth of analysis done). It depends on the concrete situation how far the planning should go. Running an optimization for proposing best combination of features to be implemented next has the potential to improve decision-making of the Scrum master and the product owner.

14.5 PLANNING FOR COMPETITIVENESS OF PRODUCTS

14.5.1 Background

For any product or service company, one of the key questions for success is: How do you ensure a strong competitive position in the future? Products are expected to contain all the mandatory "standard" features. But in addition to them, unique selling propositions are sought to distinguish from competitors and to attract additional customer interest. Often, the differentiating features might have a higher risk of implementation or risk of customer acceptance or are more cost-intensive. How to balance between being unique on the one hand and encountering high risk and increased cost on the other hand?

In a product developing unit, one needs to find an answer to the question: Which are the key product differentiators when compared to our main competitors? The question investigated in this section is: How to select product release feature sets toward becoming the most competitive? This planning objective is called *competitiveness* and is based on some assumptions which need to be fulfilled to run the proposed process:

Assumption 1: You know your main competitors (and their degree of importance)

Assumption 2: You (at least roughly) know (parts of) your competitors' future product strategy.

Assumption 3: You can judge the difference between your features in consideration and the ones the competitors are supposed to provide in future product releases.

14.5.2 Re-formulation of the problem

Following the template used previously, the problem of *planning for competitiveness of products* can be characterized as follows:

Objects:	Candidate features of a (future) product release
Stakeholders:	Stakeholders in this scenario correspond to competitors in the market space affected by the product under consideration
Time:	The next product release(s)
Resources:	All resources (cost, effort or more specific human resources) relevant for product development. All objects consume an estimated amount of the different resources.
Constraints:	Total amount of resource consumption is limited per resource type by fixed capacities. In addition, dependencies between objects (coupling, precedence) are considered.
Objectives of planning:	Maximize competitiveness of the product

There are two main phases to model the above planning for competitiveness. The first phase is to define your key competitors to become the stakeholders in the subsequent planning process defined by EVOLVE II. The difference to "traditional" release planning is that stakeholders are not really asked for their opinion (as they probably would not be willing to tell you). Instead, the degree of differentiation compared to the competitors is based on the degree of knowledge about their future products. This evaluation can be an individual or a collective one.

To accommodate the inherent uncertainty in this judgment, an additional factor is introduced. This factor describes the degree of certainty in the competitor evaluation performed for the candidate features. For feature f(n) and stakeholder stake(p) (representing competitor p), the factor certainty(n,p) defined on the interval (0,1] describes the perceived degree of certainty in the evaluation. The more confident the acting product manager is in the evaluation of being different from the competitor p with the proposed feature f(n), the closer certainty(n,p) comes to 1.

The second main conceptual step is to define the criterion of planning. One criterion in this case should be the degree of differentiation. What that means is that the nine-point scale of scoring is defined from 1 being *extremely low* to 9 being *extremely high* in terms of the level of differentiation from the competitor under consideration. If the feature under consideration is completely new with nothing comparable expected from that competitor, then a score of 9 would be appropriate. On the other hand, if the feature is expected to be offered more or less in the same way or even better by the competitor, then a low score needs to be applied.

What results out of all this is a planning objective function similar to the one introduced in Section 5.9. The only difference of this application scenario is the multiplicative factor given to all the stakeholder scores for each feature. With all the existing modeling capabilities expressing dependencies between features and describing the consumption of (limited) resources remaining the same, the objective of planning still is to maximize the number of stakeholder feature points. However, the interpretation of features points is different because now it is the measure of the degree of differentiation to customers.

14.6 PROJECT PORTFOLIO PLANNING

14.6.1 Background

Project portfolio planning is focused on the selection of the right projects versus performing projects right. The latter is the focus of project management. A *project portfolio* is a collection of all projects and programs of an enterprise or business unit to be performed. Consequently, planning for project portfolios includes the balancing of resources, business needs, business risks and changing parameters for maximum return on investment.

Project portfolio planning is part of *Project Portfolio Management* [Levine '05]. Prioritization among a larger set of candidate projects is expected to help find the right mix of projects in terms of their value, expected benefit, risk and alignment with the organizational business objectives. Once started, constant project monitoring needs to be done to support the decision if the project should still remain in the pipeline even if it no longer serves the company's best interest.

14.6.2 Re-formulation of the problem

Following the template, the problem is characterized as follows:

Objects:	Candidate projects of an organization to be implemented in the selected time horizon.
Stakeholders:	Stakeholders are the managers, executives, shareholder or customers involved in the decision on which portfolio to choose.
Time:	The planning horizon typically is in years (often between 2 and 5) to reflect the strategic nature of the decision-making process.

Resources:	All objects consume an estimated amount of different resources. All resources (cost, effort or more specific human resources) relevant for the performance of the projects are potentially relevant.
Constraints:	Total amount of resource consumption is limited per resource type and time period. Also, dependencies between projects (such as coupling or precedence) need to be considered.
Objectives of planning:	Alignment with the strategic goals and business objectives of the organization.

[Levine '05] introduced five maturity levels of project portfolio management:

Level 1:	No portfolio management (ad hoc processes)
Level 2:	Database of projects exists, value assessed for individual projects
Level 3:	Project selection prior to action occurs at department/business unit levels
Level 4:	Project portfolio is actively managed at department/business unit levels
Level 5:	Project portfolio is actively managed at enterprise level

Following [Levine '05], the current maturity status of organizations on project portfolio management is low (being 1 or 2 for most of the organizations analyzed). Among others, project portfolio planning can also be applied to the IT projects. A survey [www.scribd.com '09] of Fortune 1000 CIOs found that they believe, on average, that 40% of their IT spending brought no return to their organization. 20% of the investments is wasted, which represented an estimated annual destruction of value totaling $600 billion US. A more systematic and qualified planning process is necessary to decide where to invest and to what extent. Considering the different forms of IT spending as individual projects, the provision of optimized portfolio alternatives generated from the application of EVOLVE II might help to at least reduce the amount of wasted investment.

CHAPTER 15

HOW TO GET IT STARTED

15.1 INTRODUCTION

Having studied models, methods and tools for conducting release planning and other related planning problems leads to the follow-up question: How to get it started, after all? What needs to be looked at to improve effectiveness and efficiency of product release planning and related staffing?

Clearly, no one size fits all approach can be expected. Depending on the size and the culture of the company, and the complexity and competitiveness of the product, each case needs a specific decision on how the process should be organized. Stressing the need for customization does not mean that there are no commonalities in the effort to improve the maturity of release planning. There is a variety of factors that need to be considered in order to find out which method works best or how to customize an existing method. In what follows, some key aspects of this process are discussed. .

15.2 STEP 1: CHARACTERIZE AND UNDERSTAND

The first step of the incremental learning and improvement process as suggested by the Quality Improvement Paradigm [Basili et al. '01a] is to define the context of the process. In order to build an efficient software system, it is imperative to characterize the project environment as well as the organizational environment in which the project is embedded. The project environment is influenced by many internal factors such as the type of the product and the process to be used, the number and quality of the professionals available, and many external factors such as market demand for the intended product. A comprehensive evaluation of these factors lays a solid foundation for product development.

Any effort for qualifying a company's release planning process starts with an understanding of the impact of qualified product release planning in the context of the organization. What does it mean to fail in the market because of missed features or provision of features never used? How strong is the impact of providing the right product features, at the right point in time, to existing and potential new customers? How do you want to get ahead of your competitors?

These and other related questions constitute the starting point for qualifying the release planning process. For making proper planning into future product releases, investments into time, effort and cost are needed. The return on investment of the whole release planning process needs to be made transparent, ideally as much as possible based on objective and meaningful measures as obtained from goal-oriented measurement [Basili et al. '01a]. The amount of investment into release planning needs to be adjusted according to project and organizational needs. As a tendency, the importance of qualified planning will be higher the more competitive the product is expected to become, the bigger it is in size (measured by the number of features), and the more important the effectiveness of time and resource management is for the business success of the product.

15.3 STEP 2: DEFINE THE PROBLEM AND ITS STAKEHOLDERS

One of the decisions that have to be made in this context is how long in advance is planning reasonable. This means deciding on how long in advance we can look into the future without relying too much just on speculations. For product release planning, this requires definition of the time horizon of planning (how many releases in advance the planning should look at) and the scope of planning (looking at one versus more than one product).

Planning can only be done if objectives and constraints are known and stated properly. For planning, different objectives need to be considered. Good release plans maximize the total value of releases, minimize the risk of acceptance of the released product, and provide those features in the upcoming release which are considered most urgent and valuable. In addition, various constraints related to time, resources and technology need to be considered.

Finding the right portfolio of internal and external stakeholders in the whole process of product release planning is more than just *important*. Without their participation, essential input into the process is missing. This relates to features, their importance toward the stated business goals, and the estimated cost, time and effort to get these features implemented. There is no single category of stakeholders that can represent all the different perspectives at product development. The end-users have a different focus than the customers or sales representatives. The same is true for all the managerial and technical roles involved in the process.

Stakeholders are probably even more important for the purpose to get the created planning results realized. This requires commitments to time, financial and human resources. This commitment is hard to achieve without having these key decision-makers convinced up-front that the stated plan is indeed the best possible for the sake of the company.

15.4 STEP 3: DEFINE THE PROCESS

It is not enough to have one expert in the company perfectly knowing the planning problem and having some implicit process in place for how to approach it. As there are various people involved and impacted by the process, the problem and its intended solution approach have to be made explicit. This ensures that all the involved parties have the same understanding of the problem, and their effort to solve it can be synchronized.

Edwards Deming (1900 - 1993) formulated: *If you can't describe what you are doing as a process, you don't know what you are doing.* A process describes who is doing what in which order and is triggered by which conditions. It also describes which are the intermediate artifacts used as input and output for the different process steps. While the whole process should be well defined and highly interactive, it needs to be managed properly all the time by the responsible product or project manager.

Proper tool support is of key importance in this context. There are various considerations of what is considered *proper tool support*. The selection of the tool depends on the existing tool infrastructure (to maintain compatibility), the cost and maintainability of the tool, its ease of use, and last but not least, on the contribution the tool is able to make for improving efficiency.

15.5 STEP 4: EXECUTE THE PROCESS

Release planning is an ongoing process that includes permanent adjustment to change. Release planning implies constant demand for re-planning. As there are very different roles involved in this process, it is important to define and to follow the agreed upon process. If there is a deviation from an already existing plan, then all involved stakeholders need to be informed as well.

Release planning activities cannot be successful when carried out in isolation, without consideration of their interplay with other activities in the process. Proper requirements elicitation and project management are equally important to achieve successful products. Release planning is a part of the whole product management life-cycle. Information exchange with other organizational information systems (e.g., enterprise resource planning systems, configuration management systems) is crucial for consistency and efficiency of data handling. The organizational capability for data and knowledge management is as important as the ongoing effort to better understand the needs of the customer by performing requirements elicitation.

15.6 STEP 5: ANALYZE THE PROCESS AND ITS PERFORMANCE

As any other process, release planning needs to be checked continuously regarding its performance and the validity of the results obtained. Feedback data collected by using popular techniques such as questionnaires, interviews, discussions and regular feedback sessions must be analyzed for comparing results with stated targets. The data may show that some stakeholders did not fully understand the content of features appropriately or the effort estimates made were not appropriate. Or the proposed release plan does not look realistic enough as a whole. Or some of the key expected features have not been suggested to come in the next release.

The main quality criteria of the established planning process are the acceptance of its results and its impact on product development. Decisions formerly made related to stakeholders, resources and the number as well as the content of the selected planning objectives need to be evaluated. As a conclusion, stakeholders might need some up-front training in the future for performing the process, or the formulation of the feature content needs to be analyzed up-front. Another conclusion might be the need of early validation of the stated objectives and their degree of importance.

15.7 STEP 6: PACKAGE EXPERIENCE AND RESULTS

Not learning from mistakes made in the past was considered the deadliest sin by [McConnell '01]. In an organization where there is no provision to learn from the experience gained from previous release plans, each project is one of a kind. Every time a new product release needs to be planned, the whole process is started from scratch. This is inefficient from the perspective of the organization [Amandeep et al. '04].

As part of an overall learning and improvement cycle, data generated from various planning rounds are packaged for reuse. Such preparation would include documenting, explaining, structuring and linking the gained information to the context where it was obtained. The experience is characterized and classified, documented, explained and linked to the existing models, knowledge, and packaged in the experience base.

For retrospective analysis, it needs to be analyzed *what has worked well and what did not?* Some key questions for this analysis are summarized below:

- Were the planning objectives appropriate? Have significant criteria been missed or have criteria been used that were not so relevant?
- Was the planning horizon too long or too short?
- Was the content of the features understandable?
- Was the number and the granularity of the features selected properly?
- Did the selected stakeholders cover the main aspects of product road-mapping?
- Have the stakeholders been involved properly in the whole process? In accordance with their main expertise?
- Was the total effort spent by stakeholders worthwhile?

- Is the organizational process for estimation and re-estimation of effort mature enough?
- Were the number and the content of resources that have been taken into account properly selected?
- Have some essential resources been missed or have resources been considered not so relevant for the results?
- Have all the essential feature dependencies been taken into account?
- Was the overall effort of the process reasonable?
- Have proactive re-planning scenarios been performed to understand the implications of possible changes in the planning data?
- Was the decision-making made transparent to all stakeholders involved to get their buy-in for implementation of the final plan?

15.8 COST-BENEFIT ANALYSIS

As for any investment, the necessary efforts, directly or indirectly aimed at making "good" decisions, need to be balanced with the potential benefits. Which are the benefits of qualified decisions? Again, this is hard to describe without knowledge of the specific context. The benefit of more transparent, more understandable decisions, made with less effort and resulting in better achievement of stated objectives, might be dramatic. Proper decisions about projects, services or product features resulting in higher customer satisfaction contribute to improved competitiveness of the organization.

Harrison has analyzed managerial decision-making processes and provided the qualitative cost-benefit curve shown in Figure 15.1 [Harrison '87].

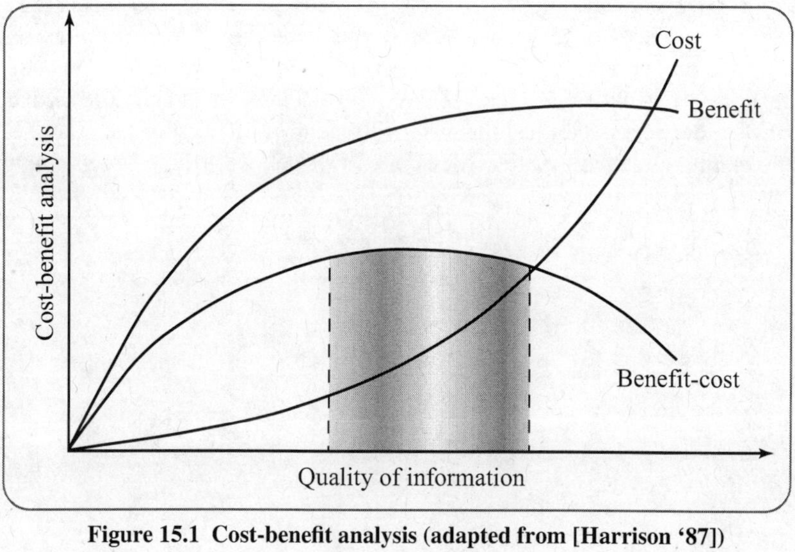

Figure 15.1 Cost-benefit analysis (adapted from [Harrison '87])

What can be seen from there is that the increasing quality of information does not result in a higher benefit/cost ratio. Instead, there is a sweet spot for qualifying the information and getting good and good enough results out of it. It can be expected that the relative effort for providing a certain quality level of information will be reduced with the number of its applications. Consequently, the investment into "good" IT decisions pays off the more frequent the information can be utilized.

15.9 FINAL REMARKS

As pointed out by Fred Brooks [Brooks '87], there does not exist a *silver bullet* technology. There is no *one size fits all* method, tool or technique for product release planning as well. A decision toward the one or against the other technology always depends on the context. The above principles were intended to provide guidance for this process. Independent of where the initial status of the product release planning process is in the organization, it is always crucial to define and start with steps of improvement for qualifying the process to achieve better results. It is important to understand this current status and to define steps of improvement in the direction that is most critical.

The main intention of the book is to provide support not only for making release decisions, but even more to define this pathway of evolutionary improvement of the whole decision-making process. In this context, three fundamental methods were studied:

- Prioritization of features
- Release planning on a strategic level
- Release planning on an operational level (staffing)

For all of these methods, tool support has been presented and discussed. To facilitate the application of results, case studies have been described. The most important lesson learned is: *Wherever the current status is, get started with some well-defined next step to move forward.* Even if it is a long way to go, it is getting on the pathway that counts, not just the results. Remember, the first of the nine deadly sins of planning as stated by Steve McConnell [McConnell '01] is *Not planning at all*!

REFERENCES

[Abdel-Hamid '89] Abdel-Hamid, T. K., Dynamics of software project staffing: A system dynamics based simulation approach, *IEEE Transactions on Software Engineering*, 15 (1989), pp. 109-119.

[Acuna et al. '06] Acuna, S. T., Juristo, N. and Moreno, A. M., Emphasizing human capabilities in software development, *IEEE Software*, 23 (2006), pp. 94-101.

[Alba and Francisco Chicano '07] Alba, E. and Francisco Chicano, J., Software project management with gas, *Information Sciences*, 177 (2007), pp. 2380-2401.

[Al-Emran et al. '07] Al-Emran, A., Pfahl, D. and Ruhe, G., DynaReP: A discrete event simulation model for re-planning of software releases, *Proceedings ICSP 2007, Lecture Notes in Computer Science,* LNCS Vol. 4470, pp. 246-258.

[Al-Emran et al. '10] Al-Emran, A., Kapur, P., Pfahl, D. and Ruhe, G., Studying the impact of uncertainty in operational release planning — an integrated method and its initial evaluation, *Information and Software Technology*, 52 (2010), pp. 446–461.

[Amandeep et al. '04] Amandeep, A., Ruhe, G. and Stanford, M., Intelligent support for software release planning, *Proceedings 5th International Conference on Product Focused Software Process Improvement* (2004), LNCS Vol. 3009, pp. 248-262.

[Antoniol et al. '04] Antoniol, G., Cimitile, A., Di Lucca, G. A. and Di Penta, M., Assessing staffing needs for a software maintenance project through queuing simulation, *IEEE Transactions on Software Engineering*, 30 (2004), pp. 43-58.

[Antoniol et al. '05] Antoniol, G., Penta, M. D. and Harman, M., Search-based techniques applied to optimization of project planning for a massive maintenance project, *Proceedings IEEE International Conference on Software Maintenance,* ICSM 2005, pp. 240-252.

[Arkhangelskii and Pontryagin '90] Arkhangelskii, A.V. and Pontryagin, L.S., General topology I: Basic concepts and constructions dimension theory, *Encyclopedia of Mathematical Sciences*, Springer, 1990.

[Bagnall et al. '01] Bagnall, A. J., Rayward-Smith, V. J. and Whittley, I. M., The next release problem, *Information and Software Technology*, Vol. 43 (2001), pp. 883-890.

[Barreto et al. '08] Barreto, A., Barros, M. D. and Werner, C. M. L., Staffing a software project: A constraint satisfaction and optimization-based approach, *Computers and Operations Research*, 35 (2008), pp. 3073-3089.

[Basili and Turner '75] Basili, V. R. and Turner, A. J., Iterative enhancement: A practical technique for software development, *IEEE Transactions on Software Engineering*, SE-1 (1975), pp. 390-396.

[Basili et al. '01a] Basili, V. R., Caldiera, G., Rombach, H. D. and Solingen, R. V., The goal question metric approach, In: *Encyclopedia of Software Engineering*, Vol. 1, Marciniak, J. (Ed.), Wiley, 2001, pp. 578-583.

[Basili et al. '01b] Basili, V. R., Caldiera, G. and Rombach, H. D., Experience factory, In: *Encyclopedia of Software Engineering,* Vol. 1, Marciniak, J. (Ed.), Wiley, 2001, pp. 511-519.

[Berander and Andrews '05] Berander, P. and Andrews, A., Requirements prioritization, In: *Engineering and Managing Software Requirements,* Aurum, A. and Wohlin, C. (Eds.), Springer, 2005, pp. 69-94.

[Berander and Joensson '06] Berander, P. and Joensson, P., Hierarchical cumulative voting (HCV) prioritization of requirements in hierarchies, *Journal of Software Engineering and Knowledge Engineering* 16 (2006), pp. 819-849.

[Bhawnani et al. '06] Bhawnani, P., Ruhe, G., Kudorfer, F. and Meyer, L., Intelligent decision support for roadmapping — a technology transfer case study with Siemens Corporate Technology, *Proceedings Workshop on Technology Transfer in Software Engineering, ICSE* (2006), pp. 35-40.

[Black '06] Black, K., *Business Statistics for Contemporary Decision-Making*, Wiley, 2006.

[Blackburn et al. '96] Blackburn, J. D., Scudder, G. D. and Van Wassenhove, L. N., Improving speed and productivity of software development: A global survey of software developers, *IEEE Transactions on Software Engineering*, 22 (1996), pp. 875-885.

[Blattberg and Hoch '90] Blattberg, R. C. and Hoch, S. J., Database models and managerial intuition: 50% model + 50% manager, *Management Science*, 36 (1990), pp. 887-899.

[Blazewicz et al. '07] Blazewicz, J., Ecker, K., Pesch, E., Schmidt, G. and Weglarz, J., *Handbook on Scheduling*, Springer, 2007.

[Boehm et al. '00] Boehm, B., Abts, C. and Chulani, S., Software development cost estimation approaches — a survey, *Annals of Software Engineering*, 10 (2000), pp. 177-205.

[Boehm and Huang '03] Boehm, B. and Huang, L. G., Value-based software engineering: A case study, *IEEE Computer,* 36 (2003), pp. 33-41.

[Bouyssou et al. '06] Bouyssou, D., Marchant, T., Pirlot, M., Tsoukias, A. and Vincke, P., *Evaluation and Decision Models with Multiple Criteria: Stepping Stones for the Analyst*, Springer, 2006.

[BPMForu] Market vigilance, product diligence, www.bpmforum.org/popups/pr_markvig.htm, accessed November 20, 2009.

[Briand and Wieczorek '02] Briand, L. and Wieczorek, I., Resource estimation in software engineering, In *Encyclopedia of Software Engineering*, Vol. 2, J. Marciniak (Ed.), John Wiley & Sons, pp. 1160-1196.

[Brooks '87] Brooks, F. P., No silver bullet: Essence and accidents of software engineering, *IEEE Computer,* 20 (1987), pp. 10-19.

[Cao and Ramesh '08] Cao, L. and Ramesh, B., Agile requirements engineering practices: An empirical study, *IEEE Software*, 25 (2008), pp. 60-67.

[Capilla et al. '08] Capilla, R., Nava, F., Montes, J. and Carrillo, C., ADDSS: Architecture design decision support system tool, *Proceedings ASE 2008 International Conference on Automated Software Engineering* 2008, pp. 487-488.

[Carlshamre '02] Carlshamre, P., Release planning in market-driven software product development: Provoking an understanding, *Requirements Engineering*, 7 (2002), pp. 139-151.

[Carlshamre et al. '01] Carlshamre, P., Sandahk, K., Lindvall, M., Regnell, B. and Nattoch Dag, J., An industrial survey of requirements interdependencies in software release planning, *Proceedings International Symposium on Requirements Engineering*, 2001, pp. 84-91.

[Carlsson and Turban '02] Carlsson, C. and Turban, E., Decision support systems: Directions for the next decade, *Journal of Decision Support Systems* 33 (2002), pp. 105-110.

[Chang et al. '01] Chang, C. K., Christensen, M. J. and Zhang, T., Genetic algorithms for project management, *Annals of Software Engineering*, 11 (2001), pp. 107-139.

[Charette '05] Charette, R. N., Why software fails, *IEEE Spectrum*, 42 (2005), pp. 36-43.

[Chegireddy and Hamacher '85] Chegireddy, C. R. and Hamacher, H. W., Algorithms for finding K-best perfect matching, *Discrete Applied Mathematics* 18 (1985), pp. 155-165.

[Choi et al. '08] Choi, J., Nazareth, D. L. and Jain, H. K., Information technology skill management: A systems dynamics approach, *Proceedings of the Hawaii International Conference on System Sciences*, 2008.

[Chrissis et al. '06] Chrissis, M. B., Konrad, M. and Shrum, S., *CMMI — Guidelines for Process Integration and Product Improvement*, Addison-Wesley, 2006.

[Clemen '96] Clemen, R. T., *Making Hard Decisions: An Introduction to Decision Analysis*, Pacific Grove, Duxbury, 1996.

[Cohen et al. '04] Cohen, D., Lindvall, M. and Costa, P., An introduction to agile methods, *Advances in Computers*, 62 (2004), pp. 2-67.

[Cohn '06] Cohn, M., *Agile Estimating and Planning*, Prentice Hall PTR, 2006.

[Colibri/Java] Colibri/Java tool, available at http://code.google.com/p/colibri-java/.

[Collofello et al. '98] Collofello, J., Houston, D., Rus, I., Chauhan, A., Sycamore, D. M. and Smith-Daniels, D., System dynamics software process simulator for staffing policies decision support, *Proceedings of the Hawaii International Conference on System Sciences*, 1998, pp. 103-111.

[Conklin '01] Conklin, J., *Dialogue Mapping: Building Shared Understanding of Wicked Problems*, Wiley, 2005. For more information see the CogNexus Institute website at http://www.cognexus.org.

[Constantine '01] Constantine, L., *The Peopleware Papers: Notes on the Human Side of Software*, Prentice Hall, 2001.

[Cormen et al. '06] Cormen, T. H., Leiserson, C. E. and Rivest, R. L., *Introduction to Algorithms*, McGraw Hill, New York, 2006.

[Davis '05] Davis, A., *Just Enough Requirements Management*, Dorset House Publishing, 2005.

[De Geus '97] De Geus, A., *The Living Company*, Harvard Business School Press, 1997.

[DeGregorio '00] DeGregorio, G., Technology management via a set of dynamically linked roadmaps, *Proceedings IEEE International Engineering Management Conference*, 2000, pp. 184-190.

[DeMarco and Lister '99] DeMarco, T. and Lister, T., *Peopleware: Productive Projects and Teams*, 2nd ed., Dorset House, 1999.

[Denne and Cleland-Huang '04] Denne, M. and Cleland-Huang, J., The incremental funding method: Data-driven software development, *IEEE Software*, 21 (2004), pp. 39-47.

[Denzinger and Ruhe '04] Denzinger, J. and Ruhe, G., Decision support for software release planning using E-assistants, *Journal of Decision Support Systems*, 13 (2004), pp. 399 - 421.

[Dieste et al. '08] Dieste, O., Juristo, N. and Shull, F., Understanding the customer: What do we know about requirements elicitation?, *IEEE Software* 25 (2008), pp. 11-13.

[Du '09] Du, G., Design and evaluation of explanation-based decision support for software release planning, PhD Thesis, Department of Computer Science, University of Calgary, December 2009.

[Du and Ruhe '09a] Du, G. and Ruhe, G., Two machine learning techniques for mining solutions of the ReleasePlanner decision support system, *Journal of Information Sciences*, Special Issue on Applications of Computational Intelligence and Machine Learning to Software Engineering, doi: 10.1016/j.ins.2009.12.017.

[Du and Ruhe '09b] Du, G. and Ruhe, G., Does explanation improve the acceptance of decision support for product release planning?, In: *Proceedings International Symposium on Empirical Software Engineering and Measurement, 2009*, pp 56-68.

[Du et al. '06] Du, G., McElroy, J. and Ruhe, G., A family of empirical studies to compare informal and optimization-based planning of software releases, *Proceedings Symposium on Empirical Software Engineering,* 2006, pp. 212-221.

[Du et al. '08] Du, G., Zimmermann, T. and Ruhe, G., Explaining product release planning results using concept analysis, *Proceedings International Conference on Software Engineering and Knowledge Engineering*, 2008, pp. 137-142.

[Dyba and Dingsoyr '08] Dyba, T. and Dingsoyr, T., Empirical studies of agile software development: A systematic review, *Information and Software Technology*, 50 (2008), pp. 833-859.

[Ebert '07] Ebert, C., The impacts of software product management, *Journal of Systems and Software*, 80 (2007), pp. 850-861.

[Efron and Gong '83] Efron, B. and Gong, G., A leisurely look at the bootstrap, the jackknife, and cross-validation, *The American Statistician*, 37(1), (1983), pp. 36-48.

[El Emam and Madhavji '95] El Emam, K. and Madhavji, N. H., Field study of requirements engineering practices in information systems development, *Proceedings International Conference on Requirements Engineering*, 1995, pp. 68-80.

[Elmaghraby '77] Elmaghraby, S. E., *Activity Networks: Project Planning and Control by Network Models*, Wiley, 1977.

[EXPLAIN-RP] EXPLAIN-RP tool, available at http://pages.cpsc.ucalgary.ca/~dug/ExplanationTool.pdf.

[Fenton et al. '04] Fenton, N., Marsh, W., Neil, M., Cates, P., Forey, S. and Tailor, M., Making resource decisions for software projects, *Proceedings International Conference on Software Engineering,* 2004, pp. 397-406.

[Figuera et al. '05] Figueira, J., Mousseau, V. and Roy, B., ELECTRE methods. In: *Multiple Criteria Decision Analysis: State of the Art Surveys*, Figueira, J., Greco, S., and Ehrgott, M. (Eds.), Springer, 2005, pp. 133-162.

[Firesmith '04] Firesmith, D., Prioritizing requirements, *Journal of Object Technology* 3 (2004), pp. 35-47.

[Garey and Johnson '79] Garey, M. R. and Johnson, D. S., *Computers and Intractability: A Guide to the Theory of NP-Completeness*, Freeman, 1979.

[Giroux and Robillard '06] Giroux, O. and Robillard, M. P., Detecting increases in feature coupling using regression tests, *Proceedings International Symposium on Foundations of Software Engineering,* 2006, pp. 163-174.

[Greer and Ruhe '04] Greer, D. and Ruhe, G., Software release planning: An evolutionary and iterative approach, *Information and Software Technology*, 46 (2004), pp. 243-253.

[Griss et al. '98] Griss, M. L., Favaro, J. and d'Alessandro, M., Integrating feature modeling with the RSEB, *Proceedings International Conference on Software Reuse*, 1998, pp. 76-85.

[Hamming '50] Hamming, R. K. Error detecting and error correcting codes, *Bell System Technical Journal,* 26(2) (1950), pp. 147-160.

[Harker '87] Harker, P. T., Incomplete pair-wise comparisons in the analytic hierarchy process, *Mathematical Modelling,* 9, (1987), pp. 837-848.

[Harman '07] Harman, M., The current state and future of search based software engineering, *Proceedings International Conference on Software Engineering,* 2007, pp. 342-357.

[Harrison '87] Harrison, E.F., *The Managerial Decision-Making Process*, Houghton Mifflin Company, 1987.

[Heckerman et al. '00] Heckerman, D., Chickering, D. M., Meek, C., Rounthwaite, R. and Kadie, C., Dependency networks for inference, collaborative filtering, and data visualization, *Journal of Machine Learning Research*, 1 (2000), pp. 49-75.

[Heikkilä et al. '10] Heikkilä, V., Jadallah, A., Rautiainnen, K. and Ruhe, G., Rigorous support for flexible planning of product releases — A stakeholder-centric approach and its initial evaluation, *Proceedings Hawaii International Conference on System Sciences*, 2010, pp.1-10.

[Hoch and Schkade '96] Hoch, S. J. and Schkade, D. A., A psychological approach to decision support systems, *Management Science*, 42 (1996), pp. 51-64.

[IEEE '08] IEEE, P1694 Enterprise strategic decision management standards working group, 2008, http://standards.ieee.org/board/nes/projects/1694.pdf, accessed July 18, 2009.

[ILOG] http://www.ilog.com/products/cplex, Cplex, accessed March 2008.

[Jadallah et al. '09] Jadallah, A., Al-Emran, A., Moussavi, M. and Ruhe, G., The how? when? and what? for the process of re-planning for product releases, *Proceedings International Conference on Software Process,* 2009, Vancouver, Springer Lecture Notes in Computer Science LNCS Vol. 5543, pp. 24-37.

[Javed et al. '04] Javed, T., Maqsood, M. and Durrani, Q.S., A study to investigate the impact of requirements instability on software defects, In: *ACM SIGSOFT Software Engineering Notes,* ACM, New York, 2004, pp. 1-7.

[Jones and Brown '02] Jones, D. R. and Brown, D., The division of labor between human and computer in the presence of decision support system advice, *Decision Support Systems*, 33 (2002), pp. 375-388.

[Jung '98] Jung, H. W., Optimizing value and cost in requirements analysis, *IEEE Software*, 15 (1998), pp. 74-78.

[Kaindl et al. '02] Kaindl, H., Brinkkemper, S., Bubenko Jr, J. A., Farbey, B., Greenspan, S. J., Heitmeyer, C. L., Do Prado Leite, J. C. S., Mead, N. R., Mylopoulos, J. and Siddiqi, J., Requirements engineering and technology transfer: Obstacles, incentives and improvement agenda, *Requirements Engineering* 7 (2002), pp. 113-123.

[Kang et al. '90] Kang, K. C., Cohen, S. G., Hess, J. A., Novak, W. E. and Peterson, A. S., Feature-oriented domain analysis (FODA) feasibility study, Technical Report CMU/SEI-90-TR-021,1990.

[Kaplan and Norton '92] Kaplan, R. S. and Norton, D. P., The balanced scorecard — measures that drive performance, *Harvard Business Review* 70 (1992), pp. 71-79.

[Kapur et al. '08] Kapur, P., Ngo-The, A., Ruhe, G. and Smith, A., Optimized staffing for product releases and its application at Chartwell Technology, *Journal of Software Maintenance and Evolution*, 20 (2008), pp. 365-386.

[Karlsson and Ryan '97] Karlsson, J. and Ryan, K., Prioritizing requirements using a cost-value approach, *IEEE Software*, 14 (1997), pp. 67-74.

[Karlsson et al. '98] Karlsson, J., Wohlin, C. and Regnell, B., An evaluation of methods for prioritizing software requirements, *Information and Software Technology* 39 (1998), pp. 939-947.

[Keeney '82] Keeney, R. L., Decision analysis: An overview, *Operations Research*, 30 (1982), pp. 803-838.

[Kellerer et al. '04] Kellerer, H., Pferschy, U. and Pisinger, D., *Knapsack Problems*, Springer, 2004.

[Kitchenham and Mendes '04] Kitchenham, B. and Mendes, E., Software productivity measurement using multiple size measures, *IEEE Transactions on Software Engineering*, 30 (2004), pp. 1023-1035.

[Kotonya and Sommerville '98] Kotonya, G. and Sommerville, I., *Requirements Engineering: Processes and Techniques*, John Wiley, 1998.

[Kruchten '00] Kruchten, P., *The Rational Unified Process*, Addison-Wesley Longman Publishing, 2000.

[Larman and Basili '03] Larman, C. and Basili, V. R., Iterative and incremental development: A brief history, *IEEE Computer*, 36 (2003), pp. 47-56.

[Lawler '72] Lawler, E. L., A procedure for computing the k-best solutions to discrete optimization problems and its application to the shortest path problem, *Management Science* 18 (1972), pp. 401-405.

[Lee et al. '02] Lee, K., Kang, K. C. and Lee, J., Concepts and guidelines of feature modeling for product line software engineering, *Proceedings Software Reuse: Methods, Techniques, and Tools*, Springer, Lecture Notes in Computer Science, 2002, pp. 62-77.

[Lehman '96] Lehman, M. M., Laws of software evolution revisited, *Proceedings 5th European Workshop on Software Process Technology,* Nancy, 1996, pp. 108-124.

[Lehtola '06] Lehtola, L., Providing value by prioritizing requirements throughout product development: State of practice and suitability of prioritization methods, Licentiate Thesis, HUT/Departure of Computer Science, 2006.

[Lethola et al. '04] Lethola, L., Kauppinen, M. and Kujala, S., Requirements prioritization challenges in practice, *Proceedings of the 4th International Conference on Product Focused Software Process Improvement*, Lecture Notes on Computer Science, 3009 (2004), pp. 497-508.

[Levine '05] Levine, H. A., *Project Portfolio Management: A Practical Guide to Selecting Projects, Managing Portfolios, and Maximizing Benefits*, John Wiley & Sons, 2005.

[Li '07] Li, J.Z., A flexible method for software effort estimation by analogy, PhD Thesis, Department of Computer Science, University of Calgary, December 2007.

[Li and Ruhe '08] Li, J.Z. and Ruhe, G., Analysis of attribute weighting heuristics for software effort estimation by analogy, *Empirical Software Engineering*, 13 (2008), pp. 63-96.

[Li et al. '07] Li, J.Z., Ruhe, G., Al-Emran, A. and Richter, M.M., A flexible method for effort estimation by analogy, *Empirical Software Engineering*, 12 (2007), pp. 65-106.

[Lindgren et al. '08a] Lindgren, M., Land, R., Norstroem, C. and Wall, A., Key aspects of software release planning in industry, *Proceedings of the Australian Software Engineering Conference*, ASWEC, 2008, pp. 320-329.

[Lindgren et al. '08b] Lindgren, M., Land, R., Norstroem, C. and Wall, A., Towards a capability model for the software release planning process — based on a multiple industrial case study, *Proceedings Lecture Notes in Computer Science*, LNCS 5089 (2008), pp. 117-132.

[Malinowski et al. '08] Malinowski, J., Weitzel, T. and Keim, T., Decision support for team staffing: An automated relational recommendation approach, *Decision Support Systems*, 45 (2008), pp. 429-447.

[Mankins and Steele '06] Mankins, M. C. and Steele, R., Stop making plans start making decisions, *Harvard Business Review*, 84 (2006), pp. 76-84+133.

[McConnell '01] McConnell, S., The nine deadly sins of project planning, *IEEE Software*, 18 (2001), pp. 5-7.

[Menzies '01] Menzies, T., Practical machine learning for software engineering and knowledge engineering, In: *Handbook of Software Engineering and Knowledge Engineering*, Vol. 1, Chang, S. K. (Ed.), World Scientific, 2001, pp. 837-862.

[Moe and Aurum '08] Moe, N. B. and Aurum, A., Understanding decision-making in agile software development: A case-study, *Proceedings of the 34th EUROMICRO Conference on Software Engineering and Advanced Applications*, 2008, pp. 216-223.

[McElroy and Ruhe '10] McElroy, J. and Ruhe, G., When-to-release Decisions for Features with Time-dependent Value Functions, *Requirements Engineering Journal*, Published online: 16 February 2010.

[Momoh and Ruhe '06] Momoh, J. and Ruhe, G., Release planning process improvement — an industrial case study, *Software Process Improvement and Practice*, 11 (2006), pp. 295-307.

[Murty '68] Murty, K. G., An algorithm for ranking all the assignments in order of increasing cost, *Operations Research* 16 (1968), pp. 682-687.

[Nerur and Balijepally '07] Nerur, S. and Balijepally, V., Theoretical reflections on agile development methodologies, *Communications of the ACM,* 50 (2007), pp. 79-83.

[Neubauer and Stummer '07] Neubauer, T. and Stummer, C., Interactive decision support for multiobjective cots selection, *Proceedings of the Annual Hawaii International Conference on System Sciences*, 2007, pp. 4743-4749.

[Ngo-The and Ruhe '08] Ngo-The, A. and Ruhe, G., A systematic approach for solving the wicked problem of software release planning, *Soft Computing* 12 (2008), pp. 95-108.

[Ngo-The and Ruhe '09] Ngo-The, A. and Ruhe, G., Optimized resource allocation for software release planning, *IEEE Transactions on Software Engineering,* 35 (2009), pp. 109-123.

[Paquet '09] http://www.quantumwhisper.com/product-management-survey-2009/, Product management survey — 2009, accessed August 30, 2009.

[Pawlak '91] Pawlak, Z., *Rough Sets: Theoretical Aspects of Reasoning about Data*, Kluwer Academic, 1991.

[Pfahl '05] Pfahl, D., ProSim/RA — Software process simulation in support of risk assessment, In: *Value-Based Software Engineering*, S. Biffl, A. Aurum, B. Boehm, H. Erdogmus and P. Grünbacher (Eds.), Springer, 2005, pp. 263-286.

[Rahman et al. '09] Rahman, M. M., Ruhe, G. and Zimmermann, T., Optimized assignment of developers for fixing bugs: An intial evaluation for eclipse projects, *Proceedings Empirical Software Engineering and Measurement,* 2009, pp. 439-442.

[Regnell and Brinkkemper '05] Regnell, B. and Brinkkemper, S., Market-driven requirements engineering for software products, In: *Engineering and Managing Software Requirements*, Aurum, A. and Wohlin, C. (Eds.), Springer, 2005, pp. 287-308.

[Regnell et al. '08] Regnell, B., Svensson, R. B. and Olsson, T., Supporting roadmapping of quality requirements, *IEEE Software*, 25 (2008), pp. 42-47.

[Reid Turner et al. '99] Reid Turner, C., Fuggetta, A., Lavazza, L. and Wolf, A. L., A conceptual basis for feature engineering, *Journal of Systems and Software* 49 (1999), pp. 3-15.

[Rittel and Webber '84] Rittel, H. W. J. and Webber, M. M., Planning problems are wicked problems, *Developments in Design Methodology*, (1984), pp. 135-144.

[ROSE2] ROSE2, Institute of Computing Science, Poznań University of Technology, available at http://idss.cs.put.poznan.pl/site/rose.html.

[Rowe and Wright '99] Rowe, G. and Wright, G., The Delphi technique as a forecasting tool: Issues and analysis, *International Journal for Forecasting*, 15 (1999), pp. 353-375.

[Rubinstein and Kroese'07] Rubinstein, R. Y. and Kroese, D. P., *Simulation and the Monte Carlo Method*, John Wiley & Sons, 2007.

[Ruhe '01] Ruhe, G., Learning software organisations, In: *Handbook of Software Engineering and Knowledge Engineering*, Vol. 1, Chang, S. K. (Ed.), World Scientific Publishing 2001, pp. 663-678.

[Ruhe '03] Ruhe, G., Software engineering decision support — a new paradigm for learning software organizations. Advances in learning organization, *Lecture Notes in Computer Science*, 2640 (2003), pp. 104-115.

[Ruhe '05] Ruhe, G., Software release planning, In: *Handbook of Software Engineering and Knowledge Engineering*, Vol 3, Chang, S. K. (Ed.), World Scientific, 2005, pp. 365-393.

[Ruhe and Ngo-The '04] Ruhe, G. and Ngo-The, A., Hybrid intelligence in software release planning, *International Journal of Hybrid Intelligent Systems*, 1 (2004), pp. 99-110.

[Ruhe and Saliu '05] Ruhe, G. and Saliu, M. O., The art and science of software release planning, *IEEE Software*, 22 (2005), pp. 47-53.

[Saaty '80] Saaty, T. L., *The Analytic Hierarchy Process*, McGraw-Hill, 1980.

[Saaty '94] Saaty, T. L., *Fundamentals of Decision Making and Priority Theory with the Analytic Hierarchy Process*, RWS Publications, 1994.

[Sackman et al. '68] Sackman, H., Erikson, W. J. and Grant, E. E., Exploratory experimental studies comparing online and offline programming performance, *Communications of the ACM*, 11 (1968), pp. 3-11.

[Saliu '07] Saliu, M. O., Decision support for release planning of software systems, PhD Thesis, Department of Computer Science, University of Calgary, October 2007.

[Saliu and Ruhe '07] Saliu, M. O. and Ruhe, G., Bi-objective release planning for evolving software systems, *6th Joint Meeting of the European Software Engineering Conference and the ACM SIGSOFT Symposium on the Foundations of Software Engineering*, 2007, pp. 105-114.

[Sassenburg '05] Sassenburg, H., *Design of a Methodology to Support Software Release Decisions: Do Numbers Really Matter?*, University of Groningen, 2005.

[Schwaber and Beedle '02] Schwaber, K. and Beedle, M., *Agile Software Development with Scrum*, Prentice Hall, 2002.

[Sharp et al. '99] Sharp, H., Finkelstein, A. and Galal, G., Stakeholder identification in the requirements engineering process, *Proceedings 10th International Workshop on Database and Expert Systems Applications*, 1999, Florence, Italy, pp. 387-391.

[Shaw et al. '07] Shaw, M. A., Feldmann, R. L. and Shull, F., Decision support with Emperor, *Proceedings 1st International Symposium on Empirical Software Engineering and Measurement*, ESEM 2007, pp. 495.

[Shepperd and Schofield '97] Shepperd, M. and Schofield, C., Estimating software project effort using analogies, *IEEE Transactions on Software Engineering*, 23 (1997), pp. 736-743.

[Smith and Reinertsen '98] Smith, P. G. and Reinertsen, D. G., *Developing Products in Half the Time: New Rules, New Tools,* John Wiley & Sons, 1998.

[Smith et al. '04] Smith, L. D., Nauss, R. M., Subramanian, A. and Beck, R., Decision support for staffing, outsourcing and project scheduling in MIS strategic plans, *INFOR*, 42 (2004), pp. 79-100.

[Standish '09] Standish, *Solutions for Enterprise Project and Portfolio Management*, The Standish Group International, 2009.

[Stark et al. '99] Stark, G. E., Oman, P., Skillicorn, A. and Ameele, A., An examination of the effects of requirements changes on software maintenance releases, *Journal of Software Maintenance and Evolution*, 11 (1999), pp. 293-309.

[Steuer '86] Steuer, R. E., *Multiple Criteria Optimization: Theory, Computation, and Application*, John Wiley & Sons, 1986.

[Takeuchi and Nonaka '86] Takeuchi, H. and Nonaka, I., The new product development game, *Harvard Business Review* 64 (1986), pp. 137-146.

[Tosun et al. '09] Tosun, A., Turhan, B. and Ayse B.B., Feature weighting heuristics for analogy-based effort estimation methods, *Expert Systems with Applications*, 36, (2009), pp. 10325-10333.

[Trial_ReleasePlanner '09] www.releaseplanner.com, Trial stakeholder account for *Releaseplanner*, accessed June 21, 2009.

[Trial_VeryBestChoice '09] http://edi.lite.verybestchoice.com:3000/login, Trial stakeholder account for *VeryBestChoice Light*, accessed June 27, 2009.

[Turban et al. '05] Turban, E., Aronson, J. E. and Liang, T. P., *Decision Support Systems and Intelligent Systems*, Pearson Prentice Hall, 2005.

[Turner et al. '99] Turner, C. R., Fuggetta, A., Lavazza, L. and Wolf, A. L., A conceptual basis for feature engineering, *Journal of Systems and Software*, 49 (1999), pp. 3-15.

[Vaidya and Kumar '06] Vaidya, O. S. and Kumar, S., Analytic hierarchy process: An overview of applications, *European Journal of Operational Research* 169 (2006), pp. 1-29.

[Valett and McGarry '89] Valett, J. D. and McGarry, F. E., A summary of software measurement experiences in the software engineering laboratory, *Journal of Systems and Software*, 9 (1989), pp. 137-148.

[Van De Weerd et al. '06] Van De Weerd, I., Brinkkemper, S., Nieuwenhuis, R., Versendaal, J. and Bijlsma, L., Towards a reference framework for software product management, *Proceedings IEEE International Conference on Requirements Engineering*, 2006, pp. 312-315.

[Van den Akker et al. '08] van den Akker, M., Brinkkemper, S., Diepen, G. and Versendaal, J., Software product release planning through optimization and what-if analysis, *Information and Software Technology*, 50 (2008), pp. 101-111.

[Van Der Poort et al. '99] Van Der Poort, E. S., Libura, M., Sierksma, G. and Van Der Veen, J. A. A., Solving the k-best traveling salesman problem, *Computers and Operations Research* 26 (1999), pp. 409-425.

[Van Lamsweerde '00] van Lamsweerde, A., Requirements engineering in the year 00: A research perspective, *Proceedings International Conference on Software Engineering*, ICSE 2000, pp. 5-19.

[VBClight] http://edi.lite.verybestchoice.com/login, accessed November 30, 2009.

[West and Allen '97] West, M. A. and Allen, N. A., Selecting for teamwork, In: *International Handbook of Selection and Assessment*, Anderson, N. and Herriot, P. (Eds), Wiley, 1997, pp. 493-506.

[Wiegers '00] Wiegers, K., http://www.processimpact.com/articles/reqtraps.html, accessed June 27, 2009.

[Wiegers '03] Wiegers, K., *Software Requirements*, Microsoft Press, 2003.

[Wille '82] Wille, R., Restructuring lattice theory: An approach based on hierarchies of concepts, In: *Ordered Sets*, Rival, I. (Ed.), Reidel, 1982, pp. 445-470.

[WinMine] WinMine Toolkit, Machine learning and applied statistics group, Microsoft Research, available at http://research.microsoft.com/~dmax/winmine/tooldoc.htm.

[www.expertchoice.com '08] http://www.expertchoice.com, Expert Choice, accessed February 10, 2009.

[www.scribd.com'09] http://www.scribd.com/doc/14531566/IT-Portfolio-Planning-LongTerm-View-ShortTerm-Results-Vfinalc, *IT portfolio planning — long-term view short-term results,* accessed October 2009.

[Wysocki '06] Wysocki, R. K., *Effective Software Project Management*, Wiley, 2006.

[Yang et al. '08] Yang, B., Hu, H. and Jia, L., A study of uncertainty in software cost and its impact on optimal software release time, *IEEE Transactions on Software Engineering*, 34 (2008), pp. 813-825.

[Zhang et al. '08] Zhang, H., Kitchenham, B. and Pfahl, D., Software process simulation modeling: Facts, trends and directions, *Proceedings Asia-Pacific Software Engineering Conference* 2008, pp. 59-66.

[Ziv et al. '96] Ziv, H., Richardson, D. J. and Kolsch, R., The uncertainty principle in software engineering, Technical Report, UCI-TR-96-33 (1996).

[Zowghi and Coulin '05] Zowghi, D. and Coulin, C., Requirements elicitation: A survey of techniques, approaches, and tools, In: *Engineering and Managing Software Requirements*, Aurum, A. and Wohlin, C. (Eds.), Springer, 2005, pp. 19-46.

INDEX

E

F

G

H

I

U

V

W